New York Murder Mystery

Andrew Karmen

NEW YORK
MURDER MYSTERY

The True Story behind
the Crime Crash
of the 1990s

New York University Press

New York and London

To the 32,600 New Yorkers

who were murdered

between 1978 and 1998

NEW YORK UNIVERSITY PRESS
New York and London

Library of Congress Cataloging-in-Publication Data
Karmen, Andrew.
New York murder mystery : the true story behind the
crime crash of the 1990s / Andrew Karmen.
p.   cm.
Includes bibliographical references and index.
ISBN 0-8147-4717-5 (cloth : alk. paper)
1. Murder—New York (State)—New York. 2. Crime prevention—
New York (State)—New York. 3. Police—New York (State)—New York.
4. Criminals—New York (State)—New York.   I. Title.
HV6534.N5 K367 2000
364.15'23'097471—dc21   00-010007

New York University Press books are printed on acid-free paper,
and their binding materials are chosen for strength and durability.

Manufactured in the United States of America

10 9 8 7 6 5 4 3 2 1

CONTENTS

A Professor Learns a Lesson about "Political Correctness"

After teaching criminology courses at John Jay College of Criminal Justice for nearly twenty years, I began to seriously study the decline in murders in New York City during the summer of 1995. Craig Horowitz, a journalist writing a feature story for *New York* magazine, was referred to me by the new director of the college's Office of Public Relations. Mr. Horowitz explained that he was working on a feature story entitled "The Suddenly Safer City: The End of Crime as We Know It." I told him that I thought it was premature to make such a bold prediction after only one and a half years of impressive declines (but his forecast was correct and I was wrong). I also volunteered the standard criminology textbook answer, which I believed then and still believe today: that the street-crime problem cannot be brought under control until its root causes are eradicated. My views were just the foil that he was looking for, so Mr. Horowitz wrote (1995:23): "Their [Mayor Rudolph Giuliani and Commissioner William Bratton] victory appears to be a repudiation of three decades of received wisdom that crime is inextricably connected to economic deprivation and social injustice. . . . Many sociologists and criminologists, however, remain reluctant to credit the Police Department. It would be an admission that they've spent careers promoting false assumptions."

After being challenged in this way, I decided to immerse myself in the available data in order to try to get to the bottom of this unfolding mystery.

John Jay College put together an interdisciplinary research team to study the ebbing crime wave. In late 1996, we held a press conference and presented our preliminary findings. I argued that improved police deserved some—but certainly not all—of the credit. I quickly learned that the politically correct answer was "All praise belongs to the NYPD." Because I failed to tow that party line, the knee-jerk "law and order" editorial page of the *New York Post* bashed me—twice, no less.

The first time they blasted me was in a piece entitled "Crime: What the Professors Don't Know." The editorial (1996:45) acknowledged that "true, Giuliani administration policies earn some kudos in the study: 'Better policing is bringing down murders,' Prof. Andrew Karmen concedes." Evidently partial credit was not good enough, so the pseudo-populist editorial writer turned up the heat: "It may not be apparent to the double-domes at John Jay. But ordinary folks understand full well that City Hall's zero-tolerance attitude towards crime, along with the Pataki administration's crackdown on prison work-release programs, have combined to produce the falling crime rates."

The tightening-up of the eligibility requirements for statewide work-release programs did not go into effect until after 1995, so it became clear to me that some parties to the intensifying controversy were more interested in promoting their political agendas than in discovering the truth. (Furthermore, this claim was rarely repeated after 1996.)

My initial curiosity deepened into a virtual preoccupation with unearthing statistics that tracked social, economic, and demographic trends that might account for the City's tumbling crime rate. As I became more knowledgeable about the facts as distinct from impressions, speculation, and public relations hype, I was able to carve out a little niche in the media as an independent observer who was skeptical about government claims and political spin. I would often take a contrary position when interviewed by reporters if the data I had collected did not support the official line. I felt comfortable in this role, since I had learned always to double-check the government's version of events when I was a campus antiwar and antiracism activist during the 1960s and 1970s.

Several years and many skeptical soundbites later, the editorial page of the *New York Post* singled me out for disseminating politically incorrect information once again, but this second time with more venom. In a polemic entitled "The War against the Crime Drop," the editorial page writer (1999:39) railed against the "Andrew Karmens of the world, who seem to believe that 'social forces' or lunar cycles or some such nonsense are the most important factors affecting crime." He ridiculed the social science approach by resorting to anti-intellectual mockery: "Karmen also opined that Mayor Giuliani and Police Commissioner Howard Safir made a mistake in taking credit for the general drop in crime by attributing it to better police techniques. In fact, the academic said, crime trends are influenced far more by demographics and social forces and yadda, yadda, yadda than by police work."

In the pages ahead, there won't be any mention of lunar cycles, and very little yadda, yadda, yadda. But evolving social conditions and demographic changes—as well as new NYPD strategies—will receive close scrutiny and, I pledge, an objective evaluation.

ACKNOWLEDGMENTS

I was fortunate to be able to draw upon the expertise of many of the faculty at John Jay College of Criminal Justice who are knowledgeable about the causes of crime, the drug problem, police administration, the courts, and prisons. In particular, I want to thank my colleagues who read a chapter or two and gave me valuable feedback, especially by questioning my interpretations or disagreeing with my conclusions: Professors Vincent Del Castillo, Michael Jacobson, Barry Latzer, Charles Lindner, Eugene O'Donnell, Aaron Rosenthal, Eli Silverman, and Barry Spunt. I also benefited from lengthy discussions with the other members of the John Jay College research team: Professors Ben Bowling (of Cambridge University, England), Richard Curtis, Rosalie Hamilton, Delores Jones, and Eli Silverman. I also appreciate the support and encouragement of Provost Basil Wilson, former Dean Barbara Price, Dean James Levine, Vice President Robert Pignatello, and President Gerald Lynch. Our research was partly supported during the mid-1990s by a grant awarded to John Jay College by the New York State Historical Trust. During the late 1990s, the Reisenbach Foundation, set up to honor John Reisenbach, who was murdered near his Greenwich Village home in 1990, provided me with additional funding that enabled me to collect crucial information directly from agency files.

I obtained as much statistical data as possible from official sources to test out all the leading hypotheses put forward by others to account for the most welcomed drop in crime. I would like to thank a number of people working for city and state agencies who supplied me with the information that academic researchers as well as members of the general public are entitled to but have had a difficult time securing during the second half of the 1990s. I won't list their names because of the controversial conclusions I have derived from the data they provided me. Besides these nine public servants, I especially want to thank Anthony De Stefano of *Newsday*, and also Michael Cooper of the *New York Times*, for sharing with me valuable statistical data they obtained from the NYPD's homicide logs.

At New York University Press, I was extremely fortunate that drafts of my chapters received the close personal attention of the director, Niko Pfund. I appreciate the editorial support provided by Tim Bartlett, Despina Papazoglou Gimbel, and Alice Calaprice.

My daughter, Emily, served as a sounding board for my ideas about the changing values of teenagers and twenty-somethings, and helped devise catchy subheadings for various chapters. I am especially grateful to my wife, Jessica, for sharing sociological insights, making editorial corrections, and patiently engaging in several years' worth of seemingly endless conversations about "What drives crime rates down?"

ABBREVIATIONS

ADAM: Arrestee Drug Abuse Monitoring, a federal urine testing program formerly known as DUF (Drug Use Forecasting).

BJS: Bureau of Justice Statistics, part of the U.S. Department of Justice in Washington, D.C.

BLS: Bureau of Labor Statistics, part of the U.S. Department of Commerce in Washington, D.C.

CBC: Citizens Budget Commission, an independent monitoring group in New York City.

CCC: Citizens Crime Commission, an independent monitoring group in New York City.

CDC: Center for Disease Control, part of the U.S. Department of Health and Human Services in Atlanta.

CJA: Criminal Justice Agency, a municipal agency that determines bail eligibility.

Compstat: A shorthand term that is a contraction of computers and statistics but embraces all the new strategies and tactics implemented since the New York City police department reengineered its operations beginning in 1994.

CUNY: City University of New York, a collection of low-tuition public senior and community colleges.

DAWN: Drug Abuse Warning Network, a data-collection system about drug abuse, linking hospitals and medical examiner's offices across the country, run by the U.S. Department of Health and Human Services.

DCJS: Division of Criminal Justice Services, a New York State agency that serves as a clearinghouse for all statistics from police departments, prosecutors, courts, and corrections agencies.

DEA: Drug Enforcement Administration, a federal agency that is part of the U.S. Department of Justice in Washington, D.C.

DOCS: Department of Correctional Services, the New York State agency that runs the prison system.

DOH: Department of Health, the municipal agency that maintains the Vital Statistics database drawn from information provided by relatives on death certificates.

FDAR: Firearms Discharge Assault Report, a compendium of shots fired by and at officers of the NYPD, discontinued as a regularly released publication after 1994.

HIDTA: High Intensity Drug Trafficking Area, a designation of the New York metropolitan region, among others, by a multiagency task force.

IAD: Internal Affairs Division, a branch of the New York City police department that ferrets out corruption.

IBO: Independent Budget Office, a watchdog group that monitors municipal spending.

IDU: Intravenous drug users, mostly heroin addicts, but also those who inject a combination of heroin and cocaine.

INS: Immigration and Naturalization Service, the federal agency in charge of deportations and criminal aliens.

LAPD: Los Angeles Police Department.

MAST: Michigan Alcohol Screening Test, a 25-question survey used to determine which new state prisoners have drinking problems.

MMR: Mayor's Management Report, an annual compendium of statements and statistics about the performance of municipal agencies, initiated in 1982.

NCVS: National Crime Victimization Survey, an annual federal survey of the public that determines how many people suffered injuries and losses from street crimes, initiated in 1973.

NIJ: National Institute of Justice, the federal organization that runs the Bureau of Justice Statistics, and the ADAM (formerly DUF) drug-testing program.

NYPD: New York Police Department, the municipal law enforcement agency for all five boroughs.

OAS: Office of Applied Studies, SAMHSA, the branch that runs the DAWN drug-monitoring system.

PBA: Patrolmen's Benevolent Association, the equivalent of the uniformed officers' union within the NYPD.

SAMHSA: Substance Abuse and Mental Health Services Administration, a federal Agency that runs the DAWN drug-monitoring system.

SCU: Street Crime Unit, an elite branch within the NYPD that patrols in plainclothes looking for suspected gunmen.

SHR: Supplementary Homicide Report, a standard form filled out by every police department after every murder is discovered, and then forwarded to the FBI for inclusion in its annual UCR.

SNAG: Street Narcotics and Guns, a unit within the NYPD.

SUNY: State University of New York, a multicampus public college system.

TNT: Tactical Narcotics Teams, a now-defunct NYPD unit that was designed to make many street drug arrests.

UCR: Uniform Crime Report, the FBI's annual nationwide report initiated in 1930.

ONE

The 1990s Crime Crash in New York

A Mysterious Outbreak of Better Behavior Sweeps over the City

> I have never seen anything as extraordinary as this, and I have been in government for 40 years.
>
> —Queens district attorney Richard Brown (quoted in Krauss, 1995a:1)

At the dawn of the 1990s, New Yorkers were slaughtering one another at a record clip. A staggering body count of 2,245 violent deaths made 1990 the bloodiest year in the City's history. The surging crime wave foretold of a nightmarish future, and many longtime residents proclaimed their intention of escaping from an unlivable and unworkable metropolis that had deteriorated into an urban battleground. But then, unexpectedly, an astonishing turnaround took place. By the close of the decade, the death toll had been halved and then nearly halved again, tumbling to its lowest levels since the mid-1960s. For some mysterious reasons, interpersonal conflict subsided dramatically and the inhabitants of the five boroughs found themselves coexisting much more peacefully. Manhattan, in particular, once again became *the* place to live and work. Such progress toward resolving a serious social problem over a short time span is rarely achieved. If cancer mortality, poverty rates, pollution levels, or even traffic congestion could be cut so substantially in just a few years, the degree of improvement would be termed "a miracle."

Pundits discussing New York City's incredibly shrinking crime rate discovered that there was no appropriate expression in the terminology of criminology or even in everyday language to describe the opposite of a rapidly spreading epidemic of lawlessness. Mild metaphors such as an "ebbing," "subsiding," or "receding" of an earlier crime wave that had engulfed the City just didn't capture the drama and novelty of the momentous reversal. Never before had double-digit declines, year after year, taken place in a major metropolitan area, so there had been no previous need to coin such an upbeat expression. Perhaps the alliterative term "crime crash" is the most appropriate way to describe an unanticipated plunge of this magnitude and importance. However, unlike an unforeseen but ruinous stock market crash that suddenly wipes out financial investments, the crime crash was greeted with sighs of relief as an oppressive burden quickly melted away.

Surprisingly, no "blue ribbon" commission of criminal justice experts was set up by the mayor, the governor, or the president to attempt to figure out why the crash took place. Even though New York City's future viability was at stake, no politician or office seeker called for a thorough investigation of the events leading up to the sudden reversal of fortune. In fact, no steps were even taken to improve public access to government records and agency files for those who wanted to seriously study this dramatic turnaround.

The outbreak of better behavior that swept across the City presented an unparalleled opportunity for researchers. The challenge was to get to the bottom of this "miracle" and discover its underlying nonsupernatural causes, so that even more lives could be saved before it dissipated or, worse yet, reversed course. A capsule history of some of the key developments as well as the mood swings that preceded the crash will shed light on the reasons for this unprecedented but most welcomed change.

Written Off as Terminally Ill: A Near-Death Experience?

Reports of New York City's impending demise have always been premature.

Even before the Civil War, a traveler (Strong, quoted in Barbanel, 1991:B1), watching the planting of trees in a muddy excavation that would become Central Park, mused that the City might succumb to the intertwined problems of poverty and crime long before the saplings grew to maturity: "Perhaps the city itself will perish before then by growing too big to live under faulty institutions, corruptly administered."

But that dire forecast was completely off-base. About one hundred years later, in 1964, the five boroughs, far from being deserted, were home to an overflow population that briefly broke the eight million mark. Yet, just as the number of residents hit an all-time high, perceptions spread that Gotham was rapidly going downhill. The frank admission that the inner city was burdened by deep-seated problems was triggered by the 1964 Harlem "riot," the first of a wave of big-city ghetto uprisings that swept across the nation. The headlines introducing a series of articles in the *New York Herald Tribune* in 1965 about the state of the City reflected a loss of confidence: "New York City in crisis," and "New York, greatest city in the world—and everything is wrong with it" (Ehrenhalt, 1992). To dispel the sense of impending disaster, Mayor John Lindsay in the late 1960s cheerfully characterized the five boroughs as "Fun City."

But pessimism about the future marred the start of the 1970s. In his first try at becoming mayor in 1973 (which failed), Congressman Edward Koch warned that unless a "tough stance" was adopted, the rising crime rate would drive away the middle class, setting into motion a chain reaction that would undercut the City's tax base and consequently lead to a deterioration in municipal services (see Newfield and Barrett, 1988:122). To restore investor confidence, an economist adopted an upbeat title for his book, *New York Is Very Much Alive* (Ginzberg, 1974). But any optimism was short-lived. In 1975, Mayor Abraham Beame discovered that New York's government had accumulated so much short-term debt that it could not repay its loans. The threat of bankruptcy and the ensuing fiscal crisis compelled the Beame administration to eliminate 65,000 jobs from the municipal payroll, impose a wage freeze on the remaining work force, severely cut back services that the poor depended on much more than the affluent, raise the fare on subways and buses, and end the century-long tradition of free tuition for students at the eighteen campuses of the sprawling City University (see Newfield and Barrett, 1988). Perhaps the most painful blow was delivered by the administration in Washington, when it refused to put the City on a life-support system. The bad news about the denial of a federal bailout was captured by the tabloid headline, "Ford to City: Drop Dead" (*Daily News*, 1975).

Even after the calamity of near-insolvency receded as belt-tightening saved the day, the damage was done in terms of lowered expectations about the quality of urban life in the foreseeable future. New Yorkers abandoned their old neighborhoods in droves and headed for the greener pastures of suburbia; census figures revealed that the population of the five boroughs emptied out by more than 800,000 (over 10 percent) during the 1970s.

Predictions about doom and gloom persisted as the 1980s began with a severe nationwide recession. Murderers claimed a record number of New Yorkers' lives (1,826 in 1981). But fears about a further downward slide melted away when the City's finance, real estate, and high-tech industries recovered, showering prosperity on the City's more privileged residents. Murders declined for four years and then bottomed out in 1985 at their lowest level in fifteen years. Mayor Edward Koch's speech inaugurating his third term in 1986 was laced with upbeat promises that local government could and should and would do more for the disadvantaged. The mayor (quoted in Newfield and Barrett, 1988:20) trumpeted a can-do chauvinism that defied the doomsayers:

> This is not a place of carefree quietude. Our city is not a refuge from reality. New York is what it always has been: it's the world's number one arena for genius, it's the battleground for new ideas. New York is the city where the future comes to rehearse, where the best come to get better. We are the leading city because we are the city of leaders. If you are trying for the top, you can't top New York.

After a brief respite of restored self-confidence, pessimism and cynicism returned with a vengeance in the latter half of the 1980s, and for good reasons. City government was rocked by a far-ranging corruption scandal, the crack-smoking epidemic swept through poor neighborhoods, AIDS seemed an unstoppable plague that was about to go mainstream, and homelessness loomed as an intractable feature of the urban landscape. A crash on the New York Stock Exchange in 1987 (with the Dow losing 22 percent of its value in a single day) triggered an economic downturn that within a few years enveloped the entire nation in another recession. Before long, a depiction of the "Rotting of the Big Apple" graced the cover of *Time* magazine. Inside, a slew of particularly brutal slayings provoked an article entitled "The Decline of New York." It read like an obituary for a once-proud and vibrant metropolis that now was "consumed with crime," where "unchecked violence" had "dulled the luster." The citizenry was "plunging into chaos" as the situation "spun out of control." The hustle and "bustle of a hyperkinetic city" had degenerated into a mad frenzy. In nursery schools, students were drilled "to hit the floor at the sound of gunfire." Epidemics of AIDS and venereal diseases had pushed the city's health care system "to the breaking point." Busy streets deteriorated into "public restrooms for people and animals." Trash collection had to be cut because the city's budget was in a "financial straightjacket." Even the banker who headed up the city's financial control board eschewed his usual optimism and confessed that he could not see any light at the end of the tunnel (see Attinger, 1989:41).

Suspicions that Gotham's lingering illness had finally turned terminal reached a feverish pitch among journalists and commentators during 1990, just as David Dinkins, New York's first African American mayor, assumed his new responsibilities. Calling New York "a city under siege" during his campaign, Mayor Dinkins vowed in his inaugural address to be the "toughest mayor on crime this city has ever seen" (quoted in "Mobilizing to fight crime," 1990:B2). Elected on a platform of racial healing and a better deal for the downtrodden, Mayor Dinkins was quickly forced by revenue shortfalls to make hard choices. At first, he planned to delay the hiring of new police recruits, declaring, "It is a mistake . . . to make sure that we have plenty of cops and cut out all of the services." But as the local economy worsened, the misery and abject poverty visible for all to see caused the editors of the *New York Times* (1990:28) to lament: "New York City is staggering. The streets already resemble a New Calcutta, bristling with beggars and sad schizophrenics tuned in to inner voices. Crime, the fear of it as much as the fact, add overtones of a New Beirut. . . . And now the tide of wealth and taxes that helped the city make these streets bearable has ebbed."

The soft-spoken mayor's reformist agenda immediately became sidetracked by demands that he allocate the City's limited resources to the fight against a rag-tag army of predators that was inflicting a slow death from thousands of cuts. One journalist warned that "A new tidal wave of crime has swept over New York, adding terrifying numbers and stories to a city already plagued by violence" (Greenberg, 1990:20). In the poorer parts of town, the sounds of gunfire punctuated the night. After stray bullets claimed the lives of four children within a nine-day span, a reporter (Attinger, 1990) for a leading news magazine condemned this slaughter of the innocents:

> The slain children are called mushrooms in street lingo—as vulnerable as plants underfoot. Their deaths have pushed New Yorkers, already reeling from a daunting inventory of urban ills, to a new depth of despair. . . . More than the epidemic of homelessness, more than inadequate schools, filthy streets, high taxes and the outrageous cost of living, violent crime is gnawing at the soul of the city that thinks of itself as the embodiment of American energy and creativity.

New York State's chief justice, Sol Wachtler, warned that crack-related offenses were overwhelming the court system. "And certainly no illicit drug epidemic in our history will produce consequences as profound and lasting," he feared, because "hundreds of thousands of children are growing up knowing only violence, abuse, neglect, addiction and hopelessness" because their mothers as well as their fathers were swept up into self-destructive behaviors (quoted in Egan, 1990:B3). He predicted that "what we are living with in New York today is not a cyclical rise and fall in the rate of crime." As 1990 went down in the record books as the bloodiest year in New York's history, marred by 2,245 murders, a tabloid headline screamed, "Dave, Do Something!"[1] The mayor was forced to devise a massive tax package to beef up the police and the criminal justice system, calling it "our battle plan against fear, a plan that will give us the tools to restore our confidence in the future" (Dinkins, 1990:B2). The mayor also was compelled to accept what pundits dubbed a "doomsday budget" because it severely cut back the municipal services that poor people counted upon (see Barbanel, 1991; Klein, 1991).

The City's image slipped another notch because of a highly publicized murder of a tourist: a son was stabbed to death while trying to protect his parents from a pack of young robbers in a midtown subway station (T. Morgenthau, 1990). Concerns about the City's moral health heightened when a young father became so infuriated with his six-day-old son that he chopped up the baby boy and fed the pieces to the family's German shepherd. A veteran journalist decried the sorry state of affairs:

In the barbarized city of New York, there is no horror these days. We no longer seem capable of that basic human emotion, which is why so many of us have begun to lose all hope for a more decent future. . . . Millions of New Yorkers have been as emotionally immobilized as anyone who lives too long in the presence of violence and death: emergency-room doctors, soldiers, Mafia hit men.

Meanwhile, as this dreadful century comes to an end, poor New York will slide deeper into decay, becoming a violent American Calcutta. The middle class will flee in greater numbers, the tax base will shrink, the criminals will rule our days and nights. Drugs, crime, despair, illiteracy, disease: All will increase into the next century. If there are twenty-five bums in the corner park now, make way for another 100. If there are two thousand murders this year, get ready for four thousand. New York is dying. (Hamill, 1990)

Back from the Dead: Was This a Great Time, or What?

As we move toward the new millennium, we as New Yorkers can take pride in the fact that our great city has regained its true stature as the Capital of the World. Our crime rate is at levels not witnessed since the 1960s, tourism in the City is at historic levels and our streets and parks are the cleanest in recent memory.

Four years ago, few would have dreamed, much less believed that these strides were possible. In fact, New York City, like other American cities, was essentially written off as a symbol of urban decay. Yet we have proven the cynics wrong and shown what is possible.

—Mayor Rudolph Giuliani (1997c:1)

Fast-forward a few years and a dramatic mood swing has swept across the social landscape. Unbridled boosterism and unabashed triumphalism has supplanted despair about the present and pessimism about the future. To many commentators, it was as if a prolonged, blinding blizzard had ended, the storm clouds were breaking up, the sun was shining once again, and people were emerging from their homes to survey the damage and make repairs. The rush was on to declare New York City back on its feet, alive and kicking, revitalized and reinvigorated. The local economy that had sputtered to a halt was picking up steam. The former U.S. attorney for the metropolitan area's Southern District in the Reagan administration, Rudolph Giuliani, had won the mayoralty on the Republican ticket even though the overwhelming majority of voters were registered Democrats. The Giuliani administration abandoned the social welfare policies and tolerance of deviant behavior that had become so closely identified with New York–style liberalism, and instead pursued a prosecutorial approach of tightening up, cracking down, and getting tough. As crime rates fell and profit margins rose, Mayor Giuliani's conservative policies were given the credit and reaped a windfall of highly favorable, accentuate-the-positive publicity, even in the reputedly liberal organs of the mass media.

From the summer of 1995 onward, story after story recounted the same theme: that the recovery was made possible by the drop in crime, which in turn was due to strict enforcement of the law. One of the more politically explicit attacks on the alleged failure of liberal policies summed up the situation this way:

> Flash back a few years. New York City had become seemingly ungovernable, a seedy place of garbage, graffiti, and crime, mired in economic decline and home to the nation's largest underclass. Who'd want to live there? No longer the hub of urbanity, Gotham was by the late eighties the very symbol of urban decay—30 years of cultural revolution had done its grievous work undermining city life. Today, astoundingly, New York is once again the place where striving men and women want to live. (Anderson, 1998:24)

The same news magazines that solemnly announced the city's impending demise in 1990 gleefully proclaimed its rebirth in the second half of the 1990s. One ran a cover story entitled, "The Big Apple comes roaring back—and other cities wonder how it was done." It focused on the signs of optimism that "were everywhere" in "Comeback City": "After three decades of economic and social malaise, Gotham has reversed its fortunes to become a national model for how cities resurrect themselves" (Marks, 1997).

A caption under some photos in a rival news magazine underscored this same spiritual renewal theme: "After decades of graffiti, muggings, and subway shootings, all this good news has even the most blasé New Yorkers taking notice. Whether it's falling crime rates or a healthy Dow, residents have new reasons to be proud of their city" (Adler, 1997).

In the media frenzy of accounts purporting to explain how the City escaped the grim reaper's clutches, the upbeat titles of the articles got the main messages across: "The end of crime as we know it" (Horowitz, 1995); "Why the Big Apple feels safer" (Beiser, 1995); "Safe? You bet your life" (Epperson, 1995); "Now, how low can crime go?" (Krauss, 1996a); "Finally, we're winning the war against crime" (*Time* magazine cover of January 15, 1996); "City coming back, New Yorkers roar" (Saltonstall, 1996); "New York City keeps getting safer" (Hampson, 1997); and "We'll take Manhattan" (Adler, 1997). The crime problem was pictured as "withering away" (Shah, 1996) because the murder rate was in "something like a statistical free fall" (Lacayo, 1996). The concomitant emergence of the "suddenly safer city" (Horowitz, 1995; also Krauss, 1995c) was described as "stunning" (Gaiter, 1997); an "astounding" and "remarkable" turnabout (Methvin, 1997), "simply breathtaking," a "marvel," and even a "miracle" (Krauss, 1995c).

As if to certify its reinstatement in good standing in the eyes of powerbrokers, *Fortune* magazine in 1997 ranked New York as the most favorable place to do business—due, in part, to its reduced crime rate. The year before, New York didn't even make *Fortune*'s list. An article in a business magazine, "New York: The Ride," likened an excursion on a double-decker sightseeing bus to a theme park trip that visited formerly "scary" sites such as Harlem or Times Square (T. Smith, 1997). In the now Disneyfied New York, tourism had expanded to such a degree that it rivaled Wall Street as the city's biggest source of revenue. The total number of visitors rose by nearly 33 percent, to about 34 million a year, and the amount of money they spent shot up 23 percent, to over 14 billion dollars, between 1994 and 1998. They came in droves largely because the fear of crime "pretty much vanished" since tourists could wander around "without being besieged by hordes of junkies and other panhandlers"(Editors, *New York Post*, 1998c). Not only had the city become the number one destination for international visitors, and the third most popular attraction for all tourists in the entire United States (right behind Orlando and Las Vegas), but pollsters reported it also rose to the top of the list as the nation's most desirable place to live, ahead of Seattle and San Francisco (Marks, 1997). Long-depressed residential real estate prices soared, and gentrification spread to neighborhoods outside of red-hot

Manhattan, as trendsetters clamored to move back. The hotel industry prospered like never before, enjoying its lowest vacancy rates despite charging the highest prices for rooms in the country (Pristin, 1999).

The growing attractiveness of New York as the "in" place-to-be greatly benefited its institutions of higher learning. Drawn by the City's refurbished image, cutting-edge vitality, night life, and job and internship opportunities, record-breaking numbers of out-of-town high school seniors inundated the admissions offices of local colleges and universities with their applications. The stiff competition for seats in the freshman class enabled prestigious universities to become much more selective and only admit students with the best GPAs and SAT scores, and thereby to rise even higher in national rankings (Arenson, 1998).

Even the Bronx shared in some of the glory. The home of the poorest congressional district in the country, it had been the target of relentless negative publicity since the 1970s for resembling a "bombed-out no-man's land," an image reinforced by mean-spirited movies like *Fort Apache, the Bronx,* and *Bonfire of the Vanities.* But in 1997 it was designated as an "All-American City" by the National Civic League (Stewart, 1997).

Eventually, the steady stream of favorable publicity and the accompanying self-congratulations lost its novelty. Reporters scrambled to discover a fresh angle to maintain their audience's interest. For example, when the level of violence among inmates behind bars on Rikers Island tumbled, headline writers put this spin on the story: "City reports a big reduction of crime in jail, of all places" (Cooper, 1997b). Other enterprising journalists pounced on any signs that the crime rate might be going back up, even temporarily, in any of the constituent categories (such as forcible rape, or domestic violence), or in particular precincts, or in specific locales such as public housing projects or subways.

Irrational Exuberance about the Reversal of Fortune? A Tale of Two Cities

Tonight we lost a battle but the war goes on. Our schools still don't work, still don't educate our kids. . . . Too many New Yorkers are out of a job. . . . We suffer police brutality instead of setting tough standards to prevent it. . . . Nearly half our kids still live in poverty. More homeless and hungry people fill our streets than ever before. The good times roll on for some, but far too many others are still left out in the cold.

—Mayoral Candidate Ruth Messinger, concession speech upon defeat, 1997

Ironically, the crime-crash years were simultaneously the best and the worst of times. In this tale of two New York cities, the situation of the poor improved a great deal in the sense that they were victimized less often by the street criminals in their midst. But it must have been particularly tough to be mired in poverty in the midst of plenty as neighborhoods gentrified to attract a more affluent clientele. The many ways that people on the margins suffered aroused far less concern than when the depredations of the destitute made headlines back in the bad old days.

The message that people without money or marketable high-tech skills no longer had a place in the new upscale social order emanated from businesses and government in many different ways. Industrial giants shifted production overseas to save on labor costs, leaving behind legions of blue-collar workers scrambling for a dwindling number of factory slots and poorly paid service jobs. Soaring demand, low vacancy rates, and conversions of rental units into expensive condominiums and cooperatives drove rents to the highest levels in the nation and created a housing crisis for low-income residents seeking decent, affordable apartments (see Bernstein, 1999a; Hevesi, 1999).[2] All but the most persistent indigents were discouraged from staying around to receive the food stamp and Medicaid benefits they were entitled to by law (Swarns, 1999). As one anti-poverty advocate put it, "the poor and homeless are intimidated, lied to, and given the runaround while they beg for help" (Jones, 1999).[3] Long lines formed in front of food pantries and soup kitchens as private charities tried in vain to make up for the reductions in government aid. Years of campaigning against "entitlements," "handouts," "chronic welfare dependency," "welfare queens," and other negative stereotypes paid off in the mid-1990s, when federal, state, and local lawmakers enacted a slew of controversial reforms. Many recipients, including mothers of small children, had to perform workfare obligations to earn their meager allotments. Changes in eligibility and maximum payment levels phased out any relative advantages that may have previously prevailed in New York, especially when the already high and rapidly rising cost of living was taken into account. The City was doing well in the "race to the bottom," in which municipalities and states competed to make themselves as inhospitable to geographically mobile poor people as possible. Compared to a 1970 baseline, welfare allotments fell substantially, down 48 percent in New York by 1996, factoring in inflation (Editors, *New York Times*, 1994; Kilborn, 1996; Krueger and Seley, 1996; Accordino, 1998).

Compassion fatigue for street people set in. The Transit Authority's management instructed subway passengers not to toss coins toward the outstretched styrofoam cups of panhandlers because such random acts of kindness only encouraged beggars to congregate at entrances or sleep on the platforms and in trains. The time was right to order the police to roust homeless persons from their encampments in subway tunnels, under bridges, and in parks. The police also evicted squatters from the abandoned tenements on the Lower East Side that they had reclaimed and fixed up with their own sweat equity. When the City Council criminalized "aggressive panhandling" as a misdemeanor punishable by a fine or even jail time, there could be no doubt that many New Yorkers had become fed up not only with the homeless, but also with other members of the highly visible underclass—especially window-wiping "squeegee pests," as they were mockingly dubbed—and disoriented mental patients who wandered through the streets. The war on poverty of the 1960s had morphed into a full-scale war against the poor by the 1990s (see Gans, 1995).

A stubbornly persistent street-crime problem served as a reminder that the surge in economic growth had not put an end to deprivation and discontent. Even after the crash, crime was down, but not out. As the 1990s drew to a close, still, on average, between one and two people were killed each day within the City's limits. The notion that the murder rate had greatly diminished was strictly relative. To people whose frame of reference was a less troubled part of the nation or a much more peaceful region of the world, boasting about this level of carnage must have seemed bizarre. Even with a murder rate that was less than one-third of what it used to be, the streets were still dangerous by any sane and reasonable standards.

Actually, the late 1990s were banner years for heartbreaking and outrageous killings. Even with far fewer tragedies to sensationalize, the tabloids still had plenty of grist for their mills. A number of despicable deeds received intense coverage, but these scattered reports were now "taken in stride" and viewed as "anomalies" because a "sense of siege" had lifted (Marks, 1997). Unlike the horror stories of the early 1990s, these equally disturbing acts of depravity failed to generate the "What is life in this city coming to?" type of handwringing and soul-searching. It seemed as if New York's new, very positive image had a teflon coating. No brutal slaying captured the media's interest and the public's attention long enough to generate enough moral outrage to build widespread demands that the social roots of the crime problem be tackled, as had happened back before the crash.

Criminological Detective Work: Following Up Leads

Murders are the most heinous of all illegal acts because lives are irrevocably destroyed—not only of victims, but also of their families and friends, and even of offenders and their kin. Murders are the most closely monitored of all crimes because killings can symbolize something more profoundly disturbing and significant: the level of conflict in a society, the intensity of its internal cleavages, and the degree of tensions among social classes, generations, sexes, and racial, ethnic, and religious groups. Consequently, the annual death toll comprises the sum total of such classic expressions of social strife as predatory behavior, resistance to exploitation, cut-throat competition, bitter rivalries, long-standing family feuds, marital discord, culture wars over clashing life-styles, the "class struggle," and even the "battle of the sexes." Clearly, the murder rate serves as a barometer of social health. A soaring body count indicates a rise in discontent, alienation, animosities, mutual antagonisms, displaced frustration, fratricidal violence, low-intensity warfare, and the readiness of many people to kill plus their willingness to die. A plunging murder rate signals a deescalation of hostilities, greater tolerance of diversity and differences, and a growing acceptance of existing social arrangements and interpersonal relationships.

As the threat of becoming a victim of murder subsided to levels far below those of other big cities, New Yorkers began to wonder, "Why us?" What was the secret? What were the underlying reasons for the unexpected outbreak of law-abiding behavior? To try to solve this mystery, reporters consulted experts like police commanders and prosecutors, and interviewed the proverbial "man in the street," as well as some "boys in the 'hood." Lots of speculation swirled about during electoral campaigns, in the news media, on talk shows, and inside college classrooms. Some explanations seemed quite plausible, but others sounded far-fetched. Certain insistent demands for credit were shamelessly self-serving and self-promoting, put forward by parties that obviously had vested interests in trying to mold public opinion.

When representatives of various constituencies contend that they surely know the reason why crime was suddenly going out of style, it is time to call for claims investigators. That's a job description for criminologists. Criminologists study illegal activities, offenders, victims, the origins and impacts of laws, the workings of the justice system, the public's reaction to the crime problem, plus the causes of individual law-breaking sprees and of waves of collective misbehavior. Criminologists have a professional responsibility to evaluate objectively the veracity of a claim for credit. Criminologists must maintain a wait-and-see attitude, and declare, with a healthy dose of scientific skepticism, "That's doubtful. Prove it! Where's the evidence to support that claim?" By exercising independent judgment, criminologists can function as members of a self-appointed truth squad. Confronted by competing theories about the reasons for the crash, criminologists have a duty to remain impartial and nonpartisan. Treating each credible hypothesis as just another lead to be followed up, criminologists must gather and analyze data that either provide empirical support or undermine the likelihood of a claim. Once these competing hypotheses have been tested, with some accepted and others rejected, the secrets behind the crash could be revealed. Then it might be possible to learn some lessons that will help to sustain the momentum, forestall any major reversals in the downward trends, and enable other jurisdictions to benefit from an understanding of the ups and downs of New York's experience with criminal violence.

When a murder is committed, detectives want to figure out "whodunit" so they can bring the culprit to justice. To solve the crime, they try to reconstruct the last few days of the victim's life, to discover who wanted this person dead. They narrow down the number of suspects who might have had the opportunity as well as the motive by tracking down leads, searching for clues, gathering evidence, interviewing eye-witnesses, checking out alibis, and sorting through lies to uncover the truth. Detectives look for patterns running through their past cases in order to enhance their crime-solving skills.

Just like detectives, criminologists want to solve mysteries by figuring out what was going on right before the violence erupted. But unlike detectives, criminologists are interested in the "big picture" and rarely immerse themselves in the particularities of a single case. As social scientists, they want to study hundreds, even thousands of slayings in order to unearth the common threads that run through many of these tragedies. The goal is to derive accurate statistical portraits of the typical offenders and their usual victims. Criminologists also need to find out the most often used murder weapons, the most likely crime scene locations, and the most frequent motives for terminating the lives of other human beings. Finally, existing patterns and emerging trends must be spotted to pinpoint the causes of rising and falling violent crime rates.

To launch their investigations, criminologists need to sift and sort through the evidence contained in detectives' case files, forensic pathologists' autopsy reports, and journalists' interviews, to see what leads they have uncovered that might be of use to help bring the big picture into focus.

Some valuable leads suggested by other observers that needed to be followed up were that crime statistics may have been manipulated; that along with murder rates, other crime rates may have plummeted, too; that crime rates also may have tumbled in other parts of the country as well; and that the differences that set New York apart from other cities may have accounted for its superior progress in reducing crime.

Two Crime Waves: Way Up, Down Somewhat, Soaring to Record Levels, Crash!

The New York that brims with health and vibrancy today seemed destined for a different ending in 1977. The city went broke and grew steadily dirtier and more disheveled. A blackout plunged millions of people into darkness punctuated by fiery riots and the screeching voices of looters. . . . Life in a city that seemed to be terminally breaking down was tense enough. But a serial killer whom the tabloids had dubbed the "Son of Sam" was stalking the streets, killing at random, taunting the police with handwritten notes.

—Editors, *New York Times* (1999:A10)

The late 1970s is an appropriate point in time to begin an analysis of the causes of homicides in New York City. The worst consequences of the mid-decade fiscal crisis, especially the lay-offs of police officers and the drastic cuts in municipal services, were winding down. The social repercussions of the widespread looting that accompanied the July 1977 power failure and that resulted in several thousand arrests which clogged the criminal justice system and polarized the population along racial lines were fading away. Accurate monitoring and accessible statistical record keeping about a number of social and economic conditions were underway.

As the 1970s came to a close, the murder rate was climbing. After reaching an all-time high in 1981, homicides fell for four consecutive years, decreasing by almost 25 percent. Unfortunately, an abrupt turnaround took place in the middle of the decade, and the city was caught in the grip of yet another crime wave that lasted five years. It culminated in 1990, when the record set back in 1981 was shattered.[4] The crash of the 1990s started slowly at first and then snowballed for the rest of the decade, driving down the homicide rate by 72 percent to levels not experienced since 1964 (see graph 1-1).

The fact that there were two time periods when murders went down and two when murders went up during the twenty years under scrutiny permits researchers to "double-check" any explanations for the two "crime waves" and the two periods of falling rates, one a modest decline, and the other a crash. A key question is, Was the crime wave of the late 1980s fueled by the same underlying problems as the crime wave of the late 1970s? And, did the same interplay of factors that drove homicide rates down in the early 1980s materialize again to bring about the crash of the 1990s?

The question arises, Was the crash of the 1990s unprecedented? If the graph were extended further back, it would become evident that never before in New York City's history (at least, not during the twentieth century) has the murder rate fallen so substantially, year after year. The only other sustained declines of considerable magnitude were registered dur-

Graph 1.1. Trends in Murders, New York City, 1955–1998

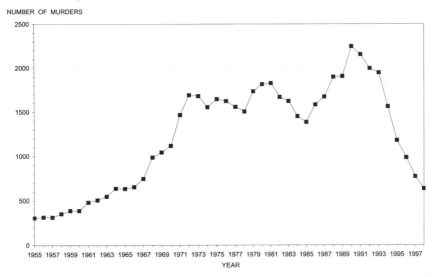

NUMBER OF MURDERS

Source: NYPD's Annual Complaints and Arrests Statistical Reports.

ing the consecutive years of 1939 to 1943 (down 31 percent), and 1946 to 1951 (down 30 percent). But these earlier multiyear drops are less impressive because they were calculated on a much smaller and therefore more statistically volatile base of just a few hundred murders per annum.

When the murder rate began to plunge during the mid-1990s, some skeptics wondered whether the welcomed relief wasn't just another example of the well-known statistical phenomenon called "regression to the mean," which can be summarized by the phrase, "What goes up must come down." But when the carnage subsided to levels not experienced in more than thirty years, it became clear that the impressive improvement could not be dismissed as just an inevitable downswing that evened-out a volatile situation after a rapid run-up (see Maltz, 1998). Furthermore, the crash took most criminologists by surprise. As crime rates dropped across the country, with New York City leading the way, skeptical headlines cautioned readers that "experts warn against seeing a trend" (Butterfield, 1995a); "experts warn of coming 'storm' of juvenile violence" (Butterfield, 1995c); and "experts on crime warn of a 'ticking time bomb'" (Butterfield, 1996a). Several criminologists were hesitant to confirm that a crash was taking place because they had predicted that the arrival of a generation of out-of-control, barely socialized "super-predators" would usher in a reign of terror before the century ended (see Annin, 1996).

Too Good to Be True? The Accuracy of Crime Statistics

During the past five years, at least two precinct captains were forced to retire after separate incidents of underreporting crime. Last year, Commissioner Safir created a special squad to review the accuracy of crime statistics. . . . Some officials say a pattern of deception may have developed because city government has become so focused on crime statistics that commanders feared they would be punished unless they produced the proper numbers.

—Kocieniewski (1998c:B1)

Many people are profoundly distrustful of statistics released by government agencies because they fear officials might try to use authoritative-sounding numbers to manipulate public opinion. An old adage warns that politicians use statistics like drunks use lamp posts: for support, not illumination. Therefore, a basic question must be addressed at the outset: Is the alleged drop in murders too good to be true? Are the impressive statistics being fudged to make the streets seem safer than they really are?

Crime statistics from police sources have proven to be unreliable on a few occasions. When the NYPD adopted a more centralized reporting system in 1966, the number of victim complaints about major crimes shot up by more than 70 percent. Precinct captains were no longer able to impress their superiors by downgrading a portion of the burglary complaints lodged by victims to mere instances of petit larceny, and of robberies to simple assaults (Weinraub, 1967). Thirty years later, the same problem reappeared. NYPD auditors caught five commanding officers from various precincts downgrading felonious assaults and grand larcenies into misdemeanors that were not counted as part of the City's crime index and did not have to be reported to Washington for inclusion in the FBI's Uniform Crime Report (UCR) (Forero, 2000). Also exposed was a decades-old tradition of keeping down the known number of crimes committed in the subways by recording them as having taken place on the streets. Although this manipulative practice did not affect the overall tallies because the incidents were counted by the nearest above-ground precincts, the scheme led to the underestimation of subway crime by about 20 percent each year. Questionable accounting practices also were unearthed in Philadelphia, Atlanta, and Boca Raton, Florida, as the incentives of promotions and pay raises generated pressures on local law enforcement officials to keep their numbers down to demonstrate improved performance. A more casual approach toward upward trends prevailed before the mid-1990s due to "a belief by the average police chief, in their [*sic*] heart of hearts, that they couldn't do anything about crime because they couldn't affect the root causes of crime," according to Philadelphia P.D. Commissioner John Timoney, formerly a high-ranking member of the NYPD brass (quoted in Butterfield, 1998:A16).

When it comes to homicide statistics, such suspicions should be laid to rest. With the eventual discovery of most corpses, the problem of underestimation is minimal for homicides, save for those missing persons who truly were victims of foul play. But the most compelling reason to trust the accuracy of body counts is that the police are not the sole source of data. Another agency, the New York City Office of the Chief Medical Examiner, independently investigates all suspicious deaths and keeps its own records. Forensic pathologists visit all crime scenes to collect the victims' bodies, upon which they later perform autopsies at the morgue to determine the cause and time of death. Decades ago, one of the pathologists reportedly was very accommodating toward detectives, who occasionally pressured him to rule suspicious deaths to be the results of suicides, accidents, or natural causes (Bouza, 1990:90), but no such accusations have surfaced in recent years. The files kept by the medical examiner's office are incorporated annually into the New York City Department of Health's vital statistics database derived from death certificates, and serve as a double-check of the yearly body count maintained by the NYPD. The degree of correspondence between the tallies from the two sources is very high. The number of homicide victims according to the Health Department's vital statistics database usually exceeds the official police body count by a few percentage points because it includes cases in which suspects deemed to be extremely dangerous were killed by the police (justifiable homicides are not murders); cases in which the deaths are later judged to be accidental (such as when youths play with a loaded gun); and people who were wounded outside the city limits but were brought to hospitals within the five boroughs for intensive care (which failed to save their lives). Since the discrepancy is recurring, insignificant, and doesn't alter trends, the general agreement between the two sets of figures should eliminate any lingering concerns that murder totals can be deliberately inflated or deflated by interested parties for some ulterior purposes.

The same degree of confidence in the accuracy of official statistics is not warranted when examining trends in the totals of the other street crimes. The biggest problem with the data is that many incidents are not reported to the police by victims, for a variety of reasons, and therefore fail to make the record books. For example, according to the findings of the U.S. Department of Justice's annual National Crime Victimization Survey (NCVS) in 1998, only 44 percent of all victims of violent crimes (rapes, robberies, and assaults) told NCVS interviewers that these incidents were brought to the attention of the police nationwide (Rennison, 1999), and even fewer, just 32 percent, were reported to the NYPD by City victims. Similarly, only 35 percent of all property crimes (household burglaries, motor vehicle thefts, and other larcenies) were reported to police departments across the country, and only 29 percent to the NYPD (Smith, Steadman, and Minton, 1999). Clearly, statistics derived from police sources are unavoidably incomplete to greater and lesser degrees, depending upon the jurisdiction and the crime category. Therefore, the possibility arises that modest trends in crimes other than murders are not genuine but merely reflect an increase or a decrease in victim reporting rates.

Just Killings? Was Murder the Only Crime to Crash?

Even if the official numbers are underestimates, what were the trends in these other street crimes since the 1970s?

Besides murder, vehicle theft—of cars, trucks, vans, and motorcycles—is the only other street crime that is not significantly underreported to the police (but only if the thief drives the vehicle away; many victims do not inform the authorities about unsuccessful attempts). The reporting rate for completed vehicle thefts approaches 90 percent, according to the yearly NCVS survey. This statistic is high because motorists hope

Graph 1.2. Trends in Murders and Vehicle Thefts

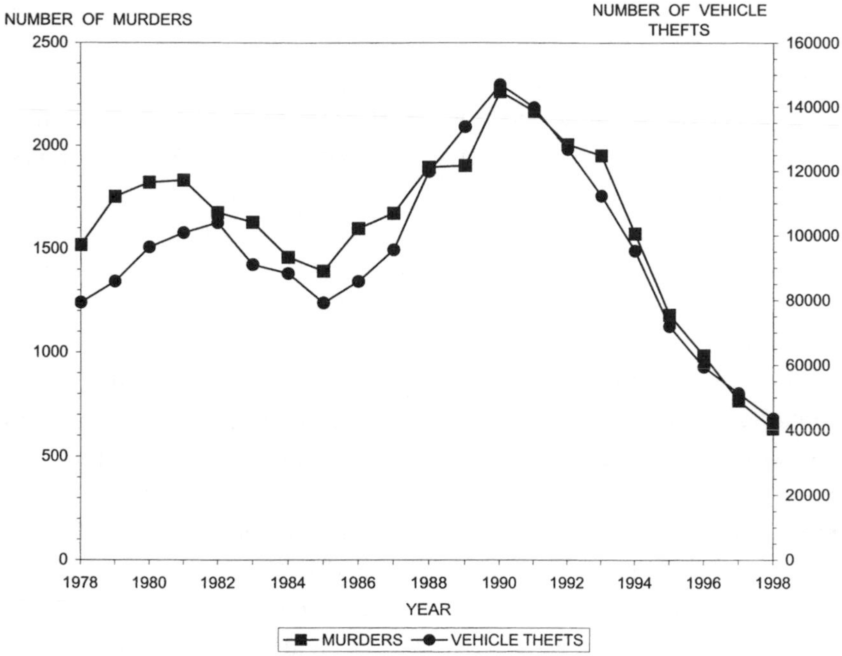

Note: Vehicle thefts include attempts.
Source: 1978–1998 NYPD Complaints and Arrests Statistical Reports.

their vehicles will be recovered intact; they want to be eligible for insurance reimbursement if the police cannot retrieve their stolen property; and they do not want to be held responsible as the presumed driver if the car is used in a crime or is involved in a hit-and-run accident.[5]

When body counts are compared to reported vehicle thefts for the years between 1978 and 1998, a striking pattern emerges. Both types of street crime increased in the late 1970s, declined in the early 1980s, rose again to new heights in the late 1980s, and plummeted after 1990, according to the two lines depicted in graph 1.2. Statisticians call the data from 1978 to 1998 a time series, and they describe the close correspondence between these two measures of distinct dimensions of the crime problem as a high positive correlation (the two variables move in lockstep, rising and falling together in tandem, with just one year out of sync).

The correlation detected in figure 1.2 furnishes an important clue about the factors or forces behind the mystery of New York's crime crash. They are not "crime specific." In other words, the explanation for the observed ups and downs does not lie in the particular nature of the crime, either life-and-death struggles or car stealing. For example, it is highly unlikely that auto theft was decreasing as a problem in the 1990s simply because new, more effective anti-theft devices (like steering wheel locks, ignition cut-offs, supersensitive alarms, or vehicle tracking systems) became available and were purchased by motorists. The companies that market theft-resistant hardware want to claim credit for the sharp decline, and this sounds like a plausible reason for the crash in auto thefts in the 1990s. But this alleged technological breakthrough would not explain the corresponding drop in murders.

Similarly, greatly improved emergency medical care in the 1990s could be helping critically injured victims recover from their gunshot and stab wounds.[6] However, hypothesizing that the murder rate tumbled because paramedics in ambulance crews, and doctors in hospital emergency rooms and intensive care units, became more proficient at saving the lives of victims who previously would have died from their critical injuries, does not explain falling vehicle theft rates. Hence, there must be some underlying change that accounts for the crash in both murders and vehicle thefts—and by extension, for the increase and decrease of other kinds of violent offenses and property crimes in New York over the twenty-year period. The observed close correspondence between body counts and stolen vehicles provides a good example of the statistician's old warning that "correlation doesn't prove causation." It doesn't make much sense to posit that murders inspire vehicle thefts, or that car stealing causes fatal encounters. It makes more sense to assume that some other force or combination of factors was driving up (and then down, up, down) the levels of both violence and theft during the twenty-year period.

Sharp drops also took place during the 1990s in the less accurate statistics monitoring the number of forcible rapes, robberies, aggravated assaults, burglaries, and larcenies reported by victims to the NYPD (see table 1.1).

Only murders and auto thefts, the two most accurately measured indicators of criminal activity, set records in 1990 (see the second column in table 1-1). Aggravated assaults (a catch-all category) and larcenies (including both grand and petit larcenies—the least often reported of all property crimes, according to NCVS findings) both peaked in 1988 and

Table 1.1. Changes in the Numbers of Reported Street Crimes, New York City, 1990–1998

Offense	Worst Year	Record Amount	1990	1998	1990–1998
Murder	1990	2,245	2,245	633	down 72%
Forcible Rape	1974	4,050	3,125	2,045	down 35%
Robbery	1981	107,495	100,260	39,355	down 61%
Aggravated Assault	1988	71,030	68,890	43,880	down 36%
Burglary	1980	210,700	119,940	46,185	down 61%
Larceny	1988	308,480	288,620	147,035	down 49%
Motor Vehicle Theft	1990	147,125	147,125	44,055	down 70%

Note: All reports rounded off to the nearest 5.
Source: FBI's Uniform Crime Reports, 1970–1999.

were already headed downward when the crash unfolded. Burglary reports had been subsiding nicely, ever since reaching an all-time high in 1980. As for forcible rapes, the least often reported of the violent offenses, the worst year had been 1974. Reports of rapes had been steadily drifting downward since the mid-1980s. In sum, all seven street crimes closely tracked by the FBI as components of its overall Crime Index in its annual Uniform Crime Report declined in frequency during the 1990s. Reports of burglaries and robberies plummeted almost as impressively as murder and vehicle theft.

Only in New York? Or Was Crime Down Everywhere?

Fear is the ugliest of emotions . . . and fear has seized American cities this summer. In Los Angeles and Atlanta, in Chicago and Milwaukee and Dallas, in Washington, Baltimore, Philadelphia, and here in New York as we know all too well, we have shattered all previous records for carnage in our streets.

—Mayor David Dinkins (1990:B2)

It is well known that within a city, some neighborhoods are much more dangerous than others. Therefore, local conditions—such as the social class of the area's residents, the extent of its unemployment problem, its drug scene, the strength of its community organizations, and the quality of its police protection—interact to influence the relative safety of a community. But the question arises: To what extent are local conditions shaped by more sweeping societal or even global forces? In 1990, most big cities were engulfed by a crime wave. But how were they faring later in the decade? Hence, another lead that criminologists need to explore carefully is, What was going on nationally while crime was crashing locally?

The answer is that crime definitely was in retreat in most other jurisdictions, according to two independent sources. People age twelve or older were experiencing fewer violent attacks and thefts by 1998 than in any previous year since 1973, according to the findings of the National Crime Victimization Survey (Rennison, 1999). Similarly, the number of serious crimes reported to the more than 17,000 police departments participating in the FBI's Uniform Crime Reporting System declined for seven consecutive years during the 1990s (FBI, 1999). The murder rate fell to its lowest levels in three decades, especially in cities with more than one million inhabitants, where it dropped from around 36 per 100,000 residents in 1991 to 20 per 100,000 in 1997 (Fox and Zawitz, 1999).

These findings yield two more useful clues. All types of street crimes were being committed less often, not only in New York, as determined above, but across the country as well; and, the steepest declines were taking place in the biggest cities. The downward trends registered in the largest urban centers merit greater scrutiny.

The decrease in the number of murders in the ten largest U.S. cities (with one million residents or more), plus several others whose crime problems were often in the news, is documented in table 1.2. It turns out that during the 1990s, the problem of criminal violence subsided in every one of the ten most populated cities. In fact, in San Diego, as well as in Boston (which is relatively small, with just half a million inhabitants), the murder rate plunged at an even greater clip than in New York. And in many of the ten biggest cities, especially Los Angeles and the three Texas urban centers of Dallas, Houston, and San Antonio, the drop in homicides was of the same order of magnitude as in New York, well over 50 percent in a time span of between five and eight years. Clearly, the decrease in murder rates was a nationwide urban phenomenon. However, only New York and Boston enjoyed a consistent drop in murders year after year throughout the entire 1990–1998 period. In most of the other big cities, the death toll began to drop a couple of years after 1990, and in a number of them (Philadelphia, Houston, Dallas, Phoenix,

Table 1.2. Changes in the Number of Murders Committed in
Large Cities during the 1990s

City	Worst Year	No. Murders	Best Year	No. Murders	Percent Decrease and Time Span	1998 Murder Rate per 100,000
New York	'90	2,245	'98	633	−72% over 8 years	9
Los Angeles	'92	1,094	'98	426	−61% over 6 years	12
Chicago	'92	939	'98	694	−26% over 6 years	26
Houston	'91	608	'97	254	−58% over 6 years	15
Philadelphia	'90	503	'98	338	−33% over 8 years	23
San Diego	'91	167	'98	42	−75% over 7 years	4
Phoenix	'94	231	'97	175	−24% over 3 years	15
San Antonio	'93	220	'98	89	−60% over 5 years	8
Dallas	'91	500	'97	209	−58% over 6 years	20
Detroit	'91	615	'96	428	−30% over 5 years	43
D.C.	'91	482	'98	260	−46% over 4 years	48
Boston	'90	143	'98	34	−76% over 8 years	6
New Orleans	'94	424	'98	230	−46% over 4 years	48

Notes: The best year and the worst year in the 1990s were chosen. In some cities murder levels went down, then up, then down again during the time interval between these best and worst years. Murder rates for 1998 were computed using 1996 population estimates, the latest Census figures available.
Source: FBI's Uniform Crime Reports, 1990–1998.

Detroit, and Washington, D.C.), body counts drifted back up during certain years.

Note that New York used to have the largest body count, since it is by far the nation's biggest city. But by 1998, New York's death toll fell below Chicago's, even though the Windy City had a population less than half the size of Gotham. This sign of progress led some people to the erroneous conclusion that New York no longer was the "murder capital of the United States." Actually, New York never was the murder capital, if population is taken into account.[7] Looking at murder rates per 100,000 rather than body counts—which is the only fair way to make comparisons between cities of varying sizes—New York's 1998 rate was much less than that of most other major cities (the streets of Detroit, New Orleans, and the nation's capital were about five times more dangerous), as is shown by the calculations in the last column in table 1.2.

In fact, even during the dismal days of 1990, New York's murder rate ranked tenth in the nation, behind (in descending order) Washington, D.C., New Orleans, Detroit, Dallas, Baltimore, Houston, Cleveland, Memphis, and Philadelphia. However, New York had the

Table 1.3. Comparison of Murder Rates, N.Y.C. and the Rest of the
United States, 1990–1998

	1990	1991	1992	1993	1994	1995	1996	1997	1998
New York City									
Body Count	2,245	2,154	1,995	1,946	1,561	1,177	983	770	633
Murder Rate	30.1	30.1	27.8	27.4	21.8	16.4	13.5	10.1	8.5
Rest of the U.S.									
Body Count	21,178	22,534	21,755	22,579	21,758	20,418	18,665	17,443	16,281
Murder Rate	9.4	9.8	9.3	9.5	9.0	8.2	7.2	6.8	6.2
Ratio of Murder Rates									
N.Y.C.:U.S.	3.2	3.1	3.0	2.9	2.4	2.0	1.9	1.5	1.4

Note: New York City murders were subtracted from the total body count for the entire country in order to derive the figure for the rest of the United States.
Sources: The N.Y.C. body counts appear in NYPD annual reports, 1990–1998. U.S. rates are from the FBI's Uniform Crime Reports, 1990–1999.

dubious distinction of being number one in 1990 when it came to reported robberies per 100,000 people. The nine other major cities with the worst robbery rates were Chicago, Baltimore, Detroit, New Orleans, Washington, Dallas, Boston, and Los Angeles, with Cleveland and San Francisco tied for tenth position (McFadden, 1991).

Another myth needs to be dispelled at this point. Not only was New York never the murder capital, but even after the crash, it still was not the safest big city, strictly in terms of the odds of getting killed. New York's murder rate was twice as bad as San Diego's, and not quite as low as San Antonio's (or Boston's) in 1998, as the last column of table 1.2 indicates.

The next logical question is whether the risks of being murdered faced by the hypothetical "typical New Yorker" were much greater than those by the fictional "average American." The drop in criminal violence during the 1990s was a nationwide phenomenon, alleviating the dangers faced by the 250 million or so people living in small towns, suburbs, and medium-sized cities, in addition to the roughly 25 million living in the largest urban areas (see table 1.3). Killings declined in the rest of the country (by 34 percent from the worst year, 1991, in terms of body counts until 1998), but not as dramatically as in New York (by 72 percent from 1990 to 1998). The N.Y.C. to U.S. murder-rate ratio had been about three times worse inside than outside the City at the start of the 1990s. But the gap narrowed to less than one and a half times as bad by 1998, as shown by the numbers in the bottom row. In other words, New Yorkers faced graver risks of getting killed than other Americans, but the City was no longer so much more of a dangerous place to live as compared to the rest of the country by the end of the twentieth century.

Note that New York suffered its worst death toll in 1990. The City already was experiencing some modest relief when the entire country endured its bloodiest peacetime casualties ever in 1993, with a total of over 24,500 lives lost, according to the rows presenting body counts in table 1.3.[8] That raises another issue: Is New York usually in step with the rest of the country, or do changes in the behavior of its residents precede shifts elsewhere or have little to do with what is going on in the lives of other Americans? New York chauvinists believe that City residents set social trends into motion that catch on in the hinterlands several years later. It's also a cliché to muse that New York is not really comparable to the rest of the United States. But are either of these views true when it comes to criminal violence?

The way to detect any connections between the ups and downs of violence in New York City vis-à-vis the entire nation is to look at percentage changes in murder rates on an annual basis, as is done in graph 1.3. Most of the time, New York City appears to be "in sync" with the rest of the country: that is, when the death toll mounts across the nation, it usually rises in New York as well. There were only thirteen exceptions (about 33 percent) during the thirty-eight years since 1960, when the body count was up in New York and down everywhere else, or vice versa. Since 1993, New York and the United States as a whole have been in step. There is no evidence of a consistent time lag, either, in which New York leads or trails the nation by a year or two. Therefore, even though four of New York's boroughs (but not the Bronx) are located on islands, the City is not cut off from the mainland in terms of social trends.

Also note that homicide rates in New York, as well as in the rest of the country, tended to rise for a number of years in a row before falling for several consecutive years, literally in a smooth, wavelike pattern. Only rarely did murder rates go up one year, then fall the next, then rebound, and then slip back in a choppy zigzag pattern (as happened in the entire

Graph 1.3. Comparing New York City with the Rest of the
United States, 1960–1998

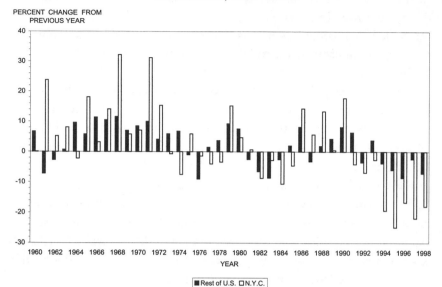

PERCENT CHANGE FROM
PREVIOUS YEAR

YEAR

■ Rest of U.S. □ N.Y.C.

Note: Rest of the United States=Entire Country, New York City.
Source: 1960–1998 NYPD Annual Complaints and Arrests Statistical Report; FBI's Uniform Crime Report.

country from 1991 through 1994; in New York, this had never taken place for over thirty-eight years). Therefore, it appears that wavelike upward and downward movements usually continue for at least a couple of years.

What's So Special about New York City?

New York City is not the center of the universe, although some Big Apple boosters believe it is and can't imagine living anywhere else. But several of the features that make New York stand out from the nation's other major cities may have some connection to its superior progress in reducing crime.

New York is at the center of worldwide communications networks. It is the home base of scores of television and radio stations, about 125 magazines, 60 trade publications, 100 ethnic and neighborhood newspapers, 90 book publishers, and over 500 bookstores (NYCVB, 1997). Madison Avenue advertising agencies churn out dreams and fantasies.

Silicon Alley crackles with internet creativity. City streets and landmarks are the settings for hundreds of movies and television shows. As a consequence, New Yorkers live in a fish bowl. Word travels fast about cutting-edge developments and emerging trends that unfold in the "backyard" of major media outlets. New life-styles—whether incorporating or rejecting defiant behaviors and forbidden pleasures—set the pace and serve as a model for others to imitate; but they evolve constantly and go out of style quickly.

New York also is more sensitive to the winds of economic change than any other place. Along with London and Tokyo, it serves as a nerve center for the global economy. Its skyscrapers house the headquarters of sixty-five corporations large enough to make the Fortune 500 list, with many more situated in gleaming glass office buildings in nearby suburbs within the metropolitan area. More than 2,500 firms doing business overseas are located within the City, as are more than one-fifth of all foreign investments in U.S. assets. The several stock exchanges handle financial transactions from all over the world. Major banks cluster nearby in downtown Manhattan. The City is the center of the international finance and business-services sector of the global corporate economy.[9] A huge underground economy thrives as well: uncountable off-the-book jobs—from construction work to making clothing in garment center sweatshops—plus rackets from surreptitiously fencing stolen goods to dealing controlled substances.

More so than ever before, New York is a city of sharp contrasts, of unabashed inequality. Right behind the citadels of power and the prestigious addresses where the planet's most affluent and privileged people work, play, dine, and reside are sprawling, run-down neighborhoods where their low-paid servants and employees struggle to survive. The largest population of wealthy people live literally down the block from the greatest concentration of families stagnating below the government's official poverty line. The city also has the country's largest number of persons living alone and the highest turnover of individuals constantly moving in and out.

As a port of entry or gateway city, New York always has been the mecca for newly arrived immigrants seeking the American Dream. It is a continuing social experiment and a perpetual work in progress, as people identifying with more than one hundred different ethnic backgrounds learn to live side by side. The metropolitan area's unique mix is a "melting pot," a "gorgeous mosaic," an "urban tapestry," a "salad bowl," and a "stained glass window" where the majority of residents are "minorities": African Americans, Hispanics, Asians, and Jews. Inner-city residents, although financially hard-pressed, are culturally prosperous and often set trends into motion. For example, hip-hop culture, with its blend of rap music, break-dancing, and graffiti-art was born in the Bronx in the late 1970s. Also, New York has the largest gay and lesbian community in the world. In addition, it can be considered one big "college town," with almost one hundred institutions of higher learning enrolling a grand total of over 400,000 students.

New York City surely has the most unnatural physical and social environment, with its high population density, tall buildings, mass transit system, ubiquitous crowds, and traffic jams. Perhaps for that reason it has been a hotbed of ideological ferment, more so than Berkeley and San Francisco, or Boston and Cambridge. New York has been the geographic and social hub for many protest groups, third parties, leftist organizations (anarchists, socialists, and communists), small independent progressive magazines and journals, and the liberal wing of the Democratic party. It has been a home-base for nearly all left-leaning causes and movements, campaigning for peace, civil rights, black power/black liberation, Puerto Rican independence, women's equality, gay rights, environmental preservation, civil liberties, and even prisoners' and mental patients' rights.

Unfortunately, New York also has been a major hub for cocaine, heroin, and marijuana trafficking, and a magnet for crack smokers and heroin injectors. As a consequence, it has the greatest concentration of people who are HIV positive or suffering from AIDS because they shared contaminated needles during intravenous drug use. All this entrenched smuggling and dealing is an outgrowth of the City's legacy as the stronghold for organized crime's rackets. Its five major Mafia families have had to fight off challenges from other mobsters belonging to ethnically based syndicates transplanted from around the world that have muscled in and carved out their own turf.

In sum, there are many good reasons to suspect that New York's unique blend of features may have played a direct or at least an indirect role in taming its formerly ferocious criminal element.

The Clues, So Far

Following up some promising leads has yielded several valuable clues that might help to solve the mystery behind the crash. The sudden and substantial drop in murdering was definitely real and not a statistical manipulation intended to fool the public. A drop of this magnitude and duration was unprecedented in New York City history. The murder rate tumbled in the 1990s faster than it went up in the late 1960s and early 1970s. Whatever forces drove down New York's murder rate also discouraged thieves from stealing cars, burglars from breaking into residences and commercial buildings, robbers from staging hold-ups, rapists from attacking girls and women, and so on. In fact, the drop in crimes reported to the NYPD was across the board, although to a more moderate degree for the other street crimes than for killings. Furthermore, the decline in murder rates was a nationwide phenomenon that was more pronounced in the biggest cities, especially in New York but also in San Diego, San Antonio, and Boston. New York City was usually in sync with the rest of the country, and its residents were affected by the same constellation of factors that shaped the behavior of other Americans. New York stood out from all other metropolises in terms of its centrality in the global economy; as a media headquarters; as a place where trends originate or are magnified; the magnitude of its crime problem; the size of its criminal justice apparatus; and the percentages of the population that were rich, poor, black, Hispanic, foreign born, college educated, drug addicted, and afflicted with AIDS.

Armed with these leads and clues, criminologists can zoom in on and take a closer look at murders in New York. That requires disaggregating or breaking up the overall yearly body count into its constituent parts: men versus women; youths versus older adults; or deaths from gunfire versus other means, and so on. This procedure enables researchers to determine what is typical about offenders, victims, weapons of choice, crime scenes, and motives (see Maltz, 1998). Once these generalizations have been derived from the data, the next step will be to pick out trends that describe murder's "changing face" as the body count rapidly shrinks. This line of analysis should yield some additional clues about why crime has crashed.

Notes

1. One of the senseless murders that shocked the conscience of the City was the apparently botched robbery of a thirty-three-year-old executive in Greenwich Village. He was using a pay phone on a quiet street on a warm night when he was shot repeatedly by a homeless man with a gun (see Kasindorf, 1990). The alleged assailant was acquitted at a trial, and no further arrests or prosecutions followed. The distraught and infuriated family and friends of the victim, John Reisenbach, set up a foundation in his honor to further antiviolence research and programs. A grant from the Reisenbach Foundation helped to support some of the data collected about homicide victims at the Office of the Chief Medical Examiner analyzed in chapter 2.

2. One out of every four renter households paid more than half its income for housing expenses, according to a study by the Center for Real Estate and Urban Policy at the New York University School of Law (Hevesi, D., 1999).

3. Statistics revealed that the proportion of indigents actually receiving all the aid to which they were legally entitled had declined substantially over the years. In the mid-1990s, of all the families living below the poverty line, only about half (49 percent) were getting public assistance, receiving food stamps (50 percent), or having their health care costs covered by Medicaid (53 percent). Those figures were down considerably from the higher averages that had prevailed over the previous ten years (59 percent, 66 percent, and 68 percent, respectively) (Aaronson and Cameron, 1997; and Jones, 1999).

4. Note that the highest-ever death toll in 1990 was inflated by a single mass killing caused by one demented arsonist; the smokey fire he set at the Happyland Social Club in the Bronx claimed eighty-seven lives, even though he was angry at only one person. If that calamity is subtracted from the 1990 figure (yielding 2,175 deaths), then 1991 (at 2,166, only 9 fewer homicides) was just about as bad a year for murders.

5. NYPD and insurance company sources estimated that between 10 and 20 percent of all auto theft complaints were phony cries for help by people pretending to be victims in order to fraudulently collect reimbursements (Blair, 1999b). If a crackdown intimidates scam artists from filing false reports about incidents that really never happened, the auto theft rate can suddenly drop.

6. If the victims survive, the crimes committed against them are recorded as attempted murders, which go into the annual reports under the heading of aggravated assaults. The number of aggravated assaults is so large each year that even a thousand saved lives would not cause an appreciable rise in this category of violent crime; hence, aggravated assaults fell, along with homicides, during the 1990s.

7. Murder rates per 100,000 are calculated by dividing the number of murders by the number of potential victims (population) and then moving the resulting decimal five places to the right.

8. Actually, the entire country suffered through its highest murder rate in history, 10.2 deaths per 100,000 Americans, in 1980, when the body count stood at 21,230 but the nation's population was smaller than in 1993; but this is not shown in table 1.2.

9. If the metropolitan area were a separate country, it would rank nineteenth on the list of the largest economic powerhouses, ahead of Australia and trailing right behind the Netherlands, in terms of total value of goods and services produced (AP, 1999b).

TWO

Deconstructing
Murders

Going behind the Numbers: Uncovering Patterns and Trends

Up to this point, the inquiry has focused on the total body count and the overall murder rate. Now, to get to the bottom of the mystery of New York's precipitously falling crime rate, murders must be deconstructed. In this context, deconstruction means breaking up the death toll into its constituent parts. The first phase of the analysis will seek to discover which kinds of murders were the most and the least common. The second phase will reveal who the typical victims were, in terms of their social characteristics. The third phase will put the spotlight on the perpetrators, in order to narrow the field in the search for the causes of criminal violence. In the fourth and final phase, murders will be disaggregated geographically, in order to reveal where crime scenes were concentrated and to pinpoint the most dangerous locations in the City. The process of deconstructing murders will piece together "murder's changing face" and yield more valuable clues about the people and the reasons behind the bloodshed, as well as give important leads about the possible causes of the crash.

What Was All the Bloodshed About?

When it comes to different "kinds" of murders, unfortunately, New York has them all, and in plentiful quantities. The first question that must be answered is: What kinds of murders are so common and make up such a high percentage of the overall body count that sudden and swift declines in these categories could account for the crash? In other words, what was all the fighting about? What were the major motives of the killers? Did certain types of killings die out in the 1990s, or were the impressive reductions across the board, affecting all the different groupings about equally?

What's Missing from This Picture?

One way to proceed is to see how many murders fall into the familiar categories that people who consume a steady diet of if-it-bleeds-it-leads tabloid news, cops and robbers television shows, and action flick imagery might suspect are disturbingly common. Many New Yorkers might share the impression that before the crash, numerous murders were the result of rampages by serial killers leaving behind a trail of corpses; by satanic cults carrying out human sacrifices; by molesters kidnaping and then slaughtering little children; by students shooting their classmates in school buildings; by violent offenders slaying Good Samaritans who dared to intervene; by stalkers hounding celebrities; by bigots seething with hatred for the victim's kind of person; by assassins hunting down major political figures; and by terrorists striking symbolic blows against the power structure.

Surely, some of the people found dead in New York City were done in by serial killers. Given Hollywood's morbid preoccupation with homicidal maniacs, it may come as a surprise to discover that only a handful of killing sprees made headlines since 1978. (The "44 Caliber Killer," also known as "the Son of Sam," was responsible for several deaths and many serious injuries before he was captured in 1977.) A twenty-eight-year-old recluse dubbed the "Zodiac Killer" slew three people and wounded five others during two separate one-man crime waves in the early 1990s (see Kleinfield, 1996). Two middle-aged men from suburban Long Island, operating independently, went on occasional forays into the City's netherworld to prey upon fallen women. Of course, these modern-day Jack-the-Rippers haven't been the only threats to ladies of the night, but over the decades a sizable body count never arose from "vice-sex-related" circumstances, as the NYPD categorizes such killings of prostitutes, as well as of pimps and johns.[1]

A panic spread across the country at the start of the 1980s about the alleged threat posed by satanic cults carrying out rituals that culminated in human sacrifices. Although many individuals on the talk-show circuit claimed to have witnessed, taken part in, and ultimately survived such nefarious ceremonies by devil worshipers, it is likely that the scare stories about a well-financed secret network were a reaction to profound social and cultural changes sweeping the country during the Reagan era (see Richardson, Best, and Bromley, 1991). Despite the enduring popularity of movies (such as *Rosemary's Baby*) about occult practices taking place in New York, no real-life case of a killing as part of a religious ceremony by an organized cult has yet come to light in a City known for its diversity of religious views and tolerance of differences.

Fears about strangers kidnaping, molesting, and then slaughtering young children also swept across the social landscape in the 1980s. Unlike satanic sacrifices, killings arising from kidnapings posed a real danger, but the actual dimensions of the problem were grossly overestimated initially, due to an absence of reliable data and imprecise definitions. A federally sponsored nationwide study discovered that many youngsters whose whereabouts were unknown to their parents were not in the clutches of dangerous strangers, but were merely runaways, were simply temporarily lost, or were snatched up by angry ex-spouses unwilling to abide by court-ordered custody and visitation arrangements. Fortunately, the most tragic missing child cases, in which a parent's worst fears about foul play were confirmed, rarely happened. New York's most widely publicized instance of child snatching took place in 1979, when a six-year-old boy waiting for his school bus on a SoHo street corner vanished, never to be seen again (Holloway, 1998). The NYPD's Missing Persons Squad reported it had only ten active cases over twenty-five years in which strangers were suspected to be behind the disappearance of children. During 1998, not one child was reported kidnaped by a stranger, although sixty-six were spirited off by family members or acquaintances (Cooper, 1999b).

In an age when many people either look the other way when a crime is committed in their presence, stand idly by, or melt away into a crowd, individuals are sorely needed who are willing to try to rescue a victim under attack. The most important murder of a Good Samaritan who dared to intervene took place in 1965. A computer programmer tried to stop a young man from harassing two elderly women on a subway train and got knifed for his troubles. After newspaper editorials highlighted the financial plight of his widow and daughter, the governor and the state legislature set up the New York State Crime Victims Compensation Fund, which provided reimbursement of losses to all innocent victims of violent crimes, not just Good Samaritans. Since then, few onlookers have been willing to risk their lives by rushing to help victims, so the deaths of Good Samaritans are rare.

Teenagers have been fighting each other in schoolyards and lunchrooms for generations. But when disputes started to be resolved with guns, parents and teachers understandably became alarmed. City schools were the sites of a rash of shootings in the early 1990s, several years before small-town and suburban schools suffered even bloodier assaults by much more heavily armed students in the late 1990s. One Brooklyn high school student shot another to death right before a scheduled visit by Mayor Dinkins (see Donaldson, 1993). Such incidents forced the Board of Education to beef up school security forces and to install metal detectors. As tragic and outrageous as these killings were, very few erupted on the grounds of a City public, private, or parochial school over the past two decades.

Bias crimes motivated by hatred can be bitterly divisive incidents that tear at the social fabric, heighten intergroup tensions, and threaten to undermine the success of the ongoing experiment in multiculturalism underway in contemporary society. To limit the aftershock of such polarizing incidents, the NYPD set up a special unit to monitor and solve bias crimes in 1980. Several vicious killings committed during the 1980s and 1990s drove wedges between New Yorkers of different racial and religious groups when they were first committed; the lengthy trials that followed reopened old wounds and stirred up further resentments. An attack in 1986 on several black people (whose car broke down) by a group of white youths leaving a party in Howard Beach, Queens, led to the death of a young black man who was chased on to a highway and accidentally run over (see Hynes and Drury, 1990). A similar "you don't belong in this neighborhood" racial incident took place in 1989 in Bensonhurst, Brooklyn, when a young black man seeking to buy a used car was shot to death by riled-up white youths who mistook him for someone else (Roberts, 1989). In 1991, a black child was run over by a car in a traffic accident involving a motorcade of Hasidic Jews in Crown Heights, Brooklyn. His death touched off several days of mob attacks by angry residents, mostly of Caribbean descent, against their Hasidic neighbors. A visiting Hasidic scholar from Australia was chased and stabbed to death (Crime File, 1998). In 1994, a Jordanian immigrant went on a rampage and shot at Jewish boys who were wearing orthodox garb and riding in a van from their religious school. The unprovoked attack, which took place on the Brooklyn Bridge, claimed the life of a sixteen-year-old (Nagourney, 1999). Fortunately, these potentially explosive acts of interethnic violence stand out as aberrations.

Celebrity stalking became such a problem in Hollywood and its environs in the 1990s that the LAPD set up a special squad to investigate and deter this kind of harassment. Plenty of famous movie stars, popular musicians, and professional athletes make New York their home or appear at events in town, but luckily only one stalking escalated into murder between 1978 and 1998. That was the senseless shooting of the Beatles' John Lennon in front of his Manhattan apartment building by a deeply disturbed fan in 1980 (Mathews, 1980).

Political assassinations dramatically changed the course of U.S. history during the 1960s, when President Kennedy was shot in Dallas in 1963, Senator Robert Kennedy was slain in Los Angeles in 1968, and Dr. Martin Luther King was killed in Memphis in 1968. In New York City, Malcolm X was gunned down in Manhattan's Audubon Ballroom in 1963 by members of the Nation of Islam, an organization he had helped build but then quit after a heated dispute. Since 1978, only two political assassinations took place within city limits. Rabbi Meir Kehane, the highly controversial founder of the Jewish Defense League who was known for his intense anti-Arab proposals and his staunch advocacy of armed self-defense, was shot after delivering a speech in a Manhattan hotel in 1990. (His assailant was linked years later to a Middle Eastern terrorist cell; see Fried, 1999.) In 1992, gunmen hired by the Cali cocaine cartel in Colombia killed, in a Queens restaurant, a former editor of *El Diario–La Prensa*, a Spanish-language daily newspaper; he had long crusaded against drug traffickers (Cauvin, Rashbaum, and Siemaszko, 1999).

Because New York is a world class city, its landmarks have attracted attacks by terrorists, both domestic and foreign. The FALN (Armed National Liberation Front in Spanish), a small clandestine leftist group

Table 2.1. The Least and Most Common Types of Murders, New York City, Selected Years, 1973–1998

	1973	1976	1980	1982	1985	1986	1991	1995	1996	1997	1998
Part A: Type of Killing											
Officers protecting the public											
Number	6	0	6	2	0	2	2	0	2	1	2
Percent	0	0	0	0	0	0	0	0	0	0	0
Organized crime rubouts											
Number	12	18	30	—	14	18	5	3	4	2	2
Percent	1	1	2	—	1	1	0	0	0	0	0
Youth-gang clashes											
Number	41	12	16	—	10	5	1	2	2	—	—
Percent	2	1	1	—	1	0	0	0	0	—	—
Innocent bystanders hit by stray bullets											
Number	—	—	—	—	—	—	92	11	12	6	11
Percent	—	—	—	—	—	—	4	1	1	1	1
Part B: Victims Slain during Felonies											
Robberies											
Number	251	289	443	298	209	342	351	135	113	86	48
Percent	15	18	24	18	15	21	16	11	11	11	8
Burglaries											
Number	30	33	24	25	14	16	7	7	6	6	2
Percent	2	2	1	2	1	1	0	1	1	1	0
Sexual assaults											
Number	27	40	18	17	10	9	2	7	2	2	7
Percent	2	3	1	1	1	1	0	1	0	0	1
Homicides arising from domestic violence											
Number	277	135	148	152	192	207	123	106	129	133	88
Percent	17	8	8	9	14	13	6	9	13	17	14
Drug-related killings											
Number	125	136	192	349	356	525	670	226	247	138	106
Percent	7	9	12	21	26	33	31	19	25	18	17
All other lethal disputes											
Number	590	655	565	438	554	525	912	332	224	229	161
Percent	35	40	31	26	40	33	42	28	23	30	25
Total murders	1,680	1,622	1,814	1,668	1,384	1,582	2,154	1,177	983	770	633

Notes: Body counts do not add up to "total murders" and percentages do not add up to 100 because of the many unsolved cases each year in which the police could not determine a motive. The years chosen in the 1970s and 1980s were ones that had fewer than 15 percent unsolved cases. Numbers and percentages were of all murders, whether solved or not. Organized crime killings include disputes over drugs. Domestic violence includes family disputes and child abuse deaths. Drug-related murders include disputes and robberies over drugs. Robberies exclude drug-related robberies. Sexual assaults include domestic and drug-related attacks. All other lethal disputes exclude drug-related and domestic disputes. Innocent bystanders include casualties from drug-related and domestic violence.
  — means that a specific figure was not available for that year.
Sources: 1972–1991: 1991 NYPD Homicide Analysis Reports; 1995–1998: NYPD Homicide Logs. Also 1991, 1995–1997: NYPD SHRs.

advocating the independence of Puerto Rico, set off a bomb in Manhattan's historic Fraunces Tavern that claimed the lives of four customers, but that was back in 1975. In 1980, Omega 7, a right-wing group of anti-Castro Cubans, bombed targets affiliated with the United Nations and assassinated a Cuban diplomat in Queens (Williams, Agrest, and Joshee, 1980). In 1993, followers of an extremist sheikh set off an explosion in a rented truck in a garage beneath the World Trade Center, hoping that the blast would topple the building over; six people died and more than one thousand were injured (Weiser, 1997a).

In sum, considering that over 32,600 people were murdered within city limits from 1978 through 1998, it is astounding how few people died because of the depredations of serial killers, satanic cults, child-molesting kidnappers, armed students, celebrity stalkers, hatemongers, assassins, and terrorists.

If these kinds of murders were the subjects of infotainment and sensationalism more often than daily news broadcasts, then what about other highly publicized killings: of officers gunned down while protecting the public, of gangsters whose days were numbered when contracts were put out on them, of street gang members who went off to rumble and never came back, and of innocent bystanders who found themselves in the wrong place at the wrong time? The relative frequency of these types of killings was greater than those on the first list; but it still was not large enough to substantially affect murder rates (see part A in table 2.1). (However, if the killers' motives could be determined even in the unsolved slayings, the body counts in the previous and following categories would be higher.)

Ultimate Sacrifices

A felonious assault leading to the death of an on-duty officer is taken very seriously by the law: it was designated as a capital offense when the New York State legislature restored the death penalty in 1995.

The NYPD has suffered more line-of-duty deaths than any other law enforcement agency because of its sheer size and its perilous mission of patrolling some of the nation's toughest neighborhoods. Between 1978 and 1998, forty-nine NYPD officers were murdered while protecting the public. The worst years were 1980 and 1989, when six men in blue were gunned down. The best years, with no line-of-duty losses, were 1985, 1995, and, surprisingly, 1990—the bloodiest year in City history (2,245 murders plus thirty-nine justifiable homicides of suspects killed by officers), as shown in table 2.1.[2]

Over 90 percent of the cop killers used guns. Bullet-proof vests as well as survival training skills saved the lives of several officers assaulted by armed criminals every year (NYPD, 1994b). The most frequent causes of loss of life were chases after robbers and attempts to break up domestic disturbances (Margarita, 1980). Even though cops run toward trouble while most everyone else flees in the opposite direction, police work actually was not the most dangerous occupation of all—driving a taxicab in the City was.[3]

Fortunately, law enforcement activities were not punctuated by as many high-speed car chases and pitched gun battles as were shown in the movies and on television. The number of line-of-duty deaths suffered by New York's Finest never made up an appreciable part of the City's overall body count, statistically speaking. Cop killings decreased in the 1990s, but that is not a reason why the murder rate tumbled.

Deadfellas Sleeping with the Fishes

Mention New York and organized crime in the same sentence, and gruesome scenes come to mind from blockbuster movies like *The Godfather*, *Goodfellas*, *A Bronx Tale*, and *Once upon a Time in America*. The best-known rub-outs of mob figures in recent decades unfolded in 1972 when Joey Gallo was slain while eating in a Little Italy restaurant; and in 1986, when Paul Castellano was gunned down in front of a fashionable East Side steakhouse on orders from an up-and-coming John Gotti.

For years, the underworld had been extracting profits from the garment industry, construction firms, private garbage collection companies, air freight deliveries to JFK airport, and exhibitors at the Jacob Javits Convention Center. But law enforcement agencies began to make considerable headway in uprooting the mob's influence and downsizing their infrastructure during the 1990s (Jacobs, 1999).

Nevertheless, the five major Sicilian Mafia families (Gambino, Genovese, Columbo, Luchese, and Bonanno) that together constitute La Cosa Nostra still call New York City their hometown. Over the past few decades, they have had to fight off the encroachments of other organized crime syndicates rooted in neighboring ethnic enclaves. Among the most prominent and notorious of the new breed of gangsters are Asian tongs and triads, and syndicates drawing their members from the Russian and Colombian immigrant communities. These newcomers apparently have muscled in on long-standing and lucrative rackets without igniting bitter mob wars.

Therefore, despite a substantial racketeer presence and plenty of opportunities for strife resulting from federal prosecutions, hostile takeovers, and shifting fortunes, gangsters don't get "whacked" too often in New York anymore. During the 1990s, only a handful of slayings each year were designated by detectives as related to organized crime, as shown in table 2.1. Assuming that police records do not seriously underestimate the actual level of killings stemming from underworld rivalries, the rapid drop in homicides in the 1990s definitely was not the result of "understandings" worked out between formerly warring mob syndicates.[4]

West Side Stories

For many years, the City had a serious youth gang problem, with periodic rumbles between fighting gangs, as depicted in the Broadway plays *West Side Story* and *The Capeman*, and in books such as *The Cool World* (Miller, 1959) and *The Warriors* (Yurick, 1978). However, unlike Los Angeles and Chicago, New York never suffered from interminable retaliatory drive-by shootings to avenge previous wrongs in endless vendettas kept alive by generation after generation of new recruits.

New York's recent experience with street gangs can be divided into three distinct time periods, according to interviews with twenty former gang leaders (Brotherton, 1999). In the 1960s and 1970s, most of the subcultural groups formed by poor young men were conflict oriented, meaning that they were preoccupied with "bopping" or "gang-banging." Their violence was largely expressive since it erupted over words, gestures, and deeds perceived to be acts of disrespect and dishonor. The Vanguards, Savage Skulls, Jolly Stompers, Nomads, Aces, Saints, Hellcats, and other notorious jacket gangs made their presence felt by wearing their symbols and colors, tagging (spray painting) their names on walls to mark the outskirts of their turf, and defending their neighborhoods against outside invaders. Their adherents could be found throughout the five boroughs because their sharply defined roles, strict membership rules, rituals, and tough-guy images attracted many recruits from economically marginalized and dysfunctional families. As the 1970s drew to a close, their numbers diminished and their territorial control dissolved as heroin addiction took its toll and landlord-inspired arson emptied out their strongholds. During the 1980s, the brisk trade in powdered cocaine transformed into a wide-open crack market, and street gangs metamorphosed into crews intent on making "crazy money" and spending it ostentatiously on gold jewelry and expensive automobiles. These loose, amorphous groups seized illegal opportunities that seemed much more attractive than low-wage blue-collar work, as New York City's manufacturing base shrunk. Whereas past gang fights were over symbolic notions of turf, drug-dealing crews went after one another for more practical, business-oriented reasons: to eliminate the competition, to protect their own strategically located selling spots, and to muscle in on their rivals' operations.

In the mid-1990s, several chieftains, particularly from the Chicago-based Latin Kings, claimed that their youth gangs were evolving into "street organizations" that eschewed fratricidal violence and would concentrate in the years ahead on building bases of political power for constructive purposes. They adopted the rhetoric of self-improvement and community empowerment and advocated an eclectic mix of self-help, cultural pride, spiritualism, and utopian visions. Their leadership spoke about finding jobs for former inmates, of running candidates for local offices, and of using mediation techniques to head off violence (Brotherton, 1999). However, as the 1990s drew to a close, stiff resistance to these reformist impulses developed within the Latin Kings, and fights between contending factions erupted. Other clashes resulted from the sudden emergence and immediate rivalry of bands of youths calling themselves "Crips" and "Bloods" in imitation of these notorious Los Angeles street gangs.

Pitched battles to wrest away territory or defend home turf from invaders, and bloody internal purges to punish renegades, flared up far more often during the 1970s than over the following two decades, according to the death tolls presented in table 2.1. Throughout the 1980s and 1990s, the NYPD attributed just a few slayings each year to clashes between rival street gangs, portraying such killings as so infrequent as to be inconsequential. It appeared that the crash could not have been furthered by "peace treaties" negotiated by enlightened reformist gang leaders. However, after drawing more heavily upon its intelligence sources for detailed and comprehensive information, NYPD detectives determined that forty-two slayings arose from gang-related disputes in 1998, and that more than twice that body count resulted from such fights during the first ten months of 1999 (Flynn, 1999c). These upwardly revised estimates pictured gang violence in an entirely different light—as a much greater threat than had been realized previously. If accurate, these much higher death tolls resurrected the possibility that a cessation of hostilities between rival youth collectives indeed may have contributed substantially to the tumbling homicide rate.[5]

Wrong Time, Wrong Place: Cruel Twists of Fate

Innocent victims hit by stray bullets meant for someone else are the unintended casualties of disputes settled with a reckless disregard or depraved indifference for the well-being of others. Eight people unfairly paid the price for being in the wrong place at the wrong time in 1971, and another six perished in 1972, according to NYPD homicide analyses. As these cruel twists of fate became more newsworthy, criminologists culled more than 50 accounts of bystander shootings from local newspapers in 1988 (Sherman, Steele, et al. 1989). When the police department began to track the number of people wounded as well as killed by stray bullets, they discovered that about 535 unintended victims were hit in 1991, about 340 in 1992, and 335 in 1993.

The most dangerous parts of town were the poorest neighborhoods and city-run housing projects. People were more likely to be hit during summer nights, when large crowds congregated on street corners, and on festive occasions like July 4 and New Year's Eve, when celebrants fired into the sky. Some people were even shot through car doors, when slugs penetrated flimsy walls in apartment buildings, or when bullets ricocheted off tall buildings. Among the most senseless deaths were incidents in which youngsters were shot while sleeping in their beds; a Bronx assistant district attorney was struck near the courthouse by a bullet aimed by one drug dealer at another; and a principal of a public school searching for one of his students in a housing project found himself caught in the crossfire between two rival gangs (see Daley and Freitag, 1990; Donaldson, 1993; and Onishi, 1994).

The seriousness of the threat posed by indiscriminate gunfire peaked in 1991, when ninety-two bystanders lost their lives, comprising about 4 percent of all killings, as shown in table 2.1. The drop in unintentional victims since then made a contribution—but not a decisive one—to the diminishing body count.

In conclusion, these four kinds of killings that readily come to mind because of intense media coverage turned out to be relatively uncommon. It is true that during the 1990s a smaller number of police officers were slain while protecting the public, not as many mobsters were rubbed out gangland style, fewer young lives were destroyed by wars between rival street gangs, and much fewer innocent people were cut down by gunfire aimed in their direction. But, contrary to widespread impressions, the actual numbers of New Yorkers murdered in these ways never added up to a massive body count, even during the worst of times in 1990 or 1991. Therefore, their dwindling down even further could not account for the enormity of the crash.

The Real Threats to Life and Limb

If the grand total of high-profile murders never reached massive levels, then, statistically speaking, what kinds of killings accounted for the bulk of the City's staggering body counts during the bad old days? The answer is that the most common slayings are depressingly familiar. Robbers murdered sizable numbers of New Yorkers during hold-ups, and family members often killed each other during heated arguments. Dealers and addicts killed huge numbers of fellow participants in the drug trade. Disputes over matters that ranged from meaningful to trivial, which escalated into life-and-death struggles, claimed the greatest number of lives, as part B of table 2.1 shows.

Predators on the Prowl

Robbery victims face the threat of losing not only their money but also their lives. Robbers may finish off their victims so that they can't turn them in to the police, or they may panic and use more force than they initially intended to compel their victims to hand over valuables. Additionally, robbers may kill resisting victims—or anyone else who gets in their way—as they make their escape.[6]

Robbers slew a substantial proportion of all homicide victims, ranging from 8 percent to almost 25 percent, according to the estimates that appear in the rows under the heading "Felony Murders" in table 2.1. Over the past three decades, the trend has definitely been downward, in terms of a smaller absolute number as well as a smaller percentage of all killings.

Burglars (who transform into robbers if they confront someone in the home or commercial property that they broke into) and rapists killed their victims much less often than robbers.[7] However, the body counts surely would have been higher if the police had been able to determine the motives in all homicides. The diminished death toll from felony murders during the 1990s was the positive fallout of an across-the-board drop in robberies, burglaries, and forcible rapes; it probably did not signal that criminals were becoming more merciful toward their victims, or that victims were learning how to survive their ordeals better.

Fatal Fallings Out: All within the Family

The oft-repeated warning that someone close might pose a graver danger than a complete stranger still contains a great deal of truth. Domestic violence in all its forms—extreme spouse abuse, patricide, matricide, fratricide, infanticide, and other intrafamily pairings—accounted for as few as 6 percent and as many as 17 percent of all slayings, as indicated by the data in table 2.1. By the late 1990s, death tolls were down substantially from the higher levels of the past two decades, and yet strife within households still claimed many lives.[8]

Most of the killings within families took place among adults, with males the offenders more than twice as often as females.[9] However, murders by husbands of their wives diminished over the years, probably because battered women became increasingly able to exercise options to end their stormy relationships or received better protection from the justice system. Of the men who did slay the females they professed to love (wives or lovers, but also mothers or daughters), nearly 30 percent also killed themselves—or attempted suicide—during the early 1990s (Wilt, Illman, and Brodyfield, 1997). The chances of the perpetrator trying to end his own life depended upon whether the two were (in declining likelihoods) married, boyfriend/girlfriend, former lovers, or if the victim was the offender's child or a close friend. A common thread running through many of the cases of romantic love was that the aggressor was jealous and insecure about unfaithfulness and felt he could not live with his partner but couldn't live without her, either. When her threat to separate aroused his anger, the violent act alleviated his sense of helplessness but provoked intense depression, guilt, and self-blame (Stack, 1997).[10]

Deaths due to child abuse were a significant component of domestic violence fatalities during the past two decades. Each year, between about twenty and thirty infants, toddlers, and children died from physical abuse and gross neglect. Some suspicious deaths from undetermined causes might have resulted from abuse as well, so the true death toll was probably larger. Most of these tragedies arose from overly punitive parenting, but others included infanticides of unwanted newborns. Particularly upsetting were murders of children by abusive parents who were "known" to child protection agencies because the family had been previously investigated in response to a complaint lodged by a neighbor, teacher, doctor, social worker, or some other person in a position to suspect or observe tell-tale signs of maltreatment.

Deaths from all kinds of family violence declined substantially, from over 275 in 1973 to just about 200 per year in the mid-1980s to less than 100 by 1998, as table 2.1 shows. However, during the 1990s, less sustained progress was made in cutting down these avoidable fatalities. Therefore, the diminution of domestic violence was a contributing factor but not a major reason for the crash.

Drug-Related Violence

Violence stemming from the drug scene emerged as a serious problem in the early 1970s and led to the creation of a special task force of NYPD narcotics detectives, Drug Enforcement Administration (DEA) agents, and state and federal prosecutors. In 1977, rival groups of dealers clashed so often (fifty shootings and eighteen murders) in the vicinity of a single Harlem street corner that the police nicknamed the area "Dodge City" (Young, 1978).

Drug-related murders can arise out of conflicts among sellers (traffickers, smugglers, wholesalers, retailers), or between sellers and buyers. Competing crews engage in turf wars over choice selling locales. Sellers and buyers might quarrel over broken promises, unpaid debts, and poor-quality merchandise pawned off by deceptive suppliers. Kingpins can order their enforcers to carry out acts of violence as a rational business practice in order to maintain discipline within the organization and to deter their subordinates from embezzling proceeds, defecting to competing outfits, or cooperating with the authorities. Profiteers must cultivate a fearsome image to fend off robbers who want to prey upon them, as well as to intimidate buyers who demand refunds for inferior merchandise. The endless cycle of violence within the drug scene leads to interminable feuds, vendettas, and acts of vigilantism; retaliatory strikes to restore pride and honor; and ambushes and double-crosses (see Brownstein, 1996; Jackall, 1997). Robbers desperate to raise money so they can purchase more drugs to get high again might kill their victims. Violent outbursts can also be the psycho-pharmacological reaction of someone intoxicated on some controlled substance, often in combination with alcohol (see Goldstein, Brownstein, and Ryan, 1992).

Homicides deemed to be related to drug selling, even though they might have been inconsistently defined or incompletely measured, climbed alarmingly from the 1970s right through the 1980s and peaked in 1991 at 670 deaths. (In terms of relative shares, 1986 may have been the worst year, when one-third of all slayings revolved around drug dealing.) After setting records, this category of killings plunged throughout the rest of the 1990s, to a low ebb of just over one hundred deaths in 1998, as documented in table 2-1.[11]

Since violence stemming from the drug trade cost so many lives over the past few decades, individuals involved with heroin and cocaine bear responsibility for significantly contributing to the oppressive conditions that burdened many New York City neighborhoods. A substantial decline in the number of people caught up in the drug scene and a big drop in the amount of drugs they consumed, coupled with a sharp decrease in the level of conflict among participants in the trade, could have furthered the crash. This important lead—the possibility of a rather sudden improvement in the City's market for illicit drugs—will be carefully investigated in chapter 5.[12]

Beefs to Kill For, to Die For

The category with the highest number of murders in New York City year after year is the residual grouping "all other disputes," as table 2.1 verifies. Unfortunately, the term conceals more than it reveals because of its catch-all nature. Family quarrels, rubouts arising from syndicate rackets, clashes between youthful street gangs, and drug-related altercations are excluded because they are counted under their own headings. But that still leaves a host of other reasons for fighting: love triangles in which a rival is eliminated, arguments over money, pitched battles over issues of great significance; but also quarrels over matters as trivial as parking spaces, perceived slights, or tragic misunderstandings.

Spontaneous and senseless killings (such as when a spilled drink in a bar leads to a shoving match and then a knife fight outside) illustrate how a fatality can result from a series of actions and reactions between an impulsive offender and a provocative victim. Such situated transactions can be broken down into six specific stages (see Luckenbill, 1977). Stage One unfolds when one person takes an initiative, either verbal or physical, whether on purpose or by accident, that is interpreted as an affront by the other individual. In Stage Two, the victim verifies the intended meaning of his adversary's actions, often by consulting with an audience of onlookers. By Stage Three, the victim is warning the aggressor to back off and apologize, or else face serious consequences. Stage Four is reached if either party persists and escalates the level of hostilities with further incitements. Stage Five is marked by a sudden explosion of violence. During the finale, Stage Six, the victor triumphs as his opponent crumples to the ground in defeat. The survivor either flees the scene of the confrontation, calls the police and claims victimhood, or tries to escape but is restrained by onlookers.

Certain disputes lead to acts of vigilantism which detectives refer to as revenge killings. They break out when individuals who feel they have been victimized retaliate violently to settle scores against adversaries who they believe deserve to suffer. Many of these revenge killings are carried out by criminals, precisely because they are involved in illegal activities and can't take their problems to the police or to court. The impulse toward vigilantism might be a common thread motivating many vicious assaults in New York City, but it eludes attention because such instances are not placed in a category of their own but rather are classified under different headings: slayings that were street-gang related, organized-crime related, or drug related, or resulted from disputes or even from intrafamily quarrels. It is possible that the murder rate declined because fewer people felt driven to resort to extra-legal measures to punish their enemies physically. Either people harboring fantasies of getting even regained faith in the criminal justice system to handle their problems; the intensity of their thirst to strike back declined; or less people were engaged in criminal activity, which translated into less aggrieved parties compelled to take the law into their own hands to pursue their versions of street justice.

In sum, the murder rate plummeted in the 1990s because there were far fewer robberies claiming the lives of their victims, not as many family quarrels leading to tragedy, many fewer showdowns among participants in the drug scene, and reduced levels of quarreling over assorted matters. However, the magnitude of the death tolls inflicted by robbers and by violent family members were substantial but not huge, in relative and absolute terms. Therefore, the crash was largely brought about by a momentous drop in vicious arguments of all sorts, and in volatile drug-related confrontations in particular.

Lost Souls Gone to a Better Place

Is it possible to characterize the more than 32,600 people who were murdered during outbursts of criminal violence in the five boroughs from 1978 through 1998? Were these lost souls a cross section of the population, selected virtually at random, or were some categories of residents more likely to be targeted by killers than others? If the burden of victimization did not fall evenly on all New Yorkers, then which groups experienced the highest and lowest risks of being murdered? And, after the crash, what kinds of people were being preyed upon far less frequently than in the bad old days?

In Harm's Way

New Yorkers of different sexes, ages, social classes, and racial/ethnic/national backgrounds endured striking differences in their odds of getting killed, according to the statistical portraits presented in table 2.2.

When it comes to murders, sex matters most. Boys and men have

Table 2.2. Trends in the Profiles of Murder Victims, New York City, Selected Years, 1973–1998

Attribute	1973	1977	1981	1985	1991	1997	1998
Sex							
Males							
Number	1,400	1,270	1,562	1,154	1,881	621	498
Percent	83	82	85	83	86	81	79
Females							
Number	280	287	270	237	316	149	132
Percent	17	18	15	17	14	19	21
Age Groups (percentages)							
1–15	5	5	4	4	3	6	7
16–20	9	11	12	12	14	13	15
21–25	18	16	18	20	21	19	21
26–30	16	18	17	19	20	14	15
31–35	12	13	13	12	13	12	12
36–40	10	9	10	9	9	11	10
41 and older	29	27	27	23	20	26	21
Race and Ethnicity							
Whites							
Number	342	361	363	231	257	122	107
Percent	20	23	20	17	12	16	17
Blacks							
Number	893	722	887	671	1,078	384	334
Percent	53	46	48	48	50	50	53
Hispanics							
Number	437	453	550	460	797	233	158
Percent	26	29	30	33	37	30	25
Asians							
Number	8	27	26	30	65	31	25
Percent	1	1	1	2	3	4	4
Total number of victims	1,680	1,557	1,826	1,384	2,154	770	630

Note: 1991 was chosen as the worst year because the 1990 body count was inflated by a single arson blaze that killed eighty-seven people.
Sources: 1972–1991: NYPD Homicide Analyses; 1997 and 1998: NYC Department of Health vital statistics from death certificates.

Graph 2.1. Trends in Murders of Males and Females,
New York City, 1980–1998

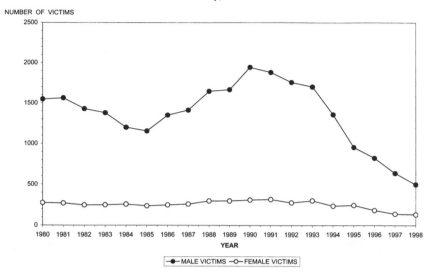

Note: Victims can be of any age and race/ethnicity.
Sources: 1981–1986 NYPD Homicide Analyses; 1987–1998 NYC DOH Death Certificates.

been slain much more often than girls and women over the past several decades. The proportion of victims who were males ranged between 79 and 86 percent since the early 1970s. Given that a little less than 50 percent of the City's population was male, boys and men obviously have been disproportionately caught up in criminal violence. Put another way, during most years, for every female killed, about four or five males were killed.[13]

Male casualties declined in the early 1980s, rose in the late 1980s, peaked in 1991, and then dropped steadily and sharply (graph 2.1). By 1998, less than one-third as many males had been slain as in the worst year, 1991. Female body counts did not rise and fall as dramatically over the decades. However, by 1998, the death toll among girls and women had been more than halved from its 1991 peak. Clearly, the murder rate soared because boys and men increasingly fought each other in the late 1980s, and it tumbled when male violence subsided. Therefore, the reasons for the rapid decline must have something to do with the behavior of boys and men, rather than girls and women.

Besides sex, age also determines homicide risks. Teenagers and young adults in their twenties and thirties made up the age groups most caught up in violence year after year. People between the ages of 16 and 40 accounted for two-thirds to as much as three-quarters of all murder victims (table 2.2). In general, the most dangerous years for New Yorkers to get through were their late teens and early twenties, but risks didn't fall off substantially until residents entered their late forties. The typical New York homicide victims during the 1990s turned out to be in their mid-twenties, in terms of the mode; and in their early thirties, using the mean. During the crash, teenagers between 16 and 19, and young adults in their twenties benefited the most. (Each group's rate fell around 70 percent between 1991 and 1998.)[14]

Members of different racial and ethnic groups also have suffered widely varying risks of getting killed. In the 1990 U.S. Census, almost 25 percent of New Yorkers labeled themselves as Hispanic, yet about 37 percent of all slain murder victims during 1991 were classified as such by their relatives on death certificates, a considerable disparity. But by 1998, this disproportionality had disappeared. New York's black community made up close to 25 percent of the City's population but suffered nearly 50 percent of the casualties, an oppressive disparity. New Yorkers of Asian descent constituted about 7 percent of the population, but they comprised a tiny percentage of all murder victims, a favorable disproportionality. Non-Hispanic whites of European descent made up about 43 percent of the inhabitants in 1990, but constituted a much smaller share of all deaths, an underrepresentation that has persisted ever since 1972 (the earliest year for which this type of breakdown is available).[15]

Changes in the composition of the population over the years must be taken into account in order to analyze trends in the victimization rate by race and ethnicity. When the growth in the proportion of blacks, Hispanics, and Asians is factored in, along with the steady net outflow of whites from the City (since the 1950s), an amended or fine-tuned picture materializes (see graph 2.2).

Hispanic New Yorkers suffered a rising victimization rate from the early 1970s until the early 1980s. Then a drop occurred, followed by a sharp rise to record levels in 1991. Rates in the 1990s rapidly declined, to a level in 1998 (at 8 per 100,000) that was just one-third the level of 1972, and better than one-fifth of the peak rate in 1991.[16] For New

Graph 2.2. Trends in Group Victimization Rates, New York City,
Selected Years, 1972–1998

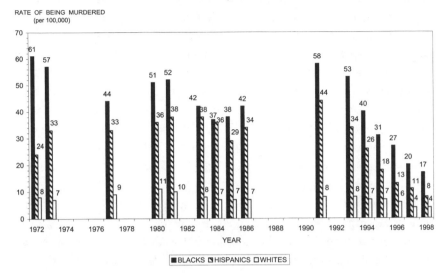

RATE OF BEING MURDERED
(per 100,000)

BLACKS HISPANICS WHITES

Note: Population by race/ethnicity interpolated from U.S. Census data, NYC Dept. of City Planning.
Sources: 1972–1991 NYPD Homicide Analysis Reports; 1993–1998 NYC DOH Vital Statistics database from death certificates.

Yorkers of African descent, the murder victimization rate was at its worst back in 1972, at sixty-one deaths for every 100,000 black New Yorkers. After dropping until 1984, it shot back up to almost as terrible a level in 1991. But by 1998, the victimization rate had fallen to 17 per 100,000, still far higher than for other groups, but an impressive improvement. Between six and nine white New Yorkers out of every 100,000 were murdered during the 1970s and 1980s, close to the national average. The crime crash knocked the white body count down to four per 100,000 in 1998, well below the level of danger experienced by the average American in other parts of the country. (The Asian rate is not shown in graph 2.2 because it was very low until the 1990s, when it nearly caught up to the level of white victimization.) In sum, dramatically different risks persisted, but the gaps were narrowing as the 1990s drew to a close. Thanks to the crash, blacks, Hispanics, and whites experienced substantial relief from the burden of victimization.

Since men were murdered much more often than women, teenagers and young adults were killed much more frequently than older or younger people, and black New Yorkers were slain at a much higher rate than other residents, it follows that people who fall into all three of these high-risk categories must face the greatest perils of all. Just how grave these dangers were for black men between the ages of eighteen to forty-four is indicated by their victimization rates. They were slain at a terribly high rate of 185 per 100,000 in 1992. By 1997, even though only one-third as many were killed, this group still suffered sixty-six murders for every 100,000 inhabitants, nearly ten times the dangers faced by the average American, and almost eight times the threat confronting the typical New Yorker.

Social class is another key factor that determines risk levels. In the absence of any direct indicators about the socio-economic status (wealth, income, occupation) of New York City's murder victims, a second-best indicator, the Zip code of the decedent's home address, can be used to estimate class. Demographers have calculated the median income of all households in a given Zip code from census data. Also, they have determined the national centile rank of this average income figure relative to other Zip codes across the country. Therefore, it becomes possible to establish in which neighborhoods the most and also the fewest murder victims had resided before they died.

Indeed, a distinct pattern emerges that indicates most victims had resided in poverty-stricken rather than affluent communities.[17] People living in the poorest parts of town—which ranked among those Zip codes with the lowest household incomes in the entire nation—endured the gravest risks of being murdered (whether close to home or elsewhere in the City), as shown in part A of table 2.3. Many victims had dwelled in the City's lowest-income communities: Upper and Lower Harlem in Manhattan; the areas of the Grand Concourse, South Bronx, Southern Boulevard, and Morrisania in the Bronx; and Bedford-Stuyvesant, Bushwick, and East New York in Brooklyn.

During the same time period, however, very few victims had been inhabiting the most prosperous areas of the five boroughs—which were among the most affluent Zip codes in the whole country, as shown in part B of table 2.3. Despite the carnage raging in the run-down parts of town, very few casualties had been residents of the most prestigious addresses: Manhattan's entire Upper East Side; Greenwich Village, surrounding Washington Square Park and New

Table 2.3. Neighborhood Victimization Rates, 1988–1993

Zip Code	Borough	Neighborhood	Median Income, 1990	National Centile Ranking	Victimization Rate per 100,000 Residents 1988–1993
Part A: Neighborhoods Whose Residents Suffered the Most Violent Deaths					
10030	M	Upper Harlem	$14,000	0	83
10026	M	Lower Harlem	$14,000	1st	73
10459	X	Southern Blvd	$14,000	1st	67
10455	X	South Bronx	$14,000	0	70
11221	B	Bushwick	$19,000	8th	61
10456	X	Morrisania	$15,000	1st	65
10451	X	Grand Concourse	$17,000	4th	62
11207	B	East New York	$22,000	18th	67
11233	B	Bed-Stuyvesant	$17,000	4th	70
10454	X	Mott Haven	$12,000	0	72
Part B: Neighborhoods Whose Residents Suffered the Fewest Violent Deaths					
11360	Q	Bay Terrace	$54,000	95th	3
10017	M	East 40s	$49,000	92nd	3
10021	M	East 60s,70s	$58,000	96th	3
10022	M	East 50s	$61,000	97th	2
10028	M	Gracie Mansion	$58,000	96th	4
10471	X	Riverdale	$48,000	91st	4
11414	Q	Howard Beach	$44,000	88th	4
11364	Q	Oakland Gardens	$47,000	90th	2
10012	M	Washington Sq	$36,000	74th	3
11426	Q	Bellerose	$48,000	91st	5

Notes: Missing Zip codes = 12% in 1988–1993; Rates are per 100,000 residents; many Zip codes have far fewer than 100,000 residents; fewer than 10,000 deemed too small to rank. 1988–1993 = six-year average. Borough abbreviations: B = Brooklyn; M = Manhattan; Q = Queens; X = Bronx. Median income = projected by *Sourcebook* from 1990 Census data. Centile = National ranking estimated by *Sourcebook*.
Sources: Zip codes of deceased persons derived from the death certificates filed with the New York City Department of Health. Zip code data drawn from *The Sourcebook of ZIP Code Demographics*, 11th edition, 1996.

York University's main campus; the Riverdale section of the Bronx; and the Bay Terrace/Bayside, Howard Beach, Bellerose, and Oakland Gardens sections of Queens. (During the mid-1990s, when the crash was well underway, no residents from some of these Zip codes were murdered during an entire year.) Therefore, it certainly appears that most of the New Yorkers who were murdered during the worst years of the late 1980s and early 1990s had been residing in poor—or at best, working-class—neighborhoods and probably were from the lower strata of the social class structure. The distinct pattern of lower income area/extremely high victimization rate versus upper income area/very low victimization rate confirms that a Zip code serves not only as a geographical locator but also as a reasonably accurate indicator of a person's social class.

Grave Danger

The disproportional victimization of young men living in the City's poorest and most segregated neighborhoods can be explained in terms of their situational vulnerability, routine activities, and life-style choices. Situational vulnerability arises from systematic disadvantages, such as being viewed by potential offenders as easy prey or fair game, living in close proximity to would-be criminals on the prowl, and suffering from inadequate police protection. Underprivileged people endure heightened risks as a result of routine activities such as attending strife-torn schools filled with hard-core delinquents, shopping in a high-crime area, commuting to work at night by subway, or interacting with neighbors who are ex-convicts.

Life-style choices can compound problems associated with limited incomes. How individuals spend their free time and their money determines the kinds of people they associate with as friends and confront as enemies. The propensity of would-be alpha males to gravitate toward thrill-seeking escapades and to engage in supermasculine posturing, incessant mutual testing, hand-to-hand combat, and face-saving fights boosts the risks they already face from situational vulnerability and routine activities. The worst odds of all are faced by those destitute young men who, despairing of their bleak future, live life in the fast line, as if there were no tomorrow. They engage in reckless behaviors and dangerous illegal activities like getting high in public places, joining street gangs and drug posses, handling lots of cash from selling stolen goods or expensive drugs, displaying flashy symbols of status, brandishing deadly weapons, and double-crossing or snitching on fellow offenders. Conversely, females tend to make different life-style choices based on available resources as well as cultural norms. These behaviors explain the relative insularity from the dangers of hanging out on street corners of females (and also the very young and the very old, and the affluent of all ages and both sexes).

If heightened risks arise from situational vulnerability, routine activities, and life-style choices, then the sharp diminution of victimization rates during the 1990s among poor young minority men must have resulted from more cautious behavior on their part as well as from more harmonious relations with their peers.

Round Up the Usual Suspects?

The profile of the street criminal is well known: male; age 15–24; born to a teenaged mother; no positive male role model present, at birth or later; school drop-out; unemployable; user of tobacco, alcohol, or illegal drugs, or a gambler; ghetto dweller; welfare client; himself an absent father; and otherwise precluded from meaningful participation in society.

So he is easy to demonize.

No one cares to ask how he was shaped, why he wasn't salvaged, why social welfare policies weren't structured to preserve his family, why he wasn't educated or employed, and why we insist on returning him, from prison, to the conditions that produced his crimes.

      —Former NYPD commander Anthony Bouza (1996:208)

The Hollywood and tabloid news images of the typical murder and the average victim were shown to be inaccurate. However, when it comes to portraying the New Yorkers usually taken into custody for homicides, depressingly familiar stereotypes are not far off the mark, according to the statistical portrait of the characteristics of suspects that appears in table 2.4. The attributes of the typical accused murderer strongly resemble those of the average victim: young, male, poor or working class, and all too frequently black or Hispanic.[18]

Portrait of the Killers

Violent offenders from privileged backgrounds and comfortable circumstances have been responsible for some headline-generating murders over the past two decades. For example, a stockbroker shot and killed a policeman while fleeing from a botched robbery (of his own father); a fifteen-year-old girl attending a fashionable private school along with her sixteen-year-old boyfriend gutted the body of a drinking buddy so it would sink to the bottom of Central Park Lake; a wealthy young man

Table 2.4. Trends in the Profiles of Homicide Arrestees, New York City, Selected Years, 1978–1997

Attribute	1978	1981	1985	1990	1991	1992	1993	1994	1995	1996	1997
Sex											
Males %	90	91	91	95	94	95	95	95	94	95	93
Number	921	1042	974	1359	1336	1185	1219	1214	1010	952	948
Females %	10	9	9	5	6	5	5	5	6	5	7
Number	98	100	90	77	82	60	58	62	70	51	70
Age Groups %											
1–15 yrs. old	2	4	3	5	5	4	5	5	3	3	3
16–20 yrs. old	24	27	22	37	36	35	34	34	32	32	31
21–25 yrs. old	25	25	27	22	24	26	25	24	27	26	27
26–30 yrs. old	17	16	18	15	15	15	15	15	16	14	12
31–35 yrs. old	12	10	11	9	9	8	10	10	9	11	11
36–40 yrs. old	7	7	8	5	4	5	4	5	5	6	9
41 + yrs. old	12	11	12	8	7	7	7	7	8	8	7
Median Age	25	24	25	22	22	22	22	22	23	23	23
Race and Ethnicity											
Whites %	19	11	12	6	7	6	5	7	7	6	6
Number	198	123	129	85	101	77	69	86	71	60	66
Blacks %	50	51	48	56	54	53	56	52	50	55	54
Number	515	586	507	801	759	663	720	670	536	555	554
Hispanics %	30	37	39	36	38	38	37	39	39	36	35
Number	308	427	416	521	532	477	470	495	426	356	360
Asians %	0	1	1	2	2	2	2	2	4	3	4
Number	0	6	12	30	26	28	22	27	47	32	38
Past Record											
Never arrested %	29	34	29	32	32	30	32	32	33	28	31
Only misd. arr. %	7	6	6	4	4	3	4	5	6	6	6
Only fel. arr. %	25	24	26	29	31	34	31	28	26	26	24
Both m. & f. arr. %	39	36	40	35	34	34	33	34	35	40	39
Never convicted %	57	58	51	59	56	53	52	54	54	51	53
Only misd. con. %	26	23	20	11	11	11	8	9	9	9	11
Only fel. con. %	7	6	10	16	17	20	22	21	20	21	18
Both m. & f. con. %	10	12	18	15	16	17	18	17	17	19	18
Number of arrestees	1021	1142	1064	1437	1418	1245	1281	1278	1080	1003	1018

Source: Arrestee database provided by the New York State Division of Criminal Justice Services.

strangled his girlfriend during what he termed "rough sex" in Central Park; and a cocaine-addled lawyer beat his adopted daughter to death. But these cases attracted sustained media coverage precisely because they were so unusual. Putting sensationalism and shock value aside, it is necessary to ask: From what social strata are most perpetrators drawn? The answer is that violent individuals come largely from the most disadvantaged depths of the City's class structure, according to evidence derived from employment and income data collected by a unique municipal agency, the Criminal Justice Agency (CJA). Its employees interview all arrestees shortly after they are taken into custody to determine their eligibility for ROR ("release on their own recognizance"—they do not have to raise money to post bail because they have sufficient "roots in the community" to give judges confidence that they will show up for future court dates); and to find out whether or not they qualify for free legal representation or are financially able to afford a private attorney.

According to a study carried out by the CJA in the mid-1990s, most persons accused of street crimes were financially hard pressed (Gewirtz and McElroy, 1997). The unemployment rate of two samples of arrestees was 60 percent and 54 percent in 1992 and 1993, respectively. Of those who worked full time, the median weekly take-home pay was around $285. Fewer than 10 percent of all these urban dwellers reported that they owned a car, and of these motorists, only about 10 percent owned a late-model vehicle (defined as less than two years old). Furthermore, only about 11 percent reported that they had a bank account of any size.

People arrested on murder charges were even more economically disadvantaged than the mixed bag of misdemeanor and felony arrestees in the 1992 and 1993 samples. These accused killers had an unemployment rate that was even higher, at about 65 percent (recall that in 1989 unemployment was not as serious a problem in the City, at 6.8 percent, as it became in 1992, with its annual average of 10.8 percent, and in 1993, when it stood at 10.1 percent). Of the forty-two murder and manslaughter defendants in the sample who had full-time jobs, the median weekly take-home pay was only $225, $60 less than the earnings of the mixed group of arrestees a few years later. With incomes this low, most fell squarely into the category of the "working poor," given the high cost of living in the metropolitan area. About 12 percent of this sample were living below the official poverty line and receiving welfare at the time of their alleged crime. Only 33 percent had been in a position to give economic support to a spouse, to children, or to parents before they were picked up by detectives, according to an analysis of the answers 150 homicide arrestees provided to Criminal Justice Agency (CJA) inter-viewers in 1989.

The suspicion that most killers ten years later still came from the mar-gins rather than the mainstream of society was confirmed by the findings of an analysis of individuals arrested for homicide in Brooklyn during 1999. Eighty-one percent of these defendants had not finished high school and 80 percent were unemployed (during an economic boom), according to the information they disclosed to CJA interviewers seeking to determine eligibility for bail and free legal representation for indigents (Hynes, 2000).

The economic standing of alleged murderers also can be discerned by the quality of legal representation they receive. It seems reasonable to as-sume that when a defendant's life is on the line, literally, as when facing murder or manslaughter charges, no expense would be spared. Yet only about 15 percent of such defendants purchased the services of private at-torneys in Manhattan in the early 1990s. Clearly, the vast majority of de-fendants facing long prison terms were indigents who had to place their fates in the hands of overburdened and underfunded lawyers supplied by the government.[19] In fact, most arrestees hauled into court met the stan-dards for free legal representation in the mid-1990s. More than eight out of every ten misdemeanor defendants and nine out of ten felony defen-dants were found eligible for publicly provided attorneys (Gewirtz and McElroy, 1997).[20]

Now that the disadvantaged socioeconomic background of most killers has been determined, in what other ways can murderers be characterized?

Unleashing deadly force has been and continues to be overwhelm-ingly a male-dominated proclivity. In 1978, 90 percent of the arrestees were boys and men. During the 1990s, the proportion of alleged killers who were male crept up to a high of 95 percent (see table 2.4). These percentages are considerably greater than the percentages of the victims who were males (which peaked at 86 percent and dipped to a low of 79 percent). Clearly, most criminal violence is male-on-male. Males are most likely to be the killers of other males, but they are also the murder-ers of most females.

Each year between 1978 and 1997, the NYPD took from nine hun-dred to more than 1,350 males into custody and charged them with killing someone. The number of females arrested hovered close to one hundred per year in the late 1970s and early 1980s, before dropping down to a range of about fifty to eighty per year in the 1990s. Widespread fears about a trend toward increasing violence by women appear to be unfounded, at least as far as New York City murders are concerned.

With respect to age, more than 85 percent of the suspects arrested for murder since 1978 have been between the ages of sixteen and forty at the time of the incident (table 2.4). Few people younger than sixteen or older than forty have been accused of causing deaths; people over forty have in fact become less involved in criminal violence over the years. However, youngsters less than sixteen became more embroiled in fights to the finish from 1978 until the mid-1990s. But as the 1990s continued, their level of participation in lethal showdowns declined. The alarm over the growing involvement of younger adolescents was justified (as it hit 5 percent), and their percent of all accused murderers has not yet fallen back to the 1978 figure of 2 percent. Similarly, the cohort of sixteen- to twenty-year-olds accounted for 24 percent of all arrests in 1978, but grew to 37 percent in 1990 before declining somewhat during the later 1990s.

The median age of murder arrestees dropped from twenty-five at the end of the 1970s down to twenty-two by the beginning of the 1990s before inching back up to twenty-three later in the decade. Therefore, it appears that the very disturbing trend toward younger and younger killers has reversed a little in the 1990s.[21]

Overall, the highest-risk ages for getting drawn into life-and-death struggles stand out as from sixteen to twenty-five, as in the rest of the United States (Blumstein and Rosenfeld, 1998). Two decades ago, young people in their late teens and early twenties made up about 50 percent of all arrestees; by the late 1990s, this age group comprised about 58 percent of all alleged killers.

With respect to the racial and ethnic composition of homicide suspects, statistics show that minorities made up the majority of the arrestees. The mix resembled that of murder victims. Over the decades, about half of the arrestees have been black; after 1978, more than one-third have been Hispanic. Added together, black and Hispanic defendants have made up about nine-tenths of all suspects taken into custody during the 1990s. In census surveys, about one quarter of all New Yorkers identified themselves as black during the 1990s, so the overrepresentation is twice what would be expected statistically. Similarly, census data indicate that Hispanic residents made up more than one quarter of all New Yorkers, so their involvement in criminal violence was also disproportional, but to a lesser degree.

Whites have made up a declining share of arrestees over the two decades. Whereas they comprised about one-fifth of all alleged killers during the late 1970s, they accounted for only about one-twentieth of arrestees by the late 1990s. The major reason was not necessarily improved behavior but demographics. The number of white teenagers and young adults living within city limits has dropped sharply since 1978. People of Asian descent also have been underrepresented among the ranks of arrestees. They made up only a small percent of suspects each year, even though their share of New York City's population has risen rapidly over the past twenty years, to nearly one-tenth.[22]

With respect to criminal histories, fewer than one-third of the suspects taken into custody each year had clean records unblemished by prior arrests. The rap sheets of six out of every ten accused killers showed a prior arrest for a felony. Surprisingly, only a small percentage had been arrested only for some minor crime, and nothing more, even though misdemeanor arrests greatly outnumber felony arrests every year. As many as two-fifths of all defendants had a past record of both felony and misdemeanor arrests.

Not only had most accused killers been arrested before for allegedly committing a serious crime, but a sizable fraction (from two-fifths to nearly one-half) had been convicted previously of either a minor or major crime. In 1978 and 1981, the bulk of the prior convictions were only for misdemeanors. But during the 1990s, about a third or more of all homicide arrestees had been previously convicted of a felony (and for nearly a fifth, a misdemeanor as well). Therefore, most of the current crop of killers have been in trouble with the law before. In fact (but not shown in table 2.4), about half of all murder suspects had fairly serious rap sheets listing at least two prior arrests for felonies.[23] Clearly, many of these suspected murderers had demonstrated by their past bad behavior that they were capable of causing serious trouble, not merely minor disturbances. As for trends, accused killers constituted a somewhat tougher, more hard-core group in the 1990s than two decades earlier. Still, in about a third of all cases, there had not been earlier warning signs of trouble ahead: the person believed to have committed a murder had never been arrested before (at least anywhere in New York State).

It is quite striking that there were no real, substantial trends, according to the data assembled in table 2.4. The statistical profile of the arrestees has not undergone any dramatic changes since 1978. During the worst of times, as well as during the crash, the majority of the people responsible for the problem of violent crime have been disproportionately drawn from the ranks of New York's most disadvantaged and disaffected subpopulation: low-income teen-age boys and young men, mostly black and Hispanic, who had not been effectively helped if they had previous entanglements with the criminal justice system.

Mortal Combat: Weapons of Choice

Corpses found bound and gagged with their throats cut, or discoveries of dismembered body parts stuffed into plastic trash bags make grisly -headlines. But how were most victims done in?

The methods favored by killers in New York City since the late 1980s are in order of preference, shooting, especially with a handgun; stabbing with a sharp instrument; clubbing with a blunt instrument; strangling; and burning by intentionally set fires, as table 2.5 shows. Perpetrators dispatched their victims much less frequently by poisoning them, beating them to death with their bare hands, pushing them off high places, holding them underwater, or even blowing them up with explosives, according to an analysis of the vital statistics database.

Firearms remain the weapon of choice, even though lives lost to gunfire dropped precipitously during the 1990s. Handguns are overwhelmingly employed as the instrument of death when males slay other males. The vast majority of the teenage boys and young men killed during 1998 succumbed to bullet wounds (and virtually all the rest were stabbed to death). Gunfire was a leading cause of death for women too, but to a lesser extent, with stabbings a close second. In terms of relative percentages, girls and women were more likely to be strangled, clubbed, or burned to death in an intentionally set fire than boys or men (table 2.5).[24]

As for changes over time in the way murderers killed their victims, two

Table 2.5. How Murderers Killed Their Victims: New York City, 1988, 1991, 1997, 1998

	1988		1991		1997		1998	
Cause of Death	No.	%	No.	%	No.	%	No.	%
Gunfire from a shotgun, rifle, or handgun								
Males	1,221	74%	1,523	81%	434	68%	341	68%
Females	109	37%	146	46%	49	33%	35	27%
Total	1,330	69%	1,669	76%	483	62%	376	60%
Stabbed with a sharp instrument								
Males	251	15%	205	11%	112	18%	74	15%
Females	79	27%	63	20%	40	27%	26	20%
Total	330	17%	268	12%	152	19%	100	16%
Clubbed with a blunt instrument								
Males	56	3%	53	3%	13	2%	10	2%
Females	23	8%	23	7%	3	2%	4	3%
Total	79	4%	76	4%	16	2%	14	2%
Strangled and otherwise suffocated								
Males	25	2%	24	1%	16	3%	10	2%
Females	51	17%	51	16%	24	16%	25	19%
Total	76	4%	75	3%	40	5%	35	6%
Burned in an arson fire								
Males	10	1%	10	1%	8	1%	7	1%
Females	9	3%	7	2%	7	5%	5	4%
Total	19	1%	17	1%	15	2%	12	2%
All other ways								
Males	82	5%	66	4%	52	8%	56	11%
Females	26	9%	26	8%	26	17%	37	28%
Total	108	6%	92	4%	78	10%	93	15%
Total homicide victims	1,942		2,197		784		630	

Notes: All other ways = mostly by unspecified means, also drowned, pushed off from a high place, poisoned, killed by an explosion, beaten to death without a weapon, starved through criminal neglect. Body count includes homicides later deemed to be justifiable.
Sources: 1988–1998: New York City Department of Health vital statistics database from death certificates; 1998: NYPD Homicide Log.

distinct trends are evident (see Karmen, 1996; Fagan, Zimring, and Kim, 1998). Fatal assaults involving blunt instruments, knifings, strangulations, poisonings, burnings, and other types of killings generally have been going out of fashion since peaking in the early 1970s (see graph 2.3). Unfortunately, over the same time period, guns grew in popularity, replacing folding knives.

Even though street gang members began to arm themselves with handguns shortly after World War II (see Wakefield, 1992), deaths from

Graph 2.3. Trends in Gun and Non-Gun Murders, New York City
and United States, 1960–1998

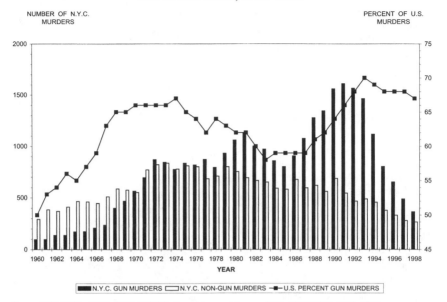

Source: FBI's UCRs, 1960–1998; NYPD's Complaints and Arrests, 1991; NYC DOH, 1991–1998.

gunfire were not a big problem at the start of the 1960s. The number of
people killed by bullets rose slowly but steadily from 1960 until 1967, as
manufacturing and importing guns became a growth industry. Although
cheap "Saturday night specials" became the focus of handgun control
legislation, the police were busy confiscating expensive, high-quality
weapons on the streets (Silberman, 1978). After 1967, gun murders
soared, catching up with killings by all other means by 1970. The number of gun murders generally matched the volume of non-gun murders
throughout most of the 1970s. But deaths from gunfire took off again
in the late 1970s, just when all other kinds of murders started their rather
steady downward drift. Firearms claimed fewer lives during the early
1980s, but the relief was only temporary. Shortly after the outbreak of
the crack epidemic in late 1985, bullets started to fly in earnest again, and
gunfire deaths reached record proportions by 1990. After that terrible
peak, fatal shootings began to drop—slowly during 1992 and 1993, and
then steeply from 1994 through 1998, down almost to the diminished
levels to which non-gun killings had sunk. Therefore, over the four

decades, three distinct escalations of an arms race took place in the City, propelling body counts to dizzying new heights. With each round, an explosive proliferation in the supply of high-tech weaponry stimulated its own demand: the more some people went about their business armed, the more other people who feared them felt compelled to play catchup by obtaining better guns of their own and carrying them around as concealed weapons whenever they left home (see Silberman, 1978).

New York's experience with gun murders paralleled developments in the entire country, but with some differences in timing. The percentage of murders across the U.S. resulting from gunfire skyrocketed in the mid-1960s, several years before New Yorkers took to arming themselves and shooting one another at a faster clip. A spurt of gun killings in the late 1970s signaled that New York's gun problem was intensifying. By 1981, it had caught up with the rest of the nation. In the late 1980s, gun murders throughout the country soared, trailing New York's surge in gunfights by a year or two. After peaking in 1993 as the cause of 70 percent of all violent deaths across the land, the ready resort to firearms subsided, just as it had in New York a year earlier. Americans in general and New Yorkers in particular definitely have not been disarmed, but they were firing their guns far less often during the late 1990s, a positive development that enabled the murder rate to crash in the City and drift downward everywhere else. Once again, what happened in New York mirrored developments throughout the United States, but with greater volatility and with a time lag—a few years behind in the 1960s, a year or two ahead in the 1980s and 1990s.[25]

Crime Scenes

Criminal activity does not break out randomly throughout the City. With the advent of computer-assisted crime mapping, more focused efforts can be undertaken to swiftly identify and neutralize local hot-spots of lawlessness (see Sherman, Gartin, and Buerger 1989). Certain mean streets suffer from a deservedly negative reputation. But what about New York's bars, subways, dwellings, and, in particular, public housing projects?[26]

Anti-drinking crusaders in the temperance movement argued that closing down establishments that served alcoholic beverages would help cut down the crime rate by preventing shoot-outs and fist fights and subsequent acts of wife beating and child abuse by liquored-up men. The Anti-Saloon League depicted bars and taverns as male watering holes plagued by boisterous boasting, loud cursing, gambling, carousing, and horseplay that could turn ugly without warning. After the enactment of the Eighteenth Amendment in 1919 ushered in the war on drinking, the crime rate—and New York City's murder rate in particular—soared. A major reason was that organized crime families, running lucrative rackets bootlegging liquor to their speakeasies, engaged in bloody mob wars to control the illegal trade. Gangsters became celebrities, if not folk heroes, as drinkers grew enamored of the underworld figures. The murder rate set records locally and nationally by the start of the 1930s, right before the "Noble Experiment" of Prohibition was abandoned.

Even though New York and the rest of the country remained in the grip of the Great Depression throughout the remainder of the 1930s, the murder rate fell rapidly. But the stereotypical images of bar patrons getting fired up and picking fights lingered in the media and in the popular imagination. These days, neighborhood taverns may no longer be the hub of working-class social life that they once were, since factories have closed and the blue-collar work force in urban areas has dwindled (see Butterfield, 1996c). This hypothesis about the declining significance of the "bar and grill" as a local troublespot has some support in the data.[27] However, slayings in bars were never all that common, even in the 1970s. By 1997, only about one percent of all slayings took place inside a bar or tavern or spilled out to the street in front of the establishment. However, to some extent, this drinking-and-fighting scene has shifted to the "social clubs," which were not such a prominent feature on the City landscape in the 1970s. By 1997, an additional 2 percent (about fifteen) of all fatal encounters had erupted in social clubs, some of which were unlicensed, after-hours nightspots that might tolerate drug taking and dealing on the premises (see Williams, 1989) and frequently attract unruly crowds. Therefore, any beneficial effects due to a decline in barroom brawls have been counteracted by a rise in violence in social clubs. In either case, killings stemming from disputes and robberies in these settings have never accounted for much of the City's body count, a misimpression cleared up by the data assembled in table 2.6.[28]

Some New Yorkers think that walking down the steps to a subway platform is a descent into hell. They conjure up images of being set upon

Table 2.6. Common Crime Scenes? Selected Years, 1972–1997

	1972	1976	1980	1982	1984	1985	1986	1991	1995	1996	1997
A residence											
Number	728	647	657	623	595	586	732	588	na	na	345
Percent	43	40	36	37	41	41	46	26	—	—	45
A housing project											
Number	na	75	89	na	na	66	138	189	124	120	99
Percent	—	5	5	—	—	5	9	9	11	12	13
A bar or club											
Number	50	53	na	na	na	na	na	na	na	na	25
Percent	3	3	—	—	—	—	—	—	—	—	1
The subway											
Number	14	7	19	16	9	12	12	26	4	3	4
Percent	1	0	1	1	0	1	1	1	0	0	0

Notes: na = not available. Some killings in residences took place on the grounds of housing projects. The two categories overlap. For housing projects, totals for 1995, 1996, and 1997 were for fiscal years. The 1976 total was unavailable, so 1975 was provided instead. For subways, the 1991 figure was not available; fiscal 1992 is provided in its place. For bars and residences, 1997 totals are an estimate projected from the M.E. files for the first six months. Residences include private homes, apartment buildings, and hotels. Nonresidential crime scenes include streets, open areas like parks, vacant buildings, commercial locations, and public buildings.
Sources: NYPD Homicide Analyses, selected years 1972 to 1986. Housing project murders: NYC Housing Authority Police; subway murders: NYC Transit Authority Police. Also, Mayor's Management Reports, 1990s. Killings in residences: 1991, from Tardiff et al., 1995, 1997, M.E. files.

by bands of marauders and chased into dark tunnels filled with roaring trains, high-voltage third rails, and scurrying rats. Although the death of twenty-six passengers in 1991 was certainly a chilling reflection of the strife going on above ground as well, killings underground from robberies and disputes never added up to more than one percent of any given year's body count (table 2.6). Therefore, subways weren't hotspots for criminal violence, and improved decorum on the platforms and trains of the mass transit system did not significantly help to bring down the City's murder rate during the 1990s.

Ironically, dwellings may be hotspots for violence. Many New Yorkers breathe a sigh of relief when they reach home, double-locking their doors, and sealing themselves off from the dog-eat-dog world of the streets. Unfortunately, for many homicide victims, entering their house or apartment and letting down their guard became their final act on earth. Either a ferocious quarrel with some other member of the household erupted, or a friend suddenly became an arch-enemy, or some robber barged in. Other victims never quite made it to their sanctuaries and were picked off right at the perimeter of their homes; in lobbies, hallways, stairwells, elevators, basements, and rooftops of apartment buildings; or right in front of their dwellings or in the immediate vicinity (e.g., a garage or driveway). Additionally, sizable numbers of victims were murdered in someone else's apartment building or home, where a family gathering, a tryst, a party, a business deal, or a drug transaction was underway.[29] Indeed, there is no place like home when it comes to murder. A large proportion—more than a third, almost a half in some years—of the people killed over the period from the late 1960s to the late 1990s were either at or close to home or visiting someone else's living quarters when the fatal encounter took place (table 2.6).

Since the 1930s, New York City has built more public housing than any other city in the nation. About 330 projects for low-income families contain 180,000 apartments, into which crowd 460,000 authorized tenants and perhaps as many as 125,000 additional members of their households (Mayor's Management Report [MMR], 1994). Unfortunately, many of these developments managed by a municipal agency have developed a reputation as a breeding ground for street gangs, gun selling, and drug dealing (see Donaldson, 1993). However, until the mid-1980s, murders in or immediately surrounding housing projects added up to just 5 percent of each year's body count. Considering that about 8 percent of the City's population was housed in the municipal projects, the death toll was disproportionately low there. Since then, the buildings and grounds of housing projects have been the scenes of an increasing number of the City's killings (by 1997, 13 percent). This growing overrepresentation took place because the murder rate was dropping more rapidly in other communities. In terms of victimization rates, 1988 was the worst year, when about two hundred murders yielded a rate of thirty-four deaths for every 100,000 project residents. By 1997, it was cut in half to seventeen deaths per 100,000, but it still was frighteningly high, and nearly twice the rate for the City as a whole. The crash brought considerable relief, but housing projects remain stubborn hot spots for criminal activity (the body count for fiscal year 1998 was 83 killings, 12 percent of the City's total). The most likely explanation is that the projects house huge concentrations of low-income people, and murderers and their victims are drawn disproportionately from the ranks of the poor and working class.

High Crime Precincts

At the height of the carnage in the late 1980s and early 1990s, some police precincts could literally be called "killing fields" (table 2.7). The threat that residents faced in these high crime precincts soared to unprecedented heights, two-and-a-half to three-and-a-half times as bad as the City's overall murder rate (of thirty slayings for every 100,000 residents in its worst year, 1990). But during the 1990s, many of these violence-torn areas experienced tremendous improvements, with their murder rates plummeting even faster than the 72 percent plunge in the entire City's murder rate (to 8.5 per 100,000 inhabitants by the end of 1998). In general, the communities suffering from the highest death tolls benefited the greatest from the crash. However, even though their

Table 2.7. How Far the Murder Rate Fell in the Most Dangerous Precincts

Precinct and Neighborhood	Murder Rate, Worst Year	Murder Rate in 1998	Percent Change
Manhattan			
14 Midtown South	111 in 1988	18	−84%
25 East Harlem	105 in 1991	15	−86%
28 Central Harlem	113 in 1991	22	−81%
32 Harlem	108 in 1988	10	−91%
34 Washington Heights	60 in 1991	8	−87%
Bronx			
40 South Bronx	109 in 1991	19	−83%
41 Hunts Point	129 in 1991	20	−84%
42 Tremont	94 in 1990	21	−78%
44 Morris Heights	74 in 1990	15	−80%
46 University Heights	73 in 1991	18	−75%
48 Fordham	69 in 1989	33	−52%
Brooklyn			
73 Brownsville	92 in 1991	31	−66%
75 East New York	68 in 1990	25	−63%
79 Bedford-Stuyvesant	100 in 1991	22	−78%
81 Brownsville/Bed-Stuy	79 in 1990	16	−80%
83 Bushwick	75 in 1990	12	−84%
All precincts	30 in 1990	8.5	−72%

Notes: Many precincts served populations of fewer than 100,000 people. The 1998 body count for the 34th Precinct includes the death toll in the 33rd Precinct, which was created from it in 1995. The worst murder rate for the 48th Precinct would be 201 in 1990 if the eighty-seven arson deaths at the Happyland Social Club were counted.
Sources: 1990 Census data: NYPD's document, "Selected Social Indicators by Precinct," 1992. Murders and murder rates by precinct: NYPD's Complaints and Arrests annual reports; 1998 Compstat summary.

murder rates tumbled to their lowest levels in decades, these precincts remained the most dangerous parts of town. The relative standing of these high crime areas did not improve because murder rates fell in all precincts, but from lower levels and to lesser degrees.

In order to determine what these high crime areas had in common and how they stood out from other neighborhoods, an analysis of each precinct's local conditions was undertaken. As anticipated from criminological theories that the causes of street crime are rooted in poverty (see Hagan and Peterson, 1995), a precinct's murder rate and its immediate demographic and social conditions were strongly correlated.[30] Murder rates tended to be higher where economic distress was greater, according to several measures (percentage of persons and families living below the poverty line; percentage receiving public assistance; unemployment rates for teenagers and adults; and proportions of persons going to college). Conversely, murder rates were lower in precincts where residents were more prosperous. As for demographic variables, higher murder rates were associated with greater concentrations of females (reflecting the absence adult men) and teenagers (a group at high risk for getting involved in violence), and ghettoization/segregation (black and Hispanic residents isolated from the mainstream of society). In areas populated mostly by whites or Asians, and where the mix of males to females as well as youths to adults was more balanced, murder rates were lower.

Since murder rates are closely tied to neighborhood demographics and social conditions, this statistical analysis implies that the crash might have been brought about by a rapid improvement in economic conditions that alleviated the serious intertwined problems of deprivation and joblessness underlying family breakdown in these beleaguered communities.

Putting Together All the Clues

Deconstructing the murder rate into its constituent parts has unearthed a number of additional valuable leads. The kinds of murders that decreased the most arose from robberies, domestic violence, the drug scene, and disputes that flared up over an assortment of issues. The crime wave that engulfed New York since the 1960s was fueled by an arms race. As guns proliferated and became the weapon of choice, all other means of killing faded in importance. The crash resulted from a sharp drop in gun violence. Most slayings before as well as after the crash could be characterized largely as youth-on-youth, male-on-male, minority-on-minority, and poor-on-poor. The areas with the highest crime rates before the crash showed the most impressive improvements by the end of the 1990s. Evidently a profound behavioral change for the better took place in these low income and highly segregated communities: many of the socially disadvantaged teenage boys and young men who had gotten caught up in reckless illegal activities during the late 1980s adopted law-abiding life-styles—as did the next generation of teenage boys during the 1990s.[31]

Add to this mix the clues that were gathered from the analysis in chapter 1: that the diminution in murders was accompanied by a decline in all reported crimes; that the drop was more pronounced in New York City but was primarily a big city phenomenon, and even a nationwide development; and that all through the years, what happened on the crime front across the country was reflected on the streets of New York as well. Finally, factor in the possibility that New York's superior progress in reducing crime might be connected to its special features: its recently overhauled police department, its huge criminal justice apparatus, its entrenched drug scene, its strong economic recovery, and its unique population mix. The time has come to speculate about all the possible reasons for the crash.

What Makes Crime Rates Rise and Fall?

Crime rates can be taken as important indicators of a community's social health. When crime rates rise, the undesirable, troublesome conditions that attract people to illegal activities must be intensifying. Either a growing share of the population is engaging in illicit behaviors, or the same number of offenders are becoming more active, or both. When crime rates fall, positive developments must be taking place either in the criminal justice system designed to suppress and control crime, and/or in the underlying social conditions that are believed to be the root causes of crime. Either fewer people are involved in deeds that the law forbids, or the same number of offenders are less active.

When crime rates began their notable decline during the 1990s, many experts expressed surprise at first. When asked by journalists why crime rates were falling, criminal justice administrators, elected officials, criminologists, and other researchers offered plausible contentions, based on recent social history, their own past experiences, or, better yet, the findings derived from ongoing research (for example, see Krauss, 1995b; Anderson, 1997; Glazer, 1997a and b; Lardner, 1997; and Witkin, 1998). Some of the more elaborate conjectures boiled down to conventional wisdom of the same sort offered by laypersons, just dressed up by sophisticated jargon. Certain speculative answers obviously were self-serving, circulated by interested parties who wished to promote some policy or program, or garner support for their ideological beliefs.

Topping most experts' lists was an assumption about improved policing, due to innovations in technology, management, coordination, interagency cooperation, and deployment strategies; the introduction of community policing; a growth in the sheer numbers of officers on patrol; proactive crackdowns on low-level quality-of-life offenses; and new antigun strategies. Following logically from better policing was an impression that dangerous persons were being removed from the streets more efficiently due to pro-incarceration policies. Most experts cited the possibility of a diminishing drug scene marked by fewer turf wars between rival drug-dealing crews, thanks to an ebbing of the crack epidemic. Many hypothesized that a surge in business activity and an expanding job market were absorbing marginal men who otherwise might be pursuing illicit ways of making money. A number of criminologists were convinced that temporarily favorable demographic situations must have reduced the proportion of the population most prone to involvement in crime and violence, low-income teenagers and young adults. Finally, some researchers believed they were witnessing a growing rejection by adolescents of a reckless life-style revolving around gangs and drugs and guns, largely due to their firsthand experiences and direct observations about the dangers of life in the fast lane.

As crime rates fell, officeholders heralded their own programs and pet projects as having turned the tide. Starting at the top, President Bill Clinton argued that the passage of his administration's 1994 crime bill contributed to the nationwide decline by putting more officers on the street to carry out community policing; by banning the sale of assault weapons;

and by imposing a background check and a cooling-off period on hand-gun purchasers (Butterfield, 1995b). Vice-President Al Gore suggested that anti-violence programs funded by the 1994 federal crime bill were working (Associated Press, 1995). FBI director Louis Freeh attributed some of the drop to the Bureau's "safe streets" campaign launched in over one hundred communities to break up street gangs (Shannon, 1995). Governor Pete Wilson asserted that California's new three-strikes-and-you're-out law had lowered that state's crime rate precipitously (Butterfield, 1996d). Governor George Pataki contended that New York was becoming a safer place thanks to his administration's new state laws, especially the one that reinstated the death penalty and another that eliminated parole for repeat violent felons (Hernandez, 1998). FBI assistant director James Kallstrom suggested that stiff sentences from successful federal prosecutions of violent street gangs in Manhattan and the Bronx had a chilling effect on "wannabes" who would have followed in their footsteps (Krauss, 1995c). Manhattan district attorney Robert Morgenthau (1995) believed that successful prosecutions of violent drug gangs by his office's Homicide Investigation Unit and of repeat offenders by the Career Criminal Bureau contributed to the decline.

But no officeholders were as insistent in claiming credit as Mayor Rudolph Giuliani and his police commissioners, William Bratton and later Howard Safir. They repeatedly argued that a reengineered NYPD was responsible for the City's widely heralded improvement (see Ward, 1997). One reporter (Krauss, 1995c) summed up the situation this way:

> New York City's murder, robbery and burglary rates have plummeted to their lowest levels in a quarter century—a development that has become a marvel of American law enforcement. But Police Commissioner William J. Bratton will not be satisfied until every last criminologist surrenders. "We'll knock them down like ducks in a row," said Mr. Bratton, speaking of all the standard criminological theories about how crime waves are tied to the size of the youth population, or to changes in the weather, or to unemployment levels, or to drug use patterns, or to the availability of guns. As an enthusiastic brawler and bragger, Mr. Bratton wants the world to believe that it is his aggressive new crime strategies, and just about nothing else, that have forced New York's thugs into a fast retreat.

Because improved policing has been cited so often as the primary reason for declining crime rates nationwide, and for New York's crash in particular, this hypothesis will be examined first.

Notes

1. Deaths among people involved in the commercial sex scene used to be monitored under the heading of "vice" by the NYPD several decades ago. But since the start of the 1980s, such killings have been classified as the result of disputes, robberies, or even drug-related conflicts, so it is no longer possible to measure their extent. Two female and two male prostitutes were murdered, and one man was found dead in a building where commercial sex took place during the first half of 1997, according to Medical Examiner files.

2. The worst gunfights took place in 1971, resulting in the most officers lost in a single year (11), and the most suspects killed by the NYPD (93) (NYPD Firearms Discharge Assault Report, 1994b).

3. In 1992, 40 drivers of livery car service taxis (not Yellow Cabs) were murdered on the job (mostly by armed robbers, but also by angry motorists). That death toll fell all the way down to 8 in 1998, 11 in 1999, and about 235 over the entire decade, according to NYPD homicide logs and other police files. The livery cabdriver workforce was about the same size as the police force, 41,000 (Kennedy, 2000).

4. The actual death tolls from organized crime rubouts were probably higher than the official numbers appearing in the homicide logs and SHRs during the 1990s. In 1991, seventeen mob hits took place on the streets of the City; five wiseguys met their fate in 1995; and seven gangland slayings were recorded in 1996, as well as in 1997, and again in 1998, according to NYPD statistics disclosed to Jerry Capeci, formerly a *New York Daily News* journalist and currently director of public relations for John Jay College.

5. If Commissioner Safir's estimate is correct, then the seriousness of the gang problem has been chronically underestimated by the NYPD's two record-keeping systems, the Chief of Detectives Homicide Logs for internal use only, and the Supplementary Homicide Reports sent to the FBI.

However, police and prosecutors in Brooklyn attributed only seven killings (3 percent) during 1998 and 10 (4 percent) during 1999 to clashes between street gang members (Hynes, 2000).

6. Although the risk of getting killed hangs over each confrontation, the overwhelming majority of robbery victims survive their harrowing encounters. For example, in 1998, forty-eight innocent victims (excluding stickups of drug sellers) died from their wounds. But nearly 40,000 people told the police that they

had been robbed, and an equal number probably didn't inform the authorities, since the reporting rate for robbery hovered around 50 percent, according to NCVS findings. Therefore, roughly one out of every eight hundred known robbery victims were murdered during the course of the holdup, and the actual figure might have been one out of every 1,600.

7. Murderers who kill their victims during the commission of a serious felony such as robbery, burglary, or rape can be executed under New York State's 1995 capital punishment law.

8. As defined by the NYPD and the FBI, the term "intra-family" includes husbands, wives, common-law spouses, estranged former spouses, sons, daughters, brothers, sisters, grandsons, granddaughters, grandmothers, grandfathers, sons-in-law, daughters-in-law, fathers-in-law, mothers-in-law, brothers-in-law, sisters-in-law, uncles, aunts, nephews, nieces, and cousins. Most deaths from child abuse are counted as "intra-family" (unless, for example, they are due to the actions of a babysitter). Many different permutations are possible: one spouse kills the other; sons or daughters kill mothers and fathers who did a poor job of raising them; sibling rivalries escalate to lethal levels; stepparents and stepchildren become embroiled into bitter conflicts; and so on.

9. In 1997, twenty-one husbands killed their wives, and eight common-law husbands murdered their partners; six wives killed their husbands, and ten common-law wives murdered their partners. In total, twenty-nine females died, compared to sixteen males. Also during that year, twenty females were slain by their boyfriends, whereas only two males were murdered by their girlfriends, according to the NYPD homicide log.

10. The sorry phenomenon of homicide followed by suicide took place thirteen times both in 1997 and 1998, according to the homicide logs.

11. The NYPD's 1991 homicide analysis report identified the following factors as necessary—but not sufficient, unless several are present—for a killing to be categorized as drug related: the crime scene is a known location for drug sales, drug taking (either a crack house or a heroin-shooting gallery) or drug preparing (a mill or factory for mixing and packaging); the victim was a known drug user or seller, from prior arrests; the suspect was a known drug user or seller, from prior arrests; and drugs or drug paraphernalia were found at the scene. Note that many "disputes" and "robberies" are "drug related," which can lead to great confusion and inaccurate estimates if consistent criteria are not applied by detectives and record-keeping personnel.

12. The proportion of all murders that were drug related varied tremendously from neighborhood to neighborhood. The highest estimates came from the 34th Precinct, which covers Manhattan's Washington Heights neighborhood with its notorious cocaine and crack problem (see Williams, 1989). In this

precinct, 38 percent of all murders were designated as drug related in 1985, and as many as 51 percent in 1991, according to the NYPD's 1991 Homicide Analysis Report. A careful reading of the precinct's case files (combined with a more inclusive definition that embraced slayings committed under the influence of drugs) yielded a higher estimate of the percentage of drug-related murders in this troubled community, where most of the residents were immigrants from the Dominican Republic: 55 percent in 1991, and 67 percent by the following year. A single drug-selling posse, the "Wild Cowboys," was responsible for as many as forty homicides throughout the City (see Jackall, 1997). However, the level of violence in Washington Heights subsided remarkably when most drug transactions took place behind closed doors rather than right out in the streets during the late 1990s.

13. Victimization rates, which take population into account, tell the same dramatic story as actual body counts. During the worst year, 1990, 57 males were killed for every 100,000 residing in the city. But by 1997, the male murder rate had plummeted by 66 percent to 18 per 100,000. Female victimization rates hovered between 6 and 8 per 100,000 over the years, before dropping to 3.5 per 100,000 in 1997.

14. When the actual number of males in each age grouping living in New York City in the census year of 1990 is taken into account, it turns out that young men twenty to twenty-four years old suffered the highest murder rate (slain at a horrific rate of 143 for every 100,000). Teenage boys ages sixteen to nineteen had the second-highest rate (at 127 per 100,000), followed by men aged twenty-five to thirty-four (at 105 per 100,000), and then men thirty-five to forty-four (at 56 per 100,000).

15. Since the beginning of the 1970s, the New York City Police Department has been following the U.S. Census classification scheme, designating victims (and offenders) as either "White Non-Hispanic," "Black Non-Hispanic," "Hispanic" (of any race), and "Other" (almost entirely Asians). Prior to that time, most Hispanics were classified as whites, obscuring an important distinction.

16. It is possible to make even finer distinctions than those offered by the broad U.S. Census categories by using the data about ancestry and birthplace found on death certificates. For example, among Hispanics, the victimization rate of New Yorkers of Dominican ancestry skyrocketed to 52 per 100,000 in 1991 before plummeting to 16 for every 100,000 in 1997. New Yorkers of Colombian descent suffered their worst losses in 1988, at 71 per 100,000, and their lowest losses in 1997, at 11 per 100,000. On the other hand, Ecuadorian immigrants were victimized at much lower rates over the ten-year period, dropping from 18 per 100,000 in 1988 to 9 in 1997. New Yorkers of Puerto Rican descent ended up with the same rate as Ecuadorians in 1997,

but suffered a higher rate back in 1991, at 27 per 100,000, according to the vital statistics database.

17. The possibility of what methodologists call an "ecological fallacy" arises whenever individual characteristics are inferred from overall group averages. In this situation, if substantial numbers of wealthy persons reside in poor neighborhoods, and considerable numbers of low-income people live among the affluent, then inferences about the social class of murder victims from their Zip codes could be misleading. But this problem would be minimal if neighborhoods are relatively homogeneous in terms of their residents' income and social class.

The deceased person's home address Zip code is available from the vital statistics database.

18. The above analysis of homicide victims was based on virtually complete data (the age, sex, and race/ethnicity of nearly all the corpses were noted in the files of the NYPD, the Medical Examiner, and the Department of Health's vital statistics database drawn from death certificates). The analysis of alleged killers is based on a database of arrestees obtained from the DCJS that suffers from inaccuracies for two reasons. The first is that only some of the perpetrators were apprehended; the rest literally got away with murder, and their attributes are unknown. The second is that some small number of innocent persons falsely accused of murder are mixed in with the truly guilty.

These same methodological problems are even more troublesome in studies of robbers, burglars, car thieves, or any other type of offenders besides murderers because higher proportions of perpetrators escape apprehension for these types of crimes.

The arrestee database obtained from the Division for Criminal Justice Services (DCJS) in Albany contains detailed information about the demographics and criminal history of 23,462 accused murderers (code PL 125) arrested by the NYPD over a twenty-year interval, from January 1978 to July 1997.

19. The rest (79 percent) were represented by court-appointed lawyers (18 percent were supplied a lawyer from the Legal Aid Society, and 61 percent were granted an attorney through the 18-B assigned counsel plan). The type of attorney was missing or unknown in 6 percent of all cases, according to an analysis of 2,122 cases supplied by the New York State DCJS of murder and manslaughter defendants in Manhattan from 1990 to 1994 (the only borough and the only recent years for which the available data were reasonably complete).

20. In New York City, persons accused of committing misdemeanors are entitled to free legal assistance if their income falls below the federal poverty line for a single individual multiplied by 250 percent (this figure is increased by $2,500 for each dependent that the arrestee supports). Using 1992 guidelines, people who earned less than about $16,600 a year or roughly $320 a week

before taxes were entitled to free representation. The standard for persons facing felony charges is the official federal poverty level times 350 percent, or about $23,200 a year or $445 a week gross pay. The threshold is higher since defending against more serious accusations will usually take more of an attorney's time and thus incur greater expenses (Gewirtz and McElroy, 1997).

21. However, a less reassuring conclusion must be drawn if the mode rather than the mean is chosen as the measure of central tendency. The modal age for arrestees was eighteen in 1978, nineteen in 1981, and twenty-one in 1985. But in 1990, it dropped back to nineteen, and in 1997 the modal age returned to eighteen, the same as in the late 1970s. Therefore, focusing on the mode rather than the mean yields a different impression, that less teenagers were drawn into violent activities in the middle 1980s than in the late 1970s; and that after this brief respite, teen killers became more of a problem once again.

22. Since a sizable proportion of murderers are not caught and their age, sex, and race/ethnicity are unknown, it would be misleading to calculate murder-offending rates comparable to the murder-victimization rates that were presented above.

23. In 1978, 46 percent of all accused killers had two or more prior felony arrests. In 1990, that figure stood at 49 percent; by 1992, it had crept up to 50 percent; and in 1996, it peaked at 51 percent, according to the DCJS database of all arrests made by local police departments throughout New York State. Their actual criminal records may have been much more extensive if they had been arrested and convicted in other states or countries.

24. Of the teenage boys fifteen to nineteen years of age who were murdered during 1998, 89 percent were killed by gunfire. Similarly, of the twenty- to twenty-four-year-old young men who were killed that year, 82 percent perished from bullet wounds. Nearly all the rest of these fifteen- to twenty-four-year-olds were stabbed to death. As for older men, 69 percent of the twenty-five- to twenty-nine-year-olds, and 58 percent of the thirty-five- to forty-four-year-olds died from gunfire, according to the 1998 vital statistics database.

25. Gun deaths accounted for only 20 to 30 percent of all killings in New York, while they comprised over 50 percent of all slayings in the U.S. from 1960 to 1967 (not shown on graph 2.3). In terms of percentages, New York did not catch up with the rest of the nation until 1981, when the proportion of gun deaths reached 62 percent, and didn't surpass the national average until 1987. New York's all-time high was 77 percent in 1992; the U.S. record was set one year later, at 70 percent. By 1998, gun deaths had tumbled to 60 percent of all homicides in New York, and had dipped to 68 percent in the rest of the country.

26. The most common type of crime scene was a city street, with 37 percent of all killings, according to the details contained in the Medical Examiner

files. About 4 percent of all the murders committed during the first half of 1997 were carried out in stores, cars, and parks. Only about one percent took place in hotel/motel rooms, abandoned buildings, empty lots, parking lots, and highways.

27. Unfortunately, it is not easy to test this proposition about a suspected drop in life-threatening bar-room brawls because NYPD homicide analyses stopped providing detailed data about the number of killings in bars after 1977. The only other source of information about crime scene locations is the Medical Examiner files, which was analyzed for murders committed during the first half of 1997.

28. Drinking—but not necessarily at bars or clubs—is implicated as a contributing factor in many murders. See chapter 5.

29. The NYPD homicide analyses make note of the location of the crime scene ("place of occurrence"), as do the files maintained at the office of the Medical Examiner. Therefore, it is possible to determine for certain years how many people were killed in their own homes or someone else's home, or a temporary home like a hotel room, locations that the police classify as "residences."

30. The statistical technique of correlation and multiple regression analysis was used to detect relationships between independent variables describing demographic and social conditions in each of New York City's seventy-four precincts (as determined by the 1990 Census) and a dependent variable—each precinct's 1991 murder rate. Regression equations were calculated by entering variables stepwise, until the most powerful yet efficient combination was derived. For the murder rate in 1991, 80 percent of the precinct-to-precinct variation could be attributed to just three variables: unemployment rate for males age sixteen and over; percentage of persons living below the poverty level, and proportion of sixteen- to nineteen-year-olds in the population). In other words, knowing the values of these three variables in a precinct permits a researcher to predict the precinct's 1991 murder rate with great accuracy. Adding one additional variable (percentage of black residents) slightly improved the prediction equation (increased the "Adjusted R Square").

31. The preponderance of "poor-on-poor" cases and the virtual absence of "affluent-on-affluent" killings might be explained in part as a function of access to institutionalized, legal mechanisms to settle disputes without bloodshed. Homicides involving high-status people were quite common in earlier and simpler societies because of the custom of dueling. In modern industrial societies, prosperous people are treated with respect, and their calls for assistance are taken seriously by the police, prosecutors, and judges. Their highly emotional conflicts over financial and private matters are handled by lawyers in civil courts, not best friends who hold their coats amidst crowds on street corners. The poor tend to

distrust a legal system that they perceive is intended to control them rather than serve them. Its lack of legitimacy in their eyes derives from the accumulated experiences in which the police serve as an army of occupation, show indifference to their problems, or even exhibit outright disdain or hostility toward their personhood; and in which the courts seem either uninterested in disentangling their personal problems, or inclined to dispose of them quickly, clumsily, and punitively (Cooney, 1997).

THREE

NYPD or Not NYPD?
That Is the Question

Everything Works?

The 1990s were the best of times for police chiefs. Since police forces are the government agencies most directly responsible for local anti-crime initiatives, chiefs across the country jumped on the bandwagon to claim what they felt was their rightful share of the credit as crime rates fell in their jurisdictions. Every strategy and tactic, old or new, that they implemented seemed to work. Officials in Los Angeles, Fort Worth, New Orleans, Wichita, and Austin believed their efforts to forge closer relationships with their communities had paid off. Denver officials attributed the decline to policies that kept 911 lines free of nonemergency calls and encouraged complainants to follow through and press charges. The police chief in Bridgeport, Connecticut, argued that the erection of traffic barricades on streets where dealers congregated chased away potential customers. Washington, D.C., officials believed that a reorganization of the homicide squad led to greater success in capturing killers on the loose. A Chicago spokesman credited his department's initiatives to disarm youths and to increase the presence of officers in high crime areas. In Buffalo, the keys to success allegedly were aggressive narcotics enforcement and a joint task force that targeted violence-prone career criminals (Bragg, 1995; "Going down," 1995; "New Orleans," 1995; Clark, 1996). Baltimore's police attributed the improvement to a revitalized Police Athletic League ("May I," 1997), while officials in Providence, Rhode Island, argued that a new court focusing exclusively on gun-related crimes and an anti-graffiti task force made progress possible

(Saltzman, 1997). Boston police officials credited a collaborative effort with probation officers to crack down on gangs and guns ("Crime rates," 1996; Kennedy, 1997).[1]

Only a few officials resisted the temptation to claim credit for falling crime rates, most notably in Albuquerque and San Diego. These police chiefs realized that if they claimed they were responsible for crime rates going down, they would get hammered the minute they went back up, too (see Bouza, 1997; Butterfield, 1997b; Dodenhoff, 1997).

In New York City, the experts—the men who have been at the helm of the police department—did not see eye-to-eye on the issue of how much even a world-class police force could influence the level of criminal activity in its jurisdiction. When crime rates were rising at the beginning of the 1980s, Police Commissioner Robert McGuire (quoted in Van Doorn, Ross, and Pelleck, 1980:31) did not accept responsibility, remarking, "Crime, as you know, for several years went down. Nobody seems to know why crime goes up and down." Similarly, when record-breaking numbers of murders were committed at the start of the 1990s, Police Commissioner Lee Brown (quoted in Krajicek, 1990:20) observed, "I don't think the police department should take credit or blame for any rise or decrease in crime. We generally react to the failures of other institutions." But as crime rates that were drifting downward started to tumble in the mid-1990s, Commissioner William Bratton (quoted in Beiser, 1995:39) asserted that his "Compstat" (explained below) strategies were behind the drop, arguing, "We don't think what has occurred here in the last 18 months has been significantly impacted by any of those other factors. It's the way the department is now policing the city." As it became evident that crime was crashing, former police commissioner Raymond Kelly (quoted in Pooley, 1996:55) was reluctant to praise the NYPD's new administration, scoffing, "It's like trying to take credit for an eclipse." But Police Commissioner Howard Safir (quoted in Clark, 1996:14) continued in the credit-claiming tradition of Mayor Rudolph Giuliani and Commissioner Bratton, contending, "Crime is continuing to go in the right direction and the citizens of this city ought to be very proud of what their police department has done."

It appears that New York's commissioners have pointed to forces beyond their control when the situation was deteriorating and have accepted full responsibility only when conditions were getting better.

NYPD Blues

The NYPD . . . frankly . . . was in deep trouble when Bratton assumed control in 1994. . . . Its troubles with abuse and corruption during the early 1990s were well known . . . but there was another story . . . far less well known—the lack of quality policing. . . . [The NYPD] was dysfunctional.
> —Professor George Kelling and Police Commissioner
> William Bratton (1998:1222)

Today, the officers of the NYPD are America's crime-fighting poster boys, with Police Commissioner William Bratton a hero.
> —Reporter Diane Shah (1996:27)

By the mid-1990s, a journalist (Pooley, 1996:55) could write without exaggeration that "Compstat has become the Lourdes of policing, drawing pilgrim cops from around the world—Baltimore, London, Frankfurt, Zimbabwe, Taiwan—for a taste of New York's magic." Even the director of the Central Intelligence Agency visited One Police Plaza to see a demonstration of the new law enforcement strategies in action (Blair, 1999d). But when Mayor Giuliani and Commissioner Bratton assumed responsibility for running the department at the start of 1994, things were not going well for the NYPD in the news media and in the court of public opinion. Its crime-fighting reputation had been badly tarnished by a series of events.

In 1992, mayoral candidate Rudolph Giuliani addressed a crowd of about 10,000 off-duty officers that had been mobilized by the Patrolmen's Benevolent Association (PBA). They rallied in opposition to a proposed change in the composition of the Civilian Complaint Review Board that investigated charges of police misconduct. Some of the demonstrators became rowdy and climbed on top of cars and then stormed the nearby Brooklyn Bridge, blocking traffic. Others leaped barricades and charged up the steps of City Hall, screaming racial epithets at Mayor David Dinkins. Police Commissioner Kelly (quoted in James, 1992b:A1) later characterized the protest as "unruly, mean-spirited, and perhaps criminal"; the behavior of some off-duty officers was "an embarrassment"; the response of the on-duty commanders and front-line uniformed officers was "lethargic at best"; and he concluded that "public confidence in the Department has been shaken."

Surveys showed that the NYPD was losing the support of City residents. In a poll taken in 1992, only 37 percent of New Yorkers gave the NYPD a positive rating (see Kocieniewski, 1996b). Another poll, conducted in early 1994, found that a sizable proportion of residents lacked faith in their police force and were anxious about its ability to protect them (see Krauss, 1994).[2]

Enthusiasm for a switchover to community policing—departments consulting with local residents and working as partners with neighborhood leaders—was sweeping the country, nurtured in part by the Department of Justice and the Clinton administration. Other police forces scrambled to catch up with the NYPD, which had initiated foot patrol experiments in 1984 under Commissioner Benjamin Ward and taken further transitional steps under Commissioner Lee Brown (1992). The NYPD aggressively marketed the changeover with posters that announced "The beat cop is back," a promise welcomed by local activists who wanted even more deployments along these lines than the department was able to deliver (Silverman, 1999). Commissioner Kelly (1993:16) proclaimed that "we have committed the entire department to community policing . . . we have seen significant declines in major crimes citywide . . . we are confident that the decline is related to our community policing strategy." The editors of the *New York Times* (1993:18) agreed that "the falling crime reports are encouraging evidence that the community policing plan is on the right track." But shortly afterward, newspapers published a series of internal memos (see Winerip, 1993) to Commissioner Kelly written by Assistant Chief Aaron Rosenthal (quoted in Marzulli, 1994a:3), which revealed that there was a world of difference between the "showroom sales spiel used to sell community policing to the public and the actual on-the-street product their tax dollars purchased."

The exposure of the NYPD's failure to effectively implement community policing meant that the department's new leadership had to quickly devise and announce some strategies to stem any further erosion of public confidence. The editors of the *New York Daily News* (1994:36) thundered:

It was heralded as the solution crime-weary New Yorkers wanted—an idea whose time had come and gone and then come back again. But . . . the city's most ambitious anti-crime effort in years—community policing—has not lived up to the hype surrounding its creation. In fact, this promising strategy is being strangled by a bureaucracy thoroughly resistant to change. . . . New Yorkers did not consent to paying for a blue army of 30,000 strong only to have cops retreat back into their cars, into their stationhouses and behind their desks. . . . Giuliani and Bratton [need] to force a radical change in cop culture, one that slashes the control of foot-dragging unions, strips a tired brass of its discredited habits and rekindles the enthusiasm that draws idealistic men and women to the job.

To distance themselves politically from the way Mayor Dinkins and Commissioners Brown and Kelly envisioned community policing, Mayor Giuliani and Commissioner Bratton disparaged it as an approach that coddled criminals and pressured cops to act as social workers, not crime fighters. First Deputy Commissioner Patrick Kelleher (quoted in Levitt, 1997:A16) buried the previous administration's version of community policing in no uncertain terms:

> Under this academic model, the beat officer is expected to reduce crime by somehow eradicating the social conditions that produce crime—inadequate education, racism, disease, inadequate health care, physical deterioration, overcrowding in housing and waves of new immigrants bringing narcotics into the country with them. . . . [This] is not the crime reduction strategy that is employed now.[3]

The new administration downplayed building bridges and instead embarked upon a zero tolerance campaign directed at the numerous petty offenders whose incessant infractions undermined the quality of life in many neighborhoods. Specifically targeted for rousting and arrest were marginal people who had no place in the high-tech economy, but had nevertheless entrenched themselves into the urban landscape: vagrants camping out in doorways and parks, mentally ill psychiatric patients wandering the streets, aggressive panhandlers who wouldn't take "no" for an answer, and "squeegee pests" who wiped windshields and then demanded coins from intimidated motorists at busy intersections. Discovering that many members of the brass did not share his enthusiasm for this crackdown, Commissioner Bratton purged the top echelons, vowed to change management's preoccupation with overtime costs, corruption, and lawsuits, and promised measures that would improve morale and re-instill pride (McQuillan, 1994). He hired a management consultant who set up twelve reengineering teams to dissect routine operations from drug-arrest procedures to directing traffic. The new commissioner (quoted in C. Smith, 1996:32–33) deliberately set out to shake up a bureaucracy that he believed needed to confront reality: "The NYPD, like the emperor, had no clothes. This was an organization that was living on reputation. . . . We forced them to come to a conclusion that, 'Hey, we're not as good as we thought we were. . . .' So we created the crisis. And with that crisis, you can then move the organization to reposition itself." The commissioner (quoted in Associated Press, 1997:B4) characterized the reengineering process he presided over in this way: "We took literally a department that was bicycling along without an engine and gave it an eight-cylinder, high-powered engine that allows us to rev it up and move it forward. . . . The culture of the organization was, 'Stay out of trouble, don't stick your neck out, don't take any risks, just go with the flow.'"

To wake the troops from their lethargy and mobilize them for battle, Commissioner Bratton (quoted in McQuillan, 1994) specifically warned "lazy cops" that they "are the ones I want to give a kick in the butt to." But his call to arms was not taken to heart by some of the old guard. Later that year, an internal review of officer productivity revealed that nearly one quarter of uniformed cops on patrol had not yet made a single arrest during the first seven months of the new commissioner's tenure, and that, up to that point, close to half had not made more than two arrests. Deputy Commissioner of Crime Control Strategies Jack Maple (quoted in Marzulli, 1994b:3) wisecracked that "there are some cops who are better at making arrests than others, but we expect everybody here to get up to the plate. There's no shortage of crooks. If they want a convenient job, they should work in a bank." "Conscientious objectors," or "couch-potato cops," as high officials mockingly called them, were warned that they faced transfers to less desirable assignments if they didn't perform better during the remainder of the year. Acknowledging that some veterans felt constrained by departmental corruption prevention rules that strongly discouraged patrol officers from arresting low-level drug sellers and users, Deputy Commissioner for Public Information John Miller (quoted in Marzulli, 1994b:3) observed bitterly that "we took the handcuffs off, but when the bell rang and the gate opened, some cops stayed in the gate."[4]

Since 1990, the NYPD had grown to record proportions. Therefore, elected officials were shocked to discover that headquarters had not met its goals of increasing patrol strength, and that the average number of cops on the streets during a tour of duty in mid-1994 was virtually the same as in 1993 (Siegel, 1994). A report critical of the new NYPD administration pointed out that an unnecessary number of officers still worked behind desks when they could be out in the field, protecting the public. Ever since the administration of Mayor John Lindsay, the department had promised to hire less-skilled civilians as a means of freeing up cops from clerical and custodial tasks so they could return to their beats (Roberts, 1994).[5]

In the early 1990s, the NYPD was in the throes of one of its periodic scandals, which seem to break out roughly every twenty years. As one reporter (Hirschorn, 1994:20) phrased it, the Mollen Commission investigation had

> laid bare the dirtiest secrets of a mammoth, Byzantine organization . . . , succeeding despite overwhelming institutional resistance. The department at times reluctantly complied, at times misled the investigators, and often pressured its officers not to cooperate. . . . The court documents brim with lurid stories—cops rampaging through black and Latino neighborhoods, snorting, stealing, dealing, selling protection, "booming" down doors, and lying to cover their tracks.

Self-policing mechanisms clearly weren't working to weed out the notoriously corrupt "rotten apples" that were giving the entire force a bad name, NYPD officials conceded. But in its report, the Mollen Commission (1994:1–2) went further and exposed the institutionalized roots of blue-coat crime:

> The problem of police corruption extends far beyond the corrupt cop. It is a multi-faceted problem that has flourished in parts of our City not only because of opportunity and greed, but because of a police culture that exalts loyalty over integrity; because of the silence of honest officers who fear the consequences of "ratting" on another cop no matter how grave the crime; because of willfully blind supervisors who fear the consequences of a corruption scandal more than corruption itself; because of the demise of

the principle of accountability that makes all commanders responsible for fighting corruption in their commands; because of a hostility and alienation between the police and the community in certain precincts which breeds an "Us versus Them" mentality; and because for years the New York City Police Department abandoned its responsibility to insure the integrity of its members.

Besides corruption, brutality also continued to smolder as a pressing and increasingly costly problem, as measured by the huge judgments awarded to injured victims by juries and in out-of-court settlements of civil lawsuits.[6] The polarizing issue flared up once again when Amnesty International, an organization known for its campaigns against torture and political oppression in other countries, condemned the NYPD for several suspicious deaths of suspects while in custody; the mayor and police commissioner dismissed the charges as unfounded.[7] But before 1994 drew to a close, the department was rocked when an officer with a history of using force under questionable circumstances strangled a suspect by using a forbidden choke-hold (see Rohde, 1998).[8]

The NYPD was fingered as having the worst record of any of the nation's ten biggest police forces in terms of integrating its ranks with members of minority groups, according to a 1994 study. Over the thirty years since the 1964 Harlem uprising, a parade of commissioners had conceded that, to be more effective, the department's racial and ethnic composition had to more closely resemble the characteristics of the residents of the neighborhoods they patrolled (see Pooley, 1993). And yet, the number of black men on the force actually had dwindled. The chairman of the House Subcommittee on Civil Rights, Brooklyn Democrat Major Owens (quoted in Kilborn, 1994:B26) characterized the department as having "the most entrenched 'old boy' network anywhere"; Michael Julian, the chief of personnel, concurred: "We're too top-heavy white male."[9] Diversifying its work force could help to forge a stronger partnership with community residents. Their cooperation is essential for effective crime fighting, since it is people in the most afflicted neighborhoods who must report incidents, volunteer eyewitness descriptions, hand over evidence, give anonymous tips about wrongdoing or the whereabouts of fugitives, testify for the prosecution, and serve as impartial jurors (see McNamara, 1999).

Despite the new commissioner's stated commitment to improve morale, 1994 turned out to be the worst year ever for off-duty suicides. Fourteen officers killed themselves, often over personal troubles after drinking heavily, by "eating" their service revolvers (see "Law enforcement," 1994; Flynn, 1999a).[10] Morale slipped further when some officers representing the department at a memorial meeting to honor fallen comrades in Washington, D.C., in 1995 drank too much and then rampaged through their hotel. As the coverage of the romp became a tabloid sensation, commentators interpreted the outbreak of disorderly conduct as evidence that a portion of the force was almost unmanageable (Kocieniewski, 1996a).[11]

When placed in context, against the backdrop of these trials and tribulations, the crime crash certainly came along at a crucial moment. As soon as the rapid improvement captured the attention of the press by the middle of 1995, the reputation of the NYPD rebounded sharply. No longer was the department pictured as troubled, ungovernable, stubbornly segregated, or plagued by a subculture tolerant of brutality and corruption. Miraculously, it had metamorphosed into a shining symbol of how corporate management principles could remake a government agency into a lean-and-mean fighting machine capable of single-handedly retaking the City's toughest streets and quelling the nation's most formidable criminal element. Simultaneously, far less attention was paid to the yardsticks traditionally employed to gauge police performance: how quickly squad cars arrived at the scenes of emergencies; how often detectives solved crimes; how frequently the police recovered stolen property; how well investigators gathered evidence and prepared cases for successful prosecution; how credible juries found the testimony of police witnesses at trials; how infrequently members of the service broke their own departmental rules and used unnecessary force; how courteous, respectful, and professional officers were in their dealings with the general public; how competently officers provided physical and psychological first aid to injured and traumatized victims; and how willing victims were to turn to the authorities for help.[12]

In an effort to distinguish the new NYPD from the old one, top officials at City Hall and Police Headquarters unleashed a torrent of "now it can be told" revelations about departmental shortcomings that formerly would have been vehemently denied as slanderous to the Finest's reputation. For example, Commissioner Bratton (Bratton and Andrews, 1999a:14) disclosed that the old NYPD was a "large, unfocused, inward looking, bureaucratic organization, poor at internal communication or cooperation and chronically unresponsive to intelligence from the outer world."

He (Bratton and Andrews, 1999b:44) also bashed the former NYPD leadership that "spent almost no time thinking about anti-crime strategies. Police brass lurched from emergency to emergency. No one looked at the overall picture." Similarly, Mayor Giuliani (1997a:28) charged that "until recently, the city's police officers were not being used to full advantage. Like many police departments, the NYPD lacked strategic direction and oversight." Commissioner Howard Safir (quoted in Associated Press, 1999a:32) hurled an even sharper criticism at the old NYPD before an audience of foreign police officials, characterizing it as a "sleeping giant." Ironically, the more these advocates argued that the revitalized NYPD was solely responsible for the impressive drop in crime, the more they were conceding, by implication, that the sluggish pre-1994 NYPD was largely at fault for crime spiraling out of control and setting records several years earlier. The more lives they said were saved thanks to smarter strategies, the more untimely deaths they implicitly attributed to previous administrations hampered by their outmoded ineffective tactics and bureaucratic mind-sets.[13]

The New NYPD: A Sea Change?

We had developed a method to reduce crime and disorder that would work in any city in America—indeed in any city in the world. . . . The turnaround of the NYPD . . . offers a potential blueprint for the turnaround of the crime situation in the entire country.
—Police Commissioner William Bratton (1998: 310)

The many anti-crime strategies, organizational innovations, and operational changes suggested by focus groups and reengineering teams and reportedly implemented since Mayor Giuliani and Commissioner Bratton assumed the responsibilities of running the NYPD in 1994 have been described as a virtual "Blue Revolution" (Massing, 1998b). Collectively, these new approaches will be referred to by the shorthand term "Compstat."[14] The sea changes in police culture brought about by Compstat have electrified the world of policing (for comprehensive descriptions of the philosophy and methods, see Bratton, 1998, and Silverman, 1999).[15]

The need for accurate and up-to-date information by decision-makers required the establishment of a new computer-based statistics-gathering and monitoring system. Precincts fed data about victims' complaints and arrests directly from the field to headquarters on a daily basis, to be used to spot crime trends and locate "hot spots" of concentrated illegal activity. This high-tech equivalent of pin-mapping functioned as both a diagnostic and early warning system that identified emerging problems that required a rapid redeployment of uniformed officers and plainclothes detectives, or the application of civil enforcement statutes to close down enterprises that were public nuisances. Long-standing barriers between bureaus concentrating on patrol services, detective investigations, and organized criminal activity were broken down to facilitate cooperation and coordination. Certain responsibilities formerly assigned to overtaxed specialized squads were returned to precinct commanders who were given more autonomy to tackle local problems and were held more personally accountable for reducing crime rates and increasing solution rates in their seventy-six precincts across the five boroughs. These commanders and other supervisors presented their accomplishments to top administrators at regular early-morning meetings in the "war room" at headquarters, and were grilled about the measures they were taking to prevent future incidents and apprehend fugitives (Bratton and Andrews, 1999a).

Ordinances against minor quality-of-life offenses were strictly enforced, generating many arrests that were formerly disparaged as "garbage cases." A virtual zero tolerance campaign was deemed an essential component of maintaining order and discouraging illegal activities. Consequently, uniformed officers were empowered to arrest small-time drug sellers and buyers, a practice that had been discouraged since the Knapp Commission uncovered widespread corruption in narcotics law enforcement in 1970. A greater number of undercover operations, stop-and-frisk searches, vehicle stops, checks for outstanding arrest warrants, and narcotics sweeps were reportedly undertaken to catch illegally armed individuals, drug sellers and users, and violators of bail, probation, and parole restrictions. Suspects taken into custody routinely were more thoroughly interrogated about their knowledge of other criminal activities, especially drug trafficking and gun selling.

Ten specific strategies were devised and publicly announced: to get guns off the street; drive drug dealers away; discourage youth violence; interrupt the cycle of domestic violence; curb auto theft; reclaim public spaces; make the roadways safer; capture fugitives; root out corruption; and restore courtesy, professionalism, and respect. Four maxims guided the department's patrol and investigative operations: collect timely and accurate intelligence; rapidly deploy troops to the hotspots identified by intelligence sources; employ effective tactics to resolve problems; and relentlessly follow up and assess situations to prevent any resurgence of problems. A new philosophy replaced the former bureaucratic mind-set: manage the NYPD like a corporation. Set crime reduction goals at headquarters. Hold local precincts responsible for meeting performance standards. Imbue commanding officers with an entrepreneurial spirit and encourage them to take initiatives and to reject the old organizational culture in which supervisors responded with caution and resisted change (see Bratton, 1998, and Silverman, 1999). As one top adviser (Andrews, 1996:4) put it, "NYPD commanders watch weekly crime trends with the same hawk-like attention private corporations pay to profit and loss. Crime statistics have become the department's bottom line."

Commissioner Bratton (Bratton and Andrews, 1999a:20) succinctly summed up why those closely watched numbers nosedived: "Since 1994, the NYPD hasn't just been solving crimes; it has been dismantling criminal enterprises and support systems. It has been taking away the things that criminals need to function: their guns, their fences, their chop shops and auto exporters, their drug-buying and prostitution customers, their buildings and apartments, their cars, and the unpoliced sectors of the city where crime used to thrive."

Sounds Convincing: Evaluating Compstat

This kind of communication [by leaders of different bureaus at Compstat meetings] has been the key to our successful fight against crime.
—Mayor Rudolph Giuliani (1997a:31)

Quality-of-life enforcement, though hardly the whole story, has been the key.

—Former police commissioner William Bratton (1999b:44)

Constant analysis and vigilance is the key.

—Police Commissioner Howard Safir (quoted in Weiss, 1997b:8)

I never measure success by arrests. That was the problem in the city for many, many years. The only thing the police measured were arrests. They were making lots of arrests but crime was going off the page.

—Police Commissioner Howard Safir (1999)

I have never been one who strongly relies on statistics as a way of measuring what we're doing. . . . I don't want the department to be overly focused on statistics.

—Mayor Rudolph Giuliani (quoted in Treaster, 1994a:B3)

The proponents of "the police deserve the lion's share of credit for the crash" point of view have put forward a seemingly compelling case: the department transformed itself and then crime tumbled. But to evaluate the effectiveness of the alleged sweeping changes brought about by the reengineering process, it is necessary to resolve the conflicting suggestions about what constituted the key developments indicated in the above quotations. Which one of these "Compstat" components, or which combination of these innovations, worked so well? To convince skeptical social scientists, it won't be sufficient merely to assert, as did Mayor Giuliani (quoted in Krauss, 1996c:B4), that "all the strategies that have been put in place are working better than anyone, including me, thought they would when we devised them."

Ideally, the way to evaluate the impact of an innovation would be to carry out a carefully controlled field experiment (see, for example, Krause, 1996).[16] Only one new strategy should be introduced in one precinct, while regular, pre-Compstat policing would go on in a demographically similar precinct that serves as a control group for comparison purposes. After a reasonable amount of time has elapsed, the two matching precincts can be examined with regard to some reliable indicator of criminal activity, such as the murder rate. The precinct that underwent a sweeping Compstat transformation should register a statistically significant drop in its murder rate, while the level of violence should stay roughly constant in the other precinct where business-as-usual prevailed. If it turns out that the murder rate dropped about equally in both precincts, then some influential variable(s) other than Compstat strategies must be behind the reductions.

If a series of carefully controlled experiments involving just one innovation at a time cannot be carried out in randomly selected pairs of matching precincts, then a second-best approach could involve a recognition that the process of changing over to the Compstat package of innovations was in itself a variable that differed from precinct to precinct. Crime rates should have dropped more rapidly in those precincts that implemented the Compstat innovations more faithfully, smoothly, and quickly than the rest. In other words, successfully implementing Compstat management strategies was a matter of degree. Perhaps the department's top administrators and strategists know which precincts fell into line first or were up and running sooner. The improved policing hypothesis could be tested if they would identify which precincts were exemplary.

Unfortunately, methodological problems undermine any attempts to perform a definitive test of the impact of the Compstat reforms (see Bowling, 1999). Each new initiative was not introduced in isolation and tested out in some model precincts but not others; the whole package of innovations was implemented citywide all at once, without identifying a control group of matched precincts for comparison purposes. And Compstat's inventors have never listed the precincts that were up and running ahead of the others. Therefore, the only way to proceed with the evaluation is to gather citywide rather than precinct-level statistics, and formulate some reasonable hypotheses that involve the same indicators that have been used by criminological researchers in other places at other times.

Therefore, the question arises: What demonstrable and measurable changes in policing strategies over the past two decades might be associated with the rising and falling and then soaring and plummeting murder rate? What evidence, in the form of statistics from official sources, might link indicators of the department's performance to the level of violence on the City's streets?

Several hypotheses can be tested with the available data. Did the murder rate, which was already dropping in the early 1990s, albeit quite slowly, begin to drop sharply after the Compstat changes were introduced during 1994? Did increases in the size of the police force enable it to take back the streets and prevent some murders from being committed right out in the open? Was the enlarged department able to shorten response times to emergency calls about crimes-in-progress and thereby save more lives? Did the Compstat strategies enable detectives to solve more crimes and make more gun arrests? Were increases in arrests for quality-of-life offenses deterring New Yorkers from going around armed and thereby reducing the number of murders committed with handguns?

It's All a Matter of Timing: Did Crime Rates Drop Sharply after the Implementation of Compstat Reforms?

To place this accomplishment [sharply falling rates] in perspective, it is important to understand that in New York City felony crime had already been declining in the previous three years. The steep drops beginning in 1994 weren't a suppression of a recent upward trend. They were an historic gain that pushed felony crime rates to their lowest levels in more than 20 years. . . .

Beginning in early 1994, twelve reengineering teams studied everything from equipment and technology to precinct organization and training. Their work was refined by a Plan of Action published in December 1994. More than 600 recommendations emerged from the re-engineering process of which about 400 have already been implemented, with others on the way.

—Andrews (1996:2–3)

Changes in the root causes of crime take place slowly, but reforms of police strategies and tactics can occur quickly. Since the crime wave receded rapidly during Mayor Giuliani's and Commissioner Bratton's first year in office, compared to 1993, the final year of the old NYPD, they were justified to advance a strong circumstantial argument that improved policing caused the crash (Editors, *New York Times*, 1995b).[17] The question arises: How quickly could the shake-up in organizational culture and management styles produce results?

New and improved approaches replaced traditional and outmoded practices throughout 1994, 1995, and even 1996, according to insider accounts of the reengineering process (see Bratton, 1998, and Silverman, 1999). New strategies were devised and announced beginning in March 1994; the twice weekly Compstat sessions started up in May, along with the first meetings of the twelve reengineering teams (Mayor's Management Report, 1994:9). Surely the major changes generated at headquarters could not have been implemented in the precincts and actually carried out on the streets any sooner than the middle of 1994. Therefore, the exact timing of the reduced volumes of reported incidents must be closely examined. If the month-by-month numbers in the second half of 1994 were much lower than those for the corresponding months in late 1993 (such comparisons are a standard police practice, to take into account seasonal variations), then the sharp declines probably resulted from the innovations. But if the drops in victims' complaints took place too soon—before the Compstat reforms were up and running and had a chance to kick in—then some other factors, and not improved policing, must have been driving down crime rates.

Fewer murders were committed in January 1994, as compared to January 1993, according to month-by-month data graphed in the NYPD's 1994 Complaints and Arrests annual report. In fact, complaints were down in every crime category during that first month. A bitter coldwave that caused unusually icy and snowy conditions seems to have helped the new administration to get off to a great start (see Treaster, 1994b). But during February, March, and April 1994, the amount of killing in the five boroughs reverted back to the levels experienced during the early part of 1993. Then, starting in May 1994, the citywide monthly death tolls began consistently to drop far below their comparable 1993 levels. This pattern supports the assertion that the Compstat reforms quickly produced positive results.

However, the levels of reported forcible rapes actually were worse during some of the months in the latter part of 1994 than they were during the comparable time periods of 1993. Aggravated assaults were as numerous during some months in late 1994 as they were during late 1993. (Both aggravated assaults and forcible rapes had been dropping slowly throughout the 1990s.) As for commercial and residential burglaries, the number of complaints were lower in 1994 than in 1993 for nearly every month, not just those late in the year. (Reported burglaries had peaked back in 1980 and had been dropping steadily since 1989.)

The numbers of reported robberies, auto thefts, and larcenies were also lower for just about every month in 1994 as compared to 1993. Holdups, car stealing, and other assorted thefts had been diminishing since 1990, so these consistent declines were also part of long-standing trends, according to graphs appearing in the NYPD's 1994 Complaints and Arrests statistical report.

Therefore, the findings of this inquiry into timing do not support the improved policing hypothesis across the board. Killings declined primarily during the second half of 1994, as predicted. But rapes and assaults did not fit this pattern; and robberies, burglaries, larcenies, and vehicle thefts fell throughout early 1994, before Compstat strategies were devised.

Size Counts? Did an Enlarged NYPD Better Fulfill Its Functions?

In safe neighborhoods, a cop is part of the scenery. . . . But in bad neighborhoods I notice people noticing me, and especially certain classes of people—older people, young kids, single women, people dressed for work or church. They look at me with positive appreciation and relief. I am proof that tonight, on this walk home, no one's going to start with them. Sometimes they express that appreciation. The exceptions are groups of young guys on the street (older, if they're unemployed). Sometimes they're just hanging out, sometimes they're planning something more ambitious, and you're a sign that a wild night's not going to happen—not as they hoped, not here.

—NYPD patrolman M. Laffey (1997:47)

It seems logical to posit that increasing the size of the force can help to cut the crime rate by adding officers to make the deterring presence of police patrols more visible; by enabling more squad cars to cruise around and race to crime scenes more quickly; by expanding the size of the detective division to lower caseloads and to raise solution rates; and by augmenting the ranks so more officers can make arrests and appear in court without leaving their beats unguarded. By maintaining a strong presence on the streets, the police can prevent violent confrontations from materializing by breaking up roaming bands of truants seeking victims to rob, by dispersing knots of idle men drinking and spoiling for a fight, by scattering youths in street gangs before they square off and attack one another, and by scaring off rival groups of drug dealers or of prostitutes before they engage in turf battles over advantageous locations.[18]

But before the crash, the consensus among criminologists was that routine police operations and even specially targeted crackdowns could repress certain kinds of criminal activities only in limited areas and only for relatively short periods of time. Supporters of this research-based viewpoint could cite more than a dozen major empirical studies that were carried out over the last twenty years that concluded that neither sheer police manpower nor community policing strategies have demonstrable substantial and sustained effects on local crime rates (see DiIulio, 1995b). But the widely touted New York experience has triggered some rethinking of the issue and stimulated the emergence of an opposing school of thought.

The prospects of a shrinking police force trying to quell a rising tide of violence provoked widespread apprehension in the late 1970s. The NYPD was undergoing a period of contraction that had started in 1975, when the City was in the throes of its most severe fiscal crisis in history. Financial problems resulting from a nationwide recession still plagued the city at the start of the 1980s. Mayor Ed Koch (quoted in Castillo, 1980) tried to reassure a nervous public: "We will have more cops . . . [but] it means loss of something else. Because in this budget, where you have limited dollars, it's robbing Peter to pay Paul. . . . But there's no question in my mind that if you can't walk the streets safely, then everything else isn't worthwhile." However, NYPD commissioner Robert McGuire conceded that hiring more cops would not necessarily turn things around: "In a sense, rising crime is somewhat independent of police manpower, though we would like to think that with more manpower we would do a better job in controlling crime. . . . But there is not a direct relationship: more men, less crime, less men, more crime" (Van Doorn, Ross, and Pelleck, 1980: 31). Crippled by a downward spiral of layoffs, hiring freezes, and losses due to attrition, the NYPD's brass adopted a triage strategy. Something had to give because the number of available patrol officers was inadequate to meet the growing volume of calls for assistance. Some highly productive plainclothes units had to be disbanded so that their officers could be returned to uniformed patrol duty. A top official (quoted in Pileggi, 1981a:25) explained that "anti-crime squads are a luxury we can't afford . . . [they are] expensive to maintain. . . . They make the best arrests and more than any unit in the department, but people want to see men in blue driving by their houses and stores."

A fearful public once again clamored for more police protection as crime rates peaked in 1990. Newly elected mayor David Dinkins had pledged to spend more of the City's limited resources on social investments that would eventually alleviate the oppressive conditions in the poverty-stricken neighborhoods of his staunchest constituents. To free up some funds, he announced that new recruits would not be sworn in as scheduled. But when a sense of crisis reached a crescendo, Mayor Dinkins (1990:B3) reluctantly revised his priorities and promised, "We will hire thousands of new officers. . . . But if we have learned any lesson from . . . the past 30 years, it is this: the police cannot stop the criminals alone."

When the crime wave began to slowly recede in the early 1990s, Police Commissioner Brown attributed the improvement to an enhanced police presence (James, 1992a). As crime rates started to tumble in 1994, Commissioner Bratton cited the expansion of the force and the deployment of officers in a highly visible way as the cause (Treaster, 1994a). By 1999, the size of the NYPD had reached record heights, topping out at over 40,000 uniformed personnel, up 25 percent from the start of the decade. With 550 officers protecting every 100,000 residents, New York's per capita staffing level was about twice the average of other large cities and was second only to Washington, D.C. Given the dramatic improvement in the crime problem, some budget experts suggested that the police force could be downsized without compromising public safety in order to free up resources to address other pressing urban ills (IBO, 1999). Surprisingly, Mayor Giuliani proposed enlarging the NYPD further, by another 1,500 officers. Admitting that the call for still more cops might sound "counterintuitive," the mayor argued (quoted in Barry, 1999:B10), "The strategy is working. Why back away from it now?" Assuming that a point of diminishing returns had not yet been reached, the *New York Times*'s editorial board (1999:A26) endorsed the planned expansion, declaring, "It makes sense to support a winning streak."

Murders Committed in "Visible" Locations Tumbled:
Did the Police "Take Back the Streets"?

Traditionally, criminologists have been reluctant to believe that police activities have a significant impact on crime. They have argued that because no empirical studies have ever shown that the number of police officers deployed within a given area actually reduces reported crime, police deployment strategies are an irrelevant variable in the crime equation.

For example, saturation patrol tactics have been shown to displace crime into other areas, and they may have some impact on reducing the types of street crimes that are readily visible to patrolling officers. However, such tactics have little effect on the number of reported crimes taking place indoors or in locations where officers cannot see and prevent them.

—Police Commissioner Howard Safir (1997:34–35)

It seems reasonable to hold the police more accountable for crimes that are committed right out in the open, in public places like streets, corners, stoops, or parks—locations that the department designates as "visible" to officers on patrol. Understandably, the police can do less to stop crimes committed out of their sight, behind the closed doors of offices, apartments and private homes, or indoors in hallways and elevators— areas deemed as "not visible" to officers on routine patrol. It follows that increases in police presence should bring about decreases in crimes committed in visible locations (but not necessarily declines in crimes committed indoors).

To measure police presence on the streets, researchers have usually used patrol strength, which includes uniformed officers walking their beats or cruising around in squad cars.[19] To test whether a beefed-up police presence on the streets sharply curtailed murders committed outdoors (and, conversely, if a diminished presence led to a resurgence of killings right out in the open), changes in patrol strength were plotted on the same set of axes as trends in murders in visible locales (graph 3.1).

One important finding is that until the late 1980s, the proportion of murders that were committed outside roughly matched the proportion that were committed inside. The mix changed radically from the late 1980s through the early 1990s, when outdoor killings greatly exceeded those taking place indoors. The NYPD apparently had a lim-

Graph 3.1. Relationship between Police Presence and Murders Outdoors and Indoors, New York City, 1982–1998

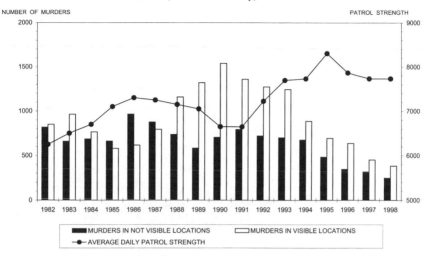

Note: Strength figures are for fiscal years. Murder figures are for calendar years.
Sources: Murders—NYPD Complaints and Arrests Reports, 1982–1998; Patrol Strength: Mayor's Management Reports, 1982–1999.

ited presence and lost control of the streets during those years. Bringing patrol strength into the picture, another discovery emerges: a weak inverse relationship existed between average daily uniformed patrol strength and the yearly number of killings at visible crime scenes. Specifically, when patrol strength went up during the early 1980s, outdoor murders went down. In the late 1980s, patrol strength diminished and visible murders soared. During 1990 and 1991, the two worst years in terms of people slaughtered right out in the open, the number of officers assigned to uniform patrol was at a relatively low ebb. When police presence rose during the middle 1990s, murders carried out on streets and in parks fell sharply. Since a few years didn't fit this inverse relationship, the negative correlation is not high. Ironically, the changes in police strength that didn't track well with the changes in murder levels occurred after the birth of Compstat. In fiscal 1995, patrol strength went up sharply and murders in visible locales dropped substantially, as hypothesized. But in fiscal 1996 and 1997, the number of officers patrolling in uniform declined (because the specialized plainclothes units like the narcotics squad expanded at their expense); nevertheless, visible murders continued to drop, in a break with the generally inverse relationship detected in prior years.

Reasonable Doubts

Although it appears that size matters, and that an enlarged NYPD deserves credit for regaining control of the streets through its enhanced presence, several reasons to doubt that conclusion must be addressed.

The first challenge, ironically, arose from Mayor Giuliani and both of his police commissioners. They have found it necessary to argue against placing great importance on the staffing levels of uniformed officers (probably because community organizations and elected officials representing fearful New Yorkers believe that size counts and generally insist upon large numbers of officers in blue patrolling in their precincts). When a reporter raised the issue of this numbers game at a press conference, Mayor Giuliani (quoted in Krauss, 1996c:B3) scolded him for not focusing on the bottom line: "The level sometimes of questions is at the point of idiocy. Patrol strength is not as important by any means as the amount of crime that goes on in a city." Commissioner Bratton (1996:790) also discouraged any emphasis on sheer size: "The luxury, the inheritance if you will, from the David Dinkins era is that we are benefiting now from that seed that was planted a while back [hiring more cops made possible by the Safe Streets, Safe City tax package]. This is one of the causal factors I think is making a difference. But more importantly, it is how they are being used." In a similar vein, Commissioner Safir (1997:35) dismissed the importance of mere numbers: "The point many criminologists and some police executives miss is that it is not how many officers are assigned to a given area that makes a difference; it is what they are doing that counts." Citizens Crime Commission president Thomas Reppetto (quoted in Krauss, 1996b:B3) summed up this point of view most succinctly: "Measuring the department by patrol strength is like counting up infantry in World War II without counting the artillery, tanks, and the Navy."[20]

A second reason to question whether a beefed-up police presence made a great deal of difference is that murders carried out behind closed doors dropped almost as sharply as murders committed outdoors during the Compstat years (table 3.1). Specifically, from 1993 through 1998,

Table 3.1. Declines in Murders in Visible vs. Not Visible Locations
since the Advent of Compstat

Time Interval	Inside Murders		Outside Murders	
	Body Count Change	*Percent Change*	*Body Count Change*	*Percent Change*
1993–1994	−26	−4%	−359	−29%
1994–1995	−192	−28%	−192	−22%
1995–1996	−137	−28%	−57	−8%
1996–1997	−28	−8%	−185	−29%
1997–1998	−69	−22%	−69	−15%
1993–1998	−452	−64%	−862	−69%

Source: NYPD's Complaints and Arrests Annual Statistical Reports, 1993–1998.

murders carried out in locations visible to officers on routine patrol tumbled more percentagewise than murders committed in places not visible to officers only during two time periods, and not all five, as would be expected. If size really mattered, why should the rate of decline of inside murders that are more difficult for the police to prevent exceed three times (1994–1995, 1995–1996, and 1997–1998) the rate of contraction of outside killings that were potentially more deterrable by an enhanced street presence? The similarity in the overall diminution from 1993 to 1998 in both inside and outside murders (down 64 percent compared to 69 percent) is puzzling from a size counts perspective and raises the possibility that other factors were at work.[21]

A third reason to question whether size really matters is that murder rates declined in cities that did not expand their police forces, especially in San Diego (where killings plummeted to the same degree as in New York—see table 1.2 in chapter 1). In fact, in Dallas and Denver crime rates fell in the 1990s even though per capita police staffing dipped a few percentage points (IBO, 1999).

If police presence really does matter, then the increased visibility of private security personnel might share some of the credit. The number of private security guards working in the five boroughs has grown dramatically in recent decades.[22] It is now commonplace to find special peace officers and lesser qualified uniformed guards (some licensed to carry guns, others just clubs) protecting the vicinity of government buildings, parks, college campuses, construction sites, sports arenas, hospitals, museums, railroad stations, and public schools.[23] They augment the ranks of such well-known security personnel as bank guards, night watchmen at factories and warehouses, store and hotel detectives, armored car drivers, burglar alarm central station field operatives, personal bodyguards, bouncers, and even doormen. Throughout the City, thirty business improvement districts, as well as merchants' organizations, gated communities, and block associations have contracted with private security firms to protect their perimeters and augment the routine patrols offered by local police precincts. An exact figure for the number of private security personnel at work in the City can't be found, but it is widely believed that they are at least twice as numerous as federal, state, and local police officers (see Carlson, 1995; Hanson, 1997; and "Welcome to the new world," 1997), which would bring their ranks to well over 80,000. In less prosperous and privileged areas, volunteers from about two hundred neighborhood watch groups and another two hundred civilian anti-crime patrols in public housing projects serve as additional eyes and ears of the police, as police auxiliary units also do (Giuliani, 1997c). Therefore, using NYPD patrol strength statistics in isolation and ignoring the contribution of private security personnel surely understates the visible presence of people working to maintain order in New York in the 1990s.[24]

Not So Fast . . . Did an Improvement in Police Response Time Help Save Lives?

The prompt arrival of officers at the scene of a crime is another dimension of police presence. It seems reasonable to hypothesize that victims under attack can be rescued if the police can intervene more quickly when summoned by an urgent call about a crime-in-progress ("C-i-P"), such as reports of screams in the night, a prowler in a backyard, or robbers pulling out guns in a bank. Besides saving victims before their assailants have time to finish them off, improved response times could have a preventive impact by deterring would-be offenders who fear capture. Catching criminals red-handed also could have an incapacitative effect by removing them from circulation so they can't strike again. Furthermore, officers who arrive at a crime scene within a few minutes are more likely to locate eyewitnesses and to collect bits of evidence that can help solve

Table 3.2. Trends in Response Times to Crime-in-Progress Calls,
Fiscal Years 1992–1999

	1992	1993	1994	1995	1996	1997	1998	1999
C-i-P radio runs (in thousands)	637	630	595	580	518	447	425	—
Average response time (in minutes)	9.9	8.0	7.9	7.7	9.1	9.2	9.8	10.3

Note: Consistent figures are available only since fiscal 1992.
Source: Mayor's Management Reports (MMR), September editions, fiscal years 1992–1999.

cases. For all these reasons, as average emergency response times decline, the number of murders should drop.

Indeed, during the early 1990s, average citywide response times shortened (by 22 percent from 1992 to 1995), and murders fell, as expected. However, the overall reductions in mean response times (fractions of a minute) were so minor during the first two Compstat years that they probably were socially inconsequential in terms of rescuing victims and nabbing offenders. Unfortunately, starting in fiscal year 1996, average response times began to creep back up and ended up worse in 1999 than they had been in 1992, when many more urgent 911 calls were logged (table 3.2).

These numbers have become highly politicized because the public and the news media interpret waiting times in life-and-death emergencies as an important indicator of police performance. The City Council passed a law in 1991 that required the NYPD to disclose this data annually. Elected officials representing communities in which local precincts have below-average response times predictably demanded that more officers be assigned to patrol duties. When anticipated improvements did not materialize, Mayor Giuliani (quoted in Topousis, 1997) declared that monitoring response times was an outmoded way of evaluating police protection and insisted that all that mattered was the bottom line: "The fact is, crime has gone down dramatically during that period of time. . . . So maybe they're looking at the wrong . . . indicators that are 3, 4, 5, maybe 10 years old as a way of measuring police performance."[25] Some researchers would agree and question whether racing to a crime scene is as crucial a factor as is commonly supposed. Considerable time can elapse before witnesses or victims regain their composure and run to a phone to summon help (see Citizens Crime Commission, 1996, and Cooper, 1999a). But the studies that concluded that improving response time was of limited importance (see, for example, Spelman and Brown, 1983) were based on data gathered many years ago, before the advent of 911 emergency hotlines, enhanced caller ID systems, computer applications to transmit information rapidly, SOS pay phones that don't require a quarter, and widespread ownership of cell phones. Arguments that rapid response times aren't crucial fly in the face of common sense and ignore the everyday realities of police work. Whenever officers call for help over the radio, squad cars with sirens blaring and lights flashing suddenly converge at the scene from all directions; their comrades-in-arms certainly believe that time is of the essence and that every second counts.

Catching Killers

Did the Murder Rate Drop Because the Solution Rate Rose?

> Murder used to be our highest priority. But nobody gives a damn about it anymore. We could be clearing a lot more homicides, but to really investigate them we'd need three times as many detectives. We're getting to be like the EMS for dead people: come to the crime scene, get whatever physical evidence or witnesses are around, put it in the file, and move on. If there's a solid lead, work the case. If not, forget it. Go to the next body.
> —Lieutenant Jack Doyle, commander of the Manhattan North Homicide Squad (quoted in Pooley, 1992)

Another way to gauge the quality of the service delivered by a police force is to look at its clearance rates. A better-managed department should be able to solve a greater percentage of the cases reported to it by victims, eyewitnesses, and its own officers. Arrest and conviction should have a deterrent effect on the offenders and all those considering the same acts. Detectives who make arrests that lead to convictions help to remove dangerous predators from circulation. If enough high-rate offenders are incapacitated behind bars, the streets should be noticeably safer.

Historically, murders have been solved at a higher rate than any other crime. Unfortunately, even these best-of-all clearance rates have been sliding for decades in law enforcement agencies across the country. In general, as the number of slayings has gone up over the years, the proportion of murderers who get caught has gone down. Nationwide, homicide clearance rates approached nine out of ten during the relatively peaceful 1950s. In the 1990s, only about two-thirds have been solved. That means that about one-third of all killers literally get away with murder—they don't even get caught (plus some who are apprehended never get convicted, or plead guilty to a much lesser offense carrying a lighter penalty).[26] One reason for the national decline is that detectives are fielding fewer "grounders" (easily solved cases, as when a husband kills his wife and then calls 911) and are grappling with more difficult-to-solve stranger-to-stranger homicides (such as corpses found in alleys after robberies). Another reason is that the sheer volume of cases overwhelms investigators; as reports of new killings pour in and bury cases at the bottom of the current pile, detectives are pressured to set aside baffling ones and move on.

Solving cases is surely a function of resources invested in them as well as the skill level of the detectives assigned to them, as the NYPD's predicament concerning burglary investigations at the start of the 1980s illustrated. Because crime was up and the size of the force was down, the vast majority of burglaries were given short shrift. Detectives could not go to the homes of victims to dust for fingerprints or search for other clues; uniformed patrolmen simply filled out reports and filed them. Chief of Detectives Daniel Sullivan (quoted in Basler, 1981) explained the department's priorities this way: "Sure, we could give more time to more burglary cases—if we took time away from the homicides, the rapes, the robberies." Not only was a triage system imposed, but the department found it necessary to put investigations on hold when manpower shortages arose. The president of the Detectives' Endowment Association (quoted in Pileggi, 1981a:25), complained:

> The Police Department is trying to get by as best it can strictly on public relations. The department feels it can look good by turning out the blue . . . but when you take a detective out of his squad and put him on a parade, his cases are just piling up unattended back at the precinct. We've got men carrying 200 cases, and there is no way any of them can get the kind of attention they need.

Besides a chronic manpower shortage, the old NYPD suffered from a lack of motivation when it came to tracking down killers who left few clues behind after dispatching marginal members of society. These kinds

Graph 3.2. Relationship between Clearance Rates and Murders, New York City, 1978–1998

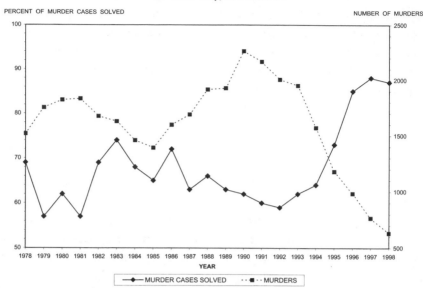

PERCENT OF MURDER CASES SOLVED

NUMBER OF MURDERS

YEAR

——◆—— MURDER CASES SOLVED ··■·· MURDERS

Note: A case is "cleared" when an arrest is made, unless there are "exceptional" circumstances.
Sources: NYPD's annual Complaints and Arrests statistical reports, 1978–1998.

of cases were assigned a low priority, according to Deputy Commissioner of Crime Control Strategies Jack Maple (1999:26-27): "Since clearances count, lives sometimes didn't. 'Misdemeanor homicide' was a pervasive term in the Detective Bureau, used whenever a less-than-upstanding citizen was murdered and understood to mean that the investigation merited no more effort than a car theft." But after 1994, the pressure reportedly was on to solve every slaying, regardless of the victim's standing in the community.

The question of whether raising the clearance rate really helps to lower the murder rate can be addressed by superimposing the ups and downs of the solution rate upon the changing body count (graph 3.2).

An inverse relationship appears, as anticipated. In general, when detectives apprehended a smaller percentage of killers, slayings rose, and in those years when more were caught, homicides diminished. In New York during the late 1970s, the clearance rate fell as the homicide rate soared. Only around 60 percent of all suspected killers were taken into custody. When murder rates subsided during the first half of the 1980s, clearance rates rebounded. As murder rates soared once more in the second half of that decade, solution rates slipped again. As crime crashed during the 1990s, clearance rates shot up. By the late 1990s, the NYPD reported that they were able to figure out who did it in nearly 90 percent of all homicides. The NYPD's ability to hunt down killers, which had been below par compared to other departments, catapulted way above the national norm to levels not seen since the 1950s.[27] It certainly looked like the new Compstat strategies were responsible for these striking gains, and more important, for suppressing homicides through deterrence and incapacitation.

Second Opinions

Part of it [an improved clearance rate] is the skill of our detectives, and part of it is that with fewer homicides we can pay more attention to each individual case.
—Police Commissioner Howard Safir (quoted in Cooper, 1997a:B2)

In 1997, the murder clearance rate reached an impressive 88 percent.[28] But a careful inspection of cases listed in the 1997 Homicide Log revealed that, at most, about 55 percent of all murders committed during 1997 were quickly closed by an arrest made before the end of that calendar year. The reason for the 88 percent overall figure was that killings that took place in 1996 or farther back in time that were solved during 1997 were credited to 1997, as they should have been, according to FBI Uniform Crime Reporting System guidelines. But a solution rate of 55 percent or so for current cases in 1997 was really no better than the track record NYPD detectives had achieved in previous years. Apparently, despite the new Compstat approaches, detectives continued to process fresh cases with roughly the same degree of success as they previously did—about half solved, half unsolved by the close of any calendar year.[29] Bringing to justice killers who thought they had gotten away with murder is always a laudatory accomplishment.[30] There is no statute of limitations for slayings, which should never be forgotten and forgiven. But inflated clearance rates may give a misleading impression to the public that Compstat strategies produced dramatic breakthroughs.

As suggested by Commissioner Safir's candid observation presented above, an opposite interpretation of causality can be drawn from the same statistical relationship. Perhaps improving the clearance rate did not drive down the murder rate; maybe it was the declining work load that enabled detectives to devote more time and effort to each murder and thereby do a better job of identifying and tracking down the perpetrators. In other words, as the crash took place, detectives enjoyed the luxury of reopening old unsolved cases because fewer urgent new matters demanded their attention.

During the Compstat years, the NYPD's crime-solving abilities improved substantially in most other categories besides murder (see table 3.3). The department made great strides in clearing robberies, felonious (aggravated) assaults, and burglaries. Compared to the national average for all 17,000 large and small police departments participating in the FBI's Uniform Crime Reporting System, the NYPD went from sub-par clearance rates in the early 1990s to stellar performance in the late 1990s in solving murders, forcible rapes, felonious assaults, and robberies. However, even with sharply reduced caseloads and the Compstat innovations, the NYPD remained stuck way below the national norm in solving grand larcenies and motor vehicle thefts.

Vehicle theft is the one other type of crime that is accurately measured (reported by victims at a very high rate), and that has plummeted as much as murder (refer back to graph 1.2 in chapter 1). Stealing cars remained a safe bet for career criminals, with an apprehension rate hovering between only 5 percent and 7 percent. The overwhelming majority of thieves escaped the long arm of the law unless they broke into and drove off other people's vehicles over and over again (statistically speaking, the odds eventually caught up with them). Even though the Auto Squad enjoyed rapidly dwindling caseloads, it apparently made little headway in nabbing more chop-shop operators, professional thieves, or even joyriders. When it came to putting car thieves out of business, the NYPD continued to lag way behind the other departments in 1998 (7 percent compared to 14 percent). And yet, despite the persistence of relatively ineffective sleuthing, this type of stealing became much less of a threat to the City's motorists.

The auto-theft anomaly demonstrates that lawless behavior can subside even if virtually no improvement takes place in the ability of the po-

Table 3.3. Trends in the Percentage of Crimes Reported to the NYPD
That Were Cleared by an Arrest in the 1990s

Type of Crime	1990	1991	1992	1993	1994	1995	1996	1997	1998	Entire Nation, 1998
Murder	62	59	59	62	64	73	87	88	87	69
Rape	49	57	49	44	51	61	52	51	59	50
Robbery	22	22	21	21	25	29	30	31	34	28
Felonious assault	50	51	50	47	53	56	55	64	69	59
Burglary	9	9	8	8	9	12	13	14	16	14
Grand larceny	7	7	6	6	7	9	9	9	10	19
Motor vehicle theft	7	7	6	5	5	7	7	7	7	14

Note: A case was considered cleared if a suspect was arrested, was already behind bars for another crime, or had died.
Source: NYPD Complaints and Arrests annual statistical reports, 1990–1998; FBI's UCR, 1999.

lice to figure out who is behind these illegal activities. Therefore, it is impossible to conclude that the City's crime rate dropped because Compstat strategies enabled detectives to bring more predators to the bar of
justice. On the contrary, the lack of a connection lends support to the
suspicion that crime must be dwindling for some other reasons than law
enforcement pressures.

Step out of Line . . . Did the Crackdown on Quality-of-Life Infractions Reduce Gun Violence?

The merits of the "Broken Windows" theory have clearly demonstrated
the fact that police agencies that aggressively address quality-of-life issues
are also those that achieve the greatest reductions in crime. . . .

Literal and metaphoric "broken windows" lead inevitably and inex-
orably to more serious crimes. These acts convey a subtle message that because such behaviors are tolerated or condoned, other and more serious
crimes are tolerated as well. The failure of police officers to correct these
offensive conditions also fosters the public perception that the police do
not care about the issues that are important to neighborhood residents.
This ultimately erodes public confidence in the police and the government
they represent.

—Police Commissioner Howard Safir (1997:31)

When press releases emanating from City Hall and One Police Plaza announced a switch-over to a policy of aggressive order maintenance in

1994, threatening zero tolerance for any lawbreaking whatsoever, this get-tough stance was welcomed in most communities.[31] Treating even the smallest quality-of-life infractions as grounds for arrest makes sense according to the "Broken Windows" thesis (see Wilson and Kelling, 1982; Kelling and Coles, 1996). It proposes that blatant signs of disorder (like graffiti covering walls, stolen and stripped cars lying abandoned in the street, drag racing, prostitutes openly plying their trade, teenagers smoking pot in parks, and men sitting on stoops drinking heavily) send out messages that "anything goes," "the authorities are not in control,""no one around here cares," and "do whatever you want, the cops won't stop you." These signals attract hard-core offenders who then feel emboldened to commit even more serious crimes. Intimidated neighbors lose their sense of community and of ownership of their immediate environment and tend to abandon public spaces and retreat into their homes to escape the dangers that they perceive to be lurking all around them (see Giuliani, 1997b; Kelling and Bratton, 1998).[32]

Stepped-up enforcement and strict compliance with the letter of the law is thought to be of preventive and deterrent value. As arrests for minor crimes rise as part of a sustained crackdown, incidents of major crimes should fall, for several reasons, according to supporters of aggressive policing. First of all, those signals that attracted criminally inclined persons would no longer emanate from the meanest streets that had earned the reputation of being virtual urban no-man's lands and free-fire zones. Second, enforcement of laws prohibiting even the most minor breaches of public decorum would lead to widespread stopping, frisking, and identity-checking that could enable officers to catch more people carrying concealed weapons and drugs. Deputy Commissioner Jack Maple (quoted in Pooley, 1996:56), explaining how one thing could lead to another, illustrated this second rationale and suggested another one as well: "It's relatively hard for a uniformed patrolman to catch someone carrying drugs. But as we'd seen, it's easy to catch someone for an open can of beer on the street. Your open beer lets me check your ID. Now I can radio the precinct for outstanding warrants or parole violations. Maybe I bump against that bulge in your belt; with probable cause, I can frisk you." Hence, the third reason for cracking down is that, mixed in with these petty violators, there may be some hard-core career criminals wanted for serious offenses who carelessly and casually broke minor laws as well.

Enthusiasm for retaking the streets and cracking down on minor transgressions is nothing new; it waxes and wanes over the years.[33] Although this conventional wisdom was elevated to the status of a self-evident truism in New York during the 1990s, it had been out of favor just a few years earlier on pragmatic grounds. Arresting large numbers of people who commit minor infractions had been derided as a waste of taxpayers' money by generating excessive police overtime costs. This policy also clogged the courts, and filled the jails with individuals who at most received a slap on the wrist and quickly returned to the streets, having learned no long-lasting lesson or received no help from passing through the revolving door of justice. In addition, the stigmatizing label of having a criminal record even for a misdemeanor conviction might damage the prospects of already marginalized poor young men of finding gainful employment in the future (see Dixon, 1998).

Just as the crime wave of the late 1970s reached its peak, a journalist (Pileggi, 1981a) lamented that "City officials may have miscalculated when they decided during the budget crisis [of the mid-1970s] to concentrate available police resources on major crimes and let 'minor' street criminals proliferate undisturbed." Overdramatizing the situation, he charged that the police and the courts had "given up." He lengthened the list of overlooked illegal acts to include some felonies, not just violations and misdemeanors:

> The situation is so bad today that the police and city officials have tacitly agreed to allow certain kinds of criminal behavior to go on without harassment or punishment. The authorities have enlarged the scope of unchallenged criminal behavior to include not only quality-of-life offenses such as aggressive panhandling, smoking in the subway, drunkenness, brawling, urinating on sidewalks and in the subways, but also certain muggings, burglaries, narcotics transactions, purse snatchings, car thefts and larcenies.

Years before the catchy phrase "defining deviance down" (Moynihan, 1993) was coined to condemn the tendency to expect and accept a certain level of lawlessness as normal and unpreventable, overlooking petty offenses was disparaged as an "open city" policy. Denying that officers had been instructed to turn a blind eye toward vice, Mayor Edward Koch (quoted in Shipp, 1981) snapped, "This is not an open city," and warned that individuals guilty of such quality-of-life offenses as prostitution, gambling, and low-level drug trafficking risked arrest.

Despite dire forecasts about a climate of license causing the collapse of governmental authority, the City experienced several years of declining murder rates during the first half of the 1980s. But the issue reemerged during the latter part of the decade when the crack epidemic hit New York hard and even more people wound up living hand-to-mouth, surviving by scavenging, begging, and stealing. The presence of this underclass was considered to be an intractable problem within the urban landscape, until, as one journalist (Pooley, 1996:55) put it: "Giuliani instructed Bratton to do something Dinkins would never have allowed: use those cops to crack down on minor offenders, public drunks, potheads, those who urinate on the street, aggressive panhandlers, graffiti scribblers and 'squeegee pests,' who converged on cars at stoplights to clean windshields for spare change."

As the pendulum of public opinion swings back and forth between tolerance and intolerance of deviant behavior, policies adopted at City Hall and at police headquarters change, causing arrest totals for minor offenses to rise and fall. Statistically speaking, that means that the degree to which patrol officers are instructed to either crack down or ease up on petty violators is a variable. One way to measure police activity against quality-of-life violations (and other lesser offenses) is to monitor misdemeanor arrests. Officers can exercise more discretion about whether to take someone in or give that person a second chance when it comes to misdemeanors as opposed to felonies. As one patrolman (Laffey, 1997:50–51) explained his options,

> If a group of guys are hanging out smoking marihuana and I'm walking by, one of two things tends to happen. Either I hear a rapid apology, the blunt is tossed—and if it's down a sewer there's no evidence to recover and no basis for a charge, you follow me, guys?—and the group gets a stern word of caution. Or someone decides to lock eyes with me and takes a drag, and someone else calls out some cute remark, like "F--- the police!" and they decline to heed my word to the wise: "Break out, guys. Bounce!" No? And in seconds, or in a minute if I decide I want backup, they're all

up against a wall. I start going into their pockets, taking names. . . . But most guys like these don't carry I.D., and you take them into the precinct to search them thoroughly, run the checks, and write the summonses. And now and then you find a prize, like a hard-core felon hiding behind a bottle of Baccardi.

Mission Accomplished?

From the intelligence we get, people are stashing their weapons rather than carrying them.

—Police Commissioner Howard Safir (quoted in "As criminals stash guns," 1997)

Of all the different kinds of slayings, gun murders should be most affected by changes in policies about misdemeanor arrests. Police spokespersons have contended repeatedly that the zero tolerance campaign associated with the Compstat reforms has not only restored a general sense of order to the asphalt jungle but specifically has deterred gun toting.

Some statistical backing emerges for pro-misdemeanor arrest policies that are so central to the "Broken Windows" approach. When the increases and decreases in total misdemeanor arrests over the past twenty years are superimposed on the peaks and valleys of gun murders, an inverse relationship becomes evident. Misdemeanor arrests fell in the late 1970s, while gun murders rose. As arrests for petty crimes went up in the early 1980s, gun murders dropped. When misdemeanor arrests declined in the late 1980s, deaths from bullet wounds soared. In the 1990s, murders involving firearms didn't plummet until misdemeanor arrests climbed to record-breaking levels during the Compstat years.[34] Cracking down harder on minor offenders seems to be a necessary but not always sufficient way of suppressing gun murders (graph 3.3).

This finding—that there seems to be a weak negative correlation between the number of misdemeanor arrests and the number of gun murders—supports the belief that stepped-up enforcement of minor laws deters casual gun toting, and that the zero tolerance campaign has saved thousands of lives since 1993.

But there are several inconvenient facts that undermine this theory. First of all, the record-breaking surge in misdemeanor arrests during

Graph 3.3. Relationship between Misdemeanor Arrests,
Gun Arrests, and Gun Murders

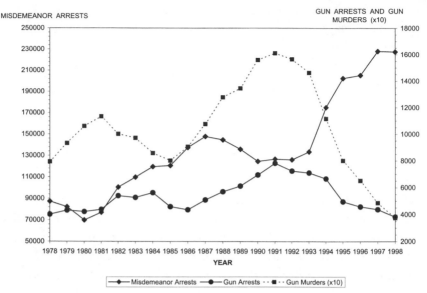

Note: "Gun arrests" includes felony arrests for other dangerous weapons like certain knives.
Source: NYPD's annual Complaints and Arrests Reports, 1978–1998.

the Compstat era gave rise to the widely held impression that never before have so many New Yorkers gotten into legal trouble for doing so little. Actually, that is not true, according to a more comprehensive indicator of officer activity, what the DCJS (Division of Criminal Justice Services) terms "Total Part II Arrests." This indicator more accurately reflects the effects of directives from headquarters on the exercise of discretion in the field because it even counts summonses for violations of local ordinances in addition to misdemeanor arrests and certain felony arrests.[35] Summonses for violating ordinances passed by the New York City Council are the kinds of infractions that officers have been instructed either to overlook in the past or focus upon during a quality-of-life crackdown. Arrest and summons activity peaked in 1986 and 1987, when the crack epidemic erupted, according to this alternative indicator. But the crackdown against even the slightest breaches of the peace during those two years was not sufficient to suppress the surge in crack selling and consuming, or the spike in violence and theft. Why didn't all that arrest activity stem the tide back then (see Bowling, 1999)?[36]

Second, proponents of the crackdown on quality-of-life offenses frequently defended all the arresting that it entailed by pointing to an alleged beneficial side-effect: apprehending suspects for minor infractions enabled officers to legitimately search them for guns, knives, and drugs (see Krauss, 1995b; Parascandola, 1996; Pooley, 1996; Kelling and Bratton, 1998). But after four members of the elite Street Crime Unit fired forty-one shots at an unarmed young immigrant from Africa (hitting him nineteen times) in the Bronx in 1999, the ensuing media spotlight and bitter controversy compelled the NYPD to reveal that it relied heavily on another tactic to catch people who were going around armed. The several hundred members of this plainclothes unit, whose motto boasted "We own the night," carried out at least 18,000 stop-and-frisks during 1997, and another 27,000 in 1998. Since many officers (not only in this unit) do not fill out the required paperwork if no arrest follows, the actual number of people accosted and searched was probably many times greater than 45,000 over two years (see Kocienewski, 1999; Roane, 1999).[37]

Apparently, NYPD officers had been given the green light to engage in aggressive preventive patrolling by exercising (civil libertarian critics would say, exceeding) the discretion granted to them by the 1968 Supreme Court decision in *Terry v. Ohio* to question and pat down individuals who aroused their "reasonable suspicion." Many street confrontations with officers cruising by were triggered by "the felon look" or "perp colors": the clothing and posturing characterizing the "Tupac-thug-for-life" imagery favored by inner-city afficionados of hip-hop culture. Black and Hispanic teenage boys and young men were particularly likely to be thrown up against a wall or spread-eagled on the ground ("tossed" in police parlance) and then sent on their way, often without an explanation or an apology, if they wore a baseball cap (at any angle), a bandanna (especially in gang colors red or blue), a hooded sweatshirt, sagging and baggy trousers, exposed plaid boxer shorts, and expensive high-top sneakers (particularly unlaced, as in prisons), according to a reporter's interviews with fifty officers (Noel, 2000). Therefore, the zero-tolerance campaign may have received too much public credit for permitting officers to initiate contact with suspicious characters and to search them for concealed weapons. In reality, many of the street encounters were triggered by a less publicized and highly controversial "pattern and practice," the mere negative stereotyping of minority youth (a form of racial profiling) that did not even require officers to catch individuals in the act of committing petty infractions in order to search them.[38]

Third, the San Diego experience demonstrates that a policy of strict enforcement resulting in massive numbers of arrests for quality-of-life infractions is not absolutely necessary to bring down the crime rate. During the mid-1990s, while the NYPD was dramatically racheting-up apprehensions for minor violations (by more than 40 percent), San Diego's police force was cutting back on misdemeanor arrests (from nearly 40,000 in 1993 to fewer than 35,000 in 1996, a drop of 13 percent); and yet this large California city enjoyed the same degree of relief from the oppressive burden of crime as did New York (see Greene, 1999).

Fourth, considering all the arresting that went on since the advent of Compstat, it might be assumed that the officers of the energized NYPD had become extremely active. However, compared to their counterparts in other cities that had similar crime problems, NYPD officers made, on average, only half as many arrests per year (IBO, 1999). This discovery casts doubt on the impression that crime crashed because Compstat unlocked a torrent of police productivity, and that sheer numbers of misdemeanor arrests drove down murder rates.[39]

In fact, Mayor Giuliani (1997b) downplayed the importance of making arrests and dismissed monitoring them—the traditional way watchdog groups have gauged police productivity—as no longer relevant: "Compstat transformed the Department from an organization that reacted to crime to a Department that actively works to deter offenses. . . . Arrests are no longer the measure of effective policing—commanders are now responsible for deterring crime." As always, the mayor focused attention on the bottom line, lower crime rates, without really specifying the precise linkages between their policies and these results.

In sum, great doubts continue to swirl around the efficacy of strict enforcement of quality-of-life ordinances. Critics argue that serious social costs undermine any alleged benefits (see Dixon, 1998; Clear and Cordner, 1999; Greene, 1999): the increased volume of hostile contacts with the public invariably leads to more incidents in which civilians complain about verbal abuse, rough handling, and the unnecessary use of force; huge numbers of poor young men who are already disadvantaged in the legal job market find themselves further handicapped by criminal records for trivial infractions; and the flood of minor cases overwhelms the lower courts' capacity to properly assess and process them (Purnick, 1996; Haberman, 1997; Rohde, 2000). Even the architects of the "Broken Windows" thesis of order maintenance warn about the ominous implications of an oversimplified and heavy-handed understanding of "zero tolerance" (see Kelling, 1998), since intolerance of minor deviations from the norm cannot be a sound foundation for law enforcement in a democratic society made up of diverse subpopulations (see Bowling, 1998). And yet, strict enforcement, New York style, has been proclaimed as the new official policy of police forces in countries as different as Britain, Norway, the Netherlands, Switzerland, Germany, Hungary, Italy, Portugal, Israel, Japan, Brazil, and China (Bowling, 1999).

Smoking Guns: Was It Really Zero Tolerance That Discouraged Gun Toting?

People carrying illegal guns quickly realized that they risked gun charges after being arrested for minor crimes. After rising briefly in 1994, gun apprehensions then began to fall; the gunslingers were leaving their weapons at home. With far fewer guns on the street, far fewer people were shot and far fewer were killed.

—Former police commissioner William Bratton
(Bratton and Andrews, 1999b:44)

This oft-repeated claim deserves a closer look.

To sidestep the heated political and philosophical debate between advocates of gun ownership for self-defense and those who believe in gun control, some criminologists (see J. Wilson, 1994) have proposed that the focus of law enforcement policies should be narrowed and fine-tuned to simply get guns "out of the wrong hands" and "off the streets." These phrases refer to tactics that disarm individuals who should not be carrying pistols or revolvers around: probationers, parolees, ex-convicts with a history of violence, drug sellers and abusers, mentally unstable psychiatric patients, street gang members, and volatile young men in general. In order to bring about this selective disarmament of just a segment of the population, officers must find legal justifications to make more stops and frisks, particularly of those hanging out in locations where illegal activities and shootings have been occurring. As gun arrests and weapons seizures increase, the level of violent crime should decrease (see Sherman, Shaw, and Rogan, 1994; and Wilson, 1994).

New Yorkers fearful about armed assailants prowling city streets received no solace from the findings of a comparative study about the ability of police forces to detect and disarm gunmen. The NYPD ranked last in 1993 among thirty large-city departments in the number of guns seized per one hundred officers, and next to last in confiscations by population size and by murder rate (Sherman and Bridgeforth, 1994).[40] Upon taking office, "Mr. Bratton realized that New York was behind in gun seizures, and made the recovery of guns a top priority," according to Deputy Commissioner for Public Information John Miller (quoted in Treaster, 1994b). The NYPD unveiled a new plan of attack in March 1994 entitled "Strategy Number One: Getting Guns off the Streets," in which the Department (NYPD, 1994b:7) bluntly conceded that "Whatever we are doing to reduce violent—especially handgun-related—crime is not working." It promised that a set of coordinated tactics coupled with a renewed commitment to a policy already on paper, but largely ignored, would produce more impressive results. Greater efforts would be made to apprehend armed individuals, make gun charges stick, pressure arrestees to divulge information about guns and drugs, catch all accomplices, trace guns used in crimes, use warrants to seize caches of illegal arms during raids, and put disreputable gun dealers out of business by denying them licenses. Officers in the elite Street Crime Unit (SCU) would undertake special anti-gun patrols, especially in high crime neighborhoods; a Special Narcotic and Gun (SNAG) squad would be set up to go after heavily armed drug dealers; a gun buy-back program would induce residents to turn in their arms, no questions asked, for cash; and a Crime-Stoppers Tips hotline would offer reward money for information about gun-law violators. The effectiveness of the program would be evaluated by monitoring gun arrests and seizures (see NYPD, 1994b; Citizens Crime Commission, 1996).

The architects of Strategy Number One expected that the relationship between gun arrests and gun crime rates would be inverse, at least for a while, as at the outset of any crackdown. The launching of the new anti-gun campaign would boost gun arrests and illegal weapons seizures, and concomitantly cause armed robberies, shooting incidents, and gun killings to subside.

But gun arrests did not spike as the new strategies kicked in.[41]

Compstat figures indicated that if there was any flurry of increased gun arrests, it must have been extremely short-lived—around the time of the announcement of the new initiative (February 1994) and the issuing of the pamphlet (March 1994). By late April 1994, the cumulative total of arrests for carrying illegal guns was lower than the comparable figure for the first four months of 1993. As the year wore on, the number of gun arrests accomplished in 1994 fell further and further behind the achievements of 1993.[42] Besides gun arrests, gun seizures also fell when compared to 1993 confiscations.[43]

At first, even the top brass apparently were confused by these disappointing results, according to a reporter's account (Treaster, 1994b:B2):

> Yet despite those efforts, the police have recovered 500 fewer guns this year than the 10,000 they seized in the first seven months of last year. . . . Neither Mr. Miller or Mr. Maple could say why seizures were down. . . . The two officials speculated that increased efforts against guns might have persuaded some people to carry their weapons less frequently and use them less frequently.[44]

As gun murders continued to tumble, a win-win situation developed. The package of new strategies could be proclaimed to be a great success whatever the data showed concerning gun arrests and seizures. If the anti-gun initiatives enabled the NYPD to nab more gunmen and seize more of their illegally concealed pistols and revolvers, the resulting incapacitation and deterrence could be cited as proof of a decisive victory in the City's nearly century-long war on guns. Alternatively, if gun arrests and seizures fell, the NYPD's "they are so scared of getting caught that they are leaving their guns at home" deterrence argument seemed credible. As long as gun crimes did not rise again, victory could be declared and credit could be claimed either way, whether gun arrests and seizures went up or down.

The belief that "they are leaving their guns at home because they are afraid of getting in serious trouble" is predicated on the assumption that New Yorkers caught packing illegal guns get stiff punishments.

On paper, the penalties are severe: people convicted of criminal possession of an unlicensed loaded handgun face a prison term of at least one year and at most seven years behind bars under New York State's long-standing 1911 Sullivan Law and its more stringent 1981 mandatory time revision. But DCJS statistics for 1998 revealed that less than half of all gun possession arrests that went to court resulted in convictions, and that just half of those convictions resulted in sentences of incarceration. Many arrests were tossed out of court because the searches were ruled to be illegal. Deputy Commissioner for Policy and Planning Michael Farrell (quoted in Rayman, 1999) blamed the high rate of dismissals and acquittals on "the vagaries of the criminal justice system," but he conceded that the conviction rate had not improved since the advent of Compstat.[45]

There can be no doubt that gun crimes, shots fired, woundings from bullets, and fatalities due to gunfire fell slowly at first, and then sharply, as the 1990s wore on. The decline in gunplay made the crash possible. Gun toting surely faded away, but why? The crackdown on quality-of-life infractions must have frightened some would-be gunmen into leaving their weapons at home. But police officers have always assigned a high priority to "gun collars." Unlike the inverse relationship between misdemeanor arrests and gun murders, the relationship between gun arrests and gun murders is direct. Over the decades, the greater the number of murders from gunfire, the larger the number of armed individuals the police were able to catch (some of these felony weapons arrests were not for handguns but for concealed knives). An inverse relationship would show that the more gunmen who got captured and the more guns the police took away, the fewer gun murders were committed—but that is not what the data in graph 3.3 reveal.

During the Compstat years, gun murders tumbled a little more than gun arrests. But other more fine-tuned, indirect measures of gun carrying, such as the yearly number of shooting incidents and shooting victims, declined less sharply than gun murders—and at about the same rate as gun arrests.[46] All these statistics make it clear that gun arrests are largely a function of gun carrying and gun usage. When more people go around armed, the police catch a larger number; when fewer people pack concealed handguns, officers catch a smaller number, but about the same proportion of them. One alternative explanation is that a major consideration governing whether or not to go around "strapped" is the perceived threat posed by potential enemies, and not simply the relatively constant threat of arrest.

After gunslinging peaked in 1990, fewer young men carried concealed handguns around with them for protection from their adversaries, real or imagined. As dropouts from the crack-dealing scene put away their guns, others in the drug trade, plus those who packed pistols for self-protection, and certainly those who brandished handguns just as a symbol of status, realized that the dangers of being caught unprepared without their equalizer had diminished and followed suit. The trends in the data suggest that a deescalation in the latest round of the arms race among poor young men had already been underway since 1990. Once again, by the time Compstat strategies were devised and implemented, a problem was diminishing; in this case, the craze of going around strapped was already winding down. The NYPD's concerted campaign helped to prod the preexisting process of disarmament along further and faster, but the innovative approaches did not cause a "turnaround" or reverse a negative trend.

Can't Stand the Heat? Good Riddance! Were Hard-Core Criminals Driven out of Town?

> The criminal element responsible for most street crime is nothing but a bunch of disorganized individuals, many of whom aren't very good at what they do. The police have all the advantages—in training, equipment, organization, and strategy. We can get the criminals on the run and we can keep them on the run. It's possible. We're doing it in New York.
> —Former police commissioner William Bratton (1995:10)

Were die-hard criminals and would-be offenders run out of town by a beefed-up police presence, improved clearance rates, and the zero tolerance crackdown?

During the crash, speculation surfaced that criminally inclined New Yorkers had been chased away in droves and had set up shop, crimewise, on new turf. Unfortunately, much of the data was anecdotal. Police Commissioner Howard Safir (quoted in Massarella, 1996:2) suggested that "the way to deal with the problem is to drive the drug traffickers out of the city, to New Jersey and Westchester. As I told [the D.A.], you take the same attitude in Westchester as we do in New York City, and you can drive them to Orange County." A few years later, Commissioner Safir (quoted in Sherman, 1998:8) reported, "We're making the environment so inhospitable they're going elsewhere. We're driving them from the city, and that's why Westchester and New Jersey are seeing spikes in drug trafficking."

Career criminals are subject to many of the same pushes (problem situations urging them to go) and pulls (opportunities attracting them) as law-abiding folks.[47] Street-level peddlers of marijuana, cocaine, and heroin might be the most mobile career criminals of all. They may simply pack up and move on to the greener pastures of underserved markets where the competition is not as keen and police pressures are not as intense.[48] By driving drug dealers out of New York—which was precisely the title of Strategy Number 3 announced in April 1994—the NYPD may be accomplishing on a grander scale the same displacement effect that neighborhood crackdowns often achieved on a local and temporary basis (see Zimmer, 1990). When police department representatives in Amsterdam, Binghamton, and Syracuse complained of a virtual "invasion" in 1998, Governor George Pataki ordered a study of the apparent shift in drug distribution from downstate to upstate urban areas (Marzulli, 1998c). Other communities that may have lost because of New York's gains included Fort Lee, New Jersey (Massarella, 1996), Rochester (Associated Press, 1998), Putnam County (Travis, 1998), Rockland County, and Mount Vernon (Glaberson, 1997). However, not many prosecutors, police chiefs, or sheriffs voiced such complaints since crime rates generally fell throughout the New York metropolitan area during the 1990s, even though the surrounding suburbs did not enjoy the same degree of relief as was registered within the five boroughs (Glaberson, 1997).

If displacement actually occurred to a significant degree, there may be some poetic justice to this reversal of fortune. For generations, tales about plentiful illegal opportunities have attracted criminals from across the country and around the world to try their luck in the five boroughs. Since the advent of Compstat, the net flow might be going the other way. But putting aside arguments about payback time, it should be clear that displacement is a short-run "solution" that really doesn't get to the root of the crime problem. Moving offenders around, scattering them here and concentrating them there, merely redistributes the burden of victimization on to other jurisdictions less able to defend themselves. The situation is analogous to target hardening measures like fortifying homes against burglars or adding anti-theft devices to make cars more difficult to steal. Unless all potential persons and property are reasonably well protected, such victimization prevention strategies don't qualify as genuine crime prevention. They merely deflect risk and harm to the more vulnerable and less privileged people and communities.

Improved Policing: Necessary, Sufficient, or Not Needed at All?

Is a vast improvement on the part of the municipal police absolutely necessary to drive down the murder rate? Or is it possible for crime rates to fall even though police services are deteriorating? Judging from the examples set by New Orleans, Washington, and Los Angeles, it seems that crime can go down even when police departments are in a reactive mode, in the throes of a severe morale crisis, embroiled in corruption scandals, and unsettled by changes in structure and leadership.

In New Orleans, late in 1996, several of the architects of Compstat were called in to reorganize that city's troubled department. And sure enough, arrests went up and murders fell sharply afterward (Maple 1999).[49] But during the years when the force was known to be one of the most corrupt, inept, and poorly paid in the nation, and before the new chief got the additional officers, increased funding, and the consultants from New York City that he sought, the city's body count dropped moderately (see Bragg, 1995; "New Orleans murder rate," 1995; Pedersen, 1996, 1997).[50]

Washington D.C.'s Metropolitan Police Department "has long been regarded as a sinkhole of corruption and mismanagement" (Massing, 1998b). After a series of scandals, a joint federal and local task force was created to win back the public's confidence. In 1998, a new commissioner reorganized the department for the fourth time in as many years. The homicide squad, which earlier had been centralized at headquarters and then decentralized into the precincts, was disbanded, with its detectives reassigned into either a violent crimes squad or a property crimes squad. And yet, amidst all this organizational turmoil, homicides fell sharply ("Capital ideas," 1998; "From the start," 1998; Thomas-Lester, 1998).[51]

The Los Angeles Police Department (LAPD) was known for its highly mobile, aggressive, pro-active, pro-arrest style of policing under Police Chiefs William Parker and Daryl Gates. But it was badly shaken by the repercussions of the brutal beating of Rodney King in 1991, the embarrassing exposés of the Christopher Commission in the wake of that incident, and the apparent bungling of the evidence that purportedly linked O. J. Simpson to the murder of his wife, Nicole, and her friend Ron Goldman in 1995. The once-proud department wound up underfunded and undermanned (Reeves, 1995) and was characterized as "disgraced and discredited . . . maligned around the world . . . for shoddy police work, perjured testimony, and racially motivated assaults on innocent people" as it sank into a "demoralized funk" because the police chief brought in to turn around the department was unable to enact any significant reforms (Pooley, 1995). Stuck in a defensive mode, officers adopted "the fine art of ostrich policing" by "rolling up their windows and looking the other way" (Director, 1996).[52] During 1996, the LAPD was described as a "broken department" with a high turnover, in which many officers felt "abandoned by their leaders and their city" (Shah, 1996). Yet all through these troubled times for the LAPD, murders tumbled.[53] This paradox led a reporter (Butterfield, 2000) to conclude: "Indeed, law enforcement experts are baffled by the decline in Los Angeles, whose Police Department has been plagued by scandals and low morale and has seen a drop in arrests. This suggests some, or much, of the nationwide reduction in crime may well stem from factors beyond better policing, like longer prison sentences, the improved economy, and changes in the attitude of young people toward drugs and crime."

A Rush to Judgment about New York's Finest? The Jury Is Still Out, but the Verdict Is Already In

The proponents of the "NYPD deserves the lion's share of the credit" school of thought contend that the reengineered department singlehandedly took back the City's streets from a legendary and fierce criminal element. It made such swift progress since the mid-1990s that its strategies and tactics served as a shining example for other police forces across the globe to emulate and imitate. But criminologists find circumstantial cases based on coincidence and on common sense insufficient as a basis for scientifically evaluating a policy change, and insist instead that claims makers prove their assertions with solid evidence that clearly demonstrates linkages. Some of the data analyzed above lends statistical support to the improved policing hypothesis, but a lot of the findings don't fit; unless and until these reasonable doubts are resolved by further research, it is premature to reach any verdict.

The Compstat innovations were not introduced as a controlled experiment that could be definitively evaluated according to the established research designs traditionally demanded by criminologists and other social scientists.

While New York's crime rates crashed, most of the big cities in the country policed by departments following a wide range of different strategies also enjoyed substantial relief. The violence problem did not "turn around" with the advent of Compstat; body counts were already drifting downward before their rate of decrease accelerated. Although the bulk of the drop in murders per month took place in the latter part of 1994 when new strategies were being introduced, the number of vehicle thefts, robberies, burglaries, and larcenies reported to the police tumbled too soon, before Compstat was developed.

In previous decades, whenever the NYPD increased its uniformed presence on the City's meanest streets, homicides right out in the open decreased. Police presence was beefed up during the beginning of Compstat, and outdoor murders dropped. But patrol strength did not continue to grow, and yet murders outdoors continued to drop. Even more baffling, during three years, the percentage change in killings committed in locations that were not visible to officers on patrol fell faster than slayings outdoors, where the police could observe unfolding events and intervene before it was too late. Overall, the rate of decline of homicides carried out inside nearly matched that of outside killings. Even with more officers chasing after far fewer perpetrators, the NYPD was not able to cut down the response time it took squad cars to race to the scenes of crimes-in-progress to rescue victims and catch perpetrators red-handed.

In years past, whenever the NYPD bettered its ability to solve murders, the number of killings declined. Clearance rates for murders rose sharply during the Compstat years, and slayings tumbled. But a closer inspection of the overall solution rate revealed that the proportion of new homicide cases that detectives solved after the implementation of Compstat reforms remained about the same as in prior time periods. The higher total apprehension rates resulted in large part from the shrinking of a formerly overwhelming work load. This enabled detectives to reopen older, unsolved cases that originally had been given short shrift. Furthermore, it is possible for crime rates to fall even if the police don't catch the culprits. Reported auto thefts dropped almost as sharply as murders did during the 1990s, even though arrest rates stagnated at very low levels—and the odds of getting away thereby remained very favorable from the offenders' standpoint.

Over the decades, whenever officers made more misdemeanor arrests for quality-of-life infractions, murders carried out with concealed handguns fell, in accord with the "Broken Windows" thesis. During the mid-1990s, the energized NYPD made many more minor arrests, and gunfire subsided. However, an even greater number of minor arrests were made during two years in the mid-1980s, but that crackdown did not slow down a surge in gun murders. Furthermore, even after rejuvenation, the NYPD averaged about half as many arrests per officer per year as some other big-city police forces confronting similar crime problems. Contrary to the expectations of Strategy Number One's architects, after Compstat innovations were in place, gun arrests and confiscations did not rise—they continued to fall in tandem with gun murders and shooting incidents, as they had since 1991.

In sum, the NYPD used high-tech monitoring and proactive tactics to prevent volatile situations from getting out of hand and to regain control of the streets and parks. Its relentless follow-up strategies pressured career criminals, especially drug dealers, to either maintain a very low profile or else get out of town. Its innovations boosted apprehension rates for violent crimes way above national norms. Therefore, the NYPD's package of Compstat reforms made an important contribution to the crime crash. But improved policing surely was not the only positive development taking place in the City during the 1990s—other crucial, constructive forces were at work as well. If the answer to the question, "NYPD or not NYPD?" is that the energized and reengineered police force deserves some but not all of the credit, then what else changed for the better?

As crime crashed, Deputy Commissioner Jack Maple (quoted in Horowitz, 1995:24) taunted academics to document their hunches:

> I'd be very happy to get all the criminologists to come in here together. They can put all their grant money in a big pile in the middle of the floor, and then we'll settle this. Winner takes all. . . . What's changed in this city in the last eighteen months other than what the police are doing? Did all the sixteen-year-olds suddenly become 50? Did all the crooks suddenly get a-scared? Did everybody leave town? Did everybody suddenly load up on heroin? Did they all go to jail? Did they all get together and decide they're not gonna shoot anybody, they're not gonna rob anybody, and they're not gonna kill anybody? And tell me about this so-called truce that's taken place to end the drug wars. I want names.

These factors, plus others, will be put to the test in the following chapters. The other components of the criminal justice system will be examined next. Did the prosecutors, courts, jails, and prisons in New York get much tougher when dealing with the City's criminals?

Notes

1. Like free agents in baseball, police executives with an apparent record of success received lucrative contracts and became objects of bidding wars whenever other municipalities tried to lure them away (Janofsky, 1998:A1).

2. The NYPD's image in the eyes of New Yorkers had greatly improved by 1998. Eighty-nine percent of whites and 77 percent of black and other non-white residents were satisfied with the service they were receiving, according to a poll of over 10,000 respondents in 1998 in twelve major cities carried out by the U.S. Department of Justice (MacFarquhar, 1999; Smith, Steadman, and Minton, 1999).

3. Only 29 percent of the residents of New York City reported that they had contact with police officers (including casual conversations) during 1998. That was the lowest level in the twelve cities surveyed by the Justice Department (MacFarquhar, 1999; Smith, Steadman, and Minton, 1999).

4. The presumption that the entire force could be energized suffered another setback when new data confirmed that the maldistribution of arrest activity persisted into 1996. Department figures revealed that about one-third of the patrol force, nearly 7,000 officers, had accomplished no more than two arrests that

year. Within that group were the one-seventh of all uniformed cops who had arrested no one (Weiss and Celona, 1997). In 1998, PBA officials complained that all beat officers were under great pressure to make arrests, but headquarters denied that any quotas existed (Celona and Massarella, 1998).

5. The City Comptroller's office released a report in 1999 which charged that the department could place 1,250 more officers on patrol by hiring lower-paid civilians to do the same work. Police Commissioner Safir contended that the report was based on "flawed numbers" and that many positions had been civilianized in the previous few years (Rohde, 1999).

6. The City Comptroller's office paid out an all-time high of $40 million of government revenue to settle 739 claims by victims of police misconduct during fiscal 1999 (Flynn, 1999b).

7. When Human Rights Watch issued a report in 1998 charging that Mayor Giuliani "automatically" publicly defended officers accused of brutality, he blasted the criticism as "left-wing ideology" (Morris and Hardt, 1998). But a 1999 poll discovered that nearly nine out of ten African American residents thought the police often engaged in brutality against blacks (Barry and Connelly, 1999).

8. The NYPD came under investigation by the City Council, the state attorney general's office, and the U.S. attorneys for the Southern District and the Eastern District after a number of highly controversial incidents, especially the sodomizing by a stick-wielding officer of a Haitian immigrant in a stationhouse bathroom in 1997, and the shooting forty-one times of an unarmed man by four plainclothes officers in a Bronx vestibule in 1999 (Investigating the NYPD? 1999).

9. Not much had changed by the late 1990s, despite the opportunities for taking affirmative action offered by a decade of expansion. The NYPD remained among the least racially diverse of the forces serving the nation's ten largest cities. Whites made up 67 percent of the sworn officers but comprised less than 40 percent of the City's residents. The underrepresentation of black and Hispanic officers was especially pronounced in the higher ranks, where over 90 percent of the captains, inspectors, and chiefs were whites (Wilgoren and Cooper, 1999).

10. By 1998, the number of suicides had dropped to 5 (Flynn, 1999a).

11. Commissioner Safir promised in 1998 to crack down on police officers who were armed when they were "not fit for duty" and involved in alcohol-related misconduct, after a spate of fatal car crashes and suicides embroiling cops drinking heavily after work (Claffey, 1998). The seriousness of the rank-and-file's drinking problem had not subsided since the mid-1990s, according to the head of the PBA-sponsored membership assistance program (Noonan, 1999).

12. For the first time in twenty years, the Department of Justice's Bureau of Justice Statistics (BJS) in 1998 carried out a city-level survey of crime victims. BJS interviewers discovered that New Yorkers were more reluctant to bring their problems to the attention of the police than residents in any of the other eleven cities in the study. Specifically, only 32 percent of the victims of violent crimes reported these incidents to the NYPD, compared to 58 percent in Springfield, Illinois, 50 percent in Washington, D.C., and 35 percent in all twelve cities combined. Similarly, New Yorkers told the NYPD about 29 percent of the property crimes they suffered, whereas the police were informed about 47 percent of the incidents by victims in Savannah, 45 percent in Kansas City, and 34 percent overall (Smith, Steadman, and Minton, 1999).

13. One of the most serious and potentially explosive charges was made offhandedly by Commissioner Bratton (Bratton and Andrews, 1999b:44) when he asserted that "the huge drop in crime has been a boon to the city's minority communities, which not long ago were left largely unpoliced and at the mercy of the lawless."

14. Sometimes the term was spelled as "CompStat" and was believed to be a contraction that evolved in police circles from either the phrases "comparison statistics" (Citizens Crime Commission, 1996) or "computerized statistics" (Safir, 1997), or even "computerized crime comparison statistics" (Giuliani, 1997b), but its actual derivation was from the software filename "compare stats" (Silverman, 1999).

15. Compstat won an award of $100,000 to promote replication of its exemplary problem-solving approaches from the Innovations in American Government competition sponsored by the Ford Foundation and Harvard University in 1996. The NYPD sponsored conferences in 1997 and 1998 to explain its strategies to representatives from more than seventy-five police departments. The National Institute of Justice has funded Compstat experiments in Indianapolis, Baltimore, and Prince Georges County, Maryland. Police forces in Boston, Washington, D.C., New Orleans, Hartford, Seattle, Los Angeles, and Broward County, Florida, have implemented their own versions of Compstat (Silverman, 1999).

16. Well-known field trials of the effectiveness of reformed police operations include the Kansas City preventive patrol experiment, the Newark foot patrol experiment, and the Minneapolis domestic violence experiment, among others (see Greene and Taylor, 1997; Cordner and Hale, 1992; Sherman, Berk, and Smith, 1992).

17. Comparing 1993 to 1994, murders went down sharply, from 1,936 to 1,561, an impressive one-year drop of nearly 20 percent. As for other violent crimes, reports of aggravated assaults dipped by 5 percent, robberies declined 16

percent, and rapes diminished by 5 percent. Complaints to the NYPD about property crimes also went down. Burglaries fell by 11 percent, motor vehicle thefts by 15 percent, and larcenies of all kinds by 11 percent, according to the NYPD's annual Complaints and Arrests report.

18. To maintain a single officer's round-the-clock presence at some visible post on the street throughout the year actually requires hiring at least six, and maybe as many as ten new recruits, when three shifts, vacations, sick leave, retraining, court appearances, and administrative duties are factored in (Bayley, 1993).

19. A parallel but broader indicator is enforcement strength, which includes officers on patrol plus plainclothes officers, detectives, undercover agents investigating mob activities or narcotics dealing, and their supervisors. Excluded from both indicators are all sworn officers assigned to executive, legal, inspection, planning, personnel, and training functions, and all civilian employees.

Since enforcement strength incorporates patrol strength, the two indicators are highly correlated and move up and down in tandem.

Patrol strength always has been used as the bellwether indicator of police visibility (Siegel, 1994). Enforcement strength was cited in the early 1990s by an NYPD report as "the most accurate measure" of police protection or presence (see CBC, 1997:22).

20. Unfortunately, the debate over the relevance of sheer size can't be pursued with data about these two indicators in the future. Starting with fiscal year 1997, the NYPD discontinued its publication of estimates of average daily patrol strength and enforcement strength and began to track a new statistic measuring police presence, called "operational strength." "Operational strength" counts uniformed personnel of all ranks who carry out patrol and enforcement duties. It includes officers working in Internal Affairs, the Detective Bureau, Organized Crime Control, Transit, and Housing as well as Patrol Services (see CBC, 1997).

21. Commissioner Bratton (1995) noted this anomaly in a speech but claimed that the NYPD should be credited for the decline in killings behind closed doors.

22. In 1970, 1.9 percent of all employed persons in New York City worked in occupations that the U.S. Census categorized as "protective service." By 1990, that figure had risen to 2.8 percent (an increase of 47 percent). The comparable work force proportions for the rest of the country were 1.2 percent in 1970 and 1.6 percent in 1990 (up 33 percent) (NYC Department of City Planning, 1992). The expansion over two decades probably reflected greater growth in the private sector than in the public sector, since the NYPD was about as large in 1970 as in 1990.

23. The two biggest supplementary forces were run by the New York City public school system, with nearly 2,900 sworn officers, and by the Port Authority of New York–New Jersey, with about 1,350 sworn officers to protect bridges, tunnels, and stations (some on the New Jersey side of the border) ("Strength in numbers," 1998).

24. Some of the "credit" for maintaining a law enforcement presence also must go to the surveillance cameras that have been installed over the last decade in many public spaces (such as streets, parks, bridges, highways, subway stations, and housing-project grounds) by the NYPD and on private property (like stores, lobbies, banks, and ATM machines) by security firms.

25. The clock starts running on response time when a 911 operator receives an emergency call, and stops running when the first officers arrive at the scene. Response time therefore is the sum of dispatch time and travel time (Roberts, 1994).

Over the years, NYPD spokesmen have blamed delays on traffic tie-ups, more time spent thoroughly handling each call, a flood of nonemergency calls to 911, and time lost in notifying dispatchers that they had arrived (see Serant and Marzulli, 1996; Citizens Budget Commission, 1997; and Cooper, 1999a).

Commissioner Safir suggested that the correct indicator to track was response time to "critical calls" (like "shots fired" or a robbery in progress), which are assigned a higher priority than other 911 calls (Ratish, 1997; Topousis, 1997). But response times to critical calls went up from 5.9 minutes in fiscal year 1997 (the first time this indicator was released to the public) to 6.1 minutes in fiscal 1998 and 6.3 in fiscal 1999, according to the annual Mayor's Management Reports.

26. Between 1978 and 1998, about 32,600 murders took place in New York and over 23,450 accused killers were taken into custody. Assuming for simplicity's sake that hardly any slayings were the work of serial killers, and that each victim was slain by just one attacker, that means that in twenty years about 8,660 killers were on the loose, if they remained in the City.

27. Back in the 1950s, when body counts remained below four hundred per year, clearance rates exceeded 85 percent (see Pooley, 1992).

28. The clearance rate for 1998 slipped to 87 percent, according to the NYPD's Complaints and Arrests annual report. By January 31, 2000, only 139 defendants had been charged with murder in the 274 homicides committed in Brooklyn during calendar year 1999, reflecting a clearance rate a little over 50 percent for thirteen months' worth of investigations (Hynes, 2000).

29. However, the NYPD did improve the way it solved cases along another dimension. A case is considered cleared if just one suspect is arrested, even if more than one perpetrator was involved. During the Compstat years, the NYPD solved cases "more thoroughly," in the sense that additional suspects were

apprehended in many cases that were already solved for record-keeping purposes by the arrest of the first defendant.

30. The excellent work of the NYPD's Cold Case Apprehension Squad contributed to the boosting of the homicide clearance rate. In fiscal 1998, it solved 93 of the old 244 cases it reopened. About 25 percent of the murders that were successfully closed were committed more than eight years earlier (MMR, 1998:14).

31. Some criminologists and police officials consider the term "zero tolerance" to be misleading to the public because it conjures up the image of strict enforcement of all laws at all times. In reality, officers always exercise discretion and do not automatically arrest all violators for minor breaches of the peace, even during a zero tolerance crackdown (Dixon, 1998).

32. Several years before the term "broken windows" was coined in 1982, the main arguments of this thesis, and many of the same examples of casual disregard for the law that were singled out in speeches by Mayor Giuliani and Commissioner Bratton almost twenty years later, were anticipated by a precinct captain in Manhattan (Rosenthal, 1997):

> I believe the erosion of the quality of life in our town began when our "system" demonstrated its inability to cope—not with murderers at the top of the scale but with the petty violators at the bottom. Once the word was out that the "system" could not and would not effectively deal with the graffiti artist, the drunk in the hallway, the aggressive panhandler, the neighbor with the blasting radio, the habitual peddler, the petty thief, the late-night noisemakers, the garbage picker, vandals, desecrators, public urinators, kids under 16, litterers, careless dog owners, and on and on . . . once that word was out, the seed was planted that has since blossomed into a full-grown disrespect for our laws.

33. Many New Yorkers, fed up with the revolting behavior of public nuisances and terrorized by violent predators, were willing to embrace a crackdown in the mid-1990s that was considered too controversial to even try out a decade earlier. During the Reagan years, the National Institute of Justice planned to sponsor tests of the effectiveness of a zero tolerance campaign against quality-of-life offenses in Newark and Houston. But when the office of the U.S. Attorney General reviewed the proposal, "His staff took one look at the idea of order maintenance and canceled the experiment. It was just too politically volatile even for a conservative Republican administration to deal with," according to "Broken Windows" theorist George Kelling (quoted in Nifong, 1997:11). The implementation of a pilot test had to be shelved until an adherent, William Bratton, was appointed chief of the Transit Police during the administration of Mayor David Dinkins.

34. However, during 1981, 1986, 1987, and perhaps 1991, this pattern did not hold. The correlation is not that strong.

35. This figure appears in the Division of Criminal Justice Services' "Crime and Justice Annual Report." It counts misdemeanor and felony arrests for both adults and juveniles, for nonfingerprintable infractions as well as fingerprintable offenses, and for violations of local ordinances for which summonses are issued. It excludes all arrests for what the FBI categorizes as serious Part One offenses— murder, rape, aggravated assault, robbery, burglary, motor vehicle theft, and larceny. Also, it does not include any traffic tickets for moving violations or illegal parking. Some of the more familiar categories within it are drug-law violations, weapons offenses, prostitution, gambling, possession of stolen property and of burglar tools, joyriding, criminal mischief, disorderly conduct, liquor-law violations, drunk driving, simple assault, and the relatively infrequent white-collar crimes of forgery, embezzlement, and fraud.

36. The grand total of Part II arrests and summonses set a record at over 750,000 in 1986 and 1987 before dwindling below 550,000 in 1990. After rising again through the early 1990s, the grand total reached 725,000 in 1994, but then dropped to about 625,000 in 1995 and 560,000 in 1996. In 1997, it bounced back to 650,000, according to the DCJS's Crime and Justice Annual Reports.

37. One former member of the SCU estimated that for every report the unit filed, they made thirty additional unrecorded stops (Dwyer, 1999).

The entire force filled out about 150,000 stop-and-frisk reports (UF250s in police parlance) during 1998, but the actual number of potentially hostile contacts with the public must have been much larger (Celona and Neuman, 1999b).

38. Street Crime Unit members reported that they felt under great pressure to meet an informal quota of at least one gun arrest and seizure per month. As a result, they found it necessary to "toss" many innocent young men who fit a crude profile until they caught one with a concealed handgun. Commissioner Safir credited the unit with making about 40 percent of all NYPD gun arrests (Kocieniewski, 1999). However, the detailed breakdown of types of arrests by different units indicated a figure of 18 percent (for felony-level dangerous weapons arrests), according to the 1998 Complaints and Arrests annual statistical report.

39. The average NYPD officer made seventeen arrests during 1996. That figure was a little less than the mean number of arrests per LAPD officer, and yet the once highly proactive police force in Los Angeles was reputed still to be in a defensive mode that year. In cities with overall crime rates about the same as in New York, the average numbers of arrests per officer that year were twenty-eight

in San Diego, thirty in San Jose, forty-eight in Virginia Beach, and sixteen in Pittsburgh. Thirty was the median number of arrests per officer per year in thirty-eight of the largest fifty cities that reported their arrest totals to the FBI's UCR, according to an analysis by the Independent Budget Office (1999: 30–31).

40. As far back as 1974, the Chicago Police Department confiscated almost three times as many firearms per 100,000 population as did the NYPD (Brill, 1977).

In 1993, the NYPD ranked last, with 47 firearms seized for every one hundred members of the department per year; the police in Phoenix (with 331 gun confiscations per one hundred) topped the list. The NYPD came in twenty-ninth out of thirty in terms of seizures compared to residents, with a ratio of 243 per 100,000 people; the Chicago PD led all the rest with 1,075 guns taken per 100,000. The NYPD also came in next to last in seizures per one hundred homicides, with 897 guns confiscated for every one hundred killings; Albuquerque came in first, with 8,333 per one hundred (Sherman and Bridgeforth, 1994; "Study of gun seizures," 1994; and Treaster, 1994b).

In 1994, the Chicago Police came in first, with 796 illegal guns taken away from every 100,000 residents; the NYPD seized 223 per 100,000. The NYPD also had the lowest ratio of gun seizures for every one hundred homicides, 1,049, while the leading department confiscated about five times as many. The NYPD was also dead last with just forty-one seizures per one hundred officers per year (Citizens Crime Commission, 1996).

41. In 1992, 7,242 felony arrests were made for possession of dangerous weapons (mostly handguns); in 1993, that number dropped by 2 percent to 7,103; it fell another 6 percent by the end of 1994 to 6,663, according to the NYPD's Complaints and Arrests annual reports.

In 1993, total gun arrests (including cases where illegal firearms possession was not the top [most serious] charge) added up to 12,076. But in 1994, that figure fell nearly 7 percent to 11,252 gun-related arrests, according to NYPD figures provided to the Citizens Crime Commission (1996).

42. Between January 1 and April 24, the NYPD made 1.5 percent fewer gun arrests than it did during that same time period in 1993. By June 23, gun arrests were down by 6.7 percent compared to that point in 1993. By the end of 1994, gun arrests were down 14.6 percent for the year, according to weekly Crime Complaint Comparison Reports for those dates during 1994.

43. The number of firearms seized by the NYPD after it adopted new strategies declined by 9 percent, from 12,953 guns confiscated in 1993 to 11,768 in 1994, according to an internal NYPD evaluation of the new anti-gun initiatives (Dunne, 1995).

Gun seizures also fell, according to other scattered reports. The department seized nearly 20,000 illegal guns during 1992, Commissioner Kelly (1993:19) reported. About 17,900 firearms were seized in 1993 (Sherman and Bridgeforth, 1994). A grand total of 14,861 firearms were confiscated during fiscal year 1995 (last half of 1994, first half of 1995), after a reporting gap of about six months. During fiscal year 1996, the number of seizures dropped by 15 percent to 12,631; seizures fell another 5 percent to 12,056 during fiscal 1997; and tumbled another 11 percent to 10,753 during fiscal 1998, according to figures in the Mayor's Management Reports for those years.

There usually is a close correspondence between the two variables, gun seizures and gun arrests, except when a single raid yields a large cache of illegal firearms. The number of guns seized depends on several factors, including the vigor and vigilance with which officers seek out concealed weapons, the prevalence or density of gun toting in public spaces and crime-ridden neighborhoods, state laws governing the rights of residents to go about their daily business armed, and departmental procedures that determine which seized guns should be counted. Many police departments do not even maintain records of how many illegal guns they confiscate (Sherman and Bridgeforth, 1994; Citizens Crime Commission, 1996).

44. Mayor Giuliani was disappointed by the data, according to Commissioner Bratton (1998:217):

[Jack] Maple tried to explain to the mayor that because of the success of our Gun Strategy, fewer people were carrying guns, and that the more we continued to pursue this strategy, the fewer gun arrests we could expect. "No!" he said, gritting his teeth. "This number goes *down* and this number goes *up!*" [Emphasis in the original.] Meaning, the higher the number of arrests, the lower the amount of crime.

This downward trend also puzzled a watchdog group (Citizens Crime Commission, 1996:66) that was undertaking an evaluation of the presumably improved anti-gun strategies: "We began this study with the assumption that in order to reduce gun crime it is necessary to make more gun arrests. In New York City, however, gun crime is down significantly and gun arrests are also down."

45. In 1972, Commissioner Patrick Murphy (quoted in Citizens Crime Commission, 1996:15) asserted that "the penalty for carrying a gun has become a joke.

46. From 1993 through 1998, shooting incidents (in which at least one person was either wounded or killed) fell 67 percent; shooting victims dropped 66 percent; and gun arrests (top charge) declined 65 percent, according to the 1998 year-end Compstat report.

47. Researchers who tracked over 100,000 prisoners released in 1983 found

that almost one-third had been arrested in a different state either before being imprisoned or within three years after being discharged (Bureau of Justice Statistics, 1992).

48. The same ounce of cocaine that sold for about $530 in the City reportedly could fetch as much as $1,500 in a small upstate city like Binghamton, where buyers were willing to pay premium prices, the risks of getting hurt or killed in a turf battle were much less, and the chances of getting caught were not as great (Marzulli, 1998c).

49. Off 24 percent, from 351 in 1996 to 267 in 1997.

50. Down 17 percent in two years, from 424 in 1994 to 351 in 1996.

51. Down 24 percent from 397 in 1996 to 300 during 1997.

52. As arrests plummeted from about 290,000 in 1991 to around 190,000 in 1995.

53. Declining 48 percent, from 1,094 in 1992 to 574 in 1997.

FOUR

Behind Bars?

Were the City's Troublemakers Shipped Upstate by a Tougher Criminal Justice System?

It took more than a decade of unbridled violence, but New York has found the formula for driving down crime.

The recipe—like most things seen in hindsight—sounds as simple as one-two-three:

More cops, more prisons, and more jail time for hardened criminals.

Toss in a dash of tighter parole and the New York recipe for fighting crime can work anywhere.

—*New York Post* criminal justice editor, Murray Weiss (1997a:18)

Many of the experts as well as pundits who believe that improved policing is largely responsible for the crime crash reserve the remaining amount of the credit for a presumably tougher criminal justice system. In fact, the argument that a reinvigorated NYPD has brought down the murder rate rested on the assumption that the City's prosecutors and judges followed through on the hundreds of thousands of arrests annually, to make sure that hard-core predators were taken out of circulation and deterred by stiff punishment from further wrongdoing.

If the City's criminal justice machinery suddenly became a much more effective means of social defense and formal control, then it could have had a substantial impact on how New Yorkers behaved toward each other. A sizable proportion of New York City's killers over the past two decades symbolically had put their neighbors on notice about their lawbreaking proclivities, as the data in chapter 2 revealed.

More than two-thirds of those charged with murder between 1978 and 1997 had criminal records (according to the database maintained in New York State; an even larger but unknown percentage must have been in trouble with the law in other states or in the foreign countries from which they emigrated). More than a quarter of them had previously been arrested for a felony; and about two-fifths had both a misdemeanor and felony arrest on their New York State rap sheet. Worse yet, almost one-half of all accused killers previously had been convicted of a crime; for one-third of them, the conviction was for a felony. Clearly, the majority of these accused murderers had previously passed through the criminal justice process. If they had been punished sufficiently for those earlier misdeeds—or were effectively helped by some court-ordered rehabilitation program—their victims might still be alive.[1]

The Bad Old Days: A Non-System on the Verge of Collapse?

At the start of the 1970s, the fear of becoming a crime victim began seriously to undermine the quality of life in "Fun City." Mayor John Lindsay appointed a blue ribbon commission to carry out the first comprehensive study of how effective the City's police, courts, and jails really were. Its disturbing findings were that law enforcement was not stemming the rising tide of street crime, and that the administration of justice was often unfair. Furthermore, even a beefed-up criminal justice system could never single-handedly quell crime, according to the mayor's Criminal Justice Coordinating Council (1971:27):

> Public discussion of the crime problem in the past has dwelt almost solely on the imagined need for more police and more "toughness." Such facile simplifications may be psychologically reassuring or politically profitable for those who advance them. But they could not be more misleading. When the courts cannot try accused criminals, when prisons reinforce criminality, when delinquent youths go unhelped, when addicts are not treated, and when criminal law is used, often arbitrarily, to deal with almost every question of social and political conduct, then 100,000 of the world's most efficient police would accomplish nothing except to temporarily pack City jails. That is the situation today [in New York City].

As the 1970s unfolded, conservative "hardliners" denounced these "liberal" views as being unrealistically "soft on crime." A "law and order" movement arose, encouraged by President Richard Nixon (before his near-impeachment because of illegal activities exposed by the investigations surrounding the Watergate break-in). It gained adherents as a backlash against anti-war protests, student demonstrations, ghetto rebellions, and a rising tide of street crime. Whenever highly politicized debates broke out about how to solve the crime problem, hardliners indicted the legal system for "coddling criminals" instead of cracking down on them (see, for example, "Revolving door justice," 1976; Glenn, 1976). Pervasive "permissiveness" (unwarranted leniency) so infected the criminal justice process that vicious predators often got off with a mere "slap on the wrist." A "revolving door" of justice enabled crooks to saunter back to the streets more quickly than cops could return to their beats. Too many arrestees routinely were released on bail, when they should have been detained in jail to prevent them from carrying out any further mayhem. New restrictions mandated by landmark Supreme Court decisions in the 1960s under Chief Justice Earl Warren (like *Mapp v. Ohio* in 1961 and *Miranda v. Arizona* in 1966) "handcuffed" police officers and detectives, hampering their ability to find corroborating evidence or extract confessions. Furthermore, these rulings from on high caused crucial evidence to be thrown out of court on some "technicality" because of the Exclusionary Rule, which stipulated that improperly obtained evidence cannot be presented at trials. Prosecutors, overwhelmed by too many cases, screened out some that looked weak but might have been won. They disposed of the rest via plea bargaining, in which leniency was offered in order to induce defendants to admit guilt to greatly reduced charges that carried mild punishments at most: suspended sentences, probation, fines, maybe community service. Unduly forgiving judges imposed the lightest possible sentences. As a result, many hard-core offenders were confined only briefly in county jails for misdemeanors when actually they had committed felonies that merited hard time in state prisons. Those who were imprisoned usually were let out by parole boards as soon as they were eligible, after serving only the minimum time prescribed by law; few habitual criminals were kept locked up until they maxed out. Prison authorities were all-too willing to take pro-rehabilitation chances at the expense of public safety, and permitted inmates to walk out the front gates on a furlough or release program to work, study, or visit their old neighborhoods. Teenagers who carried out acts as ruthless and brutal as those of adults were treated with kid gloves in a treatment-oriented juvenile justice system that at worst sent them away for very brief stints at reform schools, hardliners complained.[2]

Logically, the components of an effective criminal justice system—law enforcement, prosecution, judiciary, and corrections—should mesh together smoothly like the gears of a watch when processing cases. But in the 1970s, New York City's police, courts, and jails were depicted in the media and in political campaigns as a "non-system," uncoordinated, overburdened, and on the verge of breaking down (see Campbell, Sahid, and Stang, 1970). During the gloomy days of the fiscal crisis in the middle of the decade, Mayor Beame was urged to appoint a criminal justice coordinator to stave off an "imminent collapse" of the legal system ("Goodman demands Beame act," 1976). The first person to serve as the deputy mayor for criminal justice, Nicholas Scoppetta, readily conceded that "there was no system—just a great hodgepodge of people running around in the dark bumping into each other" (quoted in Harris, 1977:15). This pessimistic theme was echoed by other top municipal officials. NYPD commissioner Michael Codd asserted that criminals struck repeatedly because they believed that they faced very low risks of being incarcerated if they ever got caught. Chief administrative judge of the court system, David Ross, complained that backlogs and delays in holding trials undermined convictions and stiff sentences. Corrections commissioner Benjamin Malcolm conceded that prisoners were merely warehoused and not really rehabilitated while confined in the City's jails. Manhattan district attorney Robert Morgenthau noted bitterly that insufficient resources forced prosecutors to completely drop or greatly reduce charges against many of the defendants arrested for serious felonies (Harris, 1977). Bronx district attorney Mario Merola reluctantly defended the triage situation that necessitated weeding out cases involving minor quality-of-life violations, by declaring (quoted in Cook, 1978:15), "We're cutting out the garbage cases, going for the major offenses, the repeat criminals."[3] Because of all these weaknesses, limitations, and operational shortcomings, only about 4 percent of those arrested for violent crimes in the City wound up in prison, and only 30 percent of all murderers spent more than ten years behind bars, according to a state senate report (Patterson, 1978).

As the 1980s began, the ineffectiveness of the legal system was underscored by the findings of a study that projected that only one percent of New York City criminals who committed felonies ended up serving time upstate. Of those who did, most were confined for less than two years (see McGuire, 1980; Van Doorn, Ross, and Pelleck, 1980). NYPD commissioner McGuire (quoted in Rosenblatt, 1981:28) concluded in exasperation that "the criminal justice system almost creates incentives for street criminals." Mayor Ed Koch lamented that offenders faced little likelihood of being caught and punished, and made cracking down on crime a major theme in his campaign for reelection (Castillo, 1980). It certainly looked like the bad guys were winning the war on crime by overrunning the City's defenses, a crime reporter (Pileggi, 1981a:25) despaired: "The brutal truth about crime in New York is that the police, the courts, and the prison system have given up. . . . Criminals abound, and there are simply not enough cops to catch them, not enough prosecutors to charge them, not enough courtrooms in which to try them, and not enough jails to hold them."

Despite the overcrowding crisis, parole—a century-old mechanism for managing the size of prison populations—came under sharp attack whenever ex-convicts committed vicious new crimes. A panel appointed by Governor Hugh Carey called for a shift from indeterminate sentences with a chance for parole to determinate sentences with no possibility of early release, a reform that would strip the state parole board of its primary function. The Board found itself "fighting for its life, fending off attacks not only from the public but also from other members of the criminal justice system" (Basler, 1980).[4]

Whether to build additional cellblocks and open new facilities or to experiment with more alternatives to incarceration became the subject of a fierce debate (Kihss, 1980). The Citizens Crime Commission of New York weighed in on the get-tough side, arguing that (quoted in Rosenblatt, 1981:28),

Unless we make the punishment for serious crime more certain and more appropriate, we cannot expect any respite from the violence now engulfing the city. Any criminal justice system where one murder case in ten results in a murder conviction, where one arrested robber in six and one arrested burglar in twenty receives a prison sentence of even one year, is not a system where the punishment is certain and appropriate and consequently can do little to control crime.

The advocates of locking up more people for longer periods of time believed that this formula would cut the crime rate for a number of reasons: according to the doctrine of specific deterrence, the deprivations accompanying confinement teach inmates a lesson so they don't break laws again. The theory of general deterrence proposes that prisoners become negative role models whose plight serves as a warning to others contemplating the same acts. Imprisonment also accomplishes the function of incapacitation, removing predators from circulation and thereby averting future depredations against their intended prey. Furthermore, imposing years of suffering—just deserts—in an institutionalized way satisfies any vigilante impulses victims might harbor and quenches the public's thirst for retribution. Finally, restricting the activities of otherwise out-of-control individuals forces them to calm down and sample opportunities for rehabilitation (see Methvin, 1992; Bennett, DiIulio, and Walters, 1996; and DiIulio, 1996). Furthermore, common sense suggests that the streets would be a lot more dangerous than they already are if prison gates suddenly sprung open and large numbers of inmates escaped from confinement.[5] Therefore, conventional wisdom fosters the belief that the crime rate could be substantially reduced if an even greater number of incorrigible predators were locked away behind walls and bars for longer periods of time.

The rhetoric of cracking down and tightening up has dominated discussions about criminal justice policy for three decades. But how harsh has the system become, really? Is there any evidence that offenders paid a higher price for committing crimes in New York City during the crime crash years?

Lock-'Em-Up and Throw Away the Key?

There is no shortage of alternative explanations for the drop in crime both nationally and in New York. . . . But it's impossible to ignore the fact that America's prisons also are bursting. . . . A trend . . . is clear: The more felons there are behind bars, the fewer there are on the streets to mug and

murder the rest of us. . . . Full prisons help make for safe streets, and New
York has the statistics to prove it.

—Editors, *New York Daily News*, 1999

New York's justice apparatus certainly did get tougher according to one
measure: the number of felons kept under lock and key in upstate prisons. Several decades of high crime rates coupled with demands for
harsher handling brought about an expanded prison system filled beyond
its official capacity. The inmate population skyrocketed to over 70,700
by 1998. It more than tripled in size since the late 1970s, as is depicted
by the top line in graph 4.1.[6] Even when population growth is taken into
account, the results remain the same: the imprisonment rate has soared
to new heights (384 inmates for every 100,000 state residents, by 1998;
see Gilliard, 1999).

Furthermore, the imprisonment rate understates the actual degree to
which the City's known troublemakers are kept under lock and key. The
ratio is calculated by taking the number of people behind bars in all the
state's facilities plus those in federal prisons as the numerator; and by

Graph 4.1. Relationship between Incarceration and Murders,
New York City, 1978–1998

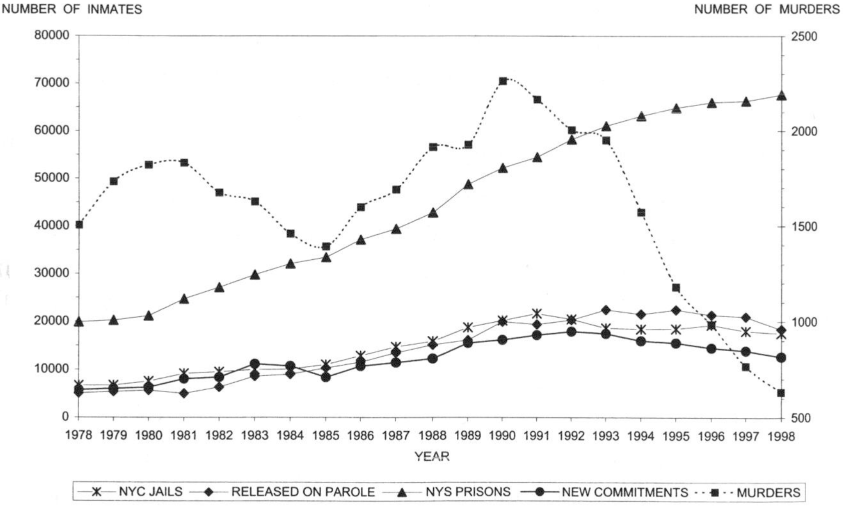

NUMBER OF INMATES

NUMBER OF MURDERS

YEAR

| —✕— NYC JAILS | —◆— RELEASED ON PAROLE | —▲— NYS PRISONS | —●— NEW COMMITMENTS | · · ■ · · MURDERS |

Note: NYS prisoner population counts federal as well as state inmates but excludes all female prisoners (about 5%
of total).
Sources: NYC Deptartment of Corrections; NYS Deptartment of Correctional Services; NYS DCJS.

using the census estimate of the whole state's population as the denominator. In this calculation, the numerator is artificially deflated by excluding persons held in jails for less than a year. And the denominator is unrealistically inflated by including groups whose members are rarely confined, such as boys, elderly men, and women of all ages. A more accurate estimate of the government's true reliance on incarceration would focus exclusively on the situation in New York City, where the crime problem is much worse than in the smaller cities and the rural and suburban counties of the rest of the state. (During a typical year, felons from the five boroughs constitute about two-thirds of all prisoners confined in the state's sixty-nine penal institutions, according to the NYS DCJS's annual reports.) To fine-tune this estimate of the real incarceration rate, add the male inmate population in the City's jails to the men from City neighborhoods confined in penitentiaries upstate, and divide that numerator by a figure representing the ranks of those actually at risk of being locked up: the number of male residents between the ages of eighteen and sixty-four living within the five boroughs.

Computations that follow this formula yield startling figures (table 4.1). A record-setting number of men (more than 61,000), and an unprecedented proportion (almost 2.7 percent) of the City's male population between the ages of eighteen and sixty-four were behind bars on a typical day, as shown in the bottom row. As always, race and ethnicity (to a large extent a proxy for social class) must be taken into account, since involvement in criminal activities is not the same for all groups, and since justice is not color-blind. Taking apart this overall incarceration rate reveals troubling disparities: on an average day, nearly 6 percent of the City's black men between the ages of eighteen and sixty-four were in a City jail or a state prison, along with over 3 percent of Hispanic men, just under one percent of white men, and less than one-half of one percent of Asian men of that age group, as is revealed in the last column in table 4.1.[7]

Comparable calculations estimating the number of African Americans under the control of the legal system in other cities have provoked grave concerns about the consequences of removing and stigmatizing such large proportions of a community's men, and touched off sharp political debates about reforming drug laws and sentencing policies (see J. Miller, 1996; Lotke, 1997).[8] Advocates of imprisonment conceded that it was a

Table 4.1. Estimated Number of New York City Men Incarcerated
on an Average Day in 1997

Group	In Jail	In Prison	Total Inmates	Rate per 100,000
Black men	9,070	22,575	31,645	5,981
Hispanic men	5,670	14,900	20,570	3,260
White men	1,135	7,225	8,360	938
Asian men	325	730	1,055	414
All men	16,200	45,150	61,350	2,664

Notes: Rates are per 100,000 men of each group between the ages of eighteen and sixty-four residing within the City. The state prison population does not add up due to rounding errors.
Sources: Jail populations = NYC DOC website. Prison populations = DCJS annual reports. Population estimates: NYC Department of City Planning projections.

sad commentary on the state of American society in the 1990s that so many marginalized men had to be locked up in order to make the streets safer in their own poverty-stricken communities. But they insisted that the data demonstrated that a willingness to incapacitate known trouble-makers could bring about substantial relief (see Becker, 1998). Critics of such a heavy reliance on imprisonment rejected the argument that this trade-off was an inevitable price that had to be paid in order to enhance public safety. They viewed these statistics as evidence of mistaken priori-ties: those in power were all too willing to incur huge economic and so-cial costs to isolate large numbers of minority men from the rest of soci-ety for long periods of time, when instead more resources could be in-vested in preventive social programs to head off criminality (see Massing, 1996; and J. Miller, 1996). As the editors of the *New York Times* (1996a) argued, these figures "should set off alarm bells from the White House to city halls—and help reverse the notion that we can incarcerate our way out of fundamental problems."[9]

But was crime really way down because imprisonment was way up?

Do the Crime, Do the Time—Or Beat the Rap?

A new report by the U.S. Department of Justice provides data to prove conventional wisdom correct: Tougher sentencing laws are resulting in more inmates spending more time behind bars. . . .

Already the poor-little-prisoners contingent is making noises. Try as it might, it cannot seem to see any correlation among harsher sentences, reduced parole and the declining crime rate. These are the same sort of people who would not be able to see a correlation between a rotting fish and a bad odor. Pure coincidence they would say. . . .

The general public—lacking as it does "expertise" in criminology and sociology—generally has a better sense of smell than the experts. That probably comes from being whacked upside the head by a violent felon out on parole.

—Editors, *New York Daily News*, 1999

According to the advocates of incarceration, the increase in the number of felons serving hard time in state prisons brought about the drop in the crime rate. But several inconvenient facts cast doubt on their contention that the two variables are closely linked in an inverse relationship.

First of all, the alleged correlation holds only for certain stretches of time in the last two decades but not others, as graph 4.1 makes clear. The number of inmates has been growing steadily ever since the early 1970s, but the volume of reported crime has not been shrinking constantly. Only in the early 1980s and again during the 1990s did this anticipated inverse relationship materialize between rising prison populations and falling crime rates, and murder rates in particular. However, during the late 1970s and again in the late 1980s, crime rates went up despite spurts in inmate populations. Why didn't the rapid expansion of the prison system prevent the rising tide of violence during those two time periods? To infer a causal relationship from a correlation that held for certain years (the 1990s but not the 1980s) is a common mistake that can be avoided by looking at a longer period of history (in this instance, the two cycles of rising and falling crime rates since 1978) (see Mauer, 1999).[10]

Second, even though New York State enjoyed the most dramatic decline in crime, it did not rely more heavily on incarceration than other jurisdictions. Despite the surge of new prison construction in New York State under Governor Mario Cuomo during the 1980s, other states were much quicker to lock up their inhabitants. New York did not have the highest imprisonment rate per 100,000 residents; in fact, it didn't even rank within the top ten states. Furthermore, the rate of increase in inmates during the mid-1990s, just when crime rates really started tumbling, barely climbed compared to most other states (see Gilliard and Beck, 1998).[11]

Third, even though the state prison population shot way up, the jail population did not grow. In fact, contrary to projections, it shrank during the 1990s. Despite the surge in arrests, the number of detainees and misdemeanants confined in City jails has declined since peaking in 1991 (see the middle line in graph 4.1).[12] Even though the municipal jail system processed a record number of admissions in 1997, these inmates did not stay behind bars awaiting trial, or if convicted, awaiting transportation upstate to their new homes, for as many days as in earlier years.[13] One likely reason for a shortened average length of stay was the lighter sentences imposed by judges on misdemeanants convicted of very minor quality-of-life infractions. It would be difficult to argue that very brief periods of confinement—which have been disparaged for decades by hardliners as evidence of a "revolving door of justice" that merely doled out "slaps on the wrist" to offenders who deserved to suffer much more—suddenly became credible deterrents and an effective means of incapacitation during the Compstat years.

Fourth, corrections officials on the state and local levels have never claimed that more effective drug and alcohol treatment, remedial education, and job training became available in their prisons and jails to rehabilitate a growing share of inmates and substantially reduce their recidivism rates. On the contrary, tight budgets and public pressures to strip away amenities and impose austere "no-frills" environments have forced wardens to cut back many of these supportive services. So why should the old practice of warehousing wrongdoers be presumed to be working unusually well as either a deterrent or a means of rehabilitation in New York State during the 1990s?[14]

Fifth, no claims have been made by the NYPD, the five district attorneys, or parole officials that somehow, during the mid-1990s, they suddenly became adept at identifying who the high-rate offenders of the future would be, and were able to convict these career criminals on serious charges in order to keep them out of circulation longer.[15] A policy of selective incapacitation of highly active robbers, burglars, and other predators holds out much more promise than mere collective incapacitation of a mixed catch of high-rate, medium-rate, and low-rate offenders (see Chaiken and Chaiken, 1991). In fact, the main reason for the expansion of the ranks of inmates has been a growing willingness of prosecutors and judges to unselectively lock up low-level drug sellers and even chronic abusers. These "drug-only" convicts are behind bars solely for the offense of taking part in a forbidden exchange between consenting parties of a controlled substance for money, and may not have any prior history of violence. The public safety payoff from this emphasis on quantity over quality in incarceration may have reached a point of diminishing returns that justifies a policy of zero prison growth (DiIulio, 1999).[16]

The population in New York's state penitentiaries reached new heights by the end of the century for an additional reason besides the stepped-up war on drugs: Parole boards became tougher. Inmates seeking parole for the first time were granted early release by members of the state board at a rate of 67 percent in 1991, and 64 percent in 1995, but only 47 percent by 1999. Also, violations of conditions of parole that might have been overlooked in the past were taken more seriously as the 1990s wore on, and led to more revocation hearings and reimprisonment. In addition, the state legislature passed a sweeping restriction on parole eligibility proposed by Governor George Pataki in 1995. The new state law required all inmates convicted of a second violent felony to serve at least 85 percent of their sentences before becoming eligible for time-off for good behavior. In 1998, the state legislature passed Jenna's Law, which mandated that even first-time violent felons must serve at least 85 percent of their terms (see Butterfield, 1997c; Editors, *New York Post*, 1998b; Perez-Pena, 1999; and Sullivan, 2000). However, by retaining the possibility of early parole release for property and drug offenses (the reasons almost half of all prisoners were incarcerated), New York did not drift as far in the direction of toughness as did fourteen other states, which abolished parole entirely and imposed the 85 percent rule on all inmates. Furthermore, the provisions eliminating early parole for violent offenders imposed in 1995 and 1998 did not apply retroactively, so the effects of these restrictions would not be felt for several years and therefore did not materialize in time to help to trigger the crash, as graph 4.1 reveals. In fact, the New York State Division of Parole released a record number of felons hardened by their experiences behind bars back onto the streets in 1993, right before the drop in crime gathered momentum starting in 1994. Equally large numbers of convicts at high risk for recidivism were let go by parole boards during the rest of the mid-1990s. The flow of parolees from upstate penitentiaries back to hard-pressed City neighborhoods (and to communities across the rest of the state) showed no real let-up until 1998.

Another way to evaluate the degree of the criminal justice system's toughness is to examine the outcomes of all the felony arrests accomplished annually by the NYPD. How many of these alleged felons wound up behind prison walls over the years? Hardliners have argued over and over again that felony arrests were of little deterrent or incapacitative value if defendants weren't indicted, convicted, and shipped upstate to serve hard time (as opposed to brief jail sentences, probation, conditional release, suspended sentences, community service, fines, and other lesser sanctions). Therefore, in addition to the clearance rate, three additional measures of the legal system's toughness in handling cases involving serious charges are the indictment rate, the felony conviction rate (excluding misdemeanor convictions for minor offenses), and the imprisonment rate (excluding confinement in Rikers Island jails for up to one year for misdemeanors). All three indicators are influenced by the quality of the NYPD's arrests and the skillfulness of the assistant district attorneys prosecuting these cases in behalf of the county's government. If indictment rates, conviction rates, and imprisonment rates all rose, the City's criminal justice system was getting tougher across the board on accused lawbreakers. But that was not what happened, according to the changes over time plotted in graph 4.2.

Looking at the first indicator, the felony indictment rate, greater toughness would be signaled by growth in the percentage of felony cases sent to upper (i.e., New York State Supreme) court. Throughout the 1980s, the system did indeed get tougher, in terms of pursuing a greater proportion of felony arrestees, according to data assembled by the NYS DCJS (see the top line in graph 4.2). But just as the volume of serious cases began to ease up during the early 1990s, the indictment rate started to fall. One explanation was that prosecutors in each borough's district attorney's office deemed many more of the felony arrests to be flawed. Instead of bringing these felony arrests before a grand jury for indictment, assistant district attorneys screened them out or accepted negotiated pleas to lesser charges for a number of reasons, including insufficient proof or improperly obtained evidence. Judges also dismissed charges against arrestees for these same reasons. If the quality of felony arrests prepared by the NYPD declined, pressures on officers and detectives to make more arrests during the Compstat years might have been to blame. But Commissioner Safir denied that arrest quality had deteriorated, and

Graph 4.2. Relationship between Court Processing of Felony Arrests
and Murders, New York City, 1978–1998

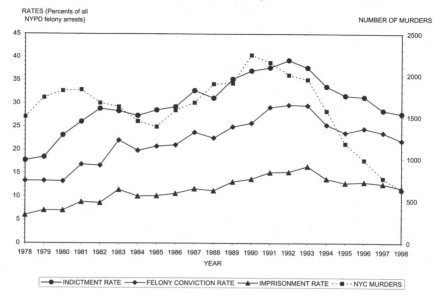

Note: Indictments = includes SCI's; Felony Convictions = excludes misdemeanors; Imprisonment = excludes jail.
Source: Data posted on the NYS DCJS web site, 2000; DCJS annual reports, 1978–1980.

insisted instead that the problem was located within the five district attorneys' staffs of lawyers, who failed to follow through on cases that
NYPD officials believed were winnable in court (Rohde, 1999). Whatever the reason, the felony indictment rate has been falling, not rising,
since 1992, even though caseloads have been dropping. Note that even
during the year when the system was "toughest," less than 40 percent of
all felony arrestees were indicted on serious charges that potentially
could have landed them in prison.

A system growing tougher would be gaining felony convictions (as
opposed to mere misdemeanor convictions) against an increasing number of indicted defendants, whether through guilty pleas via negotiations
or verdicts at trials. Plotting the felony conviction rate in upper courts
(where guilty verdicts could result in lengthy prison sentences) reveals
another surprise (see the middle line in graph 4.2). Just like the felony
indictment rate, this indicator of toughness had been rising since the
start of the 1980s. Convictions for felonies reached a peak in 1993, and

then trailed off in the mid-1990s. In other words, even though the NYPD "solved" a greater fraction of cases during the Compstat years, the police version of events usually did not prevail in court. In the mid-1990s, less than 25 percent of all persons accused by detectives of having committed serious offenses were found guilty of a felony after a trial, or pleaded guilty to a felony charge after negotiations. Some accused felons were found guilty only of misdemeanors and merely received jail time, probation, community service, a suspended sentence, and/or a monetary fine, at worst; others were not punished at all (other than the time that those too poor to make bail spent detained in jail while awaiting disposition).

An increasingly tough justice system would be shipping a larger share of convicted felons upstate than in previous years, when leniency prevailed in the form of suspended sentences, fines, community service, probation, or just short-term jail time. Imprisonment in state penitentiaries for years and years is what hard-liners clamor for; confinement on Rikers Island for less than a year is scoffed at as a mere "slap on the wrist" that sends the wrong message to hard-core troublemakers. But when imprisonment rates are graphed on the same axes as grand jury indictments and upper court convictions, another finding that undermines the "toughness" thesis materializes (see the bottom line in graph 4.2). Imprisonment rates rose fairly steadily throughout the 1980s until 1993. But then, contrary to widespread public impressions, the fraction of felony arrestees that received harsh sentences did not rise, but instead declined. Note that even in the system's "toughest" year, 1993, a mere 16 percent of all the people arrested for serious offenses—and just 55 percent of all convicted felons—were sent upstate for more than one year.

Therefore, these three indicators of toughness expose an unexpected development: a less overtaxed system was easing up, not cracking down, on arrestees accused of serious offenses at the same time that crime was crashing. During the mid-1990s (as in the City's past, and as in the nation as a whole) large numbers of people committed very serious crimes; the majority of these perpetrators did not get into legal trouble either because their victims did not report these incidents to the police or because the NYPD could not solve the felonies brought to their attention by complainants; the majority of suspects unfortunate enough to get arrested on serious charges were not even indicted, much less convicted;

and only about one-half of the convicted felons who faced stiff prison sentences actually were shipped off to state institutions.

This attrition that takes place during case processing has been called "shrinkage" or "funneling" (see Silberman, 1978; Walker, 1998) and is best pictured as a leaky fishing net. In this analogy, many suspects are swept up in the police dragnet. Truly innocent persons who were falsely accused hopefully are rescued and weeded out of the assembly line in the nick of time, before they are unjustly punished for crimes they did not commit. But factually guilty individuals also wiggle free through escape hatches and loopholes designed to protect the innocent and to keep governmental authority in check. The big losers in the adversary system are the relatively small number of offenders enmeshed like residue at the bottom of the strainer or leaky net. This imagery serves as a valuable reminder that the proportion of reported crimes that are "solved"—as far as the police are concerned—by arrest is not a true measure of the legal system's crime-fighting efficiency. The clearance rate is really just a starting point, an indicator of inputs but not of outcomes. By the time the system has finished digesting and "disposing of" the batch of felony arrests carried out each year, the percentage of convicts receiving the maximum penalties permitted by law has always been whittled down dramatically.

In conclusion, not much had changed and very little had improved. The City's unwieldy criminal justice apparatus had not suddenly and magically transformed itself into a powerful, lean and mean crime-fighting machine that some people assumed it to be. The stern rhetoric that dominated public discussions apparently did not influence case processing during the Compstat years. Actually, just the opposite took place: indictment, conviction, and imprisonment rates fell back to levels formerly denounced as reflecting "leniency" and inefficiency. The preponderance of the evidence—all the other measures except for the all-time high in the prison population—demonstrates that a retreat from toughness took place just when crime rates dwindled.

Notes

1. Since no particular crime (for example, aggravated assault or robbery) has been discovered by criminologists to be a reliable predictor of future homicidal

behavior, the following analysis will focus on arrests for felonies of all kinds, including burglary, car stealing, and drug selling.

2. Many of these arguments had been advanced for decades. Back in 1922, when 260 murders were carried out, the editors of the *New York Daily News* called for a tougher system (quoted in Maeder, 1999): "Our system is lacking in the three great essentials of law enforcement: celerity, certainty, and finality. . . . We shall be endangered and disgraced by the prevalence of crime until the apprehension and punishment of criminals are swift, certain, and conclusive."

3. During the Compstat years, the flood of "garbage cases" (retitled "quality-of-life offenses") overwhelmed the City's criminal court system, where misdemeanor cases are resolved and felony cases begin the process of adjudication (which is completed in State Supreme Court). Minor cases were disposed of in mere minutes in a cursory manner, resulting in light penalties and eroding respect for the judicial process. One out of every three cases was dismissed, and in nearly half of all misdemeanor convictions, judges imposed no jail time in 1995 (Gearty and Chang, 1996). The harried seventy-seven lower-court judges had crushing work loads of about 3,500 cases per judge per annum in 1998. Defendants, victims, and witnesses had to return to court over and over again. Discouraged victims often eventually gave up, and many cases were dismissed because the deadline for holding a "speedy" trial had passed (Rohde, 1999).

4. The parole system was still under attack in 1999. Governor Pataki, Mayor Giuliani, and Commissioner Safir called upon the state legislature to enact flat sentences and abolish parole (and also to limit "good time" reductions to trim prison sentences by no more than 15 percent). An NYPD study revealed that around 3 percent of the suspects arrested for murder were parolees, as were about 7 percent of those arrested for robbery, rape, felonious assault, and burglary during 1996 (Weiss, 1996). Of the fourteen police officers slain in the line of duty between 1994 and 1998, five were killed by parolees (MMR, 1998:18). Since the 1970s, parole had been abolished in fifteen states and in the federal system; in New York, parole was eliminated only for inmates convicted of violent felonies (Perez-Pena, 1999).

5. About one thousand state prison escapees who bolted from work release programs roamed the metropolitan area on an average day in 1993 (Editors, *New York Daily News*, 1993).

6. But it would be a mistake to assume that prison populations have been growing constantly in tandem with crime rates. For example, the inmate population in New York's state prisons dropped 37 percent from 19,860 in 1964 to 12,444 in 1973 (NYS DOCS, 1974:7), even though crime rates surged during this time period. The predominant philosophy at the time was that incarceration should be used only as a last resort, not as the default option in sentencing.

7. At the end of 1997, there were about 69,500 inmates in state and federal facilities. Of these, about 66,400 were men (see Gilliard and Beck, 1998). About 68 percent, roughly 45,150, were from New York City. Just a few percent were less than eighteen or more than sixty-four years old.

The average daily population of the sixteen New York City jails (ten of them on Rikers Island, plus one in each borough) approached 18,000, of whom about 16,200 were men, and nearly all were younger than sixty-five, according to the NYC DOC.

About 2,302,570 men between the ages of eighteen and sixty-four were City residents in 1997, according to calculations from projections made by the NYC Department of City Planning (1995) based on 1990 Census data.

Therefore, the total incarceration rate (counting jail as well as prison inmates) for adult males residing in New York City was 2,664 men for every 100,000 New York City males between the ages of eighteen and sixty-four {(45,150) + (16,200)} / (2,302,570).

The incarceration rate for black and Hispanic adult male New Yorkers was much higher because of their disproportionate involvement in street crime. In the state prisons, 50 percent of all inmates were black, 33 percent were of Hispanic origin, 16 percent were white, and less than 2 percent were of Asian descent, according to NYS DOCS records cited in the 1997 DCJS annual report. Of all jail inmates, approximately 56 percent were black, 35 percent were Hispanic, 7 percent were white, and about 2 percent were Asians in 1997, according to the NYC DOC Web page. Therefore, the incarceration rate for each group of men in 1997 varied dramatically, from nearly 6 percent to less than 0.5 percent.

8. On an average day in 1992, 15 percent of all African American males between the ages of eighteen and thirty-five living in Washington were confined in a District of Columbia jail or prison or a federal facility. Adding in those on probation or parole, plus those out on bail or being sought on arrest warrants, the percentage rose to 42 percent. By 1997, the estimate of those under direct custody dropped to 10 percent, but the total proportion under control of D.C.'s criminal justice system in one way or another shot up to 50 percent (see Lotke, 1997).

9. Spending on the state prison system grew by $761 million over the period 1988–1998, at the same time that the legislature in Albany slashed funding for SUNY and CUNY colleges by $615 million. This dollar-for-dollar shift in priorities sharply increased the number of black and Hispanic prisoners (often confined for drug offenses) and held down the number of black and Hispanic college graduates (Gangi and Schiraldi, 1999).

10. The NYS Department of Correctional Services projected that the prison population would reach 75,000 inmates by the year 2002 (Perez-Pena, 1998).

11. For example, Texas had twice as many inmates and had an imprisonment rate per 100,000 residents that was about twice that of New York State in 1997. Texas's five-year growth rate was 75 percent, the third highest in the country. New York State's was 13 percent, the third lowest of the fifty states (Gilliard and Beck, 1998).

12. In 1990, NYC correction commissioner Alan Sielaff's office anticipated that the jail population would skyrocket to over 33,000 by 1995 (Mooney, 1990). Actually, the record was set in May, 1991, when 22,615 people were confined in the aftermath of anti-drug sweeps by the NYPD's Tactical Narcotics Teams. In the mid-1990s, the Giuliani administration reduced total capacity by selling two barges anchored at Rikers Island and two other overflow facilities. On certain days during the mid-1990s, the jails were packed to 100 percent capacity (around 20,000 beds), while the overcrowded state prison system was bursting at 130 percent capacity (Mooney, 1996a, 1996b).

13. A record 133,000 admissions to the jail system took place in 1997. (However, some unknown percentage of these people were arrested over and over again and went in and out of jail several times during the calendar year.) The average length of stay actually declined that year, due to an influx of a greater proportion of quickly processed misdemeanants and fewer felons, as well as more efficient management of the City's facilities by Correction Commissioner Michael Jacobson.

14. Drug abusers placed on probation did not get in trouble if they failed to enroll in treatment programs, as the department had pledged they would, according to a study by the City Comptroller's office (Flynn, 1999c).

15. In 1981, the NYPD and the Manhattan district attorney's office set up a task force to identify, convict, and imprison career criminals who otherwise might slip out of the system without being incarcerated. The program reportedly was a success: of 1,100 chronic offenders under scrutiny, 60 percent were arrested and 90 percent of them were convicted and locked up within the first nine months (Reppetto, 1981).

16. The number of people sent to prison for drug offenses, mostly (75 percent) selling, soared during the 1980s, especially from 1985 to 1990, and then largely leveled off in the 1990s. About 45 percent of all new commitments to prison were for drug selling or possessing during the 1990s. Roughly one-third of all inmates currently are serving time for drug offenses (see NYS DCJS annual reports).

FIVE

The Drug-Crime Connection

Were More New Yorkers Just Saying "No!" to Drugs and Drinking?

New York's drug problem has made the local crime problem much worse in a number of ways: smugglers, wholesalers, sellers, and buyers of controlled substances often resort to force to settle their business disputes; intoxicated users may behave out of character and carry out acts of violence or theft that they would not have perpetrated if they were sober; and addicts desperate for cash to buy more drugs may steal and rob (see Goldstein, 1985; Currie, 1993). In addition, hundreds of thousands of City residents, from casual experimenters to hard-core addicts, are periodically guilty of possessing controlled substances before consuming them, and therefore are technically criminals by definition—and are treated as such by the police and the courts if they are caught.[1]

Many of the City's murders since the 1970s can be categorized as drug related, depending on the criteria used for classification purposes and on the degree of detailed information preserved in the sources of the data, including detectives' case files, prosecutors' indictments, trial transcripts, presentence investigation reports, or the comprehensive records about inmates maintained by state prison administrations for use in case of an emergency (see Spunt et al., 1993).[2] For example, during 1988, as many as half of all homicides in New York could be classified as drug related in one way or another (drug-induced excitable behavior, desperation for cash to pay for drugs, quarrels within the trade); of that half, about three-fourths were outgrowths of conflicts connected to buying or selling; and of these instrumental acts of lethal violence, about two-thirds were over crack rather than cocaine powder, heroin, marijuana, or some other controlled substance. Lives were lost mainly in struggles to stake out territory, to fend off robbers, to collect outstanding debts, and to resolve bitter disagreements over price and quality (Goldstein, Brownstein, and Ryan, 1992; Brownstein, 1996). Besides this drugs-crime connection, there is obviously a drugs-criminal connection as well. Of the nearly 70,000 inmates confined in New York State's penal institutions, a majority (65 percent) could be considered substance abusers or problem drinkers, according to their disclosures on a 1997 self-report (NYS DOCS, 1998).

Drugs 'R' Us: New York as the Center of the Action

I believe that 80 percent of violent crime has a nexus to the drug traffic.
—Police Commissioner Howard Safir (quoted in Marzulli, 1998b:5)

New York doesn't only attract tourists and conventioneers; it also has been a mecca for the country's substance abusers and drug sellers ever since Congress passed the Harrison Tax Act in 1914 that outlawed opium, morphine, heroin, and cocaine. In addition, it has been a battleground between drug prohibitionists and drug legalizers, a proving ground where tough new laws were first imposed, and a test site where experimental treatments like methadone maintenance and therapeutic communities were tried out. Over the decades, law enforcement officials have estimated that New York was home to somewhere between 40 and 60 percent of the nation's "narcotics addicts" (the term has always included people physically dependent on heroin, and sometimes was expanded to count heavy users of cocaine and even marijuana).

Shortly after World War II ended, a heroin-injecting epidemic erupted. The drug's false promises of instant relief and escape from life's cares and woes deceived mostly some poor young black and Puerto Rican men trapped in ghettos like the South Bronx, Manhattan's Harlem, and Brooklyn's Red Hook, Fort Greene, Bedford-Stuyvesant, and Brownsville neighborhoods (see Brown, 1999; Thomas, 1997; and Chein et al., 1964). As the 1950s began, Governor Thomas Dewey signed strict new laws mandating harsher prison sentences, including imprisonment for life for repeat offenders (Weaver, 1952). Police Commissioner Francis Adams virtually doubled the size of the NYPD's narcotics squad, declaring that desperation for money by the City's swelling addict population was one of the chief motives behind serious crimes, especially robbery ("Narcotics Squad Increased," 1954). At that time, about one in every five inmates in the state's penal institutions were known narcotics addicts (Perlmutter, 1957). After stiffer penalties against narcotics trafficking were passed by Congress in 1956, the leaders of New York's Cosa Nostra families pledged to shun the drug trade. Although some mobsters failed to abide by this ruling, the Mafia's official withdrawal from heroin distribution enabled new entrepreneurs from inner-city neighborhoods to compete for customers (Wendel and Curtis, 2000). Responding to an "alarming" increase in the number of "our children and young adolescents [who were becoming] victims of these foul dealers in death and destruction," Police Commissioner Michael Murphy announced that arresting "pushers" as well as the "higher-ups" would be a top priority of the department in the 1960s (Bigart, 1964). But by mid-decade, rebellion was in the air, and many young New Yorkers from all walks of life defied the law and experimented with marijuana, plus some new intoxicants, especially LSD and other psychedelics. Members of the hippie counterculture (particularly in the East Village and West Village, on local college campuses, and even in some high schools), believed that these psychoactive substances—as opposed to alcohol—yielded a high that unlocked creative energies and heightened their consciousness about the ugly realities besetting American society.

Police officials estimated that about half of the City's crime was linked to drugs during the middle of the 1960s (Editors, *New York Times*, 1966:28). Citing New York as suffering from the most serious problem of any city in the nation, U.S. Attorney General John Mitchell of the Nixon Administration and Mayor John Lindsay announced in 1969 the formation of a fourteen-agency federal, state, and city "strike force" to augment the anti-drug campaign waged by the NYPD's narcotics squad, which already was the largest specialized unit in any municipal police department in the world.[3] Yet, Police Commissioner Howard Leary warned that sheer numbers of narcotics agents would not guarantee success, and conceded that there was no hard evidence about the extent of law enforcement's inroads against drug trafficking (Lydon, 1969). He admitted that the drug problem had reached crisis proportions and ordered that all the department's energies and efforts should be directed at controlling it, through "arrests, arrests, arrests"(Robinson, 1970).

As the 1970s began, a corruption scandal engulfed the police force after an unusually honest officer, Frank Serpico, lost patience with the department's assurances that it was investigating itself and told reporters what he had observed firsthand. Under pressure, Mayor Lindsay set up the Knapp Commission. Its report yielded some startling admissions: corruption was widespread and organized in the enforcement of laws against gambling and prostitution (being on the "pad" for overlooking these activities was considered taking "clean" money), but in anti-drug enforcement the payoffs were even worse (even though this was considered "dirty" money). Uniformed officers, plainclothesmen, narcotics-squad detectives, and even supervisors raked in large sums of cash on a routine basis. Most of the corrupt officers merely were "grass eaters" who accepted whatever money and instructions were given to them; but others were aggressive "meat eaters," on the prowl for opportunities to "score." The corrupt practices the commission described as "typical" included keeping the money or drugs that were confiscated from pushers during raids and arrests; planting narcotics ("flaking") in order to justify an arrest; adding to the amount of narcotics seized ("padding") in order to upgrade the charges to more serious felonies; selling the confiscated drugs in exchange for stolen goods to addicts who also served as informants; offering immunity from wiretapping and arrest for a price; wiretapping suspects' telephones illegally in order to record incriminating statements to use against them or to blackmail them; selling confidential drug intelligence findings; registering individuals as confidential informants for a fee so that their alleged cooperation would qualify them for lenient treatment for prior arrests; and secretly financing heroin transactions. The commission also learned of "numerous" instances in which corrupt officers made money by introducing potential customers to drug dealers; by revealing the identities of confidential informants to higher-ups in the drug trade who were the targets of investigations; by testifying at trials in such a way that a defendant who made a payoff would be acquitted; by temporarily kidnaping critical witnesses so that they could not testify at trials; by providing armed protection for dealers; and even by offering to obtain hit men to eliminate potential witnesses. The commission noted that even though many officers were transferred out of the narcotics division after allegations about improprieties first surfaced in 1968, pervasive corruption persisted. Furthermore, susceptibility to payoffs went beyond the police department and extended to bail bondsmen, defense attorneys, prosecutors, and even certain judges (Knapp Commission, 1972:91–97). The commission's chief counsel concluded that corruption was one reason the NYPD's war against heroin was "a failure, a monumental waste of manpower and money," a charge vehemently disputed by the new police commissioner, Patrick Murphy (Burnham, 1971a:8).

Before the Knapp Commission probe, institutionalized graft enabled the major players to sell drugs without effective interference from the police. After the scandal disrupted that system of regular payoffs, the NYPD adopted a new policy that produced the same laissez-faire net effect. Uniformed officers were instructed not to attempt to arrest street-level dealers, since such interactions were fraught with opportunities for corruption. Instead, the department focused its efforts on disrupting the trade by gathering evidence against higher-ups. But in the meantime, retailers engaged in flagrant high-volume sales to strangers who walked by abandoned buildings as well as to customers who patronized stores that were mere fronts for drug-peddling operations (see Wendel and Curtis, 2000).

During the early 1970s, cocaine snorting became the rage. In 1973, NYPD undercover agents made more buys of coke than of heroin, a reflection of the growing availability of cocaine on the black market and a temporary shortage of heroin (Crittenden and Ruby, 1974). To try to stem the tide (and to enhance his politically popular tough-on-crime credentials), presidential aspirant Governor Nelson Rockefeller signed into law in 1973 state legislation that imposed even harsher penalties than those enacted in 1970 under President Richard Nixon on the federal level. Not only profiteers, but their customers as well, faced long prison sentences. But the intended deterrent effect of these strict new laws failed to materialize, and drug-related murders soared as the trade flourished. About 125 killings were classified as narcotics-related by the NYPD in its 1973 homicide analysis (7 percent of the total body count). By 1976, that figure grew to at least 136 (9 percent of the death toll), maybe more if the motives for all murders could have been discerned by the police.

As the decade ended, crack had not yet been concocted, and AIDS had not yet emerged as a terrible affliction among intravenous drug users, so heroin and cocaine were running neck and neck for the dubious distinction of being the better kick and the bigger threat. Cocaine lost its aura as the "champagne of drugs" used exclusively by those in high society, the sporting life, and Hollywood circles. It caught on among high school students, call girls, bored housewives, computer executives, writers, rock stars, and members of President Jimmy Carter's White House staff. Head shops throughout the city ostentatiously showcased the paraphernalia necessary to enjoy the powdered stimulant—gilded mirrors, straws, razor blades—accouterments that were symbols of status when worn as miniature trinkets dangling from necklaces or earrings. Sniffing went on openly in discos, at fashionable parties, and on park benches. Although state law imposed the same penalties ounce for ounce, street dealers reportedly switched from peddling heroin to cocaine because it was more profitable (they were selling to more prosperous people) and less risky (the police still were concentrating their efforts against the heroin trade) (Churcher, 1978). Sterling Johnson, New York City's special narcotics prosecutor (quoted in Ames, 1979:44), conceded that "with limited resources, we have to set priorities, so heroin, the more debilitating and addictive drug, is number one, and cocaine is number two." Yet, law enforcement officials admitted that their efforts to stop the influx of heroin were not succeeding, and that the problem had become worse than ever, fueling almost half the robberies and burglaries in the City (Maitland, 1981). Loose joints, pills by the handful, and packets of heroin and cocaine were purchased on midtown streets by young office workers wearing designer jeans or business suits "as easily as a hot dog from a street-corner vendor" (Ames, 1979). "Narcotics supermarkets" sprung up in several neighborhoods, most notably in Harlem, the "drug-trafficking center of the nation," where day or night, sellers openly hawked their wares "to the blacks who walked into the streets and to the whites who never got out of their cars" (T. Johnson, 1979). On Manhattan's Lower East Side, especially in the area dubbed "Alphabet City," the brisk commerce attracted crowds who milled around side streets congested with double-parked cars (many with out-of-state license plates). Long lines of buyers patiently lined up in front of abandoned buildings waiting their turn to enter while vendors sold refreshments. Loud music blaring from portable radios added to the din as touts shouted out the competitive advantages of their brands of heroin and cocaine.[4] To the uninitiated, the noisy open air drug bazaar could be mistaken for an ongoing block party or street fair (Zimmer, 1990). In other neighborhoods with a less lively street commerce, numerous small stores were just fronts for drug retailing (Ames, 1979). As cocaine compounded the problems caused by heroin, drug-related murders soared to a minimum of 192 (12 percent of the total body count) in 1980, and at least 349 (21 percent of all slayings) in 1982, according to NYPD homicide analyses for those years.

The Crack Attack

There has never been a problem quite like this one before. . . . Nothing so lethal, so effectively, diabolically good at the evil it does.
—Governor Mario Cuomo (quoted in Widener, 1986:17)

In the late 1970s, cocaine sniffing became a common practice in after-hours clubs, places where alcohol was served after bars and taverns had closed for the night. Dealers became regular patrons and discreetly sold their powder to the other customers. Overindulgence on the premises was frowned upon because disturbances would attract attention from the police. Soon, cocaine snorters seeking a more potent high began to experiment with a purification technique nicknamed "freebasing." But the process of adding ether and heating the mixture to inhale the vapors was a nuisance and could cause fiery explosions. Some after-hours clubs patronized by a cocaine-purifying crowd began to offer the service of converting powder to freebase. These clubs transformed into base houses, and their ambience and clientele deteriorated as norms favoring moderation were undermined by compulsive users who binged and then became argumentative and paranoid (Williams and Kornblum, 1985; Chitwood, Rivers, and Inciardi, 1996).

Then dealers discovered that a smokable, more rapidly absorbed product that yielded an instant rush and a brief but intense high could easily be cooked up in microwave ovens by mixing powdered cocaine with baking soda. The resulting "rock" cocaine that could be "cracked" into chips, or that "crackled" when it was burned in glass pipes, first appeared on the scene in New York City as early as 1982 (Johnson, Golub, and Fagan, 1995) or 1983 (NYPD, Strategy Number 3, 1994a). Crack was an immediate success among snorters tiring of freebasing. It could be marketed in smaller, less expensive units that seemed deceptively affordable to a younger, lower-income clientele—who unfortunately had weaker commitments to conventional life-styles, less to lose, and fewer resources at their disposal to help them cope with drug-induced problems.

As the pleasurable practice caught on largely among the most vulnerable and marginal of inner-city residents, especially in New York, Los Angeles, and Miami, the news media likened crack smoking to a "plague" that emanated from the netherworld and threatened to invade and destroy suburban sanctuaries. This imagery was reinforced nightly as news broadcasts featured action clips of narcotics squads raiding crackhouses, busting down doors, and carting off young black and Hispanic men in chains. During 1986, newsmagazines devoted several cover stories to what was characterized as the biggest crisis since Vietnam and Watergate. A two-hour CBS documentary watched by 15 million viewers, entitled "48 Hours On Crack Street," included a slew of New York City street scenes that contributed to a climate of near hysteria.[5]

Soon, both Republicans and Democrats, conservatives and liberals alike, were calling for an all-out war against the chemical compound which President Ronald Reagan described as "tearing our country apart" (Reinarman and Levine, 1997:24). Rekindling an old debate about whether stiffer penalties really work or merely are intended to appease outraged and frightened voters, Governor Mario Cuomo proposed life sentences for those selling as little as three vials of crack, worth about $50 (Schmalz, 1986). Mayor Edward Koch (1986:A27) concluded that even the threat of a life sentence failed to deter major traffickers from causing "an extraordinary peril," so he called for a new federal death penalty statute. City Council President Andrew Stein revealed that the municipal government inadvertently had become the largest crack-house slumlord in the country. Drug dealers operated out of apartments in an estimated one thousand buildings seized and managed by the City because their former landlords abandoned the run-down structures after failing to pay property taxes for years (Stein, 1988). Declaring crack smoking "a new form of genocide," leaders from sixty black churches organized all-night vigils on select street corners where dealing and smoking were brazenly taking place (Gately, 1986).

To impose an economic penalty on shopkeepers profiting from the brisk trade, teams of police officers raided two hundred candy stores, newspaper stands, and tobacco shops and confiscated drug paraphernalia, especially pipes used to smoke crack (Purdum, 1986b). To frighten away suburban customers who cruised City streets looking to score from curbside sellers, the NYPD employed civil forfeiture statutes to seize their cars after arresting them for buying contraband (Purdum, 1986a). To try to recapture overrun neighborhoods and parks, Commissioner Benjamin Ward launched massive roundups of both sellers and buyers (dubbed as "Operation Pressure Point"). This experimental approach became institutionalized a few years later as Tactical Narcotics Teams (TNT), which carried out sweeps and then occupied drug-ridden areas (Zimmer, 1990).[6]

In 1984, before crack smoking augmented the problems caused by cocaine sniffing and heroin injecting, at least 347 people were killed during drug-related disputes (24 percent of the death toll). The next year, that figure crept up to a minimum of 356 people (26 percent of the entire body count). But when the crack craze exploded in 1986, drug-related slayings skyrocketed to 525 (33 percent of the total death toll).

After the NYPD's Internal Affairs Division (IAD) exposed a "rotten pocket" of corruption in Brooklyn's 77th precinct in 1986, many New Yorkers were under the impression that the department was able to effectively police itself as well as drug traffickers. A total of thirteen rogue officers were charged in the "Buddy Boys" scandal with robbing addicts and dealers of their drugs and cash, pocketing the money, and then either selling or consuming the cocaine and heroin (see Editors, *New York Times*, 1986; and McAlary, 1987). However, as the 1980s drew to a close, a journalist (Marriott, 1989:A1) spotlighting the "12 Worst Drug Bazaars" in the City, reported:

> Many of the drug dealers ply their trade brazenly, with little fear of arrest. This is so despite the Police Department's announced crackdown on street-level sales. . . . The specter of widespread police corruption has also

been raised by some residents of drug-infested areas. But the police dismiss the charge that the boldness of street drug transactions is a result of officers being paid to look the other way.

In 1992, an arrest on cocaine charges of an NYPD officer who resided on Long Island by detectives working for the Suffolk County Police Department triggered another corruption scandal. Because the crooked officer had been under IAD surveillance for a long time and appeared to be the tip of an iceberg, Mayor David Dinkins appointed Judge Milton Mollen to preside over an investigation. The Mollen Commission found disturbing evidence that many clusters of officers (most notoriously in Harlem's "Dirty Thirty" precinct) accepted regular payments to protect traffickers. Those who failed to make payoffs were robbed of their money and drugs when raiding parties "boomed" (knocked) down doors and dished out "tune-ups" (beatings) to uncooperative dealers. The confiscated drugs were then consumed or resold to other dealers. To cover up their corrupt activities, officers filed false reports and "testilied" in court (see Donziger, 1996).

Over the decades, law enforcement campaigns not only have targeted major distributors operating behind the scenes, but also periodically have focused on street-level sellers and their customers. Crackdowns on the lowest echelons sometimes fall out of favor with policymakers. Critics argued that carrying out mass arrests of casual experimenters, social users, addicts, and street-level sellers (who are usually heavy users themselves) squandered taxpayers' money, used up funds set aside for police overtime needed to process important arrests, consumed valuable court time, and wasted limited jail and prison space. The punishment imposed by the criminal justice process was ineffectively adding to the misery of troubled souls who would be better served by a public health approach that emphasized treatment, vocational rehabilitation, and prevention. Advocates of this viewpont believed there were just too many customers to round up for violating the laws against possession of controlled substances, and too many replacements waiting in reserve to fill the openings that arose in selling operations after convictions (see Feldman, 1991).

However, an approach favoring low-level arrests, in accord with the "Broken Windows" thesis, has guided law enforcement strategies during the Compstat years. Proponents argued that both supply and demand could be suppressed through deterrence and incarceration via street sweeps followed by a continuing police presence, arrests of dealers in "buy and bust" stings (undercover agents pose as buyers and arrest the sellers), and arrests of customers in reverse stings (undercover agents pretend to be sellers and arrest the buyers)(see Editors, *New York Post*, 1988; Celona and Neuman, 1999a).

In the mid-1990s, the NYPD abandoned a two-decades-old anti-corruption measure that discouraged uniformed officers from arresting those who dared to sell, buy, or consume illicit substances right in front of them.[7] Also, the department reassigned many of its officers from patrol duties to anti-drug initiatives, beefing up the narcotics division to about three thousand strong by 1999 (Blair, 1999c). As Commissioner Safir (quoted in Ward, 1997:30) explained the strategy, "Our plan is to attack it on all levels. We're not just going after the major traffickers; we're gonna harass the little guys on a daily basis."

Even though many participants were taking greater precautions during the Compstat years, the NYPD still caught tens of thousands of buyers and sellers annually. In a typical undercover operation against "observation sales," a member of the narcotics squad maintained surveillance of a drug operation (a "set") by hiding on a rooftop or peering through the window of a vacant apartment. This spotter called in information to plainclothes officers lurking nearby in an unmarked van ("catch car"), identifying the purchasers as well as the "steerers" who guided them to the "pitchers" who took their money or who handed over the goods, plus any managers, "moneymen" (guarding the accumulated cash), and lookouts they could detect. Once a handful of buyers were collared as they slipped away from the scene of the exchange, the squad closed in on as many of the "players" as they could round up who visibly had "custody and control" of the growing wad of cash or the diminishing stash of contraband (usually hidden nearby, such as under a pile of trash in a vacant alley, or wedged in a crack in a crumbling lobby wall, or tucked inside the bumper of a parked car). In the game played out daily between the hunters and their quarry, the police seemingly triumphed, netting van loads of addicts and dealers, and carting off "trophies" to display at photo-op press conferences: neat rows of packages of confiscated product, piles of ten- and twenty-dollar bills, and stacks of guns. Drug spots were put out of operation, robberies and shootings were averted, and whole city blocks were reclaimed. Yet, somehow, certain locales withstood periodic assaults, other nearby spots reopened for business, captives were released, the players regrouped, the customers reassembled, and the process continued without any end in sight (Laffey, 1999).

But the NYPD reports that it has made significant headway by dismantling more than one thousand drug-dealing operations since 1996, reclaiming one formerly drug-ridden neighborhood after another. Instead of just arresting easily replaceable street dealers, undercover agents would "buy up" into the organization, purchasing increasingly large amounts until they gained the confidence of gang leaders. Individuals arrested for the large sales they had made to undercovers were secretly "flipped" (their cooperation as informants earned them reduced sentences) until enough incriminating evidence had been gathered to launch raids, seize drugs, guns, and cash, and build solid cases against entire crews that would hold up in court (Harnett and Andrews, 1999).

Although he believed that the NYPD was responsible for making great progress in the war on drugs, Commissioner Safir (quoted in Schwartzman, 1998:21) conceded, "I'm certainly not declaring victory. Drug traffickers are retrenching and relocating. But we've driven them inside."[8]

Did the Drug Trade Undergo a Transformation?

Another theory is that the trade has simply stabilized into a "mature market," as they say in the business schools, with surviving distributors less likely to clash over territory.
—*Time* magazine reporter Richard Lacayo (1996:50)

Drug-related murders hit an all-time high in 1991, accounting for at least 670 corpses (31 percent of the total body count). NYPD detectives established that in most of these drug-related slayings, the victims were street-level sellers killed by other street-level dealers.[9] In 1998, 633 New Yorkers were slain, and only a little more than one hundred of them were part of the drug trade. Since the entire body count in 1998 did not even match the number of dead drug dealers in 1991, there can be no doubt that the crash was spurred on by a sharp diminution in the amount of internal strife raging among the City's illegal entrepreneurs. The question arises, Why did formerly warring factions fight one another less ferociously as the 1990s wore on? One likely answer is that the structure of drug dealing operations within New York matured (see Lattimore et al., 1997; Blumstein and Rosenfeld, 1998; Bowling, 1999).

The emergence of the crack-smoking fad sent shockwaves through the drug business for several years, according to ethnographic reports. While the emerging market was still in its formative stage, start-up costs were minimal. Just a few hundred dollars could buy the initial batch of raw materials, several ounces of powdered cocaine hydrochloride, and baking soda; the equipment needed to process it, a microwave oven, already could be found in most kitchens; and only rudimentary networking skills were required to establish connections with suppliers and customers. Especially to youths lacking formal credentials, sidewalk selling seemed to hold great promise for upward mobility: the thrill of easy, crazy money and rags-to-riches profits; the prospects of climbing the ladder of opportunity and rising from a lookout or bodyguard or courier to become a curbside seller, then a wholesaler, and ultimately a kingpin; and the prestige of posing as a successful independent businessman.

The risks, however, were formidable: getting robbed, beaten, killed, or locked up for years. Despite these deterrents, there seemed to be no shortage of new entrants to replace fallen comrades. Cut-throat competition literally broke out between small, heavily armed crews over lucrative locations and eager consumers. Body counts ratcheted upward as the internecine warfare triggered an arms race. With the stakes so high, dealers could no longer count upon cheap, low-quality handguns, disparaged as "Saturday-night specials." They sought out fully automatic pistols, machine guns, military assault weapons, silencers, and body armor. Recklessly spraying bullets at one another, they turned urban "wastelands" into "war zones" and "killing fields," mowing down innocent bystanders along with their intended targets (Martz, 1989).[10] Since they were taking part in strictly forbidden and heavily penalized activities, participants in the trade had little choice but to resort to violence to settle their business disputes. They could not turn to the authorities for help or to the courts for redress when they felt cheated, exploited, threatened, muscled aside, or violated and deserving of compensation (see Donohue, 1998).

But when intensified police pressures drove the wide-open, free-for-all competitive arenas of drug supermarkets in run-down neighborhoods underground, the wave of violence these youthful, reckless, swashbuckling entrepreneurs had spawned quickly died down. By all accounts, since Compstat, the NYPD has successfully shut down the once flagrant open-air drug bazaars that menaced passers-by with stray bullets from endless feuds and vendettas over choice selling spots. Far fewer transactions went on right out on the sidewalk between people who did not know one another, and many more exchanges took place in low-profile indoor spots like the backrooms of corner groceries, pool halls, laundromats, video arcades, other seemingly legitimate storefronts, private apartments (house connections), crackhouses, and shooting galleries (see Schwartzman, 1998; Blair, 1999c). Some high-tech dealers made deliveries only upon receipt of orders from regular customers that came in via cloned cellular phones or beepers. Even more cautious sellers and buyers only dealt with one another through go-betweens—intermediaries whom they could trust to deliver the cash and return with the product. A complex division of labor on the wholesale and retail level emerged in response to law enforcement pressures. Permanent employees as well as day laborers assumed an assortment of roles in which they handled drugs or money but not both at the same time, if possible. Predictability became the order of the day, so that buyers and sellers could meet each other on a routine, business-as-usual basis. By forcing sellers to retreat indoors to protected settings, a formidable police presence stifled their inclination to battle one another over choice locations. By compelling dealers to be more cautious about who worked for them and whom they sold to, many of the risks of insubordination and robbery were reduced. The loss of casual customers forced selling crews to downsize their operations and employ fewer violence-prone, heavily armed workers. Also, managers of streamlined crews didn't need to unleash deadly force as often as an instrument of organizational discipline (see Johnson, Hamid, and Sanabria, 1992; Brownstein, 1996; Curtis, 1998; Frank and Galea, 1998; Bowling, 1999; Furst, Curtis et al., 1999; Johnson, Dunlap, and Tourigny, 1999; Wendel and Curtis, 2000).

Ironically, the retreat indoors and the resort to pagers and deliveries functioned as a harm-reduction measure, enhancing the safety of all concerned. Because of stepped-up police pressures, both the dealers and their customers became more discreet and businesslike, and behaved more responsibly and cautiously.

Fewer Abusers, Less Crime: Was the Drug Scene Winding Down?

At a time when many politicians and law enforcement officials are saying that their innovative police tactics are responsible for the sharp drop in homicide rates over the past five years, a new Justice Department study has found that the most important reason for the decline may be the waning of the crack cocaine epidemic.

— *New York Times* reporter Fox Butterfield (1997c:A12)

Crime rates should drop if the number of people who develop costly cocaine, crack, and heroin habits that are difficult, if not impossible, to support with income from earnings, loans, gifts, and misspent social benefit payments dwindles over the years. Fewer addicts will be out on the prowl, scavenging, hustling, dealing, shoplifting, burglarizing, stealing, robbing, and otherwise "taking care of business" (see Preble and Casey, 1969; and Johnson, Goldstein et al., 1985).[11] Also, if a diminishing number of individuals get high and behave out of character in a boisterous, hostile, and paranoid manner, less frequent outbursts will endanger them and the people around them.

Since possession of heroin, cocaine, and other controlled substances is penalized so severely, casual users as well as drug addicts wisely choose not to stand up and be counted. Consequently, it becomes very difficult for criminologists to estimate the true numbers of this hidden population that wishes to keep a very low profile. The measurement problem is compounded because the terms "user," "abuser," and "addict" lack precise, widely agreed upon meanings and are used in inconsistent ways by researchers and government agencies. Therefore, the actual size of this netherworld is the subject of guesswork.

If generating precise numbers, or even minimum and maximum ranges, seems an exercise in futility, then the next best approach is to try to detect substantial changes in the size of this shadowy population. To discern signs of expansion or contraction, trends in five sets of indicators can be monitored: NYPD arrests of sellers and customers; the proportion of arrestees (on all charges) who tested positive for controlled substances; the number of patients who sought care in hospital emergency rooms for drug-induced health crises; the number of people who died from drug-related causes; and the proportion of homicide victims whose corpses showed traces of drug use prior to death.

But do trends in all five sets of indicators provide any solid evidence that New York City's once flourishing drug scene was shriveling up, causing the crime crash?

Under Arrest

Over the last five years, the Police Department has made major headway against drug crime. Drug arrests reached an all-time high last year, and so did drug and drug currency seizures.

—Mayor Rudolph Giuliani (1997d:1)

Did an upsurge in drug arrests during the Compstat era send street crime into a tailspin? One major reason for record-breaking numbers of arrests was that the war on marijuana heated up dramatically after the zero tolerance crackdown was launched in 1994. During 1998, the NYPD made more than 40,000 arrests for marijuana possession and sale. Of all drug arrests, more than a third were merely for marijuana offenses. Yet back in 1978, when survey data showed all-time high levels of indulgence in marijuana smoking by teenagers and young adults (see Reuter, 1999), priorities were quite different: the NYPD made fewer than six thousand marijuana arrests, according to its Complaints and Arrests annual statistical report.

As for the more dangerous drugs, law enforcement pressures can be directed against sellers (usually resulting in felony arrests), or against purchasers (generally leading to misdemeanor arrests). Monitoring the year-to-year changes in felony and misdemeanor arrests for crack, powder cocaine, and heroin sheds some light on the scale of New York's drug scene and the NYPD's anti-drug activities (see graph 5.1).[12] Overall, the data show that tens of thousands of New Yorkers have gotten into legal trouble each year since the early 1980s (some individuals were caught more than once a year). Generally, felony arrests of sellers outnumbered misdemeanor arrests of abusers every year for each drug.

Specifically, as for powder cocaine, both felony and misdemeanor arrests were relatively uncommon during the late 1970s and early 1980s; they apparently rose sharply in the mid-1980s (the NYPD did not release detailed breakdowns for several years). Both types of arrests for powder

Graph 5.1. Trends in Drug Arrests, New York City, 1978–1998

NUMBER OF ARRESTS

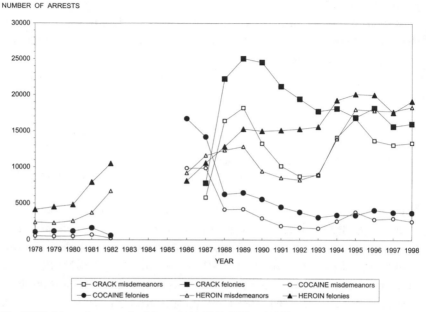

Note: NYPD did not release arrest breakdowns during 1983, 1984, and 1985.
Source: NYPD Complaints and Arrests Annual Report, 1978–1998.

declined steeply in the late 1980s as crack emerged and drew intense heat from the police. Throughout the 1990s, the level of both felony and misdemeanor cocaine arrests remained low and flat. As for crack, felony arrests for selling soared as soon as the epidemic took off in the late 1980s, tumbled in the early 1990s, and then remained fairly constant at a lower level during the Compstat years. Similarly, misdemeanor crack arrests rose in the late 1980s, plunged in the early 1990s, and then rebounded to earlier heights before drifting downward during the late 1990s. As for heroin, felony arrests for sale and possession went up in the early 1980s after remaining flat during the late 1970s. Arrests for heroin selling apparently remained about constant during the middle of the decade, drifted upward during the late 1980s, plateaued at a high level during the early 1990s, and reached all-time highs during the Compstat years. Heroin possession arrests rose during the 1980s, declined in the early 1990s, and then rose sharply before evening out at a high level during the late 1990s.

In sum, rapid changes both upward and downward took place in arrest rates during the late 1980s, when murder rates were rising.[13] In the early 1990s, drug arrests generally declined as murder rates dipped. From 1994 to 1998, when murder rates were plummeting, the levels of drug arrests of all kinds did not shoot up but remained relatively constant. Since it took many more narcotics detectives and a zero tolerance pro-arrest campaign to maintain these steady arrest figures, it could be inferred that the drug scene certainly was not growing and probably was retreating deeper underground and shrinking.[14]

The Favorite Drugs of Criminals

The drug-taking proclivities of the City's most active offenders, who broke the law so often that eventually they got caught, has been monitored since the mid-1980s. It appears that lawbreakers were heavily involved in drugs, but were using cocaine and heroin less often during the late 1990s than in earlier years (see graph 5.2).

The percentage of male suspects taken into custody for misdemeanors

Graph 5.2. Trends in Drug Use by Male Arrestees, New York City, 1984–1998

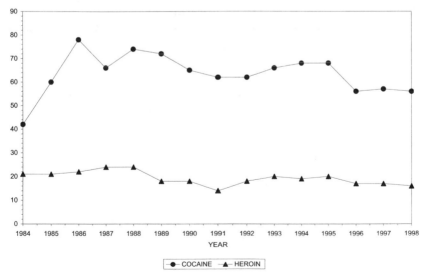

PERCENT TESTING POSITIVE

Note: Some arrestees had traces of both cocaine and heroin, plus marijuana; 1984–1987 extrapolated.
Source: NYS OASAS, drawing upon ADAM (formerly DUF) data, 1985–1999.

as well as felonies who tested positive for cocaine at the time of booking (and may have been high at the time of the crime, if they had been arrested shortly afterward) fell during the 1990s. This decline (to less than 60 percent) from the substantially higher levels (around 80 percent) registered in the mid-1980s was detected by the federal government's Drug Use Forecasting (DUF) data-collection system (see the upper line in graph 5.2).[15] The loss of interest in cocaine and crack was particularly pronounced among teenage boys, whose involvement began to wane as early as 1989.[16]

This downward trend in the number of youthful offenders who tested positive was interpreted as solid evidence that the crack epidemic was winding down because it was failing to attract new recruits. Nevertheless, a cohort of mature users (who were more than twenty-five years old in the mid-1990s) were expected to continue to smoke crack and cause trouble for many years to come, just like a hard-core of heroin addicts, who started injecting decades ago, still persisted in their habit in the 1990s (see the lower line in graph 5.2) (Golub and Johnson, 1997).[17] Even though cocaine fell in popularity among the City's criminals, it clearly continued to be their drug of choice, with marijuana a distant second (not shown in graph 5.2), and heroin holding about steady in third place. (Note that alcohol use prior to the crime was not monitored by the government's urine-testing program but may be an important factor—see below—and that most opiate abusers also indulged in cocaine use).[18]

One Too Many

But to complicate matters further, a different federal government barometer yielded an opposite impression about trends in the dimensions of New York's drug scene in the 1990s. Heavy use of cocaine as well as heroin grew more common—not less frequent—compared to the late 1980s, according to the federally financed Drug Abuse Warning Network (DAWN) data-collection system that kept track of hospital emergency-room episodes (graph 5.3).[19]

In the late 1980s, the number of patients treated in emergency rooms in metropolitan-area hospitals who mentioned sniffing or smoking cocaine as the cause of their medical crisis dropped, touching off premature

Graph 5.3. Trends in Drug Emergencies and Deaths,
New York City, 1988–1998

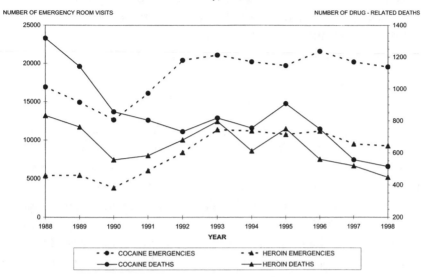

NUMBER OF EMERGENCY ROOM VISITS   NUMBER OF DRUG - RELATED DEATHS

Legend:
- ● - COCAINE EMERGENCIES   - ▲ - HEROIN EMERGENCIES
- ●— COCAINE DEATHS   —▲— HEROIN DEATHS

Note: A "mention" occurs when a drug is involved in a hospital emergency room episode or a death.
Source: SAMHSA, DAWN records.

optimism that the worst of the "snowstorm" was over, based on a mistaken assumption that a two-year downturn would continue (see Shenon, 1990; Treaster, 1990). But the volume of cocaine casualties unexpectedly rebounded in the early 1990s, before leveling off at record heights in the middle of the decade. The number of emergency room episodes due to heroin showed a similar pattern of decline, then increase, followed by stabilization during those years. The patterns in the data have been interpreted as evidence that many cocaine and heroin users are older rather than younger adults and are thus suffering the health consequences of many years of abuse (Reuter, 1999).

One Last Time

Still another reading about what happened in New York's cocaine and heroin scene can be derived from trends in drug-induced fatalities, which also are monitored by the DAWN system (see the lines depicting deaths due to drugs in graph 5.3).[20] Drug-related cocaine deaths dropped substantially from the late 1980s to the early 1990s and then fluctuated up and down, before falling further from 1996 to 1998. Apparently, a reduced number of New Yorkers were heavily snorting powder or smoking crack right before the crash. As for heroin, there wasn't such a clear-cut downturn until the late 1990s in the annual number of lives lost by the generally graying population of addicted City residents.

Killed under the Influence

One final way of discerning changes in the City's drug scene is to search for trends in the toxicology tests of murder victims' bodily fluids. Many had indulged in drug-taking or drinking before they were murdered, according to the results of autopsies performed by forensic pathologists working for the Office of the Chief Medical Examiner, which are assembled in table 5.1.[21]

Alcohol was the drug most commonly used before death. Over the years, the proportion of victims who were drinking before they were murdered ranged from 29 percent to 42 percent (see the row in table 5.1 labeled "Total alcohol"). However, drinking without drug taking appeared to be declining (compare the gap between the percentages in the row labeled "Alcohol only" with the row "Total alcohol"). In the 1990s, some of those who drank before they died were also high on cocaine. Evidence of cocaine use prior to death was rare at the start of the 1980s. Traces of metabolites indicating either cocaine snorting or crack smoking (the two routes of administration cannot be differentiated from post-mortem tests), became much more common in the corpses autopsied in 1991 and 1996. But during 1997, cocaine use among victims dropped significantly (see the rows labeled "Cocaine only" and "Total cocaine" in table 5.1), probably reflecting a sudden decline in cocaine snorting and crack smoking. Signs of recent opiate use (most commonly heroin, occasionally methadone) were not detected very often. However, there definitely was a trend in the data: fewer victims had used opiates before they died in the 1990s than in the 1970s or at the start of the 1980s (see the rows labeled "Opiates only" and "Total opiates"). The considerable involvement of heroin addicts and methadone patients in lethal violence—at least on the receiving end—had decreased since the 1970s to socially insignificant levels in the mid-1990s. One final discovery (not shown in table 5.1) was that traces of other illicit drugs were rarely pre-

Table 5.1. Findings of Postmortem Tests for Drugs in New York City
Homicide Victims, 1973–1997

Drugs Detected	1973	1974	1975	1976	1977	1981	1991	1996	1997
Alcohol only	35%	32%	31%	34%	30%	34%	21%	13%	24%
Cocaine only	—	—	—	—	—	—	13%	13%	6%
Opiates only	10%	9%	7%	8%	7%	—	2%	1%	1%
Marijuana only	—	—	—	—	—	—	—	18%	13%
Total alcohol	42%	39%	35%	42%	35%	—	35%	29%	39%
Total cocaine	—	—	—	—	—	3%	31%	29%	17%
Total opiates	17%	16%	12%	16%	13%	18%	9%	5%	2%
Total marijuana	—	—	—	—	—	—	—	21%	21%
Any drugs	52%	49%	42%	50%	42%	—	52%	44%	47%

Notes: — = not available.
Sources: N.Y.C. Medical Examiner toxicology reports. Findings for 1973–1977 were drawn from NYPD Homicide
Analyses. For 1981 (Manhattan only): from Tardiff and Gross, 1986. For 1990–1991: from Tardiff et al., 1994,
1995a, 1995b. Figures for 1996 were obtained from the M.E. files for all Manhattan homicides committed during the second half of the year; figures for 1997 were extracted from the M.E. files for all murders committed in
the five boroughs during the first half of the year.

sent in the fluids of the deceased. Toxicology results turned up just a
handful of cases in 1996 and 1997 in which the person who died had earlier indulged in amphetamines, barbiturates, designer "club drugs," or
psychedelics. The one dramatic exception was pot smoking. About a fifth
of all victims had been marijuana users. (However, since traces of
cannabis remain in the bodily fluids for weeks, it cannot be determined
if the deceased had been high before they died.)[22]

Therefore, analyses of medical examiner records have uncovered the
following trends: in New York in the 1990s, only alcohol, marijuana, and
cocaine, not heroin or any other psychoactive substances, seem to be
commonly implicated in violent deaths; and the fraction of victims with
traces of cocaine in their bodily fluids has declined dramatically since this
drug first showed up at the start of the 1980s and peaked in the beginning of the 1990s.

Down but Not Out

Hence, an analysis of trends in all five indicators—NYPD arrests, urine
test results of arrestees, hospital emergencies, drug-related deaths, and
toxicology tests at autopsies—yields contradictory findings that permit
only this conclusion to be drawn: cocaine clearly poses a bigger problem

than heroin in terms of crime and violence (and health emergencies). Cocaine use had dropped in New York during the latter part of the 1990s from its record-breaking levels, but it certainly was not disappearing. Heroin use had not withered away, but it was not supplanting cocaine, either. The preponderance of the conflicting evidence indicated that the ranks of the City's cocaine and heroin abusers have been dwindling, but these populations definitely were not disappearing.

Since the crack rage subsided in many different cities after several years, just as it did in New York, it appears that drug epidemics must run their course before winding down. These eras apparently progress through distinct phases: incubation, expansion, plateau, decline, and persistence. In New York, crack's incubation phase broke out from 1979 to 1983 among cocaine dealers and their trendy customers who were experimenting with new ways to purify the powder into combustible freebase. The expansion phase took place from around 1984 until 1986, when news spread by word of mouth that a low-cost, safe-to-handle, smokable variety of freebase could be purchased in tiny perfume vials. As the craze gathered momentum, youthful new recruits joined the older hard-core pioneers. By the end of the 1980s, most of the people already abusing powder cocaine and heroin were caught up in crack smoking, so the epidemic stopped snowballing and entered the plateau phase. A period of slow decline began around 1990, as a consensus developed among a new generation born in the 1970s that crack smoking was a very dangerous practice, to be avoided and despised. But the older cohort continued to pursue its drug of choice throughout the 1990s. Alongside them in the City's streets, courts, and jails were remnants from three earlier drug epidemics: the marijuana and psychedelic era of 1960 to 1979; the heroin era that lasted from 1965 to 1973; and the powder cocaine era that started in 1975 and was eclipsed by the advent of crack in 1984 (see Johnson, Golub, and Fagan, 1995; Golub and Johnson, 1997; and Johnson, Dunlap, and Tourigny, 1999).

Street-level researchers who observed the drug scene close up noticed signs that the initial glitter of being part of the cutting edge of the crack trade was already wearing off as the 1980s drew to a close. Get-rich-quick myths were shattered and reality set in when low-level workers realized that they toiled for ruthless exploiters around the clock, six to seven days a week, in off-the-books jobs that paid low wages, carried no fringe benefits, and exposed them to grave dangers (see Kolata, 1989). As the allure of dealing nosedived, consuming also began to fall out of favor. Crack smokers no longer were considered by their peers to be hip, cool, or part of a fashionable new trend. On the contrary, they were taunted as "scaly" and "thirsty," and looked down upon as weaklings, losers, and negative role models. The label "crackhead" became stigmatized as denoting an out-of-control addict obsessively going on "missions," binging on vial after vial, doing without food or sleep until all resources were exhausted and desperation and degradation set in. Youngsters who witnessed how the crack epidemic ravaged their families and neighborhoods also resisted the new temptation of snorting or smoking the much stronger heroin that appeared on New York streets in the early 1990s. They observed how the ranks of graying addicts who had been injecting heroin since the late 1960s or early 1970s were being thinned by AIDS and other causes of premature death. This gut-level rejection by inner-city youths (sometimes called the "little brother" learning theory) was driven by firsthand knowledge about how hard drugs had ruined lives. They generally limited their experimentation and adolescent rebellion largely to drinking malt liquor and smoking marijuana ("40 ounces and a blunt"). In sum, neighborhoods ravaged by the crack epidemic can be said to have undergone an unanticipated transformation as they healed themselves through informal mechanisms of social control (widespread disapproval of patently self-destructive behavior once the initial novelty of getting high wore off and illusions about making money from selling crack faded away). Law enforcement pressures helped local residents to reclaim their apartment buildings, streets, and parks, but the police could not have made headway without active support from the community (see Kolata, 1990; Hamid, 1992; Massing, 1996; Johnson and Golub, 1997; Curtis, 1998; Egan, 1999; Furst et al., 1999).

Even when crack smoking plummets in popularity, crime rates do not always tumble in tandem. Crack smoking quickly lost its appeal to most teenage boys in the late 1980s (according to the federal DUF monitoring system), but their disappearance from the scene did not result in an immediate decline in crime rates. A comparison with trends in Philadelphia clearly confirms this possible discrepancy. The pattern of declining crack use among arrestees in Philadelphia was almost identical to New York's, except that it fell even faster and further. Yet the murder rate in this nearby city did not drop as continuously and impressively as it did in New York. It persisted at a stubbornly high level throughout the 1990s.[23] Similarly, in Washington, D.C., and Detroit, local outbreaks of crack smoking subsided as dramatically as in New York (see Golub and Johnson, 1997), but murder rates declined less decisively.

Additional intercity comparisons shed more light on the complexity of the drugs-crime connection. No other major urban area had suffered from the heroin, cocaine, and crack epidemics as long and as severely as New York City.[24] New York's arrestees were more heavily involved in cocaine/crack at the end of the 1980s than in any other large city; and by late in the 1990s, they were still more deeply involved than elsewhere (with arrestees in Atlanta and Chicago roughly at the same level) (see Golub and Johnson, 1997; Lattimore et al., 1998; NIJ, 1998). Drug abusers experiencing medical emergencies from too much cocaine or heroin were rushed to hospitals in the New York metropolitan area more often, per capita, than almost anywhere else in the 1990s (except for three medium-sized cities: San Francisco, Newark, and Baltimore) (see OAS, 1999). The only conclusion that can be drawn from these comparisons is that New York City, even after the crash, still retained the dubious distinction of being the drug capital of the country.[25]

While campaigning for reelection in 1997, Mayor Rudolph Giuliani (quoted in Marks, 1997:8) set an ambitious goal: "The crime rate is down 45, 50 percent. Four years ago, nobody thought that was possible. Now no one thinks it's possible to cut heroin, cocaine, and marijuana use 50, 60, 70 percent. But it is possible." By the close of the 1990s, only a modest decline in the number of consumers of forbidden substances had taken place, according to the several sets of indicators reviewed above, but this diminution surely had helped to reduce the City's crime rates. And yet, New York's streets became much safer despite the continuing popularity of drug use among a stubbornly resistant portion of its residents, and not because of any sudden widespread refusal on their part to get high anymore. A profound and prolonged loss of most black-market customers could indeed trigger a crime crash—but such a virtual disappearance of the drug scene did not happen in New York City during the 1990s. Apparently, what really improved is how these users and abusers behaved toward one another, and toward their neighbors.

Down with Drinking?

Go out in Brooklyn any night of the week. . . . All these characters out there on the corner, drinking, urinating. Once they get a few drinks under the belt, out come the knives, out come the guns, out come the loud-mouths. . . . [L]ittle things count . . . like quality of life. One of the reasons why this city and this country [was] in a . . . mess . . . was nobody paid attention to those little things.

— Commissioner William Bratton (quoted in Marzulli, 1995c:12)

Because of all the attention paid to drug abuse, alcohol consumption often does not receive the scrutiny it merits as a precipitant of violence and even of property crime. Although most people who drink alcoholic beverages, even to the point of excess, do not get belligerent, there can be little doubt that drinking is connected to lawbreaking behavior. Researchers have established over and over again that many offenders have drinking problems, and that a considerable fraction were high on spirits, beer, or wine at the time that they committed a serious crime (see Bennett, DiIulio, and Walters, 1996). Many of the inmates in New York State's prisons report a history of trouble handling alcohol. During the 1990s, the proportion of City felons sentenced to prison who were classified as definite alcoholics ranged from about one-seventh to one quarter; and the fraction of new commitments who were possible alcoholics fluctuated from about one-fifth to one quarter. Adding the possible alcoholics to the definite alcoholics, as many as half of all convicted felons revealed that they had drinking problems in recent years (DOCS, 1996).[26] About one-third of inmates serving time for murder and manslaughter in upstate prisons told interviewers they had been drinking at the time of the killing, almost all of them to the point of drunkenness. On average, they had been drinking for over seven hours and had consumed a mixture of about nineteen alcohol units (bottles of beer, glasses of wine, shots of liquor), often combined with illicit drugs such as cocaine, when the incident broke out. These prisoners estimated that about two-fifths of their victims had been drunk as well (Spunt, Goldstein et al., 1994). Drunken persons might be perceived as particularly vulnerable, inviting targets, or they may provoke violence through their rash or inflammatory actions. Indeed, a sizable proportion of New York's murder victims had been drinking before they died (refer back to table

5.1). Toxicology tests revealed that the percentages ranged from a low of 29 to a high of 42.

Inebriation can result in greater aggressiveness or reduced inhibitions about the use of force. Consuming a few drinks can heighten courage and reduce fears of sanctions before engaging in risky ventures like burglaries, joyrides, acts of vandalism, and robberies. Alcohol intoxication can impair an individual's ability to process information and exercise good judgment. The motives and actions of others can be misinterpreted, while achieving immediate personal goals can become paramount. Family quarrels, fights among friends, even brawls between complete strangers become facilitated when violence-prone people drink. When crowds looking to relax and take "time out" from the everyday demands of work, school, and family responsibilities congregate near alcohol outlets like liquor stores, bars, and dance clubs, they transform these public spaces into volatile hotspots for fights, street-gang clashes, aggravated assaults, robberies, and killings (Parker and Cartmill, 1998). By cracking down on public drinking (of beer, wine, or liquor from an open container, or barely concealed by a paper bag) as part of the campaign against quality-of-life offenses, the NYPD may have prevented a great deal of needless violence among intoxicated persons from taking place during the Compstat years.

Clearly, if drinking diminished, that would be another reason why crime rates fell.

One way to determine whether New Yorkers' drinking habits changed is to examine trends in overall consumption rates over time. Changes in the overall amount of alcohol consumption have foreshadowed trends in homicide rates ever since Prohibition, according to a statistical analysis of nationwide data (see Parker, 1995; and Parker and Cartmill, 1998). In the late 1970s, the volume of beer, wine, and liquor purchased across the country peaked. Shortly thereafter, the national death toll reached an all-time high. In the early 1980s, alcoholic beverage sales began a long and steady decline that persisted through the 1990s. Homicide rates fell off during the early 1980s, but then began to climb to new heights in the late 1980s and early 1990s; this was the first time in fifty years that the two trends diverged. Since the mid-1990s, the correlation has re-emerged, as both drinking and killing have declined in tandem.[27]

This salutary national trend showed up at the local level as well, ac-

Graph 5.4. Trends in Alcohol Consumption, New York City, 1984–1998

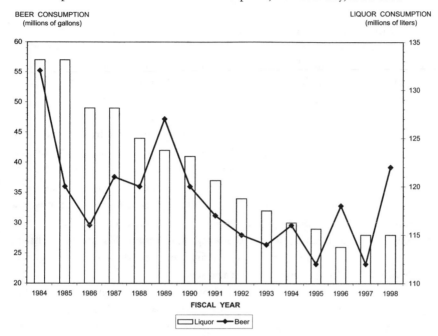

BEER CONSUMPTION
(millions of gallons)

LIQUOR CONSUMPTION
(millions of liters)

Note: NYC consumption tax on beer and liquor went into effect in 1984; NYS fiscal years end March 31.
Source: NY State Department of Taxation and Finance, 1984–1999.

cording to an analysis of revenue records that reflected alcohol sales in the five boroughs ever since a special tax on beer and hard liquor (but not wine) was imposed during Mayor Ed Koch's first term in office. The decline in liquor purchases is evident in graph 5.4.[28] Beer drinking has remained relatively popular among New Yorkers over the years since the mid-1980s. But the consumption of hard liquor dwindled steadily from the mid-1980s until the mid-1990s, and then leveled out in the late 1990s.

It is likely that crime rates have gone down because whiskey, vodka, gin, and rum consumption has diminished. However, more research is necessary to establish whether fewer New Yorkers were getting drunk and engaging in bouts of binge drinking, and whether drinking actually went down within those groups that faced the highest risks of becoming perpetrators of street crimes—males, teenagers and young adults, and members of lower-income families.

Notes

1. In the mid-1990s, a staggering 500,000 drug addicts were believed to reside in New York City, of which around 200,000 were thought to be hooked on heroin (Musto, 1995b). This projection paints a very unfavorable picture of City residents: 500,000 "addicts" divided by 6,117,000 inhabitants over twelve years of age yields an estimate that more than 8 percent of all New Yorkers are deeply involved in the drug scene.

2. In its homicide analyses, the NYPD classifies a murder as drug related if any of these distinct elements was part of the story: the lethal violence was motivated by some dispute arising from a drug transaction and either the killer or the victim was a known seller or user; the scene of the crime was a known drug location such as a crackhouse where cocaine is sold and smoked on the premises, a shooting gallery frequented by intravenous injectors of heroin, a drug mill where the raw materials are adulterated and packaged, or a spot (like an alley or stairwell) where drugs are sold; or drugs or drug paraphernalia such as syringes or crack vials were found strewn about at the scene.

3. Thirty years later, the retiring head of the NYPD Narcotics Division (see Harnett and Andrews, 1999:36) promoted teamwork as if it were an original idea derived from a Compstat session: "Commissioner Howard Safir has added a new strategy to the drug initiatives—the active participation of the federal Drug Enforcement Administration, the FBI, the Immigration and Naturalization Service, the IRS, the Secret Service, the U.S. Customs Service, the U.S. Marshal's Service, and the New York State Police. This idea of coordinating drug enforcement at every level of government is still in its infancy, but its potential is enormous."

4. Ethnographers reported that starting in the early 1970s, competition for customers became so keen that dealers stamped brand names and trademarks on the glassine envelopes in which they packaged their adulterated heroin. Their intent was to use these "dope stamps" as a way of developing consumer loyalty to their brand names, even though this way of advertising an illegal commodity attracted the attention of the narcotics squad. These brand names serve an expressive function similar to nicknames, gang colors, graffiti, and tattoos. They appropriate and subvert mainstream imagery, proclaim a manly defiance of authority, and flirt with notions of danger and death. In fact, whenever a word-of-mouth grapevine reported that injectors died from overdoses, customers flocked to that brand name, figuring it was stronger stuff than what was usually marketed (Wendel and Curtis, 2000). Popular brand names over the decades include Black Out, Could Be Fatal, Dragon Lady, Prophecy, Temptation, Terminator, Black Death, and White Death (see Zimmer, 1990). Dealers still played with self-de-

structive themes in the late 1990s, stamping their packets with names like 911, O.D., 25 to Life, Lethal Injection, and Undertaker (see Laffey, 1999). However, the changing nature of the market no longer necessitated the use of dope stamps as a means of maintaining a reputation for quality amidst stiff yet chaotic competition, so they began to fade away (Wendel and Curtis, 2000).

5. One scene pictured U.S. senator Alphonse D'Amato and U.S. attorney Rudolph Giuliani, outfitted in casual clothes and sunglasses, having no trouble purchasing vials of crack from the comfort of the passenger seat of a car driven by a federal agent down a Washington Heights street. Some officials considered their undercover mission a "feat of public-spirited bravery," but others denounced it as "shameless publicity-seeking" and a "campaign gimmick" (DeStefano and Flynn, 1986).

6. Looking back, the recently retired head of the NYPD Narcotics Division (see Harnett and Andrews, 1999:33) conceded that "TNTs focused almost entirely on arresting street dealers in 'buy and bust' operations. As a result, they could suppress street-narcotics conditions for a while but couldn't permanently uproot them. Their 90-day limit was also self-defeating. Dealers caught on, lay low for three months, and came back when the TNT was gone."

7. Headquarters authorized precincts to set up Street Narcotics Enforcement Units (SNEUs). But as the former chief of the Narcotics Division admitted (see Harnett and Andrews, 1999:32), SNEUs had to operate in uniform, and they could target only outdoor locations: "Unfortunately, in a bright blue uniform it's not easy to make observations of drug activity without being observed yourself, and once dealers figured out that SNEUs worked only out of doors, they began steering clients to hallways and vestibules, where SNEUs couldn't go. So SNEUs caught only guppies, not the bigger fish—and only guppies too dumb to adjust to the SNEUs' tactics."

8. The commander of the Narcotics Division reported that the NYPD had dismantled over 1,000 of the nearly 1,250 drug gangs operating in the City by 1999 (Blair, 1999b).

9. Detectives classified 415 (66 percent) of the 631 dead sellers as "street level" dealers; and 128 (20 percent) had been "low level," 29 (5 percent) "midlevel," and 49 (8 percent) "high level" traffickers (the organizational statuses of the other 39 were unknown). Of the 351 seller-suspects arrested for murder, 221 (63 percent) had been "street level" dealers, and 77 (22 percent) had been "low level," 13 (4 percent) "midlevel," and 34 (10 percent) "high level" traffickers, according to the NYPD's 1991 homicide analysis.

10. In 1991, twenty-one innocent bystanders were killed by the reckless shots fired by feuding drug dealers, according to a detailed homicide analysis carried out by the NYPD.

11. This phrase is derived from street slang and is the title of a study of heroin abusers in New York City (see Preble and Casey, 1969; Johnson, Goldstein et al., 1985). The researchers found that heroin injectors committed a "staggering" amount of offenses to raise money, but most of their predatory activity was confined to stealing rather than robbing. Those who did resort to force to take things of value tended to be the daily users, and they seized opportunities to strong-arm compromised targets (like men visiting prostitutes).

12. Breakdowns of "Narcotic and Drug Arrests" first distinguished crack from powder cocaine in 1987.

13. Government crackdowns can provoke violence by causing instability: disrupting de facto arrangements, dismantling near monopolies, creating fresh business opportunities. In the aftermath of raids, arrests, and convictions, rival groups clash to see who will replace distribution rings that were put out of action. Instability results from a number of possible causes: a sudden influx or loss of willing participants (both sellers and buyers) due to the ebb and flow of law enforcement pressures; a transition from one type of drug market to another: highly competitive vs. tightly controlled; anonymous outdoor sales vs. sales indoors; and rapid increases or decreases in retail prices and product quality (see Holmes, 1990; Brownstein, 1996; and Lattimore et al., 1997.

14. The NYPD was not fighting the drug war single-handedly in New York. The Office of the Special Narcotics Prosecutor for the City of New York helped to put major traffickers out of business, according to the achievements chronicled in its annual reports. In addition, the New York/New Jersey High Intensity Drug Trafficking Areas (HIDTA) multiagency task force disrupted and dismantled the organizations that imported heroin and cocaine into the City and distributed these controlled substances to the rest of the country. But despite these coordinated attacks on the highest levels of the trade, severe shortages rarely interrupted the commerce and destabilized the markets.

15. The first Drug Use Forecasting (DUF) Program urinalysis was carried out in 1984 on a sample of nearly five thousand persons arrested in Manhattan (not all of the five boroughs). A little more than 40 percent of the arrestees tested positive for cocaine. In 1986, another pilot study exploring the usefulness of urine testing detected cocaine in more than 80 percent of the male arrestees (traces of crack metabolite cannot be distinguished from powder cocaine) (Wish, 1987). These two data points are shown on the graph even though they are not quite consistent with later sampling methods.

The National Institute of Justice (NIJ) has renamed the DUF urine testing program as Arrestee Drug Abuse Monitoring (ADAM) and is expanding it to seventy-five cities from the original twenty-three localities.

16. The high point for teenage boys (more precisely, males fifteen to twenty

years old) was reached in 1988, at nearly 70 percent. During 1989 and 1990, their cocaine snorting and crack smoking nosedived. During the 1990s, it remained relatively stable, with around 20 percent to 25 percent of all arrestees in this age group showing signs of recent use in their urine samples (not shown separately on graph 5.4).

17. Less than 4 percent of the teenage boys arrested in Manhattan in 1997 tested positive for opiates (NIJ, 1999). That was a promising sign that heroin abuse might go out of fashion over the years, as existing addicts faded away and very few new recruits replaced them.

18. The overwhelming majority (about 85 percent ever since the late 1980s) of arrestees in Manhattan who tested positive for opiates also had signs of recent cocaine use in their system. However, of those who tested positive for cocaine, a much smaller percentage (nearly 25 percent) also had traces of recent heroin (or methadone) use in their urine, according to DUF monitoring (see Lattimore et al., 1997:83). Therefore, most heroin injectors have two destructive habits (in fact, they may mix their heroin with cocaine and inject the combination as a "speedball"); but most crack smokers only suffer from one affliction. Also, the relative proportions with two bad habits indicate that cocaine snorters and crack smokers must vastly outnumber heroin snorters and injectors.

19. The Drug Abuse Warning Network (DAWN) of the Substance Abuse and Mental Health Services Administration (SAMHSA) of the U.S. Department of Health and Human Services has been used to monitor changes in the drug scene by sampling the records kept by hospital emergency rooms since the 1970s.

20. Patients rushed to hospitals die there from overdoses more often than from complications from chronic use, withdrawal, or unexpected reactions. Their deaths were accidental (due to physical dependence or recreational use) more often than intentional (as a means of suicide). Some emergencies and deaths were precipitated by the interaction of a combination of drugs, often including alcohol. Deaths related to AIDS, which may have been contracted from intravenous drug use, were not counted.

DAWN emergency room records are drawn from 53 of the 108 hospitals in the New York metropolitan area (not just the five boroughs). Eight metropolitan area medical examiners' offices participate in the DAWN death reporting system. DAWN's data about drug-related deaths using consistent definitions and standard record-keeping procedures only go back as far as 1988 for the New York City metropolitan area.

21. To discover if there were any trends during the years of the crash, findings from toxicology tests were collected from the files of the Office of the Chief Medical Examiner for all Manhattan murders committed during the second half

of 1996, and all murders in the five boroughs that took place during the first half of 1997.

Unavoidably, methodological inconsistencies arose between all the studies assembled in table 5.1. During certain years, researchers relied on samples rather than test results for all murder victims. The criteria for inclusion or exclusion may have differed as well for particular categories of victims (at what ages should young children and the elderly be dropped from consideration as being virtually ineligible for getting high?). Also, should patients be excluded if they died in hospitals from wounds inflicted a day or two prior to their demise because traces of previous drug use might disappear from their systems? Despite these shortcomings, this compilation of findings furnishes some worthwhile insights and reveals several interesting trends.

22. Whether or not the victim was high at the time of the death is an important issue in court proceedings and for prevention purposes. Some victims may have been intoxicated to the point that it affected their interactions with the people around them (who also may have been high on drugs or alcohol). Because of their altered mental state, victims might have acted in a foolhardy, impulsive, or reckless manner that provoked retaliation or encouraged their adversaries to take advantage of their vulnerability and irrationality. In many ordinary disputes, drug taking can serve as a catalyst, escalating the level of violence. However, several additional factors shape the drug experience and the outcome of interpersonal conflicts: purity or dosage; the route of administration; the user's expectations of what the physical and mental effects of the intoxicant are supposed to be; and the setting (a tavern, crack house, or heroin shooting gallery may have its own peculiar norms about expressing or suppressing aggression) (see Tardiff et al., 1994, 1995a, 1995b).

23. In both cities, about 75 percent of all arrestees tested positive for cocaine/crack in 1989. By 1996, the rate in Philadelphia had fallen to 49 percent, as compared to 62 percent in New York. In both cities, among youthful arrestees, the percent testing positive fell from 70 percent to around 20 percent during those same years (see Golub and Johnson, 1997).

In Philadelphia, after peaking at 503 victims in 1990, the body count dropped to 440 in 1991, drifted back up to 432 in 1995, and then back down to 420 in 1996, according to the FBI's annual UCR reports.

24. In 1990, the State of New York had the largest percentage of cocaine abusers per 100,000 residents, with Nevada a close second, according to Senate Judiciary Committee estimates (Saul, 1990).

25. A steady stream of reports from the field confirmed the impression that not much was new in New York's drug scene during the Compstat years. The evidence came from the federal government's Office of National Drug Control

Policy's publication *Pulse Check*. This monitoring system collated information from narcotics squads, ethnographic researchers, and treatment providers in major cities. Only a handful of less-than-earthshaking changes and trends were noted during the mid-1990s.

26. The New York State prison system diagnoses and classifies all new commitments by administering the Michigan Alcohol Screening Test (MAST). Those who score between 5 and 8 points on the twenty-five-question test are labeled as "possible alcoholics," and those who score 9 or more are deemed "definite alcoholics" (DOCS, 1996).

27. However, when only beer consumption levels are the focus of a statistical analysis, variations in per capita drinking do not appear to be correlated with homicide rates (Marvell, 1998).

28. The excise tax went into effect during fiscal year 1984. It is administered by the New York State Commissioner of Taxation and Finance. Of course, to the extent that tax evasion by businesses involved in the sale and distribution of alcohol is a continuing problem, these data consistently underestimate the actual amount of consumption (hopefully by a constant and therefore unimportant amount each year).

SIX

It's the Economy, Stupid!
Or Is It?

Did the Boom Cause the Crash?

There has never been a proven connection between the state of the economy and crime, and there is absolutely no correlation between unemployment and crime.
— Mayor Rudolph Giuliani (quoted in Horowitz, 1995:23)

And I don't think it's merely coincidental that when New York is leading the nation in crime reduction, it is also experiencing the greatest job growth in 13 years.
— Mayor Rudolph Giuliani (quoted in Marzulli, 1997:B3)

The 1992 campaign slogan of presidential candidate Bill Clinton just might apply to the crime crash as well. Yet, Mayor Rudolph Giuliani's contradictory statements make it clear that a controversy surrounds the question of whether street crime has economic roots (see Hagan and Peterson, 1995; Bennett, DiIulio, and Walters, 1996; and Short, 1997). Is there a connection between enduring financial hardships and becoming embroiled in violence and theft? Are young men who are poor and without steady work at greater risk of getting caught up in life-styles revolving around drugs, guns, and gangs than other young men? Does an economic downturn drive crime rates up, and a recovery damp them down?

During the late 1990s, the nation's unemployment rate subsided to its lowest level in nearly thirty years, and the poverty rate dropped back to where it was before the last recession. Meanwhile, the nation's murder rate declined to its lowest level since 1967. It surely appeared plausible that these positive developments were correlated: that an improving economy enabled increasing numbers of poor young men to reject the siren song of illegal opportunities.

The link between lack of money and participation in street crime was confirmed by the analysis of the data from several sources presented in chapter 2. Most of the people arrested for murder clearly were drawn from the ranks of the desperately down-and-out, the working poor, and the blue-collar working class. The overwhelming majority of arrestees turned out to be eligible for free legal assistance under the government's guidelines for providing defense attorneys to indigents. Their victims tended to be their immediate neighbors, residing in communities whose average income levels ranked at or near the very bottom of all Zip codes. Also, the precincts with the highest murder rates tended to have the lowest household incomes. Overall, a large share of New York City's killings could be aptly characterized as "poor on poor."

Given this close association between poverty and street crime, a sharp drop in the ranks of the destitute would be an improvement that would go a long way toward solving the mystery of New York's falling murder rate. And if the City's business recovery was stronger and enabled more of the City's poor and unemployed to enter the work force and become upwardly mobile than in the rest of the country, these positive developments could account for New York's superior progress in crime reduction. The welcomed transition from hard times to good times could have lifted the spirits and dispelled some of the frustration and despair that for decades had enveloped underprivileged youths in the most hard-pressed communities. In essence, the key question is: Did the boom fuel the crash?

The Best of Times? Poverty Rates and Crime Rates

The second half of the 1990s were the best of times for many New Yorkers. The Gross City Product (an indicator of economic activity, parallel to the Gross National Product) rose smartly, wages moved up, and inflation remained under control. Corporate profits rolled in and the bull market on Wall Street propelled the Dow Jones average to dizzying heights. For those who were well connected to the engines of money-making and influence in the global marketplace, the last years of the century were a great time to enjoy comforts and privileges unparalleled in American history.[1]

But a look behind the business page headlines about Gotham's prosperity and renaissance revealed that times were still tough in neighborhoods untouched by gentrification.

Poverty had not been as serious a problem in New York as it was in other regions of the United States from the 1930s until the late 1960s. Even though low-wage workers struggled to make ends meet in big-city slums and ghettos, the real pockets of abject poverty were to be found in the Appalachian Mountains (mostly whites) and in the Deep South (mostly African Americans). The relative financial standing of New York vis-à-vis the rest of the country reversed in the 1950s, when several already-existing trends intensified: the widespread movement of poor black people from the rural South initially to Manhattan's Harlem and Brooklyn's Bedford-Stuyvesant; the migration of Puerto Ricans from the island primarily to "El Barrio" (Spanish Harlem); and the flight of white middle-class families to suburban "bedroom communities." While the national poverty rate dropped impressively (from a high of 48 percent of all Americans in 1935 to a low of 11 percent by 1973), the proportion of City residents living without incomes deemed adequate by government standards remained stuck at about 15 percent, as the War on Poverty wound down, and the war in Vietnam heated up at the close of the 1960s (Tobier, 1984; McMahon, Angelo, and Mollenkopf, 1997; Accordino, 1998).

Over the decades, economic and social changes transformed the face of poverty in the City. Relatively fewer elderly people suffered cruel deprivations in their final days, but substantially more children endured hardships right from the outset of their lives. Worse yet, a growing cohort of young adults, often living alone and lacking the skills, educational credentials, and work experiences sought by employers, were sinking into an "underclass" of "hard-core unemployed" persons who were not needed by the job market even during good times. Also, as most low-income whites moved up the ladder of social mobility, many members of minority groups remained confined to ghetto neighborhoods. They still were separated from the mainstream by invisible barriers of race and class, virtually excluded by subtle de facto segregationist practices from effective schooling, well-paying positions, and decent housing. The

1970 census discovered that about a quarter of all African American and a third of all Puerto Rican New Yorkers were struggling to survive on incomes that were below the official poverty line (see Auletta, 1982; Tobier, 1984; and Currie, 1993).

Paradoxically, during the prosperous second half of the 1990s, the poverty rate remained stuck in New York (at about one in four residents) at roughly twice the national average, as bad as it was right after the recession at the start of the 1990s, and worse than the City's average for the entire 1980s, according to analysts who poured over the Census Bureau's annual Current Population Survey.[2] Nearly 1.8 million residents were receiving less than $16,665 for a family of four, the federal government's definition of the minimum income needed to avoid severe hardships (Aaronson and Cameron, 1997; Bernstein, 1999b).[3] Economic marginality had become a pressing problem for even greater numbers of people of color. Hispanic New Yorkers suffered the most. About three times as many Hispanic residents as whites were poor by government standards during the second half of the 1990s. More than twice as many black New Yorkers as whites lived below the poverty line while crime was crashing. When the drop in crime accelerated in the mid-1990s, about 71 percent of all Hispanic female-headed families and nearly 58 percent of all black female-headed households were officially destitute, as were 21 percent of such families headed by white women. Despite the conspicuous consumption going on all around them as the City went upscale, shamefully 60 percent of Hispanic children, 51 percent of black children, and 12 percent of white youngsters grew up in homes deprived of some of life's basic necessities and most of its comforts (Aaronson and Cameron, 1997; CCC, 1999; Chernick, 1999).

Therefore, no statistical relationship materialized between the percentage of New Yorkers who were poor and the number who were killed (see graph 6.1). When the number of at-risk poor people—white, black, and Hispanic—went down, the body count did not necessarily fall as well. For a year or two after 1990, fewer black and Hispanic New Yorkers suffered economic deprivation, and murders began to inch downward. But in the middle 1990s, poverty intensified in the black and Hispanic communities, yet body counts dropped substantially. When poverty rates edged downward in the late 1990s, murder rates plummeted. Hence, the two factors do not seem to be intertwined in any

Graph 6.1. Relationship between Poverty and Murders,
New York City, 1979–1998

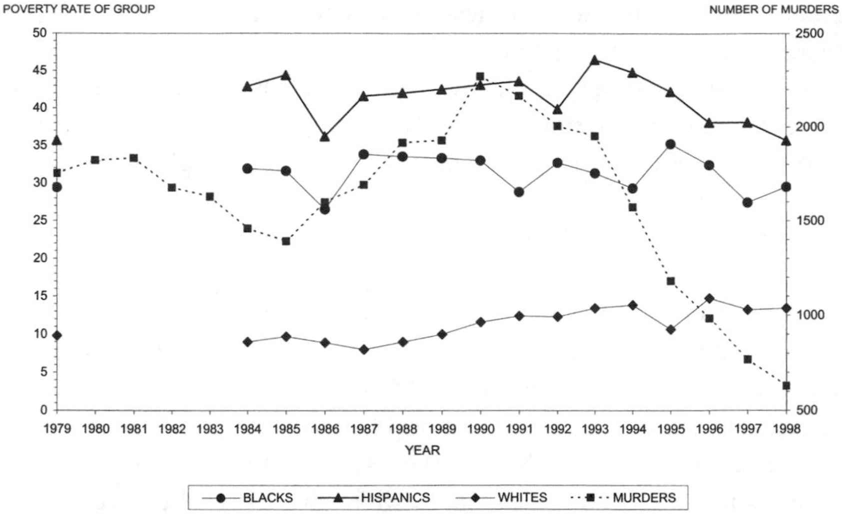

Note: Figures for 1980–1984 are not available; Figures for 1988 and 1989 are interpolated.
Source: Yearly CPS, complied by the Community Service Society (Aaronson and Cameron, 1997; Levitan, 1999).

simple and direct manner.[4] Even though poverty persisted as a very serious problem, street crime subsided. Even more puzzling, poverty remained entrenched in New York while it was less severe and on the decline in the rest of the country during the same years that the City led
the nation in crime reduction (Bernstein, 1999b). By 1998, the poverty
rate for black New Yorkers (at 30 percent) remained higher than the national average for all African Americans (26 percent). The poverty rate
for Hispanic New Yorkers (at 36 percent) persisted at a considerably
higher level than for all Hispanic Americans (at 26 percent). White New
Yorkers suffered financially more than their counterparts across the
country too (13 percent compared to 8 percent), according to census
figures.

A number of trends—suburbanization, deindustrialization, technological displacement, outsourcing, downsizing, credentialization, price
inflation, gentrification, even deinstitutionalization of the mentally ill—
conspired to make the City's class structure even more "hollow in the
middle" or "hourglass" shaped. A growing share of residents enjoyed
unprecedented affluence, and the privileged lives they were leading at-

tracted even more well-to-do people to settle beside them. But at the other end of the income spectrum, large numbers of low-wage workers sank toward or slipped beneath the poverty line as the purchasing power of their stagnant real wages failed to keep pace with a rising cost of living as the City became a more desirable and therefore more expensive place to reside. Consequently, the size of the middle-income class in the late 1990s was smaller than it had been in 1977 (see McMahon, Angelo, and Mollenkopf, 1997). Furthermore, the income gap between the City's major racial/ethnic groups widened. Hispanic New Yorkers had a median income that was only 41 percent of white income; for black residents, the figure was 51 percent. Across the country, the gap between the rich and the poor became a chasm. But it opened even wider in New York State than anywhere else in the United States (see Perez-Pena, 1997; Johnston, 1999). Worst of all, the bulk of the City's poor was sinking even deeper into the pit of absolute deprivation. In the mid-1990s, roughly three-quarters of New Yorkers living below the poverty line were situated way below it, suffering from what was termed "extreme poverty." Nearly eight thousand youngsters were homeless and living in shelters (up 21 percent during the 1990s). Soup kitchens and food pantries estimated that they were feeding 650,000 hungry people per month in 1997 (up from 360,000 three years earlier), many of them unable to pay for necessities on meager welfare allotments (Aaronson and Cameron, 1997; CCC, 1999).

Government public assistance programs have ameliorated the suffering of those unable to pay for necessities in the competitive economy ever since the economic system's shortcomings became obvious during the Great Depression of the 1930s. In general, welfare rolls contracted during periods of prosperity and expanded during hard times, thereby regulating the attitudes and behavior of a surplus population (see Piven and Cloward, 1972). By fiscal year 1995, in the aftermath of a severe recession, the City's public assistance caseload (consisting mostly of mothers and their children) reached an all-time high of 1.1 million. As the economy recovered, the rolls were sharply cut by stringent new federal, state, and municipal regulations and workfare requirements designed, in President Bill Clinton's words, to "end welfare as we know it." Mayor Giuliani (quoted in Giuliani, 1998a) proclaimed that "we can end welfare by the year 2000. Once New York City was the welfare capital of the

Graph 6.2. Relationship between Public Assistance and Murders,
New York City, 1978–1998

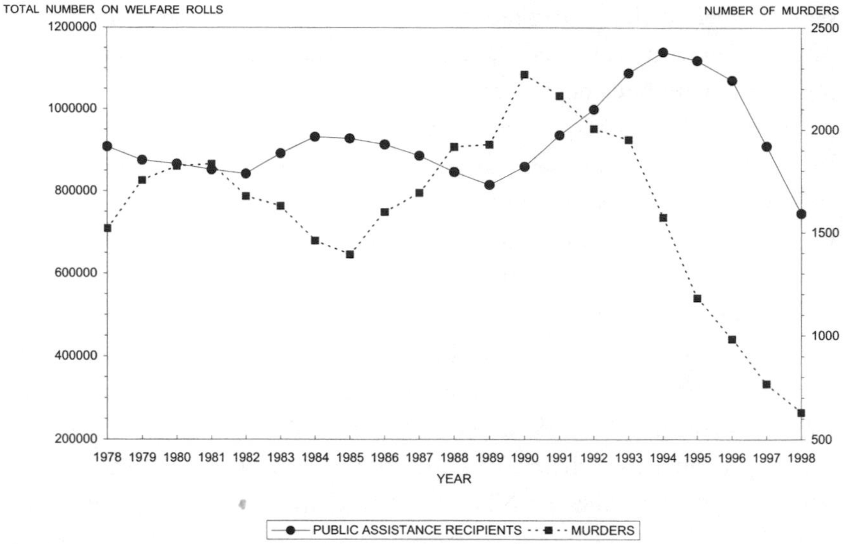

TOTAL NUMBER ON WELFARE ROLLS NUMBER OF MURDERS

YEAR

PUBLIC ASSISTANCE RECIPIENTS · · ■ · · MURDERS

Note: Welfare Rolls are per fiscal year. Includes AFDC, Home Relief, PG-ADC, and AFDC-U.
Source: Mayor's Management Report, Fiscal Years 1993, 1999; figures from NYC Human Resources Administration.

world—now we're the work capital of the world." Did this policy of slashing the welfare rolls contribute to the crash?

The impact was beneficial only if the new restrictive qualifications drove away and scattered many criminally involved people who were also abusing the system rather than the truly needy unable to fend for themselves.[5] Otherwise, the relationship between welfare and crime was just the opposite over the previous twenty years (graph 6.2). When more needy people were granted public assistance, murders tended to decline; and when some of these indigents were denied relief, killings generally increased. Since some years didn't fit this pattern, the inverse relationship was weak. But the disruption of this pattern since 1994 casts doubt on any contention that cutting welfare rolls knocked down the crime rate. Just the opposite, offering public assistance to more people might have eased the violence problem, according to the track record of past experience.

Clearly, the data demonstrate that poverty and crime are not linked in any simple and direct manner. Poverty by itself cannot be an automatic "cause" of crime, since more people were poor and yet better behaved during the 1990s than in prior decades. Also, most of the needy are not deeply involved in stealing, robbing, and other illegal money-making ventures. Furthermore, Hispanic New Yorkers were poorer than black New Yorkers, yet their rate of involvement in homicidal violence and other street crimes was not as disproportionally high, according to the data assembled in chapter 2. Finally, the rate of criminal involvement of Asian New Yorkers, especially the most recent arrivals, was disproportionally low, despite their high rate of poverty.[6] Therefore, poverty might best be conceived of as one of several important risk factors, along with many others, including limited educational and occupational opportunities, intense social discrimination, self-defeating cultural values, and profound alienation.

Perhaps participation in the job market has a greater effect than impoverishment on the willingness of poor young men to either abide by the law or engage in illegal activities.

As Good As It Gets? Unemployment Rates and Crime Rates

The relationship between unemployment and crime is complex, just like the relationship between poverty and crime. Researchers have had little success in documenting a clear-cut connection between the ups and downs of the unemployment rate and the rise and fall of crime rates (see Hagan and Peterson, 1995; Bennett, DiIulio, and Walters, 1996; and Short, 1997). Most of the people who are out of work at any given time are not resorting to illegal activities to raise money to support themselves and their families. But many of the individuals who are hauled into court and who wind up behind bars had no job when they committed the offense that got them into legal trouble. If they were employed, most held only marginal (seasonal, occasional, or part-time) positions, or were limited to low wage work in what economists call the "secondary labor market." Usually, they had no particular trade or profession or regular means of earning a living that they could count upon during hard times. Ill-prepared to succeed in a highly competitive environment, they were under constant temptation to gravitate to illegal activities to make the money that others gain from honest labor. Furthermore, the demoralization from chronic unemployment or sporadic work can be a risk factor that causes men to acquire a drinking or drug habit; and the loss of their status as breadwinner can disrupt or destroy family ties. Since a good job is an indispensable prerequisite for gaining income, status, acceptance, and influence in the larger community, it follows that those who are entirely excluded or just marginally connected to the legitimate opportunity structure will be less integrated or bonded to society and less committed to conventional life-styles (see Currie, 1985; and Wilson, 1987).

Indeed, most of the New Yorkers arrested for murder had spotty work histories and held minimum-wage jobs or were unemployed at the time of the killing. Also, the precincts with the highest murder rates tended to have the highest unemployment rates, according to the findings presented in chapter 2.

If young men caught up in illegal activities suddenly found decent jobs and began to enjoy heightened self-esteem, steady incomes, and some degree of financial security, it seems reasonable to hypothesize that their stake in conformity would increase and their involvement in street crime would wither away. If the male unemployment rate dropped sharply in New York during the 1990s, that positive development would go a long way toward explaining the sudden outbreak of law-abiding behavior. If joblessness declined much more impressively in New York than in other major urban centers, that could largely account for the crash. Was participation in illegal activities waning because the City's chronic job shortage was easing?

Unfortunately, a close reading of the economic data revealed that the unemployment rate did not fall impressively in New York; in fact, joblessness, just like poverty, remained an intractable problem all through the 1990s.[7] Even after six years of solid economic recovery, the unemployment rate remained stalled at recessionary levels in 1998, with nearly twice as many job hunters unable to find a paid position in the City as in the rest of the nation (8 percent compared to 4.6 percent). Actually, the annualized unemployment rate did not even drop smoothly. After falling in 1994 and 1995, it crept back up during 1996 and 1997, before declining again in 1998. The unemployment rate remained high, even while the local economy was generating more jobs, mainly because of an influx of a new cohort of job seekers—adults on public assistance forced to search for paid employment under new workfare requirements (Bram et al., 1997; Levitan, 1998). Job seekers had a tougher time finding work in New York than in any other major city. In about fifty-five other metropolitan areas, the local job market was as good as it gets—unemployment rates below 3 percent in 1999. But in the New York vicinity, nearly 7 percent of the labor force was unable to find a job as the decade drew to a close (Levitan, 1998; A. Hevesi, 1999; and Wysocki, 1999).[8]

Breakdowns in joblessness rates by race/ethnicity demonstrated that black and Hispanic New Yorkers did not benefit as much as whites from the celebrated recovery. Black city residents suffered an unemployment rate that was about two-and-one-half times that of whites. The rate for Hispanics was about two times higher than the white rate. One reason minority job seekers found it more difficult to land good positions was that a historically important avenue for upward mobility into white-collar occupations and middle-class status—civil service employment in government agencies—dwindled because of a tax-cutting policy of shrinking the size of the federal, state, and municipal work forces. Positions in City agencies alone were cut by 10 percent from 1993 to 1998 (MMR, 1999).[9] Minority teenagers had particular trouble breaking into the job market, suffering an unemployment rate that hovered around 33 percent. Adults without a high school diploma had a very hard time getting hired and endured double-digit jobless rates during the mid-1990s. Those with a high school degree and even residents with some postsecondary education still experienced recession-type unemployment rates. Only college grads enjoyed low rates (down to about 4 percent) in the 1990s (Levitan, 1998).

In theory, a direct relationship should exist between unemployment rates and crime rates; they should rise and fall in tandem. In reality, there appears to be a more complicated relationship between unemployment rates for the two most at-risk groups—black and Hispanic men—on the one hand, and murder rates on the other (graph 6.3). During the first half of the 1980s, the very high unemployment rate for black men fell; the high unemployment rate for Hispanic men did not improve; yet the murder rate dropped considerably. During the second half of the 1980s, unemployment rates dropped sharply for both black and Hispanic males, but murder rates climbed when they theoretically should have tumbled. After the recession of the early 1990s ended, unemployment rates diminished modestly for black

Graph 6.3. Relationship between Unemployment Rates and Murders, New York City, 1981–1997

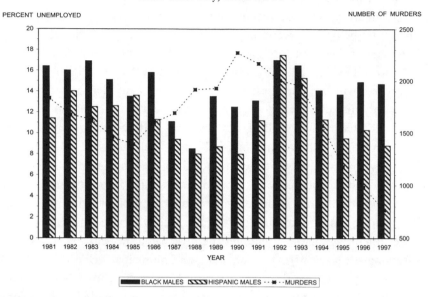

Note: Hispanic unemployment rates were not tracked until 1981.
Sources: 1981–1993 = BLS Geographic Profiles; 1994–1997 = BLS CPS in Levitan, 1998.

males (but stalled at a depression level of 15 percent) and fell substantially for Hispanic males (down to about 8 percent, but still at recessionary levels, and only as good as in 1988 and 1990, terribly crime-ridden years); and murder rates dropped, but much more than anticipated. Therefore, the hypothesized correlations only materialized after the early 1990s, and even then the expected relationships were strong only for Hispanic males but not for black males. In sum, male minority workers were not able to fully participate in the boom of the latter 1990s. The objective economic conditions improved considerably for only one of the two groups at high risk of getting caught up in theft and violence—unemployed Hispanic males—but not very much for the other, out-of-work black males.[10]

Boom and Bust: The Business Cycle and Crime Rates

The 1990s began on a sour financial note. A journalist (Stone, 1990:36) wrote: "A sobering economic reality has settled over New York, a cold, hard morning after the high times of the 1980s. Sales are down, unemployment is up, real estate prices are sinking, companies are cutting back, and the city itself is facing a big budget deficit." A professor of urban planning (Salins, 1990:23) observed that "Confronted with a string of highly publicized crimes, a flagging economy and a potential budget gap of $2 billion for next year, New York City is facing new predictions of its imminent demise." Was it just a coincidence that the amount of blood spilled on City streets set a new record that year?

When the recession finally loosened its stranglehold, an infectious enthusiasm swept the ranks of commentators and pundits. A heady mood of self-confidence, self-congratulation, triumphalism, even euphoria swept across the City and the nation because the sizzling economy was generating so many new jobs without touching off another round of inflation. New York's private sector created jobs "at a record pace, the best since 1950," at an annual growth rate that was even a bit better than the average for the whole country (2.9 percent compared to 2.8 percent) in 1998 (A. Hevesi, 1999; and MMR, 1999:37).[11] Optimism reached such heights that some economists even speculated that hard times could be staved off indefinitely (see Uchitelle, 1998; and Wysocki, 1999). Meanwhile, crime crashed. Was that just a coincidence, too? Could the boom and bust of the business cycle influence the crime rate?

The resurgence in New York's private-sector activity did not substantially reduce the poverty rate or dramatically alleviate the high unemployment rate, as the analysis above illustrated. Perhaps the most significant impact of financial upturns and downturns was psychological. Could the prosperity ostentatiously enjoyed by some have lifted the spirits of others—even those not immediately or directly benefiting from the recovery—and renewed their faith in the "system"? Even if objective conditions did not improve much, did the subjective outlook of the populace, as reflected by such measures as consumer confidence, turn around to such a degree that it profoundly shaped collective behavior?[12] According to the concept of relative deprivation, what really matters is how unemployed and poor people perceive their plight, their expectations about their situation in the near future, and to what groups they compare themselves when assessing the adequacy of their standard of living. Was there evidence that even the "other half" felt they were making progress, or at least would soon be able to climb the ladder of mobility?

Graph 6.4. Relationship between Job Growth and Murders,
New York City, 1960–1998

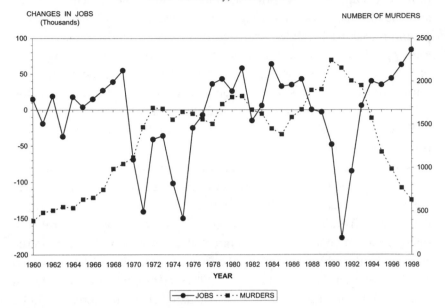

CHANGES IN JOBS
(Thousands)

NUMBER OF MURDERS

Note: Annual job gains or losses are in thousands.
Source: Job growth = BLS, in 1999 Mayor's Management Report.

Or does upward mobility by some but not others breed frustration and resentment?

Whatever theoretical links may be proposed, it appears that in actual practice changes in the City's business cycle were not correlated with changes in the number of murders (graph 6.4). If the two variables were tied together in a simple inverse relationship, periods of substantial job growth should be accompanied by falling murder rates; and periods of net job losses should be marked by a rising tide of violence. But there seems to be no solid evidence to support this hypothesis about an inverse relationship when the job gains and losses defining the business cycles were plotted against net changes in the murder rate since 1960.[13]

During the socially and politically turbulent 1960s, murder rates climbed every year save one, even though the local economy was strong, generating more jobs during seven years out of ten. During most of the next decade, the City's labor force suffered a crippling loss of economic opportunities, yet the murder rate didn't soar. By the end of the 1970s, the job market was improving but violence increasingly marred everyday life. After the brief recession at the start of the 1980s, job creation picked up and the murder rate dropped. But times were still good when the crack epidemic exploded and murders took off. When the local economy faltered and then went into a tailspin after the 1987 stock market crash, murders soared. During the recession in 1990, the loss of jobs reached painful levels, and the loss of life reached intolerable levels. In 1991, the shrinking private sector imposed record-setting layoffs, yet the murder rate began to inch downward. In 1992, even though contracting businesses continued to shed a huge number of jobs, the death toll again drifted lower. Then, as a recovery picked up steam, the hypothesized inverse relationship between more jobs and less crime finally showed up clearly. Overall, one variable rose when the other fell, as predicted, only about half the time (nineteen out of thirty-nine years). Unless it is posited that an entirely new psychology gripped the populace as the millennium approached, this retrospective analysis of the historical record reveals no consistent link between business cycles and murder rates in New York City.[14]

In sum, the booming economy of the 1990s did not alleviate the misery endured by a quarter of the City's population. Even though the unemployment rate for Hispanic men declined, decent jobs remained very hard to find for black men. Poverty and joblessness continued to be more serious problems in New York than in other metropolitan areas, yet crime rates fell more decisively in the City than in other parts of the country. If the economy sank into a tailspin during the 1990s, the crash really would have been baffling. But the improvements in the job market and in earned income were so modest for hard-pressed New Yorkers that these positive economic developments apparently played a minor role, at best, in furthering the crash.

Trickle Down: Was the Underground Economy Thriving?

Before deciding conclusively that the twin problems of poverty and unemployment were not significantly reduced by the recovery of the 1990s, it is necessary to question the accuracy of the data by addressing the issue of the "underground" economy of off-the-books jobs. Official statistics fail to capture the untaxed transactions that go on at all levels of society and, in particular, the actual ways that poor people survive under harsh conditions (see, for example, Rosenthal, 1997; and Pozo, 1998). Some job seekers who tell census and BLS survey interviewers that they are not employed or have low incomes actually may have devised ways of making money in this "twilight" sector. They may benefit from the prosperity of those above them through trickle-down pathways—by working strictly for cash in such service occupations as housekeepers, nannies, home health attendants, gardeners, construction workers, home improvement craftsmen, handymen, drivers, waiters, busboys, dishwashers, and day laborers. Illegal aliens are forced to eke out an off-the-books living in this manner because of stringent document-checking regulations imposed on employers. Surely, many other apparently down-and-out New Yorkers also made ends meet in myriad ways that rendered official statistics quite misleading (see Kacapyr, 1998). To the extent that the lavish spending of money that flowed through recorded and taxable transactions also trickled down to those participating in the underground economy, the 1990s recovery may have reached farther down the social ladder than government measurements of employment and income indicated. In addition, another realm of the "subterranean" economy continued to provide jobs and income: crime as work. Illegal opportunities constantly compete with—and sometimes appear more promising than—legitimate jobs (see Cloward and Ohlin, 1960). Despite law enforcement's victories against mob activities and the black market during the 1990s, some unknown proportion of New Yorkers still were earning money from rackets like gambling, prostitution, fencing stolen items, selling counterfeit and pirated goods, dealing drugs, and perpetrating countless money-making scams and schemes.[15]

Furthermore, the changing nature of New York's economy may have driven down the crime rate in two other ways. First, the growing demand for educated labor rather than manual labor could have inspired increasing numbers of young New Yorkers to prepare for careers that required higher education, and going to college may have enabled them to transcend street culture and thereby resist the temptations of street crime. Second, the long-standing worldwide reputation of New York's economic engine as a vehicle for upward mobility may have attracted record numbers of immigrants to the City, and these newcomers could have been better behaved than the native born, especially in terms of enduring adversity without resorting to illegal ways of coping with frustration and anger.

Higher Learning, Lower Criminality? Did the College Experience Counteract Street Smarts?

The personal benefits of a higher education are dramatic and fairly easy to substantiate using available census data on earnings. However, the collective social and economic benefit to society of having a more highly educated citizenry may be even greater, although these impacts are difficult to impossible to quantify.

—New York State comptroller H. Carl McCall (1998:A20)

When it comes to murder, offending rates remain at their highest levels between ages eighteen to twenty-four (Blumstein and Rosenfeld, 1998). This range usually is characterized as "college-aged youth." How teenagers and young adults spend their time during these turbulent years greatly determines whether or not their behavior will make the crime problem worse. The subculture of college students differs markedly from street culture. Dropping out of high school and not working raises the odds of criminal involvement. But what about finishing up and then going to college? Does pursuing a higher degree substantially lower the chances of causing serious trouble? And were more New York City high school grads college-bound in the 1990s?

Since the late 1970s, the proportion of high school graduates who have opted not to continue their studies (by either going to work, staying home to raise children, or joining the armed services) has diminished steadily. As a matter of occupational necessity in the high-technology and information-processing global economy, increasing percentages of career-oriented young adults have been enrolling in postsecondary institutions. As a result, the proportion of New Yorkers whose outlook on life has been influenced by the campus experience has been growing rapidly (see graph 6.5). The share of the senior class (male and female) continuing its education (full time or part time, in-state or out-of-state, in two- or four-year institutions) rose from about 76 percent in 1977 to nearly 87 percent in 1991, and after slipping a bit rebounded to an all-time high in 1997 of just over 87 percent, according to the government's annual

Graph 6.5. Trends in College Entrance Rates, New York City, 1977–1997

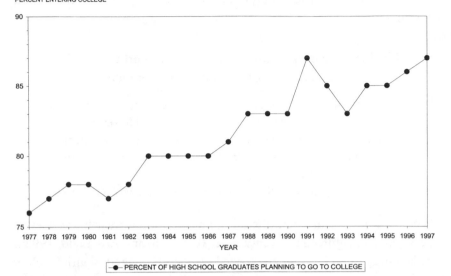

Note: Includes all high school graduates intending to go to two- and four-year colleges throughout the country.
Source: State Education Department of New York, 1978–1999.

survey of high school principals (State Education Department of New York, 1978–1999).[16] The comparable college-going figures for high school graduates across the country were considerably lower, 49 percent in 1979 and 65 percent in 1997 (see Foote et al., 1997; BLS, 1999).

During the 1990s, college-going rates for black and Hispanic high school graduates throughout New York State (largely residing in New York City) became available from the annual survey of principals. Although the comparable figures were several percentage points lower than for white students, and way below the levels for Asian students, they were far better than in the rest of the country. By 1997, 81 percent of black as well as Hispanic high school graduates across the state were enrolling in either two- or four-year institutions (State Education Department of New York, 1991–1999). The nationwide college enrollment rates (for 1998) were substantially lower for black grads (62 percent) and even more so for Hispanics (47 percent) (see BLS, 1999).

One of the major reasons for the increase in the college-going rate for young New Yorkers of all backgrounds was that access to educational opportunities remained student-friendly at the multicampus public college system, the City University of New York (CUNY).[17] The CUNY system struggled to continue to fulfill its historic mission to serve the disadvantaged and recent immigrants by educating about half of all the college students in the City. Adding in the private and religious-based institutions (some of which have dormitories for out-of-towners), the roughly one hundred colleges and universities (including law, medical, and other professional schools) in New York City enrolled a total undergraduate and graduate student body of over 400,000 during the 1990s (Department of City Planning, 1993, 1999). Therefore, although it was seldom characterized in this manner, with so many students living in the metropolitan area, New York actually was the country's—and the world's—largest "college town."

The cumulative effect of the year-after-year processing of large numbers of students by local institutions of higher learning (plus in-migration exceeding out-migration) has brought about the development of an increasingly well-educated populace in New York. Back in 1970, the proportion of City residents who had ever enrolled in college was less than 19 percent (of the population over twenty-five years old, the standard census cut-off point). By 1980, that share had grown to almost 30 percent. By 1990, it had risen to 42 percent, according to the complete U.S. Censuses for those years. Projecting these trends to the end of the century, at least half the adults (twenty-five and older) in New York have probably attended college.

As for graduating from college as opposed to just completing some courses, degree holders made up 8 percent of the City's population (at least twenty-five years old), and 6 percent of the nation's, in 1960. By 1970, the corresponding figures were 11 percent for the City compared to 7 percent for the country; and in 1980, 17 percent versus 11 percent. By 1990, New York's relative proportion of college graduates was even more favorable, 23 percent, in contrast to 16 percent for the rest of the U.S., according to the Census Bureau's decennial surveys (Department of City Planning, 1993, fig. 5.3). Clearly, the achievement gap has been steadily widening to New York's advantage, causing the City to stand out in yet another way. Local residents, including low-income and black and Hispanic New Yorkers, were more likely to have attended college and to have completed a degree than people living in most other cities in the

Table 6.1. Years of Schooling Completed by Accused
Murderers, New York City, 1989

Number of Years of Schooling Completed	Percent of All Male Arrestees
Less than 12 (dropped out)	60
12 (graduated high school)	28
GED (diploma)	3
13 (one year of college)	5
14 (two years)	3
16 (four years)	0
19 (graduate degree)	1

Notes: Based on a sample of 87 men accused of murder in 1989. All arrestees under the age of twenty were excluded as being too young to complete a year of college.
Source: Database of 1989 arrestees for homicide, based on interviews carried out by the New York City Criminal Justice Agency (CJA).

nation. Could the growing presence of all these current and former college students have been another economy-related development that facilitated the crime crash?

When students enter college, they are socialized to respect new sources of knowledge sharply different from "street smartness" (see Miller, 1958) that is prized as the fount of survival skills by those who are forced to live day-to-day by their wits. When college students break the law, they typically limit themselves to drug-taking and low-level selling, drunken brawls, rowdiness, vandalism, petty thefts, and date rapes. More mature criminally inclined former college students gravitate toward white-collar crimes like embezzlement, tax evasion, and sophisticated frauds rather than crude thefts and applications of brute force. Murders carried out by well-educated offenders are few and far between. Not very many of New York's suspected killers twenty years old or older had ever attended college, according to the database accumulated from arrestees interviewed in 1989 by the New York City Criminal Justice Agency (CJA) (see table 6.1). Only 9 percent of the men had been exposed to higher education, and just one man of eighty-seven homicide arrestees had graduated from college. In fact, most of the killers had not even finished high school.

Not only are people who have taken some college courses underrepresented among murderers, they are also disproportionately uninvolved in other types of serious felonies like robbery, burglary, or drug dealing.

A mere 8 percent of all incarcerated felons had ever enrolled in college, according to data about the educational background of the inmates in the New York State prison system during 1995–1997 (NYS DCJS, 1996, 1997, 1998). Of the nearly 68,000 convicts confined during 1998, hardly any had previously completed a course of study, earning a one-year certificate (0.4 percent), a two-year associate degree (2 percent), a four-year bachelor's degree (1 percent), or a graduate degree (0.2 percent)(NYS DOCS, 1998).[18]

Exposure to higher education not only lowers the odds of committing murder but even reduces the chances of getting killed (probably through its influence on occupation, income, and life-style). The rate of victimization of former college students remains relatively low, considering that the proportion of New Yorkers who have ever enrolled in an institution of higher learning was approaching 50 percent by the close of the 1990s. The overwhelming majority of men killed in the midst of the crime crash had never attended college, as indicated by the data in table 6.2. Most were high school graduates. Among the deceased Hispanic men, more had been high school dropouts than had been college students; among black men, the numbers were about equal. Among the young white and Asian men (who probably had many more former

Table 6.2. Educational Background of Men Twenty Years of Age or Older Murdered in 1995, 1996, and 1997

	High School Dropouts	High School Graduates	Attended College	Total Number of Victims
Part A: All Men 20 Years Old or Older				
White	12%	66%	22%	299
Black	13%	76%	12%	1,227
Hispanic	22%	68%	11%	580
Asian	15%	61%	24%	62
Part B: All Men Born in New York City and Murdered during 1995–1997 When They Were in Their Twenties				
White	17%	64%	19%	36
Black	26%	54%	20%	233
Hispanic	30%	58%	12%	33
Asian	36%	45%	18%	11

Notes: Part B includes only men between twenty and twenty-nine years of age who were born in New York City. Excluded are cases in which years of school completed or victim's race/ethnicity was missing.
Source: NYC DOH vital statistics database, 1995, 1996, 1997.

collegians than dropouts in their midst), more of the casualties were college educated rather than high school dropouts. But still the proportion of homicide victims who had been to college was nowhere near the almost 50 percent share of the general population over age twenty-five.

Young men born (and presumably raised) in New York before they were cut down in the prime of life are the focus of Part B of table 6.2. Virtually all of these victims had the chance to pursue higher education because they had grown up in the City at a time when going to college (including part time and at night) was easier (due to CUNY's open admissions policies and low tuition) than anywhere else in the country—or the world. The proportion of graduating high school seniors enrolling as college students has exceeded 75 percent for two decades (minus a dropout rate of about 15 percent to 20 percent), so it is reasonable to anticipate that a high percentage (in the vicinity of 55 to 60 percent) would have attended college among the men in their twenties murdered during the mid-1990s. But former college students were obviously underrepresented among these casualties of criminal violence, as the data in Part B make clear. Most of the deceased men had only graduated high school, and more had dropped out than had gone on for more schooling (except among whites).

In conclusion, college attendance functioned as an effective risk-reduction factor—in terms of killing or being killed—especially for black and Hispanic young men. Furthermore, some college was better than no college at all, since the enhanced safety benefits were not only enjoyed by those who earned degrees, but also by those who took courses but did not graduate. The inverse relationship between the number of years of schooling completed and a New Yorker's likelihood of participating in predatory behavior or falling victim to it can be explained in terms of rational economic choices. As the ranks of the college educated grew, the number of potential recruits attracted to high risk/low reward activities like street gang membership, drug dealing, robbing, burglarizing, car stealing, and gun toting dwindled. Sending a growing share of young people to college served, among other functions, as a wise crime-prevention strategy. This long-term social investment policy embarked upon in the late 1960s finally started to pay dividends in the 1990s. As it became the norm for eighteen- to twenty-four-year-olds of all racial/ethnic groups to go to college rather than straight to work or, worse yet, to idleness in the streets, a lifetime spent in pursuit of ill-gotten gains increasingly lost its appeal. Higher aspirations to pursue a career competed successfully against baser impulses to seize illegal opportunities. New York stood out from all other cities in the level of access to postsecondary education that it provided to all of its residents, especially the disadvantaged. Therefore, the extra-rapid expansion of a populace influenced by the promise of self-improvement and upward social mobility that college offered contributed significantly to the crime crash.

Foreign Aid: Did Immigrants Help Turn the Tide?

For those people in New York who are concerned—'Oh, there are too many foreigners coming here and there are too many people that look different or act different'—please remember that has been the key to our success.

—Mayor Rudolph Giuliani (quoted in Dugger, 1997:A1)

New York always has been a major destination and port of entry for new arrivals from abroad. But during the 1980s and 1990s, unusually large numbers of immigrants settled within the five boroughs, bringing about unprecedented ethnic diversity.[19] The growing presence of new arrivals contributed to the City's revitalization, as noted by Mayor Giuliani in the above quotation. These newcomers were willing to settle into an urban environment that other City dwellers were abandoning in droves for the greener pastures of suburbia. Their influx helped to avert the destructive chain reaction that has burdened many of the older cities of the Northeast and the Midwest: population loss leads to a decrease in tax revenues, which then results in a deterioration in municipal services.[20] Immigrants were willing to rent apartments in run-down buildings for which landlords were having trouble finding tenants (see Schill, Friedman, and Rosenbaum, 1998). Otherwise, the owners of these brownstones and tenements might have abandoned these deteriorating structures as not worth the upkeep and property taxes, or even sought out arsonists to burn them down as part of insurance scams (as some unscrupulous slum lords did in the 1970s).[21] Immigrants also were willing to accept menial, dirty, difficult, dangerous, and low-paying jobs (some in "sweatshops") that American workers turned down; and they were willing to undertake risky business ventures to fill marginal entrepreneurial niches that may or may not prove to be profitable in the long run (see Groneman and Reimers, 1995; Millman, 1996; Waldinger, 1996; Jordan, 1997; and Lobo and Salvo, 1997).

At the start of the 1970s, the proportion of foreign-born residents slipped to its lowest point in the twentieth century, around 18 percent of all New Yorkers (about 1.5 million people), according to the Census Bureau.[22] By the late 1990s, the foreign-born population had soared to an all-time high, comprising about twice the proportion, 36 percent, of all residents of the five boroughs (more than 2.7 million people).[23] Factoring in their children, roughly 55 to 60 percent of all New Yorkers were either immigrants or their immediate offspring. These figures would be even larger if the estimated 400,000 "illegal aliens"—newcomers without the proper papers to stay in the country who therefore try to keep a very low profile—were counted (see Dugger, 1997; Siemaszko and McKoy, 1998; and Sontag and Dugger, 1998).

Wretched Refuse or Huddled Masses Yearning to
Breathe Free: Were the Newest New Yorkers
Criminally Inclined or Disinclined?

This continuous stream of new residents from other countries could not have directly caused the murder rate to rise in the late 1970s, fall in the early 1980s, soar in the late 1980s, and then crash during the 1990s. But, on balance, how has the buildup of immigrants affected the City's street crime problem? The key question centers on the overall degree of involvement in illegal activities of recent arrivals from overseas. To borrow some phrases inscribed on the base of the Statue of Liberty, did this latest wave of immigration bring to New York a lot of "wretched refuse" whose lawless ingratitude boosted the City's crime rate, or mostly "huddled masses yearning to breathe free" who were so thankful to escape their oppressive homelands that they made extra efforts to steer clear of the murder and mayhem going on around them? Relatively speaking, were the new arrivals from overseas more or less likely to be drawn into illegal activities than native New Yorkers and internal migrants who moved in from other parts of the country?

Judging from historical accounts, criminological research, alarmist politicians,[24] and news reports, there are sound reasons to be concerned about the impact massive immigration can have on crime rates. When waves of European immigrants settled into the hastily built tenements in the City's overcrowded Lower East Side at the turn of the century, the murder rate went up. Even after restrictive laws cut the flow of foreigners down to a trickle, violent crime rates continued to soar during the Prohibition years of the Roaring 1920s and did not begin to fall until after the ban on drinking was lifted and the Great Depression had set in, during the 1930s. However, researchers believe that immigrants who arrived as adults generally were hard working and law abiding; it was their children who experienced the severe adjustment problems that led to high rates of involvement in delinquency and street crime (Haskell and Yablonsky, 1970; Silberman, 1978). In fact, a social movement during the Progressive Era around the turn of the century was so fearful about the destructive potential of what were quaintly referred to as "street urchins," "urban waifs," and "wayward youth" that it set up separate juvenile courts and justice systems specifically to save and salvage these high-risk youngsters (see Platt, 1969). Reportedly, the children of successive waves of immigrants grew up confused about right and wrong in "interstitial" downtown neighborhoods that suffered from rapid population turnovers, large numbers of transients, mixed land use, substandard housing, and social disorganization (Shaw and McKay, 1942). These youths had unusual trouble negotiating the turbulence of adolescence because they felt pulled in different directions: they were torn between observing the traditions inculcated by their parents at home and adopting the norms of the popular culture they were being socialized into by their peers in the streets and in school, according to the Wickersham Commission that analyzed the crime wave of the 1920s in 1931 (see Silberman, 1978).[25] Imbued with the American dream, some children of immigrants resorted to illegal opportunities during the Depression in order to climb out of poverty when they encountered the frustrating restrictions and discrimination that the dominant society imposed on individuals branded as foreigners (Sellin, 1938).

Immigrants have been particularly vulnerable to the lure of racketeering as an avenue for upward mobility. Organized crime families emerged and thrived in tightly bonded ethnic enclaves of newcomers who had suffered brutal repression in their native lands and continued to harbor deep distrust of the authorities (Sanoff, 1996; Ianni, 1998). Transplanted gangsters from Sicily's secret Black Hand organization became the forerunners of the Mafia's five crime families that took root in New York's Italian American immigrant neighborhoods earlier in this century (see Cressey, 1969). Decades later, the same pattern was followed by members of Russian organized crime rings who recreated rackets familiar to them as they reassembled and then mingled with, recruited among, and preyed upon their countrymen in Brooklyn's Brighton Beach, starting in the 1970s (see Friedman, 1994).

Since the 1960s, trafficking in cocaine, heroin, and marijuana has served as the primary rags-to-riches racket. The lucrative drug trade has attracted to New York members of Colombia's Cali and Medellin cartels, Jamaican possees, Chinese Tongs and Triads, and of other less well known smuggling rings hailing from the Dominican Republic, Nigeria, Afghanistan, and Pakistan (Natarajian, 1998).

Street gangs also have sprung up among immigrant youths from dysfunctional families in conflict-ridden neighborhoods. During the 1990s, the new recruits included some youths from Mexico (organized into eleven gangs with roughly six hundred members) (see Donohue, 1998), El Salvador (forming the gang "MS13"), and Vietnam (joining "Born to Kill").

The "Marielitos" who fled from Cuba in 1980 stand out as the most maligned of any group of recent immigrants. Their exodus took place when pressure from exile groups compelled the Castro regime to permit a "Freedom Flotilla" of thousands of small craft to ferry about 120,000 refugees from Mariel Harbor to nearby Florida ports. Tired of losing some of the island's most talented people, the government took advantage of the situation to export some malcontents and troublemakers. Somewhere between 5 percent and 20 percent of the asylum seekers had been inmates of Cuban prisons and mental institutions. (However, many of the refugees with criminal records had been punished for political crimes like refusing mandatory sugar-cane-cutting assignments or military service, were guilty merely of minor black market offenses, or were under psychiatric confinement for their homosexuality). Most settled in the Miami area, and when that city's homicide rate soared during the 1980s, the drug-related carnage was blamed on them (to some degree unfairly: they were more likely to be victims than offenders). About two thousand of the former convicts gravitated to New York. Within about a year, the NYPD had arrested over four hundred of them, and they were thought to be responsible for about five thousand incidents, including several murders (Martinez, 1997).[26]

But are the notorious criminals cited above the exceptions to the rule, feeding negative stereotypes that unfairly slander largely law-abiding, hard-working newcomers to New York? This issue can be examined in two ways, given the limitations of the available data: by establishing the proportion of known serious offenders—state prison inmates—who were foreign born; and by determining the fraction of foreign-born homicide victims who had used illegal drugs before they were murdered.

New York State's Department of Correctional Services (DOCS) began to monitor the presence of the foreign-born among convicted felons shipped upstate in 1985, in order to bolster the argument that the state government deserved financial support from Congress to help pay for their upkeep, since the federal government controls immigration policies. The DOCS discovered that these inmates were serving some-what longer sentences for committing more serious drug and violent crimes. For example, the foreign born comprised 17 percent of the in-mates in 1998 (2,035 of 12,183) who were being punished for killing someone (convicted of either first- or second-degree murder, first-or sec-ond-degree manslaughter, vehicular manslaughter in the first or second degree, criminally negligent homicide, or murder and manslaughter as "juvenile offenders" or "youthful offenders"). Furthermore, the number of foreign-born inmates had risen dramatically. Back in 1985, only about 2,630 inmates claimed they were born outside the United States. But by the end of 1998, roughly 9,180 prisoners were immigrants, a jump of nearly 250 percent. Put another way, 8 percent of all the men and women under lock and key had been born in some other country in 1985. By 1991, their ranks had swelled to roughly 12 percent of all in-carcerated felons. For the rest of the 1990s, their share held steady at around 13 percent (see Clark, 1992–99).

But was the rise from 8 to 13 percent hard evidence of a crime wave fueled by immigration, and of overinvolvement in illegal activities on the part of newcomers? Was the 1998 figure of 9,180 prisoners way out of line and far too high? Before drawing any conclusions, one cal-culation must be made, and several factors need to be taken into account. First of all, from 1985 until the late 1990s, the City's immigrant population rose from about 26 percent to 36 percent of all residents. Meanwhile, the prison population doubled from roughly 35,000 inmates to just about 70,000. Therefore, the ranks of foreign-born inmates would be anticipated to swell for both of these reasons. As for the calculation, the 8 percent, 12 percent, and 13 percent figures have to be placed into context, in terms of how many prisoners would be expected to be foreign born if immigrants were perpetrators of serious offenses strictly in proportion to their share of the City's population. Taking various factors into account, the expected numbers of foreign born prisoners that theoretically ought to be confined can be calculated. These expected frequencies, the actual counts, and the departures from the predicted amount appear in table 6.3.

Clearly, year after year, the estimated number of foreign-born inmates who were New York City residents turned out to be far below what would be expected statistically, given the assumption of proportional representation (see the last column of table 6.3).[27] In 1985, the calculated number of foreign-born inmates from the City was 63 percent less than anticipated. Admittedly, during the next five years, the proportion of immigrant inmates grew rapidly (by 50 percent). Presumably, this surge reflected the recruitment of large numbers of young men from other countries into the City's burgeoning crack cocaine market during the height of the epidemic. But even in the worst year, 1991, the estimated number of foreign-born inmates in the state prison system who had committed felonies in New York City was roughly half of what was expected on the basis of proportional representation. During the rest of the 1990s, the actual ranks of immigrants behind bars fell even further behind projections. In other words, immigrants have been much less involved in serious crime than nativist fears would predict.[28]

Furthermore, to their credit, immigrants overcame several demographic disadvantages that placed them at higher risk of becoming involved in street crime. First of all, any population that is disproportionately young and male should have a higher level of participation in violence and theft. The newest New Yorkers had many more young men in their midst during the 1980s and 1990s than nonimmigrants (see Rose, 1997). Second, communities of new arrivals tend to be harder hit by poverty than more established New Yorkers, according to the 1990 U.S.

Table 6.3. City Immigrants Incarcerated in New York State Prisons,
Expected versus Actual Numbers, 1985–1998

Year	NYC Foreign- Born Pop.	NYS Prison Pop.	Percent Foreign- Born Inmates	NYS Actual Foreign- Born Inmates	NYC Expected Foreign- Born Inmates	NYC Calculated Foreign- Born Inmates	Departure Number and Percent
1985	26%	34,620	8%	2,630	6,120	2,287	−3,835 = −63%
1991	29%	57,795	12%	7,140	11,400	6,215	−5,190 = −46%
1992	30%	61,735	12%	7,730	12,595	6,725	−5,870 = −47%
1993	31%	64,570	13%	8,200	13,610	7,135	−6,476 = −48%
1994	32%	66,760	13%	8,575	14,526	7,460	−7,060 = −49%
1995	33%	68,485	13%	8,775	15,370	7,635	−7,735 = −50%
1996	34%	69,685	13%	9,050	16,110	7,875	−8,235 = −51%
1997	36%	69,800	13%	9,100	17,085	7,915	−9,170 = −54%
1998	36%	70,005	13%	9,180	17,135	7,985	−9,200 = −54%

Notes: Two constants were used in the calculations to derive the NYC estimates: % NYS inmates from NYC = 68%; % of NYS foreign-born inmates from NYC = 87%. All figures rounded to the nearest 5. Figures for 1997 were interpolated.
Sources: NYS DCJS (68% of inmates from NYC); U.S. INS (87% foreign-born from NYC). New York State Department of Correctional Services prisoner files, as reported in Clark (1991–1999).

Census. Since living in poverty raises the risks of becoming involved in street crime and being sent to prison, the City's lower-income immigrants should be more numerous among prisoners than in the overall population, but they weren't. Finally, if the Census Bureau had counted all the illegal aliens living in the City accurately, the proportion of foreign-born New Yorkers would be greater on the outside and therefore should be higher on the inside as well. For all these reasons, it is reasonable to suppose that immigrants would be overrepresented behind bars. Since their actual presence among convicted felons serving time turned out to be way below expectations, it appears that the disproportionately youthful, male, and poor immigrants living in New York City in the 1980s and 1990s were surprisingly law abiding, just like their counterparts at the turn of the century.

There is another way, albeit indirect, to double-check the extent of immigrant involvement in illegal activity. Their participation in the drug scene can be investigated by examining the results of toxicology tests performed on the bodily fluids of homicide victims.[29] The findings from these postmortems indicate that compared to other New Yorkers, fewer foreign-born persons indulged in drug use before dying (table 6.4). Of

Table 6.4. Prior Drug Use by Foreign-Born and U.S.-Born
Homicide Victims, New York City, 1997
(number and percentage testing positive by drug)

Birthplace	Cocaine	Opiates	Marijuana	Alcohol
Foreign born	6/86 = 7%	0/86 = 0%	13/85 = 16%	32/87 = 37%
U.S. born	30/143 = 21%	5/143 = 4%	42/143 = 31%	57/143 = 40%

Notes: Dichotomizing the victims into just two categories (foreign born vs. American born, including Puerto Rico) and excluding the unknown birthplace cases, the differences in drug use are statistically significant (at the 0.05 level) for cocaine (chi square = 7.9) and marijuana (chi square = 6.1) and almost for opiates (chi square 3.1), but not for alcohol.
Source: Files maintained by the Office of the Chief Medical Examiner of all homicides committed during the first six months of 1997.

all those who were murdered in New York City during the first half of 1997, the foreign born had a rate of positive test results for cocaine in their corpses that was only one-third the rate for American-born victims, and that difference was statistically significant (see rows 1 and 2 in column 2). As for marijuana smoking, the gap was narrower but still turned out to be statistically significant. Foreign-born victims used pot prior to their demise half as frequently as U.S.-born victims (see rows 1 and 2 in column 4). None of the foreign-born victims had heroin in their system that year; a very small number and percentage of other victims did (see rows 1 and 2 in column 3). Alcohol consumption (which, of course, is a risk factor for violence but not a sign of participation in the illegal drug scene) by immigrants who subsequently got slain took place to a lesser degree, but hardly so when compared to other groups (see rows 1 and 2 in column 5); this slight difference was not statistically significant.[30]

Up to this point, immigrants have been treated as a monolithic group or single entity when, in reality, all they actually have in common is their initial status as new arrivals. Since they have gravitated to New York from all over the globe, the various immigrant groups can have very different educational backgrounds, work experiences, cultural practices, and degrees of difficulty with the English language. The young men in each community become more or less involved in street crime for a number of reasons: the social classes from which they come, their average educational and occupational background, the legitimate job possibilities open to them, the illegal opportunities that beckon to them, the presence or absence of street gangs and organized crime syndicates in their midst, their cultural and religious traditions, and their overall family stability.

Furthermore, immigrants may be visitors and students on visas, legal permanent residents ("green card" holders), undocumented ("illegal") aliens, and new, naturalized citizens. Consequently, immigrant groups ought to differ substantially in their rates of involvement in street crime. This hypothesis is confirmed by the discovery by the state prison authorities that although foreign-born inmates hailed from 126 different countries, over three quarters of them came to the United States from Caribbean islands or South America. In fact, nearly two-thirds emigrated from just four source countries: the Dominican Republic, Colombia, Cuba, and Jamaica (Clark, 1999). The obvious explanation for the higher involvement rates in the Jamaican, Colombian, and Dominican communities is that some of their members were drawn into the drug trade, especially during the height of the crack epidemic in the late 1980s until the start of the 1990s. Many of the Cuban inmates had arrived during the Mariel boatlift.

Throughout the 1990s, even more people from abroad poured into New York than during the 1980s. Immigration from the Dominican Republic shot up 52 percent. But the number 2 source country switched from Jamaica (which fell 27 percent to become the fourth-biggest supplier) to the former Soviet Union (skyrocketing 884 percent from twelfth place in the 1980s). China (including the mainland, Taiwan, and Hong Kong) maintained its position in third place, but its pace picked up (increasing 33 percent) (see NYC Department of City Planning, 1997; and INS, 1999).

Newcomers from Russia and China have been able to steer clear of trouble much more successfully than other groups in the 1990s. The surge of over 66,000 new arrivals from 1990 through 1994 from Russia (and a few other republics of the former Soviet Union, particularly the Ukraine) helped bring down the crime rate. Russian and other European newcomers (largely from Poland) encountered fewer difficulties and discrimination than their Third World counterparts when searching for gainful employment or decent affordable housing (see Schill, Friedman, and Rosenbaum, 1998). The less hostile reception they received meant that fewer of their members would be vulnerable to the lure of the streets. For example, of the roughly 70,000 convicted felons in the prison system during 1998, fewer than 70 (one-tenth of one percent) from across the state were born in the republics of the former Soviet

Union (see Clark, 1999). Similarly, of the roughly 780 homicide victims in 1997, only 5 (less than one percent) were listed as of "Russian" ancestry, according to the Vital Statistics database. If the City is home to roughly 200,000 Soviet émigrés (Lewine, 1999), then their victimization rate was a very safe 2.5 deaths per 100,000 per year.

A parallel set of statistics confirms the low rate of involvement as offenders or homicide victims of New Yorkers of Chinese descent. Just 2 percent of all foreign-born prisoners (206 out of 9,180) were from mainland China (in 1998), and only 8 Chinese were murder victims (in 1997). In sum, the data confirms that the City benefited in a largely unacknowledged way from the political developments that shook the world as the 1990s began. The sudden end of the Cold War and superpower rivalry touched off a massive exodus of people who had been brought up in authoritarian communist societies. The relocation of these unusually law-abiding political refugees to New York helped to dampen the crime wave.[31]

Several factors might explain why immigrants in general have been disproportionately less involved in street crime. In the 1990s, more women than men came to the City from all points on the globe. A greater percentage of the newcomers were well educated and highly skilled (Rose, 1997). The foreign-born black and Hispanic immigrants had higher labor force participation rates and lower poverty rates than their native-born counterparts (NYC Department of City Planning, 1996).[32] New arrivals with darker skins landed in the United States after the worst was over in terms of racial discrimination. Even though exiles and refugees didn't find the streets paved with gold, many apparently have concluded that America remains the land of opportunity. Their struggle to survive economically, despite the legendary high cost of living and cut-throat competition, evidently pales in comparison to the oppressive conditions they endured in their homelands. Perhaps this sense of relative improvement overrides feelings of relative deprivation that otherwise breed bitter resentment among longer-term City residents who feel they are not making progress quickly enough in comparison to the good life being led by affluent pace-setters. This grateful-to-be-here frame of mind could account for the general willingness of immigrants to move into housing units and work at jobs that other New Yorkers reject, and their relative unwillingness to surrender to the seduction of risky illegal opportunities that some of the more acculturated residents pursue.

Newcomers off to a rocky start had reasons to be optimistic that their prospects and situations would improve with time. They had landed in the United States during a period of unparalleled prosperity and relatively low unemployment. The longer immigrants remained in the country, the better-off they became, census data showed. Legal immigrants generally earned as much as other New Yorkers, and the children of immigrants tended to make the same amount of money as their U.S.-born counterparts. After fifteen years of residence, the foreign-born on average earned greater incomes than nonimmigrants (Clark and Passel, 1998).

Furthermore, those who have not yet become naturalized citizens might feel particularly vulnerable to deportation, and therefore might take extra precautions to avoid becoming caught up in illegal activities that could jeopardize their treasured status as visa and green-card holders and legal permanent residents. In other words, their tenuous position might deter them from committing crimes that could carry the extra penalty, besides imprisonment, of expulsion from the country.

On balance, the particularly heavy flow of immigrants to New York during the 1980s and 1990s was a very positive social and economic trend.[33] By settling in decaying neighborhoods that were emptying out, they prevented severe population losses. Through hard work, they helped to revitalize these areas as vibrant, bustling places to live, do business, and shop, thereby reclaiming public spaces and deterring outdoor criminal activity. The largely unplanned social experiment in multiculturalism of bringing together people speaking 121 different languages seems to have worked out very well, in the sense that it put a brake on spiraling crime rates and even helped turn the tide. The unprecedented ethnic diversity of New York in the 1990s—what Mayor David Dinkins termed a "gorgeous mosaic"—was another reason why crime crashed.

Notes

1. New York had more upper-income residents than any other major urban center in the mid-1990s; nearly 2 percent of City families had incomes of $150,000 or more, and thanks to the millionaires among them, these households averaged more than $300,000 a year (Craig and Austin, 1997).

2. The analysts at the Community Service Society, a group that advocates in behalf of the poor, drew these conclusions from the yearly CPS surveys. The Census Bureau considers the annual CPS for New York City to have too great a margin of error because of its relatively small sample size to make such precise determinations. The federal government will not derive official estimates of the City's poverty rate until the massive data set collected by the census of 2000 is thoroughly analyzed.

3. The poverty line serves as the income cutoff for eligibility for many social welfare programs. It is based on the number of persons in a household and is adjusted upward periodically to take inflation into account. However, it does not reflect the local cost of living. Poor people in New York must pay much more for rent, food, and certain other necessities of life than in most other parts of the country (Editors, *New York Times*, 1994).

4. On the national level, no simple relationship emerged until 1993. Then all three indicators—the murder rate, the unemployment rate, and the poverty rate—moved downward in tandem for the rest of the 1990s.

5. Mayor Giuliani was reported to have said that New York had more than its fair share of welfare recipients, and that it would be a positive development if some left town in response to more stringent eligibility requirements. He told a journalist in 1995, "That's not an unspoken part of our strategy. That is our strategy." Later, he amended his public statements which he felt were taken out of context, and declared that an exodus of poverty-stricken residents who had formerly received aid "could be a natural consequence," though "not the intention of our policy." One of the mayor's chief policy architects told the press that "the poor will eventually figure out that it's a lot easier to be homeless where it's warm" (Barrett, 1997:32; Tumposky, 1995:2).

6. Nationally, 14 percent of all Americans of Asian and Pacific Island descent lived below the poverty line in 1997 (compared to 9 percent for whites, 27 percent of blacks, and 27 percent of Hispanics), according to the annual Current Population Survey carried out by the U.S. Bureau of the Census (Dalaker and Naifeh, 1998).

7. One of the sharpest methodological controversies among social scientists surrounds how to measure unemployment rates. The official government figures derived from Bureau of Labor Statistics (BLS) surveys only count people who are actively looking for work. Discouraged workers who have given up trying to find a job, at least at survey time, are not counted as unemployed. Therefore, the official estimates understate the true dimensions of the problem of joblessness.

8. Unemployment in the New York City metropolitan area (including several prosperous suburban counties) stood at 6.9 percent during 1998. The Miami–Dade County area had the second-highest unemployment rate, at 6.4

percent, and greater Los Angeles the third highest at 6.3 percent. The Minneapolis–St. Paul area had the lowest unemployment rate of all, with just 1.6 percent of its local job seekers unable to find work (A. Hevesi, 1999).

9. At the start of the 1990s, New York's public sector work force was much larger than in other cities (at almost 13 percent, nearly twice the big-city average) (Craig and Austin, 1997).

10. Unemployment rates can fall for the wrong reasons. If job seekers grow disillusioned and stop searching for positions, they no longer are counted as out of work in periodic BLS surveys. Any apparent statistical improvement in the unemployment rate for this reason would not have a corresponding beneficial effect on crime rates. In fact, an exodus of discouraged workers from the labor market usually translates into an influx of new recruits seeking out marginal, even illegal ways of making money. To prevent false readings, the unemployment rate needs to be supplemented by other measures of economic well-being, the employment rate (the total number of people holding jobs divided by the size of the group between the ages of sixteen and sixty-five), and the labor force participation rate (which includes job seekers as well as job holders). Good times have arrived only when the number of "officially" unemployed people goes down at the same time that the proportion of employed persons goes up. When employment rates and labor force participation rates were graphed (not shown), patterns emerged that were very similar to graph 6.2 linking unemployment and murder rates.

11. Critics pointed out that many of the new positions in the service sector and in sales and clerical work were entry-level jobs that paid low wages. However, from an immediate crime-reduction perspective, these were precisely the kinds of jobs that could be filled by people without many marketable skills who were at risk of becoming involved in stealing and violence.

12. Across the country, consumer confidence soared during the late 1990s to its highest levels since 1952, when the University of Michigan began to survey the public to calculate its Index of Consumer Sentiment.

13. Statistics about job gains and losses are derived from the BLS's survey of employers. These numbers are believed to be more accurate than unemployment figures estimated from surveys of individuals.

14. Some peculiarities of the 1990s boom caused a rethinking of certain virtually immutable laws of economics, such as the tenet that low unemployment inevitably leads to wage inflation (see Nasar, 1998).

15. As many as "several hundred thousand" New Yorkers were estimated to still be employed by the drug trade after it had been forced to contract by intense police pressures during the late 1990s (Johnson, Dunlap, and Tourigny, 1999).

16. A parallel but more volatile indicator of the same trend measures the

intentions of graduating seniors in the City's public high schools (the poorest students academically and financially) who are surveyed almost every year by the Board of Education. The proportion anticipating that they would go on to college leaped from 77 percent in the late 1980s (fiscal years) to 84 percent in 1991. But then it fell to 73 percent in 1993 before rebounding up to 87 percent in fiscal 1997 (NYC Department of City Planning, 1993, 1999).

17. A prolonged building occupation of the City College campus in Harlem by radical students in 1969 forced the CUNY Board of Trustees to accede to demands for an open admissions policy guaranteeing a seat for all high school graduates, even those needing remediation in basic skills. In the aftermath of the financial crisis of the mid-1970s, the century-long tradition of free tuition was ended. When another price hike was imposed in the early 1990s at the thirteen senior colleges and six community colleges, a noticeable number of financially strapped students could no longer afford the cost of tuition, books, and fees.

Many CUNY students needed to take remedial courses to overcome the deficiencies in their college readiness skills because they attended the City's ineffective public school system. In the late 1990s, Mayor Giuliani and Governor Pataki proposed policies that would raise admission standards but also limit opportunities to take remediation courses. Such changes could substantially reduce the size of the student body in the near future.

18. Among identified substance abusers in the state prison system in 1997, about 8 percent had taken some college courses (NYS DOCS, 1997).

Among jail inmates across the country surveyed in 1978, about 10 percent of the white males and 9 percent of the black males had completed a year or more of college; whereas among the general population of males eighteen to fifty-four years old, the corresponding figure was 40 percent (BJS, 1980).

Among state prison inmates interviewed nationwide, 11 percent said they had taken at least some college courses in a 1986 survey, and 12 percent in 1991 (Beck et al., 1993). Adding in jail inmates and prisoners in federal institutions, 16 percent reported they had been to college in a 1991 survey, compared to 43 percent of the general population of adults (Lynch et al., 1994).

19. A wave of immigration that lasted from the late 1800s through the early 1900s brought to the City Europeans fleeing from political and religious persecution as well as economic hardships, boosting the foreign-born population to an all-time high of 40 percent by 1910. But by the 1960s, the flood had dwindled down to a trickle; many of the immigrants from the earlier wave had either retired and moved away or died of old age.

Just then, a new surge of immigration gathered steam. It was made possible by federal legislation that abolished a national origins quota system, which had strongly favored northern and western European countries at the expense of the rest of the world since the 1920s. The revised quotas of this Immigration and Naturalization Act of 1965, in conjunction with the Immigration Reform and Control Act of 1986 and the Immigration Act of 1990, greatly changed the racial and ethnic composition of the City. Most of the newest New Yorkers hailed from the Caribbean, Africa, Latin America, Asia, and Europe. Compared to the rest of the nation, New York received fewer people from the major source countries (Mexico, El Salvador, Cuba, Iran, Canada, and Vietnam), and many more from the Dominican Republic, Jamaica, Haiti, Guyana, Trinidad, Ecuador, Colombia, Pakistan, Bangladesh, the former Soviet Union, Poland, Italy, Ireland, and China (plus Taiwan and Hong Kong) (Groneman and Reimers, 1995; Lobo and Salvo, 1997; and Sontag and Dugger, 1998).

20. If immigrants had not gravitated to New York City, the number of residents would have shrunk by a crippling 9 percent during the 1980s (as happened during the 1970s) instead of expanding, as it did, by 4 percent, and then by 3 percent more during the first half of the 1990s (Lobo and Salvo, 1997).

21. There were so many fires of suspicious origin in New York and other big cities that Congress asked the FBI in 1978 to make arson its eighth index crime and to monitor the problem more closely. Although reliable statistics never materialized about intentional blazes, arson-for-hire schemes are no longer destroying substantial numbers of deteriorating buildings as in the 1970s. In fact, in many neighborhoods the economic boom of the 1980s and 1990s encouraged landlords to renovate their buildings so they could charge higher rents or sell off the apartments as cooperatives and condominiums.

22. Partly in response to the hard times surrounding the fiscal crisis, the number of inhabitants of the five boroughs shrank from 1970 to 1980 by a staggering 800,000 people; but the number of immigrants rose by roughly 250,000. By 1980, immigrants (mostly from the post-1965 wave) made up 24 percent of City residents. During the 1980s, the pace accelerated to an average of about 86,000 new arrivals per year. The 1990 census determined that 28 percent of the City's population came from abroad. During the 1990s, the flow picked up even more, to well over 115,000 immigrants per year (peaking at 133,000 during fiscal 1996). This influx exceeded previous record levels processed at Ellis Island roughly one hundred years earlier. Between 1990 and 1998, more than 850,000 legally admitted foreigners poured into New York. Projecting these U.S. Census figures for the additional two years, roughly one million immigrants entered the City during the 1990s (Groneman and Reimers, 1995; Waldinger, 1996; Lobo and Salvo, 1997; Siemaszko and McCoy, 1998; and Sontag and Dugger, 1998).

23. Because the City was less populated in 1910, the foreign born made up a greater share in relative terms, at 40 percent, but were far smaller in absolute numbers, at about 1.9 million (Groneman and Reimers, 1995). By 1920, an

estimated 78 percent of all New Yorkers were either foreign born or the children of at least one immigrant parent (Siemaszko and McCoy, 1998).

For the entire country, the percentage of the population that was foreign born was about 9 percent in 1995, according to the U.S. Census Bureau's Current Population Reports. The figure had been as low as about 5 percent in 1970.

24. Congressman Robert Deal (1999) of Georgia reported that 220,000 foreign-born troublemakers were confined in federal and state prisons and local county jails across the nation; over 140,000 were on probation or parole, and 160,000 more were fugitives who had disappeared underground after receiving deportation orders.

25. Internal migrants fleeing to large cities from economically stagnant agricultural communities experienced many similar problems of discrimination and culture conflict as did earlier waves of immigrants. The impact of dislocation was especially serious for African Americans uprooted from the Old South and Puerto Ricans leaving the island's rural areas. Their city/country disorientation probably accounted for much of their disproportionate high rate of participation in street crime during an adjustment period in the 1950s and 1960s (Haskell and Yablonsky, 1970:282–283).

26. By 1998, they still had a noticeable presence behind bars: 404 of the 602 Cuban-born inmates (67 percent) in New York State prisons had entered the United States during the boatlift (Clark, 1999:10).

27. For example, as a first approximation, immigrants made up roughly a third of all inhabitants of the five boroughs in 1995, so they "ought" to comprise about 33 percent of all inmates, if they were guilty of committing serious felonies no more or less often than other residents. However, 33 percent is too large because only about two-thirds of all prisoners (68 percent in 1995) were sent upstate by courts in the City. Also, most (87 percent) but not all of the immigrant inmates probably came from the five boroughs; 13 percent of New York State's immigrant population lives in upstate communities (INS, 1999). Therefore, if the foreign born comprised 33 percent of all City residents, and felons from the City made up 68 percent of all the roughly 68,500 prisoners at that time, then about 15,370 of the inmates shipped upstate from the five boroughs should have come from abroad if the level of involvement in serious crime was the same for immigrants as for nonimmigrants ($68,500 \times 0.33 \times 0.68 = 15,370$). But only about 7,635 were immigrants from New York City, since 13 percent of all the foreign-born men and women probably were from upstate communities ($8,775 \times 0.87 = 7,635$). The departure between the expected and calculated numbers of foreign-born inmates from the City was about -7,735. Therefore, in 1995, their estimated presence in state facilities was 50 percent less than was anticipated ($7,635 - 15,370 = -7,735; -7,735/15,370 = -50\%$).

28. Researchers analyzing 1980 and 1990 census data concluded that among men between the ages of eighteen and forty, immigrants were less likely than their U.S.-born counterparts to be institutionalized in correctional facilities and mental hospitals, even though immigrants have more trouble in the labor market. Furthermore, earlier immigrants were more likely to suffer institutionalization than recent immigrants. However, all immigrant cohorts experienced higher rates of institutionalization as their time in the U.S. increased (Butcher and Piehl, 1998).

29. Unfortunately, in 21 percent of the cases, information about place of birth was missing.

It would be unreasonable to expect that traces of marijuana, cocaine, and/or heroin or other opiates like methadone (maybe even alcohol) would be found in the corpses of the very young or the very old. Therefore, homicide victims under the age of thirteen or over the age of sixty-five were excluded from this analysis. Also excluded were cases in which the body was not discovered for a day or more, or corpses that were not tested within twenty-four hours of death (after that amount of time elapsed, traces of drug use could disappear); and files that did not yet contain autopsy results when the data were extracted and coded.

30. Drinking has been identified as a serious violence risk factor among immigrant men. For example, a review of toxicology tests performed on male Mexican American homicide victims found that alcohol was present in the bloodstream of 70 percent of 25–34-year-olds, 55 percent of 35–44-year-olds, and 65 percent of 45–54-year-olds (Gilbert and Cervantes, 1986). Also, researchers who studied several communities of Mexican immigrants in California concluded that levels of violence were highest in the vicinity of concentrations of alcohol outlets like liquor stores and bars (see Alaniz, Cartmill, and Parker, 1998).

31. Approximately the same size flow of immigrants from China and the former Soviet Union continued to enter the country legally during fiscal years 1994 to 1997 (see INS, 1999).

32. The poverty rate for foreign-born blacks was about 15 percent, far less than the 27 percent rate suffered by native-born African Americans. For Hispanic New Yorkers, the poverty rate was 25 percent for the foreign born and 37 percent for native-born residents, according to the 1990 census (NYC Department of City Planning, 1997:5).

33. Other cities that may have benefited from receiving large numbers of immigrants during the 1990s include Los Angeles, Chicago, Houston, San Diego, San Francisco, and Washington, D.C. (Frey, 1998). Also, refer to table 7.1 for a listing of arrivals from abroad as a percentage of a big city's 1990 population.

SEVEN

Where Have All the Criminals Gone?

Did Favorable Demographic Trends Facilitate the Crash?

Demographic changes take place very slowly. But the steady buildup of positive trends could have laid the foundation for the crime crash. If favorable demographic shifts took place during the years leading up to the crash, then changes in the composition of the City's population might explain much of the drop in crime.

What trends would constitute favorable demographics, in terms of crime reduction? One beneficial development would be an out-migration of individuals deeply involved in street crime. Another positive trend would be a reduction in the number of vulnerable potential recruits coming of age who could replace those who have outgrown criminal activity. A third way of thinning the ranks of high-rate offenders would be attrition caused by the finality of death or permanent removal via deportation.

Escape from New York

Huge numbers of New Yorkers were born, entered adolescence, reached middle age, moved in, moved out, grew old, and died while the crash was taking place. What happened to the criminal element?

The City's population peaked in 1966 at a little over 8 million. The number of people living within the five boroughs dropped by over 10 percent to less than 7.1 million by 1980. The grand total of residents rebounded to 7.3 million by 1990, and inched up to 7.4 million by 1998, according to the U.S. Census Bureau's annual Current Population Survey. So, it may seem that the City stagnated, but this apparent stability during the first eight years of the 1990s masked tremendous underlying shifts in the composition of the population. Just about one million babies were born and over half a million people died, yielding what demographers call a "natural increase" of close to half a million inhabitants. Because the total population barely grew (up less than 100,000), the "net migration" out of the City must have totaled about 380,000 former residents. But even this net loss obscured underlying trends because it was the product of large population influxes and outflows. More than 850,000 newcomers from foreign lands settled in New York, at least for awhile, during the 1990s. Also, an unknown number of Americans from other parts of the United States moved to the City, temporarily if not permanently. Hence, the "net domestic migration" figure for 1990–1998 was estimated by the U.S. Census Bureau to be a dispersal of over 1.2 million former New Yorkers to the rest of the country (NYC Department of City Planning, 1997; and U.S. Census Population Division, 1999). Therefore, during the 1990s, the City's population underwent a significant turnover of more than 15 percent. About one in seven New Yorkers in the late 1990s had not been around during the bad old days when crime ran rampant, and almost as many cleared out. A considerable number of repeat offenders, career criminals, mobsters, street-gang members, drug dealers and addicts, and other troublemakers may have joined the exodus. This circumstantial evidence lends credibility to the argument that the NYPD deserves some credit for bringing down the crime rate by driving drug dealers—and their ilk—out of town through intensified pressures (the explicit aim of Strategy Number 3, promulgated in April 1994).

Furthermore, the twin processes of attrition (primarily through out-migration rather than death) and replenishment (from in-migration from within the United States and from abroad, plus births) generated more turnover in New York than in any other of the ten biggest urban centers with populations of one million or more (table 7.1). Even though the crash was accompanied by an economic boom and a much-heralded revitalization in the quality of daily life, more people

Table 7.1. Turnover in New York Compared to Other Major Cities, 1990–1996

City	1990 Population (millions)	Net Domestic Migration (% of 1990 population)	Net International Migration (% of 1990 population)	Net Migration (% of 1990 population)
New York	7.3	−13%	+9%	−4%
Los Angeles	3.5	−14	+8	−6
Chicago	2.8	−9	+4	−6
Houston	1.6	−3	+5	+2
Philadelphia	1.6	−12	+2	−10
San Diego	1.1	−7	+5	−3
Phoenix	1.0	+11	+2	+13
San Antonio	1.0	+1	+2	+3
Dallas	1.0	−4	+4	0
Detroit	1.0	−9	+1	−8

Notes: Overall population changes are not shown. Natural increase not shown because births and deaths (generally of elderly people) do not affect crime rates. Figures are for counties. Some cities have suburbs within the same county. New York includes five counties (boroughs) and no suburbs.
Source: New York City Department of City Planning, 1999.

"escaped" from New York (not just in absolute numbers, but also percentage-wise) than from any of the other urban centers, with the possible exception of Los Angeles (see column 2).[1] Also, more people from abroad made the "pilgrimage" to New York than to any other major city, with Los Angeles a close second (see column 3). (Recall that recent immigrants tended to be less involved in crime than native-born residents, according to the analysis in chapter 6.) This process of population turnover—attrition and replacement—was so much more extensive in New York than in other urban centers that it could account for New York's superior progress in crime reduction via displacement of active criminals and replacement by more law-abiding newcomers. Or, to put it differently, if New York's population had not experienced such turnover, it would be difficult to make the case based on circumstantial evidence that a substantial displacement and dispersal of the City's criminal element took place, and to a degree greater than anywhere else.

What about the people who died right before and during the crash? How many were deeply involved in crime, and to what extent might their absence from the City's streets have been noticeable? Attrition through untimely death, a most disturbing and politically unappealing explanation, will be examined next.

Grisly Arithmetic: Did Untimely Deaths Eliminate Many Active Criminals?

The state's prisons have doubled their population in the last 10 years, removing from circulation many criminals who were not already killed in the streets.

—Editors, *New York Times* (1995a:12)

Incapacitation of career criminals via imprisonment rather than execution has been the civilized solution favored by government officials as well as the general public whenever the clamor to "do something" about predators preying upon innocent victims reached a crescendo. Whether the criminal justice system really got tougher and significantly contributed to the crash was examined in chapter 4. Now the possibility that high-rate offenders also put themselves out of action—permanently—through their own reckless behaviors must be addressed. To put it bluntly, have untimely deaths—murders by fellow criminals, drug overdose fatalities, and mortality of intravenous drug users due to AIDS—substantially thinned the ranks of highly active criminals before and during the crash, far more than would be expected in an actuarial sense from the normal course of events?[2]

Criminals Killed Off by Other Criminals

The best detectives—and plenty of good ones are still out there—try to approach every murder the same way, but after the fiftieth dead crackhead, it's hard to do; many cops these days refer to drug murders as "misdemeanor homicides," "public-service killings," or worse. There's little pride in solving a murder that no one cares about, and little encouragement from above.

—Correspondent Eric Pooley (1992:27)

It would be naive to assume that all murder victims were innocent, law-abiding citizens just minding their own business when disaster struck. Some casualties of shoot-outs and knife fights surely were dangerous persons themselves and could be branded as dead offenders who were actively involved in boosting the crime rate before their demise. Could internecine warfare among hard-core lawbreakers have taken so great a toll

Table 7.2. Criminal History of Murder Victims, New York City,
Selected Years, 1976–1991

		Victims with Prior Arrest Records					
		Any Arrests		Just One		Two or More	
Year	Death Toll	Number	Percent	Number	Percent	Number	Percent
1976	1,622	867	53%	—		—	
1977	1,557	820	53%	—		—	
1983	1,622	816	50%	195	12%	621	38%
1984	1,450	737	51%	191	13%	546	38%
1985	1,392	634	46%	148	11%	486	35%
1986	1,598	638	40%	189	12%	449	28%
1991	2,166	889	41%	—		—	

Note: — = Not available
Source: NYPD Homicide Analyses carried out by the Office of Management Analysis and Planning, 1976–1991.

during the record-setting years that the streets became noticeably safer? The question boils down to, What percentage of murder victims had been serious troublemakers themselves?

To cite some extreme cases, a small number of the casualties of lethal violence had killed others in prior confrontations. In 1975, sixty-two homicide victims had previously been arrested for murdering someone; in 1976, that figure was thirty-five, and in 1977, thirty-six, according to the NYPD's earliest statistical analyses of homicides.[3] Although dead ex-killers only constituted a tiny fraction of the entire body count, an even greater share had a past record of illegal activities when they were slain by their former victims or current enemies or even by their accomplices. Judging how these people spent their lives by the worst things they are known to have done (perhaps too harsh a yardstick) yields estimates about criminals killed in action.

More than half of all murder victims had records of prior arrests during the late 1970s (see table 7.2). That proportion dropped to about two-fifths by the beginning of the 1990s. All through these decades, of those who had criminal records the average number of prior arrests hovered between three and four, according to calculations made by the NYPD's Office of Management and Planning. To assume that a homicide victim who had just one run-in with the law had been responsible for an appreciable amount of theft or violence might lead to a serious overestimate. So, to err on the side of caution, those with just a single arrest, even if it was for a felony, are not counted as "deceased criminals." Therefore, only the figures appearing in the last column indicating two or more arrests were taken as indicative of serious involvement in street crime. Taking into account an apparent downward trend, one-fourth of all homicide victims were deemed to have been active offenders before they were killed from the late 1980s onward. This conservative figure of 25 percent was used in calculations to derive the body counts that appear in column 2 of table 7.3. The toll imposed by criminal-on-criminal violence drifted downward from over five hundred deaths annually to about two hundred as murder rates plummeted during the 1990s.

Drug Abusers Overdosing to an Early Grave

Some of the most predatory and dangerous offenders have heavy cocaine and heroin habits. These drug abusers face serious health consequences if they take too much of a psychoactive substance all at once, either by accident or intentionally, or mix one powerful intoxicant with another. Each year in the past decade, overdoses have claimed the lives of between one and two thousand New Yorkers. Most of the fatalities were caused

Table 7.3. Estimated Attrition of Active Offenders, New York City, 1988–1997

	Murdered by Other	IV Drug Abusers Succumbing to AIDS		Dead from	Deported Criminal
Year	Criminals	In NYC	In Prison	Overdose	Aliens
1988	470	1,290	100	1,860	—
1989	480	1,460	90	1,790	—
1990	540	1,580	120	1,540	—
1991	540	1,790	150	1,450	—
1992	500	1,980	140	1,400	—
1993	490	2,090	150	1,470	870
1994	390	2,430	160	1,330	—
1995	290	2,410	170	1,510	—
1996	250	1,710	120	1,290	1,320
1997	200	900	40	1,080	3,060
Totals	4,150	17,640	1,240	14,720	5,250

Notes: All estimates rounded off to the nearest ten persons. Deportations are for federal fiscal years. NA = not yet available.
Sources: Murders: NYPD homicide analyses; AIDS deaths in NYC: NYC DOH AIDS Surveillance reports; AIDS deaths in prison: Maruschak, 1997; Wright and Smith, 1999; overdose deaths: DAWN Medical Examiner annual reports; deported aliens: INS Statistical Yearbooks.

by taking too much cocaine (whether smoked, snorted, or injected) or too powerful hits of heroin (or other opiates such as methadone), or excessive use of alcohol in conjunction with these or other dangerous substances (see Office of Applied Studies, SAMHSA, 1988–1999). The majority of City residents who died from overdoses were black or Hispanic males between the ages of twenty-five and forty-four who came from poverty-stricken neighborhoods. In these depressed areas, the accidental drug overdose rate exceeded national rates for homicide and suicide combined. Most of the decedents were persistent heavy abusers rather than casual experimenters, according to an analysis of autopsy records kept by the Office of the Chief Medical Examiner (Marzuk, et al. 1997).

Drug overdoses exacted a heavy toll each year from the late 1980s through the late 1990s, as column 5 in table 7.3 indicates.[4]

Lives of Intravenous Drug Abusers Lost to AIDS

Scientists and doctors detected the emergence of a new, deadly and incurable disease—Acquired Immune Deficiency Syndrome (AIDS)—spread by the Human Immunodeficiency Virus (HIV), at the start of the 1980s. By 1990, AIDS was the leading cause of death of young men in the City. Worse yet, figures about the prevalence of AIDS and the death toll it imposed were considered minimum estimates because many cases went undiagnosed or were not reported to health authorities (Morbidity and Mortality Weekly Report, 1991). From the outset, New Yorkers suffered a higher rate of infection than inhabitants of any other city in the United States. City residents made up about 16 percent of all the AIDS cases diagnosed across the U.S., even though they made up barely 3 percent of the nation's population. Since the epidemic began, more than 110,000 people in the five boroughs had been diagnosed as afflicted with AIDS, and about 68,000 of these patients had died. At the close of the 1990s, about 41,000 residents with full-blown AIDS were struggling to stay alive, and as many as 100,000 were harboring the HIV virus (Altman, 1997, 1998; and NYC DOH, 1999).

One reason for the disproportional toll imposed by AIDS on New Yorkers was that the disease spread rapidly through the large community of homosexual men who had sought refuge in the City from the social discrimination that was more intense elsewhere. But there is no reason to believe that the widespread suffering ravaging the gay community had any impact on the crime crash. Violence and stealing have never been identified as problems associated with male homosexuality.

Another important reason for the high death rate from AIDS among New Yorkers was that the virus was transmitted by intravenous drug users (IDUs) who shared hypodermic syringes to mainline heroin and/or cocaine directly into their veins. IDUs have such costly habits that most of them must turn to street crime to raise money. Therefore, these addicts who perished from AIDS probably were deeply involved in theft and, to a lesser degree, robberies and other acts of violence before they got deathly ill. (An even larger number than those who died were too debilitated to engage in street crime any longer, but it is difficult to estimate the size of this gravely ill population.)

As early as 1986, epidemiologists estimated that about three-fifths of all the heroin addicts in the City already had spread the virus to one another by using the same dirty needles or contaminated water (Musto, 1995). By the late 1990s, some modest progress had been made in stopping the spread of this infection by the many high-profile educational outreach efforts and by several low-profile needle exchange programs, some legal but others in defiance of the law. As few as one-fourth to as much as one-half of New York City's estimated 200,000 IDUs were believed to be HIV positive (Richardson, 1998; Talan, 1998; Hartel and Schoenbaum, 1999). A cumulative total of about 38,500 men in New York City had contracted full-blown AIDS from injecting drugs from the early 1980s until 1999.[5] These IDUs made up 45 percent of all the known adult male AIDS cases (the rest of the infections were attributed to engaging in unprotected homosexual or heterosexual sex acts or transfusions of contaminated blood products). Males made up 76 percent of all AIDS patients (Office of AIDS Surveillance, 1999). Therefore, in the calculations that yielded the estimates in column 3 of table 7.3, it was assumed that 76 percent of all those who died from AIDS-related causes were males, and 45 percent were IDUs.[6]

AIDS-related deaths climbed steadily throughout the 1980s and peaked at over twenty per day in late 1995. Then an effective "AIDS cocktail" of protease inhibitors mixed with other antiviral medicines was discovered, prolonging the symptom-free period in people who were HIV positive. Although the disease was still deadly and incurable, at least it was treatable. The mortality rate plunged dramatically (by 30 percent in 1996, another 48 percent in 1997, and a further 26 percent during 1998), to the level of about five deaths a day (Musto, 1995a; Altman, 1997, 1998; and NYC DOH, 1999). However, most of the AIDS patients who were able to survive indefinitely by taking expensive medications were not impoverished drug addicts.

Since many intravenous drug users wind up in New York State's prisons, facilities run by the Department of Corrections house the largest population of inmates known to be HIV positive in the country (9,500 felons in 1995, 14 percent of all convicts in the state's institutions and 40 percent of all the roughly 24,000 infected prisoners across the country). Most (84 percent) of these inmates were described as still "asymptomatic" in the mid-1990s, but the rest were showing signs of illness. However, when the combination of retroviral therapies offered to AIDS patients in hospitals became available to prisoners, their mortality rate also tumbled in the late 1990s (Maruschak, 1997; Wright and Smith, 1999).

AIDS exacted a terrible toll among intravenous drug users on the streets and behind bars from the 1980s through most of the 1990s, as columns 4 and 5 reveal in table 7.3. Of the three causes of untimely deaths, AIDS depopulated the ranks of the criminally active more than drug overdoses or fratricidal violence.

Criminal Aliens Expelled from the United States

We applaud the I.N.S. for its efforts, but several hundred deportations from Rikers, or a thousand from the state prisons, make only a small dent in a city of this size.

—NYPD deputy commissioner Michael Farrell
(quoted in Sontag, 1997:A8)

Deportations do not have the finality of death, in terms of permanent incapacitation to prevent recidivism. But expulsions of lawbreakers who were not citizens also reduced the size of the City's active offender population. Therefore, the number of criminal aliens sent packing was added in table 7.2 to the totals of offenders who were murdered by fellow criminals, died from drug overdoses, or perished from AIDS contracted from intravenous drug use.

An Immigration and Naturalization Service (INS) get-tough policy of hunting down and expelling offenders who by law did not have a legal right to stay in the country gained support in Congress during the 1980s. Stepped-up deportations were seen as a means to cut the crime rate, free up prison space for home-grown outlaws, and save American taxpayers from having to spend more money for criminal justice and victim assistance (see Sontag, 1994; McDonald, 1997; and Rohter, 1997).

Consequently, the number of noncitizens kicked out of the United States for breaking the law skyrocketed. Back in 1981, the INS had deported only about 365 convicts who were not citizens after their sentences had been served in various state and federal institutions. By 1990, that figure had soared to almost 11,000. During fiscal year 1996, over 33,000 were forced to leave the country. By fiscal year 1999, the INS sent nearly twice that number, about 62,000 lawbreakers, back to where they came from (over 80 percent to Mexico), largely (47 percent) because they had broken U.S. drug laws. More than 4,000 aliens convicted of crimes were deported from the New York City area, up 12 percent from the previous year (Office of Public Affairs, INS, 1999; Sachs, 1999).

Could this policy have helped to cut the crime rate significantly, especially in areas like New York with disproportionately large concentrations of undocumented and recent immigrants, some of whom were deeply involved in illegal activities? The crackdown could have made a difference if the deportables were in fact expelled, if alien ex-cons who wanted to reenter New York and wreak more havoc could not get back in the country, and if this get-tough policy had the intended effect of deterring unlawful impulses among recent immigrants who were not yet naturalized citizens (see Sontag, 1994; McDonald, 1997; and Rohter, 1997).

By the late 1990s, New York State prisons housed the third-biggest criminal alien population, after California and Texas (Sontag, 1994; Rohter, 1997)—about 9,000 strong and constituting 13 percent of the total inmate population. Only about 7 percent of these foreign-born inmates had become naturalized citizens before getting into trouble with the law; most (51 percent) were legal permanent residents; but a substantial number (29 percent) were illegal aliens, and the remainder (13 percent) were awaiting INS determination of their status (Clark, 1999). New York was one of the few states that had a special program that sped up deportation proceedings against illegal immigrants convicted of nonviolent crimes (half of which were drug related). From its inception in 1995 through 1997, about 1,200 convicts meeting the criteria had been approved for early parole, and roughly 900 had been released from state facilities and expelled from the U.S. (Goodnough, 1998).[7]

Deportations did not make a significant dent on the City's criminal element until fiscal year 1996, as is indicated by the last column in table 7.3. But deportations picked up just when attrition from other causes faded away.

For All the Wrong Reasons: The Ugly Bottom Line

Adding up the various causes of permanent removal, it turns out that AIDS was the major factor in reducing the ranks of active offenders in New York. Over the ten-year period from 1988 (as crime rates were nearing their peak) to 1997 (well into the crash), AIDS claimed the lives of almost 19,000 intravenous drug users. The second most serious source of attrition was from drug overdoses. More than 14,000 abusers of heroin and cocaine (and alcohol in combination with other drugs) died over the ten-year period. About 4,150 criminals were killed off by other offenders during the 1988 to 1997 period. Another 5,250 at minimum were removed from the streets, jails, and prisons, and expelled from the country. Combining the attrition from all four sources, about 43,000 fewer lawbreakers roamed City streets for these four reasons by the end of the ten-year period.

Could the annual loss of several thousand troublemakers and the cumulative disappearance of over 43,000 active offenders after a decade of attrition translate into noticeably safer streets? There is no definitive answer, but some comparisons might be instructive. By coincidence, the total strength of the NYPD was about the same size (40,000) as the cumulative death toll. The number of heroin addicts receiving methadone maintenance treatment at all the clinics across the City was a few thousand less (36,000) (Massing, 1998a). On any given day in the late 1990s, the jail system held less than half this many men (18,000 inmates), and the entire state prison system with seventy facilities incapacitated several thousand more (about 47,000 felons from the City).

It is a sad fact that taken cumulatively, these four causes of permanent removal inflicted heavy casualties on the criminal element over the years.

It would have been preferable to thin their ranks in a humane and enlightened way via breakthroughs in rehabilitative treatment programs or more effective preventive educational approaches, rather than vigilantism among criminals, the ravages of an incurable ailment, and the self-destructive recklessness of those who couldn't control their drug cravings. Even sending hardened troublemakers back to where they came from is nothing more than displacing a problem elsewhere.[8] The attractiveness of the New York "miracle" as a model to be emulated diminishes to the extent that crime rates were brought down appreciably by these deplorable causes of needless deaths and preventable removals.

Was the drying-up of the pool of potential new young recruits to replace these fallen comrades another reason that crime crashed?

Generations on the Move: Did the High-Risk Population of Young Males Shrink?

And there are widespread predictions that another tidal wave will break as soon as the milk-toothed children of the '90s crowd into their saw-toothed teens. Whoever called economics the dismal science must not have heard about criminology.

—*Newsweek* correspondent Richard Lacayo (1996)

One of the most striking truisms in criminology is that involvement in street crime varies tremendously by sex and age.

Basically, street crime is a young man's game. The stage of life during which the likelihood for committing an act of violence or theft is greatest ranges from the late teens into the twenties, according to data collected by criminologists at different times and places (Hirschi and Gottfredson, 1989; Blumstein and Rosenfeld, 1998). For example, burglaries are carried out by culprits who are seventeen years old more often than any other specific age, according to FBI arrest statistics collected from police departments from across the country. The level of involvement in burglary drops by one half by age twenty-one. As for robbery, seventeen is also the peak year, but the loss of inclination with increasing maturity takes longer; twenty-five-year-olds carry out half as many robberies as seventeen-year-olds. For murders, the most dangerous years range from eighteen up to about twenty-four. Unfortunately, the willingness to kill tapers off even more slowly than to rob or burglarize; nationwide statistics show homicide arrests aren't halved until people reach their mid-thirties (see Blumstein, 1995).

In New York, the pattern of "age-specific" arrests for murders resembled what the FBI statistics showed for the United States as a whole. From 1978 to 1997, the majority of killers and their victims were teenage boys and young men, according to the data presented in chapter 2. The median age of accused killers was twenty-five in 1978 and remained so throughout most of the 1980s, before it slipped down to ages twenty-two and twenty-three between 1990 to 1997. Put another way, about 50 percent of all accused killers were between the ages of sixteen and twenty-five during the late 1970s and 1980s. During the 1990s, an even greater share, about 60 percent of all homicide arrestees, were in their late teens or early twenties. Including the remainder of the twenty-something age bracket, more than 70 percent of suspected perpetrators were between the ages of sixteen and thirty. Adding in arrestees in their thirties and early forties, over 90 percent of the people thought to have slain their fellow New Yorkers were between sixteen and forty-five years old.

As a consequence of this strong correlation between sex, age, and offending, whenever the cohort of male teenagers and young adults swells in relative size, local crime rates rise; when it shrinks, crime rates fall. Furthermore, as offenders grow older, "spontaneous remission" or "maturational reform" takes place on its own, lessening their chances of recidivism even in the absence of effective rehabilitation programs. Graying has-beens lose their urge to fight and steal as the passions and fires of their youth die down during adulthood and then burn out entirely after middle age. Therefore, crime waves caused by a proliferation of young people have the potential to dissipate without outside intervention.

Even though a small number of youth are responsible for most of the mayhem blamed upon the entire group, sheer numbers do matter. The "baby boom" generation (those born between 1945 and 1965) of record-breaking size produced a bulge in the nation's and the City's age structure that touched off many social repercussions, including a surge in street crime. Baby boomers ranged in age from fifteen to thirty-five when the 1980s began. By the start of the 1990s, most of this cohort was

Graph 7.1. Trends in Male Age Cohorts, New York City, 1960–1998

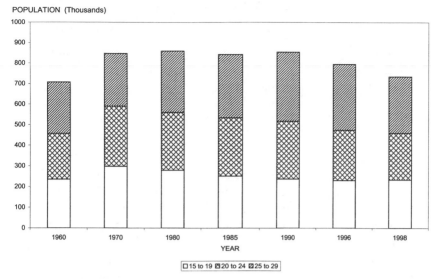

Note: Includes males of all races.
Sources: U.S. Census Bureau (1960, 1970, 1980, 1990) and Current Population Surveys (1985, 1996, 1998) from NYC Dept. of City Planning.

passing out of its high-risk for misbehavior years into a more mellow middle-age stage of life. Meanwhile, the leading edge of the next, much smaller "baby bust" generation was entering its turbulent adolescent and young adult phase. The total number of boys in their late teens, and young men in their early and late twenties declined significantly during the 1990s. The sharpest drop (down 19 percent over eight years) took place within the 20–24 year old group. The population of men in their late twenties contracted almost as much (off by 18 percent). The number of boys in their late teens also fell a little (by 2 percent). Since all three age cohorts were shrinking during the 1990–1998 period (all together, down by roughly 120,000 or 14 percent), these demographic changes in the local male population were quite favorable, in terms of crime reduction potential, for the first time since 1960. These shifts are pictured in graph 7.1.

The analysis presented in chapter 2 revealed that the City's several broad racial/ethnic groupings were responsible for dramatically different rates of offending. Black teenage boys and young men were arrested for acts of violence at a much higher rate than their Hispanic counterparts.

Table 7.4. Decline in the City's Young Male Population during the 1990s, by Age and Race/Ethnicity

	Year		Population Change	
Group	*1990*	*1998*	*Number*	*Percent*
White Males				
15–19	71,900	62,300	–9,600	–13%
20–24	103,800	72,900	–30,900	–30%
25–29	143,500	102,200	–41,300	–29%
15–29	319,200	237,400	–81,800	–26%
Black Males				
15–19	71,900	66,600	–5,300	–7%
20–24	71,100	56,800	–14,300	–20%
25–29	76,800	62,700	–14,100	–18%
15–29	219,800	186,100	–33,700	–15%
Hispanic Males				
15–29	74,300	80,300	6,000	+ 8%
20–24	83,500	72,600	–10,900	–13%
25–29	88,100	77,400	–10,700	–12%
15–29	245,900	230,300	–15,600	–6%

Notes: Asian males were excluded from this tabulation. Hispanics can be of any race. Census categories re-calculated to yield non-Hispanic whites and non-Hispanic blacks.
Sources: 1990 Census, as broken down in Technical Report 2, Population Projections for the Year 2000, by the NYC Department of City Planning, 1995; and the 1998 Current Population Survey of the U.S. Bureau of the Census, as analyzed by the NYC Department of City Planning memo, 2000.

Both of these groups were charged with murder far more often than white youths of the same age bracket (mostly because New York's African-American and Hispanic-American communities were much harder hit by poverty than were whites, as chapter 6 confirmed). Therefore, it is necessary to disaggregate the overall population shift into its components in order to discover which groups contracted the most. The shrinking of the ranks of the City's young males by race/ethnicity is documented in table 7.4. The Bureau of the Census data shows that far fewer young white males lived in the City by the end of the decade. But the rate of white involvement in violent street crime was disproportionately low, so this demographic trend was not of major importance. However, the population of young black male residents declined considerably, and that would have an impact. Also, the size of the 20–29 year old cohort of Hispanic young men (but not of teenage boys) decreased, and that population shift also could contribute to a reduction in street crime. Overall, the passage into better-behaved middle age of the inflated baby boom generation definitely could account for some of the decline in the City's crime rate, since dwindling ranks of potential new recruits became available to replace participants who were aging-out of the street scene as the 1990s wore on.

Besides the use of census data, another way to monitor the size of the youth cohort from year to year is to track the number of graduates of New York City public and private/parochial high schools. Assuming that the typical high school grad is about eighteen years old, and that the dropout rate has been fairly constant over the twenty-year period, then these annual tallies might be reliable indicators of the number of eighteen-year-olds living in the five boroughs. Combining six consecutive years yields cohorts of eighteen- to twenty-four-year-olds, the age group responsible for a substantial amount of street crime. The estimated minimum number of eighteen-year-olds in the City declined from 1977 until 1991, as is shown in graph 7.2. As a result, the size of this eighteen- to twenty-four-year-old cohort remained at a relatively low ebb throughout

Graph 7.2. Trends in High School Graduates, New York City, 1977–1998

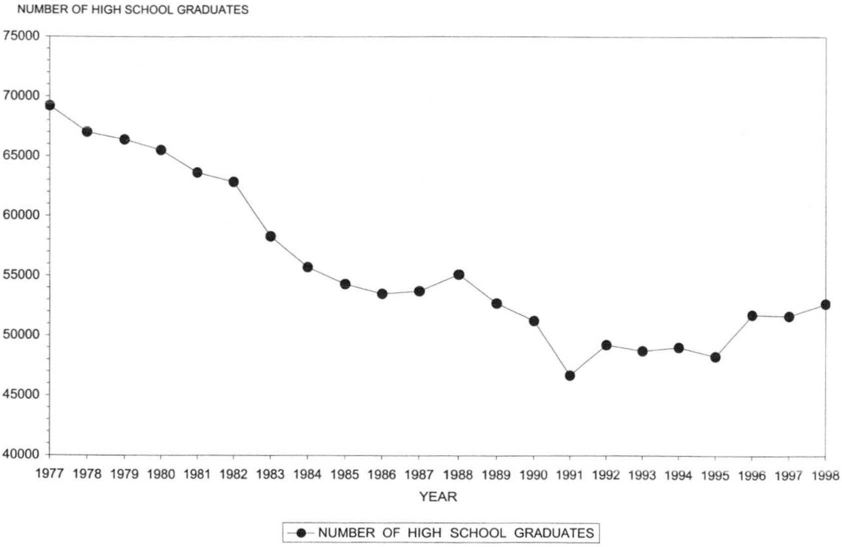

Note: Graduates completed both public and nonpublic high schools.
Source: State Education Department of New York, 1978–1999.

the decade, even after an up-tick occurred in 1996 due to the six-year time lag (diminishing numbers of eighteen-year-olds annually replacing larger numbers of twenty-four-year-olds). Therefore, this continuing favorable demographic trend of year-after-year reductions in the high risk cohort could have furthered the crime crash, according to this set of population data from a government source other than the U.S. Census Bureau.

Fewer Potential Recruits? Young Males with Many Strikes against Them

Idle youth with unpromising futures serve as the cannon fodder for recruitment into socially harmful and self-destructive fads like crack smoking, drug dealing, street gang rivalry, and gun toting, and they face grave risks of winding up as either perpetrators or casualties of lethal violence, according to the data analyzed in chapter 2. The individuals in greatest danger have at least five strikes against them: they're males; teenagers between sixteen and nineteen; no longer in school; not high school graduates; and not at work (or even actively hunting for a job). They suffer additional disadvantages if they are from poverty-stricken homes and if they are subject to the negative stereotyping and discrimination that still burdens black and Hispanic youth in the City. So, to further explore the impact of demographic changes, the empirical question can be framed as follows: Were far fewer high-risk teenage boys living in the City during the 1990s than in previous decades?

Between 1970 and 1980, the number of sixteen- to nineteen-year-old male high school dropouts unsuccessfully searching for jobs or not even looking for work rose by about 8 percent (up roughly 2,000, from 23,790 to 25,780). Fortunately, between 1980 and 1990, the ranks of these young males with five strikes against them tumbled by 30 percent (down about 7,800, from 25,780 to 17,990) (see the census data in NYC Council on Economic Education, 1974:132; Schaffer, 1993:11; and NYC Department of City Planning, 1994, fig. 1.8).[9]

Census figures for the year 2000 probably will show that this highest-risk population diminished even further. The number of youth in this age group declined over the decade. The citywide high school dropout rate dipped to 16 percent for the class of 1997, the lowest level since the Board of Education began longitudinal tracking of each yearly cohort in 1986 (NYC Department of City Planning, 1998). At the same time, the retention rate for teenagers who had not completed the requirements to graduate from high school within four years also improved slightly, to 36 percent (Wasserman and Gonzalez, 1998). Another positive development further reducing idleness and aimlessness was the easing of the unemployment problem, even for the least-skilled sector of the labor force. For these four reasons, it seems reasonable to optimistically predict that the number of teenage boys not in school and not at work, or even looking for a job, fell even further during the 1990s. This shortfall of very vulnerable youth with five strikes against them surely aided the crime crash.

Exercising Their Right to Remain Silent: Did a Dramatic Change in Attitudes Lead a Generation to Turn Away from Crime?

The final demographic factor might be the most important of all because it has the power to explain not only the crash in New York but also the ebbing of the crime wave in urban areas across the nation, and the reduced level of involvement by black, Hispanic, Asian, and white youth. The shift is not even strictly demographic in nature: it is attitudinal and behavioral as well as generational. An apparent sea change in underlying outlooks shaped the actions of teenagers and young adults during the 1990s. Unfortunately, the existence of this suspected evolution in subcultural values defies precise statistical measurement. It is not clear what kinds of evidence and statistics could prove or disprove it.

In concise terms, it seems that a widespread rejection of lawbreaking life-styles revolving around drug taking, stealing, gang fighting, and gun toting took place. Instead, a growing acceptance of conventional lifestyles centering on working, earning, and consuming swept across the social landscape.

What could have caused such profound changes in the prevailing norms of urban youth culture? One explanation, sometimes referred to as the "little brother syndrome" (Curtis, 1998) or the "younger sibling effect" (Golub and Johnson, 1997), emphasized learning from direct observations and firsthand experience. The baby bust cohort of teenagers and young adults had witnessed how crack smoking, cocaine snorting, heroin injecting, gun toting, and gang fighting decimated the ranks of their older family members, friends, and neighbors. Realizing the devastation wrought on their communities by these risky and reckless behaviors, they made the conscious decision to steer clear of these activities formerly considered as emblematic of hipness and coolness.

But it is likely that another source of these changes in values had deeper roots and grew out of the personal experiences and outlooks of entire generations, particularly the aging baby boomers and their prime-of-life children. The baby boom generation entered its high crime-prone years during the 1960s, a turbulent decade marked by fast-paced social developments, political upheavals, and the rise of mass movements seeking fundamental changes in everyday life. A painful generation gap opened up when many young baby boomers found themselves locked into conflict with their parents in particular, and older adults in general. Their sharp disagreements revolved around the goals and tactics of the civil rights, black power, and student power movements, and the peace movement against the war in Vietnam and the nuclear arms race. The young and old also were divided over the sexual revolution and the rise of a new wave of feminism; the hippie counterculture and drug experimentation; and the credibility of conspiracy theories about the assassinations of charismatic political figures—John F. Kennedy, Malcolm X, Martin Luther King, Jr., Robert Kennedy. As baby boomers pondered whether they really wanted to "sell out" and become part of the "Establishment" as they grew into adulthood, a small but influential portion developed and promoted an oppositional youth culture. Its main themes were to question authority, challenge conventional mores, experiment with new forms of social relationships, criticize the policies of both big government and big business, and to remain wary of the personal and social costs imposed by the unbridled pursuit of wealth and power. One of the social consequences of all this reexamination of what earlier generations had taken for granted was a generalized condemnation and rejection of unfair rules and unjust laws requiring racial segregation, the exclusion or subordination of women, the disempowerment of youth and students, sexual abstinence until marriage, drug abstinence other than drinking and cigarette smoking, and universal military service (the draft). By extension, hostility also grew among adherents of this oppositional culture toward law enforcement agencies that buttressed conventional norms, and the criminal justice system that punished the youth who defied them. Surely, part of the crime wave that broke out during the 1960s was fueled by this deep polarization and bitter conflict between teenagers and young adults who were fighting for greater autonomy versus their elders who held the reins of power.

The sixties lasted part of the way into the 1970s. As the late 1970s merged into the 1980s, the baby boomers entered middle age and played a much greater role in running the families, schools, government agencies, businesses, and other important institutions and organizations they had earlier challenged, criticized, or even opposed. As they matured, lost their rebellious spirit, and dropped out of protest activities—and also, for some, street crime—in droves, the next generation, their children, took over center stage as the subject of attention and concern.

It may be an exercise in futility to even try to characterize the common threads that run through the thinking and pursuits of roughly 40 million members of the age cohort commentators have dubbed as twenty-somethings, or post–Baby Boomers, or Baby Busters, or Generation Xers. All they surely have in common is that they were born between 1965 and 1978 (which means that the older twenty-somethings entered their thirties during the crash). In New York, a considerable portion of this generation was not even born in the United States and came of age elsewhere, as highlighted in the analysis of immigration presented in chapter 6.

A barrage of negative stereotypes was hurled at Generation Xers as they reached young adulthood. Hostile Baby Boomer critics branded them as slackers, whiners, malcontents, drifters, cynics with an overly gloomy worldview, and conservative young fogies. But there was no consensus over their common traits, as other commentators praised them as independent, ambitious, savvy, pragmatic, and self-sufficient. The only conclusion all observers could agree upon was that they were thoroughly depoliticized. Compared to their Baby Boom predecessors, most members of the next generation were much less engaged, less inclined to protest collectively or demonstrate in favor of their positions, less civic minded, and less trustful of political parties, leaders, governmental institutions, or even their fellow Americans, according to the findings of survey research. They rejected ideological consistency, and shunned what were considered to be outmoded political labels like Left and Right. Throughout the 1990s, twenty-somethings showed little interest in short-lived wars, electoral campaigns, voting, debates over divisive issues, presidential scandals, and impeachment proceedings. They were quite familiar with the problem of crime and violence, having watched countless acts of murder and mayhem on TV, but they generally didn't tune into the news or follow current events. Instead of concerns about the state of the union and the rest of the world, they were largely preoccupied with the state of affairs in their own immediate personal lives. Compared to their parents at a similar age, they were much more self-absorbed about their individual well-being and much more intent upon enjoying the material possessions, conveniences, and comforts offered by the ever-expanding consumer culture (see Hamilton and Gegax, 1995; Loysk, 1997a, 1997b; Craig and Bennett, 1997; and Halstead, 1999).

But what might be the impact of the thorough depoliticization of Gen Xers on the crime rate? It all depends upon the degree to which certain acts of fighting, robbing, thievery, defrauding, vandalism, looting, rioting, gang joining, weapons carrying, drug selling, and drug taking are considered to be embodiments of the seeds of primitive rebellion.

To some extent, illegal acts committed by rebellious youth, especially by young men from poor and working-class families, are expressions of their anger at their plight, their frustration with the barriers they face, and their hostility toward the institutions they perceive hold them back. These outbursts are misdirected and distorted acts of protest. The wrong methods of struggle are employed against inappropriate, usually totally innocent targets. Pent-up rage is vented on scapegoats who are close at hand, like family members, neighbors, and friends, individuals who certainly are not the real sources of their misery. Fratricidal aggression is freely unleashed against other young men who suffer under the same conditions. Internecine warfare breaks out between bands of youths who ought to be allies, not enemies. Some bottled-up anger is directed inward and follows self-destructive paths such as heavy sedation via drugs or brawling. Of course, these inchoate explosions of rejection and defiance do not alleviate their suffering. If anything, lawless acts and reckless behavior ruin their lives, destroy their families, undermine their communities, and provoke severe repression from the criminal justice system.

To their credit, a greater proportion of the post–civil rights, post-feminism, post–Vietnam generation has arrived at the pragmatic conclusion that illegal acts tinged with political protest are ultimately not just ineffective but downright counterproductive, in terms of making constructive, lasting changes and solving problems. The falling rate of violence and theft is the result of their collective refusal to make the same mistakes as many members of their parents' generation did. As a group, they firmly condemn their peers who wander down these self-defeating paths.

Very specifically, what changes in the values of youth culture could bring about a sharp drop in street crime? The first prerequisite would be a rejection of Hollywood's and popular music's subterranean, smirky admiration of fast-talking con men, high-stakes gamblers, swashbuckling pimps, good-hearted prostitutes, cunning drug smugglers, free-spending drug dealers, cold-blooded professional hit men, short-fused wiseguys, ruthless mob chieftains, and other "gangstas," hellraisers and low-riders.

The new outlooks would have to involve a profound redefinition of what is considered by youth to be admirable, hip, and cool: that it is no longer cool to be an outsider; to defy conventional norms by remaining in a drug-induced stupor; to carry around a concealed handgun as a symbol of status and power; to look up to predators and exploiters as role models; to view the authorities with hostility and honest, hard-working, law-abiding persons with disdain; to identify with outlaws and to be unwilling to turn them in and testify against them; and to regard doing time behind bars as a rite of passage into manhood, proof of toughness, a source of pride, and a badge of honor (for an in-depth analysis, see Canada, 1995; Connor, 1995; Frank, 1998; Anderson, 1999).[10]

The tumbling crime rate is the positive fallout from the passage from a rebellious to a thoroughly depoliticized, uncritical, and self-absorbed generation. There are many negative consequences of a falling rate of participation in conventional politics, of course. Clearly, the widespread insistence by people in their late teens and twenties that they have a right to remain silent about major foreign policy and domestic issues imperils the workings of a representative government and stymies any attempts to create a genuine participatory democracy. But at least the streets are safer.

Summing Up the Numbers

Demographic trends played an important role in building favorable conditions that enabled crime rates to crash during the 1990s. Many active criminals fled the City. Others disappeared from the scene due to homicides by fellow offenders, drug overdoses, AIDS contracted from injecting drugs, and deportations by the INS. The number of young men in their high crime-prone years shrank considerably. In particular, the ranks of teenage boys who had dropped out of high school and were not working probably declined sharply. And most members of the generation in its late teens and twenties acted in ways that reflected disinterest not only in conventional politics but also in the distorted, counterproductive, self-destructive, illegal ways of expressing social protest and personal rebellion that had been adopted by a portion of their parents' generation. Demography may not be destiny, but these incremental changes profoundly shape collective behavior.

Notes

1. The census-derived data are by county. Los Angeles, and some smaller cities, are ringed by suburbs within the same county, so any population shift to the immediate suburbs is obscured.

2. For example, poor people receiving public assistance who abuse drugs and/or alcohol face much higher than average odds of becoming involved in theft and violence and of sinking into even deeper difficulties. Researchers found that of roughly 850 welfare recipients who were substance abusers in 1984, within eight years over 20 percent had died from various causes and almost another 10 percent were gravely ill from AIDS. This high-risk group was ten times more likely to become infected with the HIV virus and five times more likely to die than the City's population in general (Friedman, Williams, et al., 1996).

3. This kind of detailed information did not appear in subsequent analyses of homicides carried out by the Office of Management Analysis and Planning during the 1980s or in the latest one to date, in 1991.

4. The Drug Abuse Warning Network tabulations include deaths due to

drinking alcohol in combination with drug taking, but exclude cases in which the patient died strictly from drinking, from AIDS and its complications, from homicide while high on drugs, or due to ingesting an unknown chemical substance (Office of Applied Studies, 1994).

5. Of all the 38,500 known AIDS patients over the years who were male IDUs, about 45 percent were black, 39 percent were Hispanic, 15 percent were white, and 1 percent were Asians and others (Office of AIDS Surveillance, 1999).

6. Infection via injection was a more common source of contracting AIDS in New York City (42 percent) than in the country as a whole (29 percent) as of 1991, according to the Centers for Disease Control (NYC Council on Economic Education, 1994).

7. Intended to save taxpayer's money and free up prison space for violent offenders, the program became controversial when it was exposed that four drug lords facing lengthy sentences had been quickly granted parole and then deported to their native lands. Eligibility criteria were tightened up to exclude major traffickers from early release (Goodnough, 1998).

8. In the home countries to which these ex-convicts were forcibly repatriated (primarily to Mexico, El Salvador, and other Central American countries, and to Caribbean Island nations like Jamaica), the local authorities reported severe repercussions, in terms of stepped-up, more sophisticated street-gang warfare and drug dealing (Rohter, 1997).

9. The Census Bureau counts the numbers of these high-risk youths every ten years. Therefore, just three sets of figures are available for the City: for 1970, 1980, and 1990. In 1970, about 34 percent of these very vulnerable teenage boys were white, 40 percent were black, 24 percent were "Puerto Rican" and 2 percent were Asian (NYC Council on Economic Education, 1974:132). Twenty years later, only 18 percent of these teenage boys were white, while the Hispanic portion had risen to 39 percent (partly reflecting shifts in the City's population); the proportion who were black remained at 40 percent, and 3 percent were Asian (NYC Department of City Planning, 1994).

10. The contention that these shifts have taken place has some preliminary empirical backing from the findings of a pilot survey administered to a nonrandom convenience sample of about two hundred low- to middle-income largely black and Hispanic college students at several public and private campuses in the New York City metropolitan area during 1993 and 1994. They were asked to list some behaviors or activities that they considered to be "cool" as well as "uncool." There was considerable consensus about what was uncool: hurting people in general, selling or consuming drugs, carrying a gun, fighting, and stealing

in particular. Most of the respondents identified hipness and coolness with being popular, chic, trendy, and successful; few supplied adjectives that would indicate that they approved of rejecting mainstream values and seeking ways to be part of a youth-oriented underground value system or counterculture (Karmen, 1994).

EIGHT

Lessons from the
New York Experience

The Anatomy of a Crime Wave

The mystery behind New York's crash has been solved. No single factor—such as innovative policing strategies—deserves the lion's share of the credit for the rapid improvement in public safety. The turnaround at first took place gradually but then accelerated suddenly as a number of positive developments all kicked in and pulled together in the same direction—downward. The best way to describe the City's situation in the 1990s was that a "fortuitous confluence" of underlying factors materialized. Luckily for City residents—and for those in positions of authority and trust—every one of the causal factors known to affect crime rates moved in the desired manner. No force or condition was out of step. The local economy recovered and the problems of unemployment and poverty in inner-city neighborhoods, although stubbornly persistent, were not as severe. More importantly, the dream of occupational mobility attracted greater numbers of generally hard-working, law-abiding people from around the world to seek their fortunes in New York, and it motivated increasing numbers of students, even from low-income families, to finish high school and enroll in college. The crack epidemic that devastated entire communities in the late 1980s subsided because it failed to recruit new adherents. While crack smoking was waning, heroin was not making its anticipated comeback, in part because an entire generation of potential victims recoiled in horror after witnessing firsthand how these twin vices had wrecked the lives of their families, friends, and neighbors. Although pot smoking and beer drinking remained popular, the consumption of another crime-facilitating drug—hard liquor—kept declining. At the same time, the NYPD was reengineered, and became energized, better managed, more technologically advanced, and more proactive. The new NYPD regained control of the streets and shut down the open-air drug bazaars that had lured poor young men into selling crews that fiercely fought one another for competitive advantages. As the drug scene downsized and customers and providers were driven behind closed doors, the arms race that the once-flourishing trade had spawned quickly deescalated. The upstate prisons continued to fill up with dangerous persons whose absence from the streets became noticeable. Throughout the period, a predicted contraction took place in the ranks of young people in their most crime-prone years. The number of teenagers who had dropped out of school and couldn't find work dwindled even further. The ranks of the City's criminal element took a further hit when substantial numbers of high-rate offenders either killed another off, died prematurely from AIDS contracted by IV drug use or from overdoses, were expelled as undesirable aliens, or fled due to intensified law enforcement pressures. Most important of all—and this "changing values of youth" factor could explain crime's reduction across all categories and throughout the nation—a shrinking number of young people expressed their angst via drugs/guns/gangs as a large share of members of their parents' generation had done during their youth amidst more turbulent political times.

However, one single factor did stand out as more important than the rest. New York's murder rate definitely soared in the late 1980s because of the crack epidemic. Otherwise, underlying conditions were becoming increasingly favorable for a continuation of the drop in crime that materialized in the first half of that decade. The police force was growing in sophistication and in size, as was the prison population, and the courts were processing felony cases more seriously. Poverty and unemployment rates were slipping, drinking was declining, increasing numbers of students were going to college, immigrants were pouring in, the size of the youth cohort was shrinking, and the values of young people were changing. The explosion of the crack-smoking craze, with its abusers desperate for money, and flagrant curbside selling provoking turf battles among heavily armed dealers, ruined everything. The crash could not begin until the epidemic ran its course and wound down.

The best way to conceptualize the dynamics behind the building-up, cresting, and receding of a crime wave is to focus on inputs and outputs (see fig. 8.1).

Crime waves are the product of the interaction of a wide array of forces and conditions. These affect the collective actions of many potential offenders. If the ranks of street criminals grow larger, or if each member becomes more active, more incidents will take place, boosting crime rates. The pool of active offenders grows through recruitment if additions exceed subtractions through attrition. Crime waves resemble epidemics. At some point on the way up, a critical mass develops that encourages even more people to join in. For example, once a sufficient customer base is established, a drug market can flourish; similarly, an

Figure 8.1. Dynamics of a Crime Wave

Additions	Impact	Subtractions
Attraction of offenders from across the globe →	RANKS	→ Displacement and dispersal by police action
Growth of the high-risk youth population →	OF	→ Execution by other criminals → Expulsion via deportation → Incapacitation in jails and prisons
Desperation from poverty and unemployment →	HIGH	→ Absorption into the middle class through college and upward job mobility
Drug abuse epidemics and drinking binges →	RATE	→ Maturation out of street gangs and drug scene
	OFFENDERS	→ Deaths of IDUs from AIDS → Overdose deaths
Distorted protest and primitive rebellion →		→ Depoliticization of local youth → Initial rejection of protest by immigrant youth

adequate number of thieves makes fencing operations and black market distribution channels profitable. Conversely, at some juncture on the downward spiral, a tipping point is reached (see Gladwell, 2000), wherein involvement in street crime becomes a rejected, even despised life-style. As former participants abandon these activities in droves, crime rates tumble faster.

Certain specific factors are particularly difficult to evaluate and require much more careful and thorough investigation because they virtually defy measurement. More attention must be paid to the role of private security forces, surveillance cameras, and antitheft hardware; the out-migration of active criminals displaced by intensified police pressures; the underground economy as a source of off-the-books, uncounted employment and income; and community organizations combating the street culture values that youths pick up during adolescence.

They Said It Couldn't Be Done: Ideological Stakes in the Search for Crime's Causes

Lurking behind the dispute are powerful ideologies. The success of New York City, and of the many other cities that have established similar efforts to restore order, directly contradicts the ideology that has reigned in American criminology since the 1960s. According to the older view, poverty, racism and social injustice cause crime. To deal with crime, society must deal with its causes. Therefore, police can do little about crime except respond after it occurs and, perhaps, "displace" it—move it around a bit.

—Rutgers University professor George Kelling (1997:25)

As the impressive drop in crime gained national attention during the latter part of the 1990s, self-interested parties advanced competing claims for credit with unusual vehemence. As always, professional lives hung in the balance. Incumbents tried to further their careers by insisting they were responsible for the improvement, vaguely tracing it back to some policy or program they had instituted or favored a few years earlier. But soon the situation became highly politicized, not just in the contest-for-elected-office sense, but ideologically. An entire school of thought was put on trial. Conservatives interpreted the falling crime rates as evidence of the intellectual bankruptcy of liberal thinking about crime. Criminologists on the political left remained convinced that street criminals are "drawn" to illegal opportunities or "driven" to commit desperate acts by the deprivations and injustices imposed upon them. Criminologists on the political right maintained that the crime problem arises from personal shortcomings and spiritual or "moral poverty" that afflict deviant individuals who "choose" to commit antisocial acts because they cannot fit into an essentially fair and sound social system (see the contrasting views of Bennett, DiIulio, and Walters, 1996, and Currie, 1998, 1999). To conservatives, New York City's meanest streets became the proving grounds for one of their most cherished ideologically driven proposals: that crime rates can be substantially reduced through get-tough policies, and that it is not necessary to tackle the alleged "social roots" of crime that would take vast sums of money and many years of intensive social intervention to correct. Advancing this argument rhetorically, Governor George Pataki (quoted in Nagourney, 1998:B4) described as "nonsense" the view that a criminal's actions stemmed from "a culmination of social factors beyond his control . . . we, as servants of the people, are not charged with carrying out a sociological study. We are charged with maintaining public order and saving lives." His alternative explanation was "to embrace what—for you and I—is an incredibly simple principle: that criminals cause crime." Clearly, the attack on "root cause theory" was based on a belief that offenders exercise free will, and on a faith in the efficacy of punishment and the repressive potential of strict policing and a ready resort to imprisonment.

As this political debate intruded itself into the controversy surrounding the reasons for the drop in crime in New York, tremendous confusion arose concerning the distinctions between "root causes of crime," crime theories, and crime rates. Crime rates indicate how much illegal activity is going on. Social roots generate criminal activity. Crime theories that focus upon social roots explain why certain people are more vulnerable to the temptation to violate the same laws that most others obey. But crime theories that identify economically hard-pressed people as being more "at risk" do not predict with any precision how many of these individuals at any given time will succumb to pressures and get swept up into illegal activities, thereby influencing the crime rate. Even though murder rates declined by more than two-thirds during the 1990s in New York, the characteristics of the remaining one-third of perpetrators and their victims did not vary. Before, during, and after the crash, they continued to be drawn disproportionately and predominantly from the ranks of lower-income young men. This poor-male-on-poor-male carnage, proceeding at a much diminished level, actually confirmed that economic hardships were still deeply implicated as a root cause of street crime. As long as this pattern persists, there is no reason to abandon the traditional criminological theories that locate the risks of involvement in social deprivation. "Liberal" criminological theories were not really on trial in the social laboratory of New York neighborhoods, and these explanations certainly have not been negated by the evidence that crime rates can fall sharply, suddenly, and unpredictably in just a few years, even though poverty persists, or even intensifies.

However, the New York experience does cast doubt on two widely held beliefs in criminology: that growing inequality inevitably generates greater dissatisfaction; and that a "revolution of rising expectations" causes an upsurge in crime if conditions are improving but not rapidly enough. The gap between the City's rich and poor widened, while the problems endured by lower-income people were ameliorated to only a small degree amidst incessant talk of prosperity, and yet crime rates tumbled.

Actually, sharp increases and decreases in crime rates undermine the credibility of theories that involvement in criminal behavior is somehow genetic and inherited or otherwise biologically determined and fixed by human nature. Similarly, those psychological explanations that focus upon individual pathology and personality disorders as the underlying cause of criminal behavior also cannot account for sudden yet profound short-run changes in collective lawbreaking versus law-abiding behavior, since child-rearing practices and treatment modalities evolve slowly. Only social and economic conditions and subcultural outlooks can vary dramatically over a period of a decade or less.

What Really Works?

A summary of the findings of this research project appears in table 8.1. This summary indicates the results that emerged when the leading hypotheses were tested with the available data. It is clear that many of the widely circulated—and firmly believed—explanations for New York's

Table 8.1. Summary of Findings

Possible Reason for the Crash	Qualifications, Anomalies, and Contradictions
Improved Policing by the NYPD	
New NYPD strategies since the advent of Compstat reengineering quickly produced results.	The claim is difficult to evaluate because the innovations were not introduced piecemeal, as a controlled social experiment.
	Some types of street crimes were already falling in early 1994 before Compstat innovations were implemented.
	Murder declined in cities even if their police forces were demoralized or poorly managed.
A greater uniformed presence deterred murders in outdoor locations visible to officers on patrol.	Murders committed indoors declined almost as much.
	Police presence in the aftermath of crimes (response time) did not improve.
	The increasingly visible presence of private security personnel plus greater use of surveillance equipment and anti-theft devices may account for some of the deterrence.
New tactics enabled detectives to solve more murder cases, as well as other violent crimes, to above average levels.	The same percentage of current cases were solved; more old cases were solved, boosting the annual clearance rate.
	Vehicle theft rates fell as much, yet this clearance rate did not improve.
Zero tolerance for quality of life infractions restored order, as hypothesized by the "Broken Windows" thesis.	A crackdown on minor offenses did not stem the tide shortly after the outbreak of the crack epidemic.
	Murder dropped as much in other cities in which mass arrests were not made.
Zero tolerance deterred gun toting.	Gun arrests did not rise; they kept falling ever since the 1990 peak in gun murders.
	The proportion of gun arrests that led to indictment and conviction did not improve.
More aggressive tactics chased career criminals out of town.	Reports of displacement remain largely anecdotal.
A Tougher Criminal Justice System	
More offenders than ever before were incarcerated in upstate institutions, incapacitating them and deterring others.	New York's incarceration rate and prison expansion rate does not top the list.
	The proportion of felony arrests leading to indictment, conviction, and imprisonment actually declined after 1993.
	Crime rates did not decline in the late 1970s and late 1980s even though inmate populations grew rapidly.
	The number of new commitments to prison fell along with the felony arrest rate.
	Parolees reentered the City in large numbers.
	Jail inmates declined even though total arrests increased.

(continued)

| 263 |

Table 8.1. (continued)

Possible Reason for the Crash	Qualifications, Anomalies, and Contradictions
The Drug Scene Dwindled	
The crack epidemic began to wane after 1990, especially in terms of young new recruits.	The crack epidemic declined as much in Philadelphia without producing the same relief.
As the drug market matured and as it was driven indoors by intensified police pressures, violence broke out less often.	The overall proportions of arrestees with cocaine and heroin in their systems did not dramatically decline.
The narcotics squad dismantled many of the City's drug-dealing operations.	Fewer victims had used cocaine before they died, and overdose deaths diminished but hospital emergency room episodes increased. Large numbers of sellers and users continued to carry out transactions and get arrested.
Overall alcohol consumption declined.	It can't be established that alcohol consumption by poor young men declined.
The Local Economy Boomed	
The recovery and prosperity alleviated the stresses on poor people, from whose ranks street criminals are disproportionately drawn.	Poverty rates of black and Hispanic New Yorkers did not fall.
More jobs were created during the second half of the 1990s than in recent decades.	Other metropolitan areas enjoyed much lower unemployment rates. Unemployment rates for Hispanic men dropped, but did not improve dramatically for black men. Perhaps a growing underground economy of off-the-books jobs enabled those who were officially poor and unemployed to earn money.
More people were able to make the transition from welfare to work	In the past, expanding welfare rolls were associated with lowered murder rates.
Greater numbers of at-risk youth were absorbed into student culture at two- and four-year colleges across the country.	The college-going rate has been increasing for decades.
Record-breaking numbers of generally law-abiding immigrants settled in the City.	Immigration to New York has been increasing for decades.
Favorable Demographic Trends Materialized	
The number of active offenders declined through attrition.	Death and expulsion are not admirable social policies for others to emulate.
The number of young males dropped after the baby boomers matured.	Much of the decline took place among white youth, who were far less involved in street crime.
The number of at-risk youth not in school and not at work dropped.	This vulnerable group shrank during the 1980s, and is only inferred to have diminished further during the 1990s.

Table 8.1. (continued)

Possible Reason for the Crash	Qualifications, Anomalies, and Contradictions
Changing Values of Teenagers and Young Adults	
This could explain the nationwide decline in crime across-the-board.	It is difficult to verify that a change took place, other than through opinion poll results.

crash contain at least a kernel of truth, but qualifications, anomalies, and contradictions abound for many of these assertions. Policymakers must commission further studies before accepting any of these explanations and acting upon their implications.

Four policies merit special emphasis. First, encouraging most high school graduates, even those who are underprepared and are unlikely to graduate, to enroll in college serves the worthwhile social purpose of reinforcing crime-resisting tendencies. Universal exposure to higher education is a sound collective investment for a number of reasons, and counteracting the values of street culture can now be added as a demonstrable beneficial side effect. Second, welcoming hard-working immigrants into the City's multicultural mix is a wise social policy that is rarely presented as an anti-crime measure, but it serves that purpose as well. Third, discouraging drinking, especially to excess and in public, through law enforcement strategies and educational efforts, has the potential to substantially curb violence as much as other anti-drug strategies. Fourth, a job creation program that would offer meaningful occupations at a living wage would go a long way toward luring the remaining car thieves, burglars, and others engaged in property crime, rackets, and scams to try their hand at legitimate opportunities.

An unprecedented massive and sustained offensive against drugs launched in tandem with the advent of Compstat was able to drive some cocaine, crack, and heroin dealers out of town, and force the remaining participants to discreetly carry out their transactions behind closed doors, but it was not able to deliver a knock-out punch. The resulting stalemate underlines the necessity of investing more resources in the two other anti-drug strategies, treatment and prevention through education.

Until the law enforcement strategies accounting for some of the drop in crime are identified and evaluated with greater precision, and their impacts "weighted" statistically, it is premature to draw the conclusion that expensive and controversial anti-crime tactics (like zero tolerance, aggressive stop-and-frisk practices, and mass imprisonment) are "worth it," in terms of the social costs they exact: the alienation of minority youth from the police, the negative stereotyping that leads to racial profiling, and the stigmatizing long-term impact of criminal records on job prospects.

Finally, more efforts must be undertaken toward improving race relations. Most low-income young black and Hispanic males were law-abiding even in the bad old days when crime rates were much higher. Yet, ironically, after the crash, when they collectively were behaving so much better in the statistical sense, they were still treated indiscriminately as potentially dangerous persons by the NYPD, and were not given any credit for turning their backs on hard drugs and violence by commentators in positions of authority and influence. A "reachable" moment materialized but was largely missed. The latter 1990s were a time when discriminatory barriers based on class and race should have been dismantled—in housing, schooling, job training, hiring—much more thoroughly and enthusiastically than they were.

Imagine . . .

Some of the most important lessons from the New York experience concern policy shifts and events that never happened.

One striking conclusion is that allowing law-abiding people to go about their business armed with handguns is not necessary to prevent crime. Advocates of armed self-defense have succeeded in 31 states since 1987 in passing "shall issue" laws that make it easier for individuals with clean records to get permits to carry guns for self-protection (Ratnesar, 1996). Criminologists have not found any solid evidence that a more heavily armed populace was a safer one (see McDowall, Loftin, and Wiersenna, 1995), but gun enthusiasts proclaimed that these new laws brought down the crime rate in a number of states (Kopel, 1995; Polsby, 1995; Lacayo, 1996; Lott, 1998). If the New York State legislature had enacted a right-to-carry law that enabled apprehensive residents to go about the city with handguns in their pockets, briefcases, and purses at the start of the 1990s, wouldn't the gun lobby trumpet the New York miracle as definitive proof that would-be "bad guys" can be deterred by the threat of an armed citizenry, causing them to either leave town for greener pastures where unarmed victims are still ripe for the taking, or to stifle their urges to rob, rape, and assault complete strangers? But New York State did not loosen up its gun permit laws. In fact, the NYPD became much stricter about issuing right-to-carry permits within city limits (Marzulli, 1999a).

Nor is a reliance on capital punishment needed to quell murderous rampages. Death penalty proponents argue that the prospect of execution can be a persuasive general deterrent that can cow would-be killers into abandoning their deadly plans. However, the potential benefits of executions can't be realized until they occur with regularity (see DiIulio, 1995a). Imagine if the New York State legislature had pushed through a death penalty statute by overriding Governor Mario Cuomo's veto during the 1980s, and a spate of successful prosecutions and a well-publicized series of executions of cold-blooded killers had taken place at the start of the 1990s. Wouldn't people who have faith in the power of punishment have concluded that the government can stifle interpersonal violence by making a negative example out of certain murderers to scare others into behaving? But execution did not loom as a deterrent until 1995, when the legislature and the newly elected governor, George Pataki, restored capital punishment as a penalty for certain types of slayings. And by the close of the century, just one murderer out of several thousand killers apprehended within the five boroughs had been sentenced to die, and no execution date was in sight because of a lengthy appeals process. As Kings County district attorney Joe Hynes summed up the situation (quoted in Barrett, 1999:6): "It has not proven to be a deterrent. It's no small irony that I've asked for the most death penalty cases in the state, and the numbers of murders [in Brooklyn] have gone up." Therefore, execution's supposed chilling effect could not account for the plunge in homicides, and certainly could not cause auto thefts, burglaries, and robberies to tumble.

An even longer list of strictly hypothetical candidates for the honor of helping to bring down the crime rate in the City could be drawn up. Imagine if some brilliant doctor had discovered an effective cure for drug addiction and had set up a chain of clinics to help addicts break their habits. What if some new rehabilitation programs were training and educating prisoners and finding good jobs for them after they were released back into society? Suppose techniques of "fair fighting" (with words) and of conflict resolution were part of the curriculum in every high school, and had to be mastered before graduation. What conclusions would be drawn if the City Council had imposed a strict curfew on juveniles, as was done in hundreds of other cities? What claims would be made if early in 1994 several massive religious revival rallies to inspire errant men to change their ways had been held in Yankee Stadium or Central Park? Or if a tough new law had sent a stern message to criminals with two strikes against them that one more felony conviction would seal their fate? This kind of speculation could go on and on. Although these factors might account for some of the drop in crime in other parts of the country, they must be eliminated from consideration as the reasons behind New York's crash because none of these sudden changes actually took place before crime rates tumbled. The lesson to be learned is that when a new policy is implemented or a social event takes place and then crime rates go down (or up), what appears to be linked might really be unconnected or merely coincidental.

Final Days: When Did the Crash End?

It is quite unlikely that street crime has permanently gone out of style and will never make a comeback. It is probable that another crime wave will engulf the City in the near future. What changes could usher in another painful period of fear and suffering? And what factors might stave off the inevitable? A deadly combination of several of the following developments hitting the City at once would bode ill for the foreseeable future.

First, the prosperity bubble will surely burst, triggering a severe downturn in the local economy. This shift in the business cycle will set adrift once again many of the poor young men who finally had been absorbed into the world of legitimate work by years of sustained economic growth. They will be cast out by the principle of last hired, first fired when massive layoffs take place. Second, a predictable boomlet or bulge currently moving through the age structure unavoidably will provide a larger pool of potential new recruits for street crime. Third, if restrictive admission and retention policies force a contraction in the size of the student body attending the metropolitan area's low-tuition public colleges, a reduced share of eighteen- to twenty-four-year-olds will be involved in student culture and inoculated against the self-defeating norms of street culture and the temptations of illegal money-making schemes. Fourth, a new drug epidemic, perhaps of "crank" or "ice" (smokable speed), which appeared on the West Coast years ago but whose spread eastward stalled during the 1990s, could wreak havoc in impoverished communities, the way the crack attack did. Fifth, an upsurge in binge drinking, especially in public spaces, would be ominous. Sixth, any choking-off of the flow of new immigrants also could be deleterious. Seventh, a return to a reactive mode by a deenergized NYPD would endanger public safety. Finally, and most damaging of all would be a shift in the values and lifestyles of adolescents and young adults back toward self-destructive, counterproductive forms of superficial rebellion, ineffective protest, and misdirected hostility, as had developed after the idealism and optimism of the 1960s dissipated into cynicism and despair.

During 1999, the crime crash came to an end, at least as far as murder was concerned. The body count rose to roughly 667 (unofficially), up about 6 percent from the year before (McQuillan, 2000). During the first few months of 2000, the death toll continued to mount at a frightening pace (Flynn, 2000). This was ominous, since several decades of past experience indicated that whenever New York's murder rate went up, it kept on climbing for several years in a row before reversing direction. It rarely fluctuated in a choppy fashion, up one year and down the next (refer back to graph 1.1). Furthermore, both gun and non-gun killings increased during 1999 (Marzulli, 1999b). The rebound in fatal stabbings was particularly troubling since non-gun murders had been falling steadily for decades (refer back to graph 2.3), and knives were more difficult for the police to go after than guns. On the other hand, the crash was not over in terms of less-than-lethal violence and stealing. The additional six closely watched street crimes, including automobile theft, continued to drift downward throughout 1999 (off another 10 percent)(Flynn, 1999e). This decoupling was puzzling, since vehicle thefts are very reliably reported and had been rising and falling in lockstep with murders since 1978 (refer back to graph 1.2).

No one knew for sure why murder was making a comeback. Even though the decade of the 1990s was heralded as the Information Age, no comprehensive monitoring and data-retrieval system had been set up to integrate the record-keeping systems of the NYPD, the five district attorneys, the medical examiner's office, the courts, the jails, the prisons, and the Health Department's death certificate database. Up-to-date social, economic, and demographic data won't be accessible to researchers for years.

Although the NYPD labored mightily, applying all the Compstat strategies it claimed it had perfected, it could not stem the rising tide of killings at the turn of the century. Since its champions had proclaimed that improved policing deserved all the credit for the crash, they were in no position to suddenly point to social, economic, cultural, or demographic factors as the culprits for the resurgence in lethal violence. As a result, the NYPD accepted responsibility—but actually didn't. Top officials at City Hall and Police Headquarters seized the opportunity to blame a growing chorus of critics for interfering with the department's ability to continue to carry out the aggressive stop-and-frisk and zero-tolerance policies that had (allegedly) worked so well since 1994. Their official explanation was that the condemnation of the Street Crime Unit in particular (after four members killed an unarmed young black man, Amadou Diallo, in the Bronx in February 1999) caused a drop-off in gun arrests and seizures and a consequent spike in killings (for example, see Herszenhorn, 1999; and Flynn, 1999d, 1999e). This version of events, although repeated over and over again by a host of top officials, never was directly challenged in the media, even though it lacked empirical support and seemed illogical on its face. First of all, the rebound in murders did not take place after the Diallo shooting and the subsequent protests in early 1999, but actually began during the second half of 1998, months earlier. This fact was masked by the substantial drop that had continued into the first half of 1998, which was sufficient to bring down the rate for all of 1998 compared to 1997.(Therefore, the crash in murder rates technically ended around July 1998, not at the end of December.)[1] Second, the murder rate continued to fall in the immediate area of the Diallo shooting, the Bronx, throughout 1999 (Kapstatter, 1999). Third, gun arrests had been dropping ever since 1990, not just since February 1999 (refer back to graph 3.3). Fourth, the overall importance of the Street Crime Unit in ferreting out gunmen was being exaggerated.[2] Fifth, the alleged "virtual handcuffing" of the NYPD by the unfavorable public outcry against its aggressive tactics did not explain why aggravated assaults, forcible rapes, robberies, burglaries, grand larcenies, vehicle thefts, and larcenies kept falling while killings started rising.

The rise and fall of murders in New York City generally has been in step with negative and positive developments throughout the rest of the United States (refer back to graph 1.3). Therefore, something greater than just deteriorating conditions within the City might be behind New York's latest woes, and tougher times may loom for the nation as a whole after a time lag of a year or two. A new mystery is materializing, one that needs to be solved with far greater urgency than the reasons for the much-welcomed crash of the 1990s—the mystery surrounding the ominously rebounding murder rate of the twenty-first century.

Notes

1. Ever since the beginning of 1994, succeeding half year (January to June, July to December) totals were lower than the previous time period, until the second half of 1998. The totals for 1998 and 1999 were as follows, according to the FBI's UCRs for 1998 , and the NYPD's figures released to the media: first six months of 1998, 303 murders; second six months, 330; first six months of 1999, 341; second six months, 326. Therefore, it turns out that after two consecutive six month periods of rising body counts, murders fell in the second half of 1999, even though protests continued.

2. Commissioner Safir repeatedly claimed that the Street Crime Unit was responsible for 40% of all gun arrests (for example, see Kocieniewski, 1999). But the 1998 NYPD Complaints and Arrests annual report credited the SCU with just 610 dangerous weapons possession arrests, less than 20 percent of the total force's 3,830 felony weapons arrests that year.

Descriptions of the Different Data Sets Obtained and Compiled for This Study of New York City Murder Rates

Vital Statistics Database, Compiled from Death Certificates, 1988–1998

Obtained from the New York City Department of Health; submitted annually to the National Center For Health Statistics, mortality branch, in Atlanta. Variables include the victim's sex, age, race, ethnicity, nationality, place of birth, borough and Zip code of residence, place of death (scene, ambulance, hospital), marital status, job status, educational attainment, and cause of death.

Supplementary Homicide Reports (SHRS), 1976–1997

Obtained from the New York City Police Department, the State Division of Criminal Justice Services (DCJS), and the ICPSR. Compiled by the New York City Police Department, and submitted to the FBI's Uniform Crime Reporting Division. Based on data from the NYPD's SHR form filled out early in the homicide investigation, and submitted monthly to the DCJS. Variables include the victim's age, sex, race, ethnicity; the arrestee's age, sex, race, ethnicity; the victim-offender relationship, the circumstances surrounding the crime, and the method of killing.

Homicide Arrestees, 1978–1997

Obtained from the New York State Division of Criminal Justice Services from the state database of arrests and dispositions. Variables include arrestee's age, sex, race, and prior record of arrests and convictions.

Social Conditions and Crime Rates by NYPD Precincts, 1990–1995

Obtained from published sources. Based on data from the NYPD's Annual "Complaints and Arrests" reports, and demographic data from the 1990 U.S. Census. Compiled on a precinct-by-precinct basis. Variables include the precinct's racial/ethnic composition, its economic conditions as of 1990 (income levels, unemployment rate, college attendance rate), and its murder rate from 1988 to 1995.

Data on Arrestees Seeking Bail, 1989

Obtained from the Criminal Justice Agency in New York City. Based on applications for free legal representation and bail. Variables include arrest code, personal background (age, sex, race), and socioeconomic status (job, income, savings).

NYPD Homicide Logs, 1995–1998

Obtained from *New York Newsday* (1995–1997 case-level data) and the *New York Times* (1998 summary). Includes the arrestee's age, sex, and race, the victim's age, sex, and race, the weapon used, and the circumstances surrounding the crime.

Profile of Detainees Held on Murder Charges on Riker's Island, 1996

Obtained from the NYC Department of Corrections. Based on data extracted from the jail's files of approximately 950 persons facing murder or manslaughter charges. Variables include the defendant's age, sex, race, ethnicity, borough of residence, Zip code, prior record (felony conviction), date of admission, and number of days in custody.

REFERENCES

Aaronson, S., and Cameron, S. (1997). Poverty in New York City, 1996: An update and perspectives. New York: Community Service Society.

Accordino, J. (1998). "The consequences of welfare reform for central city governments." Journal of the American Planning Association 64, no. 1, pp. 11–18

Adler, J. (1997). "We'll take Manhattan." Newsweek, August 18, pp. 33–37.

Alaniz, M., Cartmill, R., and Parker, R. (1998). "Immigrants and violence: The importance of neighborhood context." Hispanic Journal of the Behavioral Sciences 20, pp. 155–176.

Altman, L. (1997). "Deaths from AIDS decline sharply in New York City." New York Times, January 25, pp. A1, A28.

———. (1998). "AIDS deaths drop 48% in New York." New York Times, February 3, pp. A1, B6.

Ames, W. (1979). "The three-joint lunch." New York Magazine, August 27, pp. 43–44.

Anderson, D. (1997). "The mystery of the falling crime rate." American Prospect 32 (May), pp. 49–55.

———. (1998). Sensible justice: Alternatives to prison. New York: New Press.

Anderson, E. (1999). Code of the street: Decency, violence, and the moral life of the inner city. New York: W. W. Norton.

Andrews, W. (1996). "The new NYPD." Spring 3100 special internet edition.

Annin, P. (1996). "Crime: 'Superpredators' arrive." Newsweek, January 22, p. 57.

Arenson, K. (1998). "Big metropolis on campus." New York Times, September 9, pp. B1, B10.

"As criminals stash guns, NYC murder toll plunges." (1997). Law Enforcement News, January 31, p. B4.

Associated Press. (1995). "Murder rate fell in 1994 for 3rd consecutive year, agency says." New York Times, October 24, p. A19.

———. (1996). "Bill: Border crime dip my doing." New York Daily News, June 11, p. 28.

Associated Press. (1997). "N.Y.C. reaches goal of fewer than 1,000 homicides." Bergen Record, January 1, p. A4.

———. (1998). "Slaying of cousins is seen as part of crime's upstate migration." New York Times, February 17, p. B7.

———. (1999a). "Israelis press Safir about NYPD blues." New York Daily News, June 16, p. 32.

———. (1999b). "Report shows the economic might of urban areas." New York Times, November 4, p. A21.

Attinger, J. (1989). "The decline of New York." Time, September 17, pp. 36–41, 44.

———. (1990). "The littlest victims." Time, August 20, pp. 44–45.

"Attitudes: Police rank their priorities." (1994). New York Times, p. B8.

Auletta, K. (1982). The underclass. New York: Vintage.

Baden, M. (1978). Alcohol, other drugs, and violent death. New York: Oxford University Press.

———. (1989). Unnatural death: Confessions of a medical examiner. New York: Random House.

Barbanel, J. (1991). "Some signs of hope glint from New York's clouds." New York Times, July 30, pp. B1, B2.

Barrett, D. (1999). New York's death penalty: No quick fix." New York Post, September 27, p. 8.

Barrett, W. (1997). "50 reasons to loathe your mayor." Village Voice, November 4, pp. 30–43.

Barry, D. (1997). "For a suspect in an officer's killing, a long slide into ruin." New York Times, May 25, pp. A29, A36.

———. (1999). "Mayor says adding officers is key to city's health." New York Times, January 30, p. B8.

Barry, D., and Connelly, M. (1999). "Poll in New York finds many think police are biased." New York Times, March 16, pp. A1, B8.

Basler, B. (1980). "State parole board fights those who would sentence it to death." New York Times, December 13, pp. 31.

———. (1981). "Burglaries increase, but arrests fall as New York's police try to cope." New York Times, May 17, p. A1, A36.

Bayley, D. (1993). "The cop fallacy." New York Times, August 16, p. A17.

Beck, A., Gilliard, D., Greenfeld, L., Harlow, C., Hester, T., Jankowski, L., Snell, T., and Stephan, J. (1993). BJS Survey of state prison inmates, 1991. Washington, D.C.: U.S. Department of Justice.

Becker, G. (1998). "Economic viewpoint: How the U.S. handcuffed the crime rate." Business Week, December 28, p. 28.

Beiser, V. (1995). "Why the big apple feels safer." Maclean's, September 11, pp. 39–40.

Bennett, W., DiIulio, J., and Walters, J. (1996). Body count. New York: Simon and Schuster.

Bernstein, N. (1999a). "With a job, without a home: Low-wage workers turn to shelters." New York Times, March 4, p. B1.

———. (1999b). "Poverty rate persists in City despite boom." New York Times, October 7, pp. B1, B6.

"Big Apple's big assault." (1996). Forbes, January 1, p. 26.

Bigart, H. (1964). "1,100 police get narcotics duty in drive to curb rise in addicts." New York Times, September 10, p. 8.

Blair, J. (1999a). "Striking drug bosses, not street dealers, pays off, the police say." New York Times, June 17, p. B16.

———. (1999b). "22 are charged with insurance fraud in stolen-car sting." New York Times, August 11, p. B3.

———. (1999c). "New tactic goes citywide after it ends drug bazaars." New York Times, October 3, p. B47.

———. (1999d). "CIA chief slips in to study police department." New York Times, November 6, p. B2.

Blumenthal, R. (1991). "Numbers game: Putting more police on the streets." New York Times, February 17, p. A44.

Blumstein, A. (1995). "Violence by young people: Why the deadly nexus." National Institute of Justice Journal, Spring, pp. 2–9.

Blumstein, A., Cohen, J., and Nagin, D. (1978). Deterrence and incapacitation: Estimating the effects of criminal sanctions on crime rates. Washington, D.C.: National Academy of Sciences Press.

Blumstein, A., and Rosenfeld, R. (1998). "Explaining recent trends in U.S. homicide rates." Journal of Criminal Law and Criminology 88, no. 4 (Summer), pp. 1175–1216.

Bouza, A. (1990). The police mystique. New York: Plenum.

———. (1996). The decline and fall of the American empire. New York: Plenum.

———. (1997). "NYPD blues—good, lucky, or both?" Law Enforcement News, January 31, pp. 8, 10.

Bowling, B. (1998). "Book review: N. Dennis (ed.), 'Zero tolerance: Policing in a free society.'" British Journal of Policing 38, no. 2, pp. 318–321.

———. (1999). "The rise and fall of New York murder: Zero tolerance or crack's decline?" British Journal of Criminology 39, no. 4 (Autumn), pp. 531–554.

Bragg, R. (1995). "New Orleans's hopes rise as crime rate decreases." New York Times, December 25, p. A12.

Bram, J., Brauer, D., and Miranda, E. (1997). "New York City's unemployment picture." Current Issues in Economics and Finance (Federal Reserve Bank of New York) 3, no. 14 (December), pp. 1–3.

Bratton, W. (1995). "Great expectations: How higher expectations for police departments can lead to a decrease in crime." Paper delivered at an NIJ Conference entitled "Measuring what matters," November 28, Washington, D.C.

———. (1996). "New strategies for combating crime in New York City." Fordham Urban Journal 23 (Spring), pp. 781–793.

———. (1998). Turnaround: How America's top cop reversed the crime epidemic. New York: Random House.

Bratton, W., and Andrews, W. (1999a). "What we've learned about policing." City Journal, Spring, pp. 14–27.

———. (1999b). "A good police state." New York Daily News, May 2, p. 44.

Brill, S. (1977). "Firearm abuse: A research and policy report." Washington, D.C.: Police Foundation.

Brotherton, D. (1999). "Old heads tell their stories: From gangs to street organizations." Free Inquiry in Creative Sociology 27, no. 1, pp. 1–15.

Brown, C. (1999). Manchild in the promised land. New York: Simon and Schuster.

Brown, L. (1992). "Community policing: Bring the community into the battle against crime." Vital Speeches 58, no. 18 (July 1), pp. 567–570.

Brownstein, H. (1996). The rise and fall of a violent crime wave: Crack cocaine and the social construction of a crime problem. Guilderland, N.Y.: Harrow and Heston.

Bureau of Justice Statistics (BJS). (1980). Profile of jail inmates. Washington, D.C.: U.S. Department of Justice.

———. (1992). Multi-state offenders: A report concerning state prisoners who were criminally active in more than one state. Washington, D.C.: U.S. Department of Justice.

Bureau of Labor Statistics (BLS). (1999). College enrollment and work activity of 1998 high school graduates. Washington, D.C.: U.S. Department of Labor.

Burnham, D. (1971a). "3 ex-policemen tell state inquiry of their involvement in heroin traffic." New York Times, April 7, p. 8.

———. (1971b). "Police shift tactics to curb heroin sale." New York Times, April 21, p. 8.

———. (1996). Above the law. Scribner: New York.

Butcher, K., and Piehl, A. (1998). "Recent immigrants: Unexpected implications for crime and incarceration." Industrial and Labor Relations Review 51, no. 4 (July), pp. 654–680.

Butterfield, F. (1995a). "Serious crimes fall for third year, but experts warn against seeing a trend." New York Times, May 23, p. A15.

———. (1995b). "Major crimes fell in '95, early data by F.B.I. indicate." New York Times, May 6, pp. A1, B8.

———. (1995c). "Crime continues to decline, but experts warn of coming 'storm' of juvenile violence." New York Times, November 29, p. A18.

———. (1995d). "Grim forecast is offered on rising juvenile crime." New York Times, September 8, p. A16.

———. (1996a). "Experts on crime warn of a 'ticking time bomb': Cite demographics and 'revolving' justice." New York Times, January 6, p. A6.

———. (1996b). "Successes reported for curfews, but doubts persist." New York Times, June 3, pp. A1, B7.

———. (1996c). "Barrooms' decline underlies a drop in adult killings." New York Times, August 19, pp. A1, A11.

———. (1996d). "'Three strikes' rarely invoked in courtrooms." New York Times, September 10, pp. A1, D23.

———. (1997a). "Crime keeps falling, but prisons keep on filling." New York Times, September 28, sec. 4, pp. 1, 4.

———. (1997b). "Property crimes steadily decline, led by burglary." New York Times, October 12, pp. A1, A26.

———. (1997c). "Drop in homicide rate linked to crack's decline." New York Times, October 27, pp. A12.

———. (1998). "As crime falls, pressure rises to alter data." New York Times, August 3, pp. A1, A16.

———. (2000). "Cities reduce crime and conflict without New York–style hardball." New York Times, March 4, pp. A1, B4.

Campbell, J., Sahid, J., and Stang, D. (1970). "Law and order reconsidered." Staff report to the National Commission on the Causes and Prevention of Violence. Washington, D.C.: U.S. Government Printing Office.

Canada, G. (1995). Fist, stick, knife, gun. Boston: Beacon Press.

"Capital ideas: DC chief unveils blueprint for top-to-bottom overhaul." (1998). Law Enforcement News, October 15, pp. 1, 9.

Carlson, T. (1995). "Safety, Inc.: Private cops are there when you need them." Policy Review 73 (Summer), pp. 66–73.

Castillo, A. (1980). "Koch seeks policy role to toughen administration of criminal justice." New York Times, November 16, p. 42.

Cauvin, H., Rashbaum, W., and Siemaszko, C. (1999). "Suspect arrested in '92 slay of editor." New York Daily News, April 19, p. 5.

Celona, L., and Massarella, L. (1998). "'Collar' shortage puts Queens cops in doghouse." New York Post, June 11, p. 12.

Celona, L., and Neuman, W. (1999a). "600 cops set to launch city's new drug blitz." New York Post, February 22, p. 8.

———. (1999b). "NYPD to bare 'stop and frisk' data." New York Post, April 12, p. 19.

Chaiken, M., and Chaiken, J. (1991). Research in Action: Priority prosecution of high-rate dangerous offenders. Washington, D.C.: U.S. Department of Justice.

Chein, I., Gerard, D., Lee, R., and Rosenfeld, E. (1964). The road to H: Narcotics, delinquency, and social policy. New York: Basic Books.

Chernick, H. (1999). "Commentary." Federal Reserve Bank of New York Economic Policy Review, September, pp. 165–167.

Chitwood, D., Rivers, J., and Inciardi, J. (1996). The American pipe dream: Crack cocaine in the inner city. New York: Harcourt Brace.

Churcher, S. (1978). "Heroin versus cocaine: The drug of choice." New York Magazine, September 25, p. 54.

Citizens Budget Commission (CBC). (1997). The state of municipal services in the 1990s: The New York Police Department. New York: CBC.

Citizens Committee for Children (CCC). (1999). Keeping track of New York City's children. New York: CCC.

Citizens Crime Commission of New York City. (CCC). (1996). "Reducing gun crime in New York City: A research and policy report." New York City: CCC.

Claffey, B. (1997). "Ranking bests that of other major cities." New York Daily News, December 1, p. 2.

———. (1998). "Cop booze woes spur crackdown." New York Daily News, December 11, p. 8.

Clark, D. (1992–1999). The impact of foreign-born inmates on the New York State Department of Correctional Services. Annual report by the Division of Program Planning, Research, and Evaluation, 1991–1998. Albany: NYS DOCS.

Clark, J. (1996). "As crime rates continue to dip, police credit community efforts—and their own." Law Enforcement News, September 15, pp. 1, 14.

Clark, R., and Passel, J. (1998). Immigrants in New York. Washington, D.C.: Urban Institute.

Clear, T., and Cordner, G. (1999). "Does 'zero tolerance' really reduce crime? A look at New York's experience." Community Corrections Report on Law and Corrections Practice 6, no. 4, pp. 53–54.

Cloward, R., and Ohlin, L. (1960). Delinquency and opportunity. New York: Free Press.

Connor, M. (1995). What is cool? Understanding black manhood in America. New York: Crown.

Cook, J. (1978). "Five men waging war against street crime." New York Post, November 12, p. 15.

Cooney, M. (1997). "The decline of elite homicide." Criminology 35, no. 3, pp. 381–407.

Cooper, M. (1997a). "New York City takes a bow as homicide rate plunges." New York Times, January 1, p. B2.

———. (1997b). "City reports a big reduction of crime in jail, of all places." New York Times, November 15, p. B3.

———. (1999a). "Police are criticized for responding more slowly to 911 calls." New York Times, September 24, p. B9.

———. (1999b). "Officials say bureaucratic snag kept suspect in boy's kidnaping on streets." New York Times, October 26, p. B3.

Cordner, G., and Hale, D. (1992). What works in policing? Cincinnati: Anderson.

Cottman, M. (1992a). "Black cops want probe: Actions of Giuliani, Caruso eyed." New York Newsday, September 21, p. 5.

———. (1992b). "Giuliani calls mayor divisive." September 22, p. 9.

Craig, S., and Austin, A. (1997). "New York's million missing jobs." City Journal, Autumn, pp. 43–51.

Craig, S., and Bennett, S. (1997). After the boom: The politics of Generation X. Boston: Rowman and Littlefield.

Cressey, D. (1969). Theft of the nation: The structure of organized crime in America. New York: Harper and Row.

"Crime file: Crown Heights chronology." (1998). New York Daily News, April 1, p. 8.

"Crime rates just keep on dropping." (1996). Law Enforcement News, December 31, p. 9.

Criminal Justice Coordinating Council. (1971). "Crime and punishment in New York City." New York Post, March 20, magazine section, p. 5.

Crittenden, A., and Ruby, M. (1974). "Cocaine: The champagne of drugs." New York Times, Sunday Magazine, September 1, pp. 8–10.

Currie, E. (1985). Confronting crime: An American challenge. New York: Pantheon Books.

———. (1993). Reckoning: Drugs, the cities, and the American future. New York: Hill and Wang.

———. (1998). Crime and punishment in America. New York: Henry Holt.

———. (1999). "Reflections on crime and criminology at the millennium." Western Criminology Review 2, no. 1 (online at wcr.sonoma.edu.).

Curtis, R. (1998). "The improbable transformation of inner-city neighborhoods: Crime, violence, drugs, and youth in the 1990s." Journal of Criminal Law and Criminology 88, no. 4 (Summer), pp. 1233–1266.

Daily News. (1975). "Ford to city: Drop dead." New York Daily News, October 30, p. 1 (headline on cover).

Dalaker, J., and Naifeh, M. (1998). Poverty in the United States. Washington, D.C.: U.S. Government Printing Office.

Daley, S., and Freitag, M. (1990). "Wrong place at the wrong time: Stray bullets kill more bystanders." New York Times, January 14, pp. A1, B3.

Deal, R. (1999). "Immigration and its impact on the future of our nation." Congressional Record, March 23, pp. H1574–1575.

Department of Correctional Services (DOCS). (1996). Profile of 1995 new commitments with suggested alcohol abuse problems based on MAST scores. Albany: NYS DOCS.

———. (1998a). Identified substance abusers, December 1997. Albany: NYS DOCS.

———. (1998b). The hub system: Profile of inmates under custody on January 1, 1998. Albany: NYS DOCS.

DeStefano, A., and Flynn, K. (1986). "Al and Rudy show gets mixed reviews." New York Newsday, July 11, p. 2.

DiIulio, J. (1995a). "Retrieve the death penalty from symbolism." The American Enterprise, May–June, pp. 40–41.

———. (1995b). "Why violent crime rates have dropped." Wall Street Journal, September 6, p. A19.

———. (1995c). "Arresting ideas: Tougher law enforcement is driving down urban crime." Policy Review 74 (Fall), pp. 12–15.

———. (1996)."Prisons are a bargain, by any measure." New York Times, January 16, p. A17.

———. (1999). "Two million prisoners are enough." Wall Street Journal, March 12, p. 14.

Dinkins, D. (1990). "Mobilizing to fight crime." New York Times, October 3, p. B2.

Director, R. (1996). "The Barney wave: Where, oh where, have all the bad guys gone." Los Angeles Magazine 41, no. 5 (May), p. 17.

Dixon, D. (1998). "Broken windows, zero tolerance, and the New York miracle." Current Issues in Contemporary Justice 10, no. 1 (July), pp. 96–106.

Dodenhoff, P. (1997). "A LEN interview with Joseph Polisar." Law Enforcement News, December 15, pp. 8–10.

Donaldson, I. (1993). The ville: Cops and kids in urban America. New York: Anchor Books.

Donohue, J. (1998). "Understanding the time path of crime." Journal of Criminal Law and Criminology 88, no. 4 (Summer), pp. 1423–1451.

Donziger, S. (1996). The real war on crime. New York: Harper Perennial.

Dugger, C. (1997). "City of immigrants becoming more so in 90s." New York Times, January 9, pp. A1, B6.

Dunne J. (1995). "Getting guns off the streets of New York." Unpublished NYPD evaluation of Police Strategy No. 1.

Dwyer, J. (1999). "Stats don't justify frisks." New York Daily News, April 20, p. 10.

Editors, *New York Daily News*. (1993). "They're on the lam, and they're near you." May 27, p. 58.

———. (1994). "The sad, short life of community policing." January 24, p. 36.

———. (1999). "Throw away more keys." January 13, p. 30.

Editors, *New York Post*. (1988). "No drug buyers, no drug dealers." March 2, p. 22.

———. (1996). "Crime: What the professors don't know." November 9, p. 45.

———. (1998a). "The murder drop: Give prisons the credit." January 4, p. 58.

———. (1998b). "The prison population problem." August 9, p. 48.

———. (1998c). "The best place to visit." September 2, p. 30.

———. (1999). "The war against the crime drop." June 27, p. 39.

Editors, *New York Times*. (1966). "Slow war on narcotics . . . and a shocking statistic." March 30, p. 28.

———. (1986). "The cops caught the crooked cops." September 26, p. A34.

———. (1988). "Should cocaine cost more? Less?" July 28, p. A26.

———. (1990). "To restore New York City: First, reclaim the streets." December 30, p. A28.

———. (1993). "The mayor's record on crime." April 10, p. 18.

———. (1994). "Poverty is unfairly defined." August 7, p. E16.

———. (1995a). "Bringing the murder rate down." July 17, p. A12.

———. (1995b). "Crime is down, again." December 23, p. A26.

———. (1996a). "Effective drug crime tactics." September 2, p. A20.

———. (1996b). "The changing face of AIDS." November 4, p. A26.

———. (1997a). "The Cedeno report." July 3, p. A22.

———. (1997b). "Crime is down all over." October 14, p. A26.

———. (1999a). "Sizing the police force." February 4, p. A26.

———. (1999b). "The summer of evil." July 3, p. A10.

Egan, T. (1990). "Chief judge says crack may overwhelm courts." New York Times, December 3, p. B3.

———. (1999). "A drug ran its course, then hid with its users." New York Times, September 19, pp. A1, A46.

Ehrenhalt, S. (1992). "Retrospect and prospect: The dynamics of the labor market." Pp. 25–55 in Challenges of the changing economy of New York City, 1992. New York: New York City Council on Economic Education at Baruch College.

Epperson, S. (1995). "Safe? You bet your life." Time, July 24, p. 35.

Fagan, J., Zimring, F., and Kim, J. (1998). "Declining homicide in New York City: A tale of two trends." Journal of Criminal Law and Criminology 88, no. 4 (Summer), pp. 1277–1324.

Federal Bureau of Investigation (FBI). (1978–1999). Crime in the United States: Annual uniform crime reports. Washington, D.C.: U.S. Department of Justice.

Feldman, D. (1991). "Let the small-time drug peddlers go." New York Times, February 23, p. A25.

Flynn, K. (1999a). "Police officer facing disciplinary charges commits suicide." New York Times, September 25, p. B5.

———. (1999b). "Lax follow-up for drug offenders is cited." New York Times, September 30, p. B8.

———. (1999c). "Record payout in settlements against police." New York Times, October 1, pp. B1, B5.

———. (1999d). "Rebound in city murder rate puzzling New York officials." New York Times, November 5, pp. A1, B6.

———. (1999e). "Experts wonder if crime drop is near end." New York Times, December 19, p. B55.

———. (2000). Shooting raises scrutiny of police antidrug tactics." New York Times, March 25, p. B4.

Fooner, M. (1979). "Where the system breaks down." Pp. 163–167 in D. MacNamara (ed.), Criminal justice: Annual editions, 1981/82. Guilford, Conn.: Dushkin.

Foote, D., Kaufman, L., McGinn, D., and Winegert, P. (1997). "Are diplomas destiny?" Newsweek, June 16, p. 46.

Forero, J. (2000). "Precinct's rosy crime rate was a distortion, the police say." New York Times, January 7, pp. B1, B3.

Fox, J., and Zawitz, E. (1999). BJS crime data brief: Homicide trends in the United States. Washington, D.C.: U.S. Department of Justice.

Frank, B., and Galea, J. (1998). Current drug use trends in New York City. Annual report. New York: New York State Office of Alcoholism and Substance Abuse Services.

Frank, T. (1998). The conquest of cool. Chicago: University of Chicago Press.

Frey, W. (1998). "The diversity myth." American Demographics, June, pp. 39–50.

Fried, J. (1998). "Killer of Hasidic student won't talk in court." New York Times, March 21, p. B5.

———. (1999). "Man suspected of playing a role in Kahane assassination plot." New York Times, August 21, pp. B1, B3.

Friedman, L., Williams, M., Singh, T., and Frieden, T. (1996). "Tuberculosis, AIDS, and death among substance abusers on welfare in New York City." New England Journal of Medicine 334, no. 13 (March 28), pp. 828–834.

Friedman, M. (1991). "A war we're losing." Wall Street Journal, March 7, p. A14.

Friedman, R. (1994). "The organizatsiya: Brooklyn's booming Russian mob is slicker, smarter, and much meaner than La Cosa Nostra." New York Magazine, November 7, pp. 50–58.

"From the start, acting DC chief acts to shake things up." (1998). Law Enforcement News, January 15, pp. 1, 6.

Furst, T., Curtis, C., Johnson, B., and Goldsmith, D. (1999). "The rise of the street middleman/woman in a declining drug market." Addiction Research 7, no. 2, pp. 103–128.

Gaiter, D. (1997). "Color blind? To Rudolph Giuliani, the race issue isn't much of an issue at all." Wall Street Journal, September 19, pp. A1, A6.

Gangi, R. (1995). "Continuing the lie: New York's sentencing reforms. The Correctional and Osborne Associations Newsletter 3, no. 4 (August), p. 1.

———. (1997). "Why is the crime rate going down? It's the demographics, stupid!" New York Daily News, January 14, p. 43.

Gangi, R., and Schiraldi, V. (1999). New York state of mind? Higher education vs. prison funding in the Empire State, 1988–1998. New York: Correctional Association.

Gans, H. (1995). The war against the poor: The underclass and anti-poverty policy. New York: Basic Books.

Gately, G. (1986). "Street drug vigils set up by black church leaders." New York Times, July 22, pp. B1, B4.

Gearty, R., and Chang, D. (1996). "Justice at a sale price." New York Daily News, March 11, pp. 7, 22.

Gewirtz, M., and McElroy, J. (1997). Assigned counsel eligibility screening project. Final report. New York: Criminal Justice Agency.

Gilbert, M., and Cervantes, R. (1986). "Patterns and practices of alcohol use among Mexican Americans: A comprehensive review." Hispanic Journal of the Behavioral Sciences 8, pp. 11–60.

Gilliard, D. (1999). BJS Bulletin: Prisoners in 1998. Washington, D.C.: U.S. Department of Justice.

Gilliard, D., and Beck, A. (1998). BJS Bulletin: Prisoners in 1997. Washington, D.C.: U.S. Department of Justice.

Ginzberg, E. (1974). New York is very much alive. New York: Praeger.

Giuliani, R. (1997a). "How New York is becoming the safest big city in America." USA Today Magazine 125, no. 2620, pp. 28–32.

———. (1997b). "Innovative computer mapping program has reduced crime to its lowest levels in 30 years." City Hall press release, May 13 (NYC official Internet website: ci.nyc.ny.us/).

———. (1997c). "Further evidence of New York City's resurgence: A cleaner, safer, more prosperous city." Mayor's Message press release, September 29 (NYC Internet website).

———. (1997d). "Removing drugs from our neighborhoods and schools." City Hall press release, October 1 (NYC Internet website).

———. (1998a). "Why we will end welfare by 2000." New York Post, July 21, p. 27.

———. (1998b). "HRA study finds 54% of former welfare participants left public assistance because they found work." Press release 442–98, September 21, Office of the Mayor.

Glaberson, W. (1990). "Trapped in the terror of New York's holding pens." New York Times, March 23, pp. A1, B4.

———. (1997). "Crime in region is dropping, but some pockets defy trend." New York Times, February 27, pp. A1, B4.

Gladwell, M. (2000). The tipping point: How little things can make a big difference. Boston: Little, Brown.

Glazer, S. (1997a). "Can police take credit for lower crime rate?" Associated Press, syndicated in many newspapers, April 18.

———. (1997b). "Declining crime rates: Does better policing account for the reduction?" Congressional Quarterly Researcher, April 4, pp. 289–312.

Glenn, G. (1976). "Crime does pay." The Police Chief Magazine, January, pp. 8–10.

"Going down for the third time: UCR shows another decrease in Part I crime in '94." (1995). Law Enforcement News, June 15, pp. 1, 6.

Goldstein, P. (1985). "The drugs/violence nexus: A tripartite conceptual framework." Journal of Drug Issues 15, no. 4, pp. 493–506.

Goldstein, P., Brownstein, H., and Ryan, P. (1992). "Drug-related homicide in New York: 1984 and 1988. Crime and Delinquency 38, pp. 459–476.

Golub, A., and Johnson, B. (1997). Crack's decline: Some surprises across U.S. cities. NIJ Research in Brief. Washington, D.C.: U.S. Department of Justice.

"Goodman demands Beame act to stop collapse of criminal justice system." (1976). Bronx Home News, October 28, p. 8.

Goodnough, A. (1998). "Tighter rules on deporting state inmates." New York Times, April 10, p. B5.

Greenberg, J. (1990). "All about crime." New York Magazine, September 3, pp. 20–32.

Greene, J. (1999). "Zero tolerance: A case study of police policies and practices in New York City." Crime and Delinquency 45, no. 2 (April), pp. 171–187.

Greene, J., and Taylor, R. (1997). "Community-based policing and foot patrol: Issues of theory and evaluation." Pp. 195–223 in J. Greene and S. Mastrofski (eds.), Community policing: Rhetoric or reality? New York: Praeger.

Greenfeld, L. (1998). Alcohol and crime. BJS Guide. Washington, D.C.: U.S. Department of Justice.

Groneman, C., and Reimers, D. (1995). "Immigration." Pp. 581–587 in K. Jackson (ed.), The encyclopedia of New York City. New Haven: Yale University Press.

Haberman, C. (1997). "Crime down, but courts are clogged." New York Times, January 3, p. B1.

Hagan, J., and Peterson, R. (1995). Crime and inequality. Stanford, Calif.: Stanford University Press.

Halstead, T. (1999). "A politics for Generation X." Atlantic Monthly, August, pp. 33–42.

Hamid, A. (1992). "The developmental cycle of a drug epidemic: The cocaine smoking epidemic of 1981–1991." Journal of Psychoactive Drugs 24, pp. 337–348.

———. (1997) "The heroin epidemic in New York City: Current status and prognosis." Journal of Psychoactive Drugs 29, no. 4, pp. 375–391.

Hamill, P. (1990). "City of the damned." Esquire, December, pp. 61–65.

Hamilton, K., and Gegax, T. (1995). "Young fogies." Newsweek, October 28, pp. 54–59.

Hampson, R. (1997). "New York City keeps getting safer." USA Today, July 2, p. 3A.

Hanson, G. (1997). "Private protection is secure industry." Insight on the News 13, no. 36 (September 29), pp. 19.

Harnett, P., and Andrews, W. (1999). "How New York is winning the drug war." City Journal 9, no. 3 (Summer), pp. 29–37.

Harris, R. (1977). "A reporter at large: Crime in New York." New Yorker, September 26, pp. 8–18.

Hartel, D., and Schoenbaum, E. (1999). "Methadone treatment protects against HIV infection: Two decades of experience in the Bronx, New York City." Public Health 113 (June), pp. 107–115.

Haskell, M., and Yablonsky, L. (1970). Crime and delinquency. Chicago: Rand McNally.

Hernandez, R. (1998). "Pataki says he delivered on promises; Experts aren't so sure." New York Times, January 4, p. B6.

Herszenhorn, D. (1999). "The statistics: Arrests drop and shootings rise as the police, Giuliani says, are distracted." New York Times, March 29, p. B3.

Hevesi, A. (1999). "NYC's Economy, 4Q98: Momentum sustained." Economic Notes from the New York City Office of the Comptroller 7, no. 1 (February), pp. 1–12.

Hevesi, D. (1999). "New home costs found highest in New York." New York Times, July 28, p. B1.

Hinds, M. (1990). "Number of killings soars in big cities across U.S." New York Times, July 18, pp. A1, A19.

Hirschi, T., and Gottfredson, M. (1989). "Age and the explanation of crime." American Journal of Sociology 89, pp. 552–584.

Hirschorn, M. (1994). "Good cop, bad cop." New York Magazine, July 11, pp. 16–24.

Holloway, L. (1998). "Boy who vanished in 1979 is dead, ex-prosecutor claims." New York Times, May 21, p. B8.

Holmes, S. (1990). "Fewer turf battles, more drug arrests." New York Times, January 21, p. E22.

Horowitz, C. (1995). "The suddenly safer city: The end of crime as we know it." New York, August 14, pp. 21–27, 82.

Hynes, J. (2000). An analysis of Brooklyn homicides in 1999: Strategies for saving lives. Brooklyn: Kings County District Attorney's Office.

Hynes, J., and Drury, R. (1990). Incident at Howard Beach: The case for murder." New York: G. P. Putnam's Sons.

Ianni, F. (1998). "New Mafia: Black, Hispanic, and Italian styles." Society 35, no. 2 (January–February), pp. 115–130.

Immigration and Naturalization Service (INS) Office of Policy and Planning. (1994, 1999). Annual report: Legal immigration, fiscal years 1993, 1997. Washington, D.C.: U.S. Department of Justice.

Independent Budget Office (IBO). (1999). New York City's fiscal outlook, January 1999. New York: NYC IBO.

"Investigating the NYPD? Wait your turn." (1999). Law Enforcement News, June 15, p. 6.

Irwin, J., and Austin, J. (1997). It's about time: America's imprisonment binge. 2nd ed. Belmont, Calif.: Wadsworth.

Jackall, R. (1997). "Wild cowboys: Urban marauders and the forces of order." Cambridge, Mass.: Harvard University Press.

Jacobs, J. (1999). Gotham unbound: How New York was liberated from the grip of organized crime. New York: New York University Press.

James, G. (1992a). "In every category, crime reports fell last year in New York City." New York Times, March 25, pp. A1, B4.

———. (1992b). "Police dept. report assails officers in New York rally." New York Times, September 29, pp. A1, B3.

Janofsky, M. (1998). "Flush and crime-wary cities bid up pay for police chiefs." New York Times, April 20, pp. A1, A12.

Johnson, B., Dunlap, E., and Tourigny, S. (1999). "Crack distribution and abuse in New York." Paper delivered at the International Workshop on Drug Markets, April 9, John Jay College, New York City.

Johnson, B., Goldstein, P., Preble, E., Schmeidler, J., Lipton, D., Spunt, B., and Miller, T. (1985). Taking care of business: The economics of crime by heroin users. Lexington, Mass.: Lexington Books.

Johnson, B., and Golub, A. (1997). "Trends in heroin use among Manhattan arrestees from the heroin and crack eras." Pp. 210–222 in J. Inciardi and L. Harrison (eds.), Heroin in the age of crack-cocaine. Thousand Oaks, Calif.: Sage.

Johnson, B., Golub, A., and Fagan, J. (1995). "Careers in crack, drug use, drug distribution, and non-drug criminality." Crime and Delinquency 41, no. 3 (July), pp. 275–295.

Johnson, B., Hamid, A., and Sanabria, H. (1992). "Emerging models of crack distribution." Pp. 56–78 in T. Mieczkowski (ed.), Drugs, crime, and social policy: Research, issues, and concerns. Boston: Allyn and Bacon.

Johnson, D. (1996). "Nice city's nasty distinction: Murders soar in Minneapolis." New York Times, June 30, pp. A1, A18.

Johnson, T. (1979). "Police clear 'drug supermarket' off block." New York Times, September 19, p. B3.

Johnston, D. (1999). "Gap between rich and poor found substantially wider." New York Times, September 5, p. A16.

Jones, D. (1999). "Targeting the poor." New York Amsterdam News, March 11, p. 5.

Jordan, H. (1997). "Dominicans in New York: Getting a slice of the Apple." NACLA Report on the Americas 30, no. 5 (March–April), pp. 37–43.

Kacapyr, E. (1998). "Notes from underground." American Demographics, January, pp. 30–31.

Kaplan, D., and King, P. (1996). "City slickers." Newsweek, November 11, pp. 29–35.

Kapstatter, B. (1999). "Murders in Bronx drop, defying trend in city." New York Daily News, September 30, p. 11.

Karmen, A. (1994). "What college students consider cool: Results of a survey." Proceedings of the New York State Sociological Association, Dowling College, Oakdale, N.Y., October 12.

———. (1996). "What's driving New York's crime rate down?" Law Enforcement News, November 30, pp. 8–10.

Kasindorf, J. (1990). "Nightmare on Jane Street." New York Magazine, September 17, pp. 30–38.

Kelling, G. (1997). "The assault on effective policing." Wall Street Journal, August 26, p. B22.

———. (1998). "Broken windows and cultural pluralism." Pp. 13–14 in National Institute of Justice, Crime control, the police, and culture wars. Perspectives on crime and justice lecture series. Washington, D.C.: U.S. Department of Justice.

Kelling, G., and Bratton, W. (1998). "Declining crime rates: Insiders' views of the New York City story." Journal of Criminal Law and Criminology 88, no. 4 (Summer), pp. 1217–1232.

Kelling, G., and Coles, C. (1996). Fixing broken windows: Restoring order and reducing crime in our communities. New York: Free Press.

Kelly, R. (1993). "Toward a new intolerance of crime and violence." FBI Law Enforcement Bulletin 62, no. 7 (July), pp. 16–20.

Kennedy, D. (1997). "Pulling levers: Chronic offenders, high crime settings, and a theory of prevention." Valparaiso University Law Review 31, no. 2 (Spring), pp. 449–481.

Kennedy, R. (2000). "As crime surges, livery drivers keep a wary eye in the mirror." New York Times, March 28, pp. B1, B6.

Kihss, P. (1980). "State urges alternatives as prisons fill." New York Times, November 13, p. B4.

Kilborn, P. (1994). "New York police force lagging in recruitment of black officers." New York Times, July 17, pp. A1, B26.

———. (1996). "Welfare all over the map." New York Times, December 8, p. E3.

Klein, J. (1991). "Less than zero: For the City, the bad news follows the bad news." New York Magazine, February 25, pp. 35–37.

Kleinfield, N. (1996). "Police say suspect admits fatal 'Zodiac' shootings 'because they were evil.'" New York Times, June 20, p. B1.

Knapp Commission to investigate allegations of police corruption. (1972). Final report. New York: Fund for the City of New York.

Koch, E. (1986). "An arsenal for the federal war on drugs." New York Times, July 18, p. A27.

Kocieniewski, D. (1996a). "2 more officers dismissed for Washington partying." New York Times, February 24, p. B25.

———. (1996b). "Two polls give Bratton major credit for drop in crime." New York Times, April 21, p. B41.

———. (1997). "New York City murder rate may hit 30-year low." New York Times, December 25, pp. B1, B5.

———. (1998a). "Officers facing added scrutiny over shootings." New York Times, January 1, 1998.

———. (1998b). "Police's use of deadly force in New York is low for nation." New York Times, January 2, pp. B1, B6.

———. (1998c). "Safir is said to seek to punish a chief over false crime data." New York Times, February 28, p. B1.

———. (1998d). "Police effort to speed 911 lagging badly." New York Times, June 12, pp. B1, B8.

———. (1999). "Success of elite police unit exacts a toll on the streets." New York Times, February 15, pp. A1, B5.

Kolata, G. (1989). "Despite its promise of riches, the crack trade seldom pays." New York Times, November 26, pp. A1, A42.

———. (1990). "Old, weak, and a loser: Crack user's image falls." New York Times, July 23, pp. A1, B4.

Kopel, D. (1995). "Get more guns into law abiding pockets." The American Enterprise, May–June, pp. 38–39.

Krajicek, D. (1990). "Newest cop on the beat." New York Daily News, February 21, p. 20.

Krause, D. (1996). Effective program evaluation. Chicago: Nelson-Hall.

Krauss, C. (1994). "Poll finds a lack of faith in police." New York Times, June 19, pp. A1, B30.

———. (1995a). "Murder rate plunges in New York City." New York Times, July 8, pp. 1, 22.

———. (1995b). "Crime lab: Mystery of New York, the suddenly safer city." New York Times, July 23, sec. 4, p. 1.

———. (1995c). "Shootings fall as more guns stay at home." New York Times, July 30, pp. 29, 32.

———. (1995d). "The commissioner vs. the criminologists." New York Times, November 19, p. B43.

———. (1996a). "Now, how low can crime go?" New York Times, January 28, p. E5.

———. (1996b). "Report sets off questions on police patrol strength." New York Times, September 18, p. B3.

Krauss, C. (1996c). "New York crime rate plummets to levels not seen in 30 years." New York Times, December 20, pp. A1, B4.

Krueger, L., and Seley, J. (1996). "The return of slavery: Lessons from workfare in New York City." Dollars and Sense 208 (November–December), pp. 28.

Lacayo, R. (1996). "Law and order." Time, January 15, pp. 48–54.

———. (1997). "Good cop, bad cop." Time, September 1, pp. 26–30.

Laffey, M. (1997). "Cop diary." New Yorker, November 10, pp. 46–50.

———. (1999). "Cop diary: Inside dope." New Yorker, February 1, pp. 29–33.

Lardner, J. (1997). "Can you believe the New York miracle?" New York Review of Books 44, no. 13 (August 14), pp. 54–58.

Lattimore, P., Trudeau, J., Riley, K., Leiter, J., and Edwards, S. (1997). Homicide in eight U.S. cities: Trends, context, and policy implications. National Institute of Justice Research Report. Washington, D.C.: U.S. Department of Justice.

"Law enforcement around the nation, 1994: New York." (1994). Law Enforcement News, December 31, pp. 21–22.

Levitan, M. (1998). New York City's labor market, 1994–1997: Profiles and perspectives. New York: Community Service Society.

Levitt, L. (1997). "Family in blue abandons cop." Queens Newsday, May 27, p. A16.

Lewine, E. (1999). "The wave of immigrants began 25 years ago." New York Times, March 14, section 11, p. 1.

Lobo, A., and Salvo, J. (1997). "Immigration to New York City in the '90s: The saga continues." Migration World Magazine 25, no. 3 (March–April), pp. 14–18.

Lotke, E. (1997). Hobbling a generation: Young African-American men in D.C.'s criminal justice system five years later. Washington, D.C.: National Center on Institutions and Alternatives.

Lott, J., Jr. (1998). More guns, less crime: Understanding crime and gun control laws. Chicago: University of Chicago Press.

Loysk, B. (1997a). "Generation X: What they think and what they plan to do." The Futurist 31 (March–April), pp. 39–44.

———. (1997b). "Generation X: What are they like?" Current 392 (May), pp. 9–13.

Luckenbill, D. (1977). "Criminal homicide as a situated transaction." Social Problems 25, pp. 176–186.

Lydon, C. (1969). "U.S. and City plan narcotics fight." New York Times, June 16, p. 8.

Lynch, J., Smith, S., Graziadei, H., and Pittayathikhun, T. (1994). BJS profile of inmates in the United States and in England and Wales, 1991. Washington, D.C.: U.S. Department of Justice.

MacFarquhar, N. (1999). "Police get good ratings from most, but not all, New Yorkers." New York Times, June 3, p. B3.

Maeder, J. (1999). "Rites of passage: Kid dropper." New York Daily News, June 16, p. 15.

Maitland, L. (1981). "Heroin trade rising despite U.S. efforts." New York Times, February 15, pp. A1, A32.

Maltz, M. (1998). "Which homicides decreased? Why?" Journal of Criminal Law and Criminology 88, no. 4 (Summer), pp. 1489–1496.

Maple, J. (1999). The crime fighter: Putting the bad guys out of business. New York: Doubleday.

Margarita, M. (1980). "Killing the police: Myths and motives." Annals of the American Academy of Political and Social Science 452, pp. 63–71.

Marks, J. (1997). "New York's comeback: New York, New York." U.S. News and World Report, September 29, pp. 45–54.

Marriott, M. (1989). "The 12 worst drug bazaars: New York's continuing blight." New York Times, June 1, pp. A1, B4.

Martinez, R., Jr. (1997). "Homicide among the 1980 Mariel refugees in Miami: Victims and offenders." Hispanic Journal of Behavioral Sciences 19, no. 2 (May), pp. 107–123.

Martz, L. (1989). "A tide of drug killing." Newsweek, January 16, pp. 44–45.

Maruschak, L. (1997). HIV in prisons and jails, 1995. Bureau of Justice Statistics Bulletin. Washington, D.C.: U.S. Department of Justice.

Marvell, T. (1998). "The impact of beer consumption on crime rates." Paper delivered at the meeting of the American Society of Criminology, November, Washington, D.C.

Marzuk, P., Tardiff, K., Leon, A., Hirsch, C., Stajic, M., Portera, L., and Hartwell, N. (1997). "Poverty and fatal accidental drug overdoses of cocaine and opiates in New York City: An ecological study." American Journal of Drug and Alcohol Abuse 23, no. 2 (May), pp. 221–229.

Marzulli, J. (1994a). "Community cops: Memos show few arrests, fudged reports." New York Daily News, January 24, pp. 2, 3, 18.

———. (1994b). "A new club for Finest." New York Daily News, August 19, p. 5.

———. (1995a). "Slay plunge highlights dramatic drop in crime." New York Daily News, September 25, p. 5.

———. (1995b). "Major city crime hits skids again." New York Daily News, October 27, p. 3.

Marzulli, J. (1995c). "Bratton says judges killing city's quality of life." New York Daily News, November 8, p. 12.

———. (1997). "Crime decline suits city fine: Extends trend of past 4 years." New York Daily News, December 1, p. 3.

———. (1998a). "Homicides plunge 31%." New York Daily News, March 31, p. 8.

———. (1998b). "Crime plummets." New York Daily News, June 29, p. 5.

———. (1998c). "Narco agents weed out bad apples upstate." New York Daily News, August 17, p. 8.

———. (1999a). "Gun permits KOd: NYPD shoots down 55% of requests." New York Daily News, May 4, p. 5.

———. (1999b). "Nongun slays lead growth in homicides." New York Daily News, November 9, p. 8.

Massarella, L. (1996). "Crime takes a timeout." New York Post, October 22, p. 2.

Massing, M. (1996). "Crime and drugs: The new myths." New York Review of Books, February 1, pp. 16–20.

———. (1998a). "Winning the drug war isn't so hard after all." New York Times Sunday Magazine, September 6, pp. 48–50.

———. (1998b). "The blue revolution." New York Review of Books, November 19, pp. 32–36.

Mathews, T. (1980). "Lennon's alter ego." Newsweek, December 22, pp. 34–35.

Mauer, M. (1999). Race to incarcerate. New York: New Press.

"May I have the envelope, please." (1997). Law Enforcement News, April 30, p. 1.

Mayor's Management Report (MMR). (1982–2000). Issued in September for prior fiscal years. New York City Office of the Mayor.

McAlary, M. (1987). Buddy boys: When good cops turn bad. New York: G. P. Putnam's Sons.

McCall, H. (1998). New York State's higher education policy vacuum. Albany: Office of the State Comptroller.

McDonald, W. (1997). "Crime and illegal immigration: Emerging local, state, and federal partnerships." National Institute of Justice Journal 232 (June), pp. 2–10.

McDowall, D., Loftin, C., and Wiersenna, B. (1995). "Easing concealed firearms laws: Effects on homicides in three states." Journal of Criminal Law and Criminology 86, no. 1 (Fall), pp. 193–206.

McFadden, R. (1991). "New York leads big cities in robbery rate, but drops in murder." New York Times, August 11, p. B2.

McGuire, R. (1980). "For the Finest, a tough job gets tougher." New York Daily News, September 28, p. 49.

McMahon, T., Angelo, L., and Mollenkopf, J. (1997). Hollow in the middle: The rise and fall of New York City's middle class. New York: City Council Finance Division.

McNamara, J. (1999). "Giuliani cop system doesn't work." Newsday, April 15, p. 40.

McQuillan, A. (1994). "Bratton plan targets lazy cops." New York Daily News, January 29, p. 10.

———. (2000). "Crime dips overall, but murders up 6%." New York Daily News, January 2, p. 8.

Messinger, R. (1997). "Opening statement, mayoralty debate." New York Times, October 10, p. B4.

Methvin, E. (1992). "Doubling the prison population will break America's crime wave." Corrections Today, February, pp. 28–40.

———. (1997). "Where the police are winning." Reader's Digest, February, pp. 84–89.

Miller, J. (1996). Search and destroy: African American males in the criminal justice system. Cambridge, U.K.: Cambridge University Press.

Miller, W. (1959). The cool world. New York: Fawcett Books.

Miller, W. B. (1958). "Lower class culture as a generating milieu of gang delinquency." Journal of Social Issues 14, pp. 5–19.

Millman, J. (1996). "Ghetto blasters." Forbes 157, no. 3, pp. 76–81.

Mollen Commission (1994). Report of the Commission to investigate allegations of police corruption and the anti-corruption procedures of the police department. July 7. City of New York.

Monkkonen, E. (1995). "New York City homicides: A research note." Social Science History 19, no. 2 (Summer), pp. 202–214.

Mooney, M. (1990). "City jail population to increase 50%." New York Post, May 22, p. 12.

———. (1996a). "B'klyn, E. Side drug busts flood city jails." New York Daily News, June 11, p. 8.

———. (1996b). "City's jails, and hands, full." New York Daily News, September 19, p. 16.

Moran, R. (1995). "More police, less crime, right? Wrong." New York Times, February 27, p. A15.

Morbidity and Mortality Weekly Report. (1991). "Mortality attributable to HIV infection/AIDS—United States, 1981–1990." Journal of the American Medical Association 265, no. 7 (February 20), pp. 848–850.

Morgenthau, R. (1995). "Credit district attorney's office also for drop in murder rate." New York Times, July 25, p. A14.

Morgenthau, T. (1990). "New York's nightmare." Newsweek, September 17, p. 35.

Morris, V., and Hardt, R. (1998). "Rudy rips report he's soft on cop brutality." New York Post, July 8, p. 8.

Moynihan, D. (1993). "Defining deviancy down." American Scholar 62, no. 1 (Winter), pp. 17–30.

Musto, D. (1995a). "AIDS." P. 11 in K. Jackson (ed.), The Encyclopedia of New York City. New Haven: Yale University Press.

———. (1995b). "Drug abuse." Pp. 345–346 in K. Jackson (ed.), The Encyclopedia of New York City. New Haven: Yale University Press.

Nagourney, A. (1998). "Warming up with a Washington visit." New York Times, March 13, p. B5.

———. (1999). "U.S. reopens inquiry into Yeshiva student's '94 shooting death on Brooklyn Bridge." New York Times, August 27, p. B9.

"Narcotics squad increased to 200." (1954). New York Times, November 5, p. 8.

Nasar, S. (1998). "Unlearning the lessons of Econ 101." New York Times, May 3, pp. E1, E4.

Natarajan, M. (1998). "Drug trafficking in New York City." Pp. 72–79 in A. Karmen (ed.), Crime and justice in New York City. New York: McGraw Hill Custom Publishing.

National Institute of Justice (NIJ). (1999). Drug use forecasting: Annual reports, 1987–1997. Washington, D.C.: U.S. Department of Justice.

Newfield, J., and Barrett, W. (1988). City for sale. New York: Harper and Row.

"New Orleans' murder rate, highest in nation, cut by 20%." (1995). Jet, November 13, p. 38.

New York City Council on Economic Education. (1974, 1994). New York Metropolitan Region Fact Book. Baruch College, CUNY, New York: City Council on Economic Education.

New York City Department of City Planning. (1987–1999). Annual report on social indicators, 1985–1997. New York: City Planning Department.

———. (1995). Population projections for the year 2000. Technical reports 1 and 2. New York: City Planning Department.

New York City Department of Health (NYC DOH). (1998). Mayor and health commissioner announce dramatic decrease in deaths due to AIDS. Press release, February 2. New York: NYC DOH Office of External Affairs.

———. (1999). Health department announces significant decrease in deaths in NYC due to HIV/AIDS. Press release, February 1. New York: NYC DOH Office of External Affairs.

New York City Visitor's Bureau (NYCVB). (1997). Facts about New York. New York: NYCVB.

New York Police Department (NYPD). (1994a). Police strategy No. 3: Driving drug dealers out of New York. New York: NYPD.

———. (1994b). Firearms discharge assault report. New York: NYPD.

"New York's finest." (1996). The Economist, August 10, p. 30.

New York State Department of Correctional Services (NYS DOCS). (1974). Annual statistical report, 1973. Albany: NYS DOCS.

———. (1997). Idenitified substance abusers, December 1997. Albany: NYS DOCS.

———. (1998). The hub system: Profile of inmates under custody on January 1, 1998. Albany: NYS DOCS.

New York State Division of Criminal Justice Services (NYS DCJS). (1977–1998). Crime and justice annual report. Albany: DCJS.

Nifong, C. (1997). "One man's theory is cutting crime in urban streets." Christian Science Monitor, February 18, pp. 1, 10–11.

Noel, P. (2000). "Portraits in racial profiling: When clothes make the suspect." Village Voice, March 21, pp. 47–48, 51.

Noonan, D. (1999). "NYPD booze: The silent struggle." New York Daily News, April 18, p. 26.

Nossiter, A. (1996). "2 crime busters for New Orleans." New York Times, December 5, p. A32.

Office of AIDS Surveillance. (1999). AIDS New York City, update, first quarter 1999 (May). NYC Department of Health.

Office of Applied Studies (OAS), Substance Abuse and Mental Health Services Administration (SAMHSA). (1986–1999). Preliminary estimates from the drug abuse warning network. Advance reports 11–19. Rockville, Md.: U.S. Department of Health and Human Services.

———. (1988–1999). Annual medical examiner data from the drug abuse warning network (DAWN). Rockville, Md.: U.S. Department of Health and Human Services.

Office of Public Affairs, INS. (1999). News release: INS breaks previous removals record. January 8. Washington, D.C.: U.S. Department of Justice.

Onishi, N. (1994). "Stray gunfire kills man in Bronx." New York Times, May 26, p. B3.

Parascandola, R. (1996). "Cutting edge of crime." New York Post, August 18, p. 3.

Parascandola, R. (1998). "Judges fire blanks when it comes to enforcing gun law." New York Post, April 29, p. 4.

Parker, R. (1995). "Bringing 'booze' back in: The relationship between alcohol and homicide." Journal of Research in Crime and Delinquency 32, pp. 3–38.

Parker, R., and Cartmill, R. (1998). "Alcohol and homicide in the United States, 1934–1995—Or one reason why U.S. rates of violence may be going down." Journal of Criminal Law and Criminology 88, no. 4 (Summer), pp. 1369–1398.

Patterson, M. (1978). "The violent get easier bail: Study." New York Daily News, February 14, pp. 2, 24.

Pedersen, D. (1996). "Bullets in the Big Easy: Can New York–style justice save New Orleans?" Newsweek, December 23, p. 29.

———. (1997). "Go get the scumbags: A very odd couple tries to clean up New Orleans." Newsweek, October 20, p. 32.

Perez-Pena, R. (1997). "Study shows New York has the greatest income gap." New York Times, December 17, pp. A1, B6.

———. (1998). "Governor's inmate estimates were too high, memo says." New York Times, January 28, p. B2.

———. (1999). "Governor to emphasize fighting crime." New York Times, January 6, p. B5.

Perlmutter, E. (1957). "City called hub of U.S. narcotics." New York Times, November 26, p. 8.

Pileggi, N. (1981a). "Open city: The bad guys are winning the war on crime." New York Magazine, January 19, pp. 20–26.

———. (1981b). "Inside Rikers Island." New York Magazine, June 8, pp. 18–22.

Piven, F., and Cloward, R. (1972). Regulating the poor: The functions of the welfare system. New York: Random House.

Platt, A. (1969). The child savers. Chicago: University of Chicago Press.

Polsby, D. (1995). "Firearms costs, firearms benefits, and the limits of knowledge." Journal of Criminal Law and Criminology 86, no. 1 (Fall), pp. 207–220.

Pooley, E. (1992). "Getting away with murder: The cops can't catch half the city's killers." New York Magazine, September 28, pp. 26–33.

———. (1993). "Bulldog." New York Magazine, February 22, 32–41.

———. (1995). "Heat on the beat: Looking more corrupt and inept than ever, the LAPD resists change." Time, October 16, pp. 66–67.

———. (1996). "One good apple." Time, January 15, pp. 55–56.

Pozo, S. (1998). Exploring the underground economy. Kalamazoo, Mich.: Upjohn Institute.

Preble, E., and Casey, J. (1969). "Taking care of business: The heroin user's life on the street." International Journal of the Addictions 4, pp. 1–24.

Pristin, T. (1999). "Occupancy at hotels falls slightly as prices rise." New York Times, June 3, p. B3.

Purdum, T. (1986a). "New York police now seizing cars in arrests for possession of crack." New York Times, August 5, pp. A1, A24.

———. (1986b). "Police searching for crack pipes raid hundreds of stores in city." New York Times, August 22, pp. A1, B4.

Purnick, J. (1996). "Petty crimes are swelling the dockets." New York Times, May 31, p. B1.

Ratish, R. (1997). "Study says cops slower to respond." Queens Newsday, August 15, p. A33.

Ratnesar, R. (1998). "Should you carry a gun?" Time, July 6, p. 48.

Rayman, G. (1999). "Possession not so easy to prove." Queens Newsday, February 23, pp. A4, A32.

Reeves, R. (1995). "The cops we deserve." Los Angeles Magazine 40, no. 12 (December), pp. 40–43.

Reinarman, C., and Levine, H. (1997). Crack in America: Demon drugs and social justice. Berkeley: University of California Press.

Rennison, M. (1999). Criminal victimization, 1998. Washington, D.C.: U.S. Department of Justice.

Reppetto, T. (1981). "Keep criminals off streets." New York Daily News, November 1, pp. 53–54.

Reuter, P. (1999). "Drug use measures: What are they really telling us?" NIJ Journal, April, pp. 12–18.

"'Revolving door justice': Why criminals go free." (1976). U.S. News and World Report, May 10, pp. 50–53.

Richardson, J., Best, J., and Bromley, D. (eds.). (1991). The satanism scare. New York: Aldine de Gruyter.

Richardson, L. (1997). "U.S. urging identification of patients with H.I.V." New York Times, October 21, p. B5.

———. (1998). "Agencies defend needle exchange programs." New York Times, April 22, p. B5.

Roane, K. (1997a). "Despite fears, little evidence is seen of a rise in gang violence." New York Times, October 12, p. B37.

———. (1997b). "Clues of robbery prompt charges in officer's death." New York Times, November 30, p. B46.

———. (1998). "Rape resists the inroads of the city's war on crime." New York Times, August 23, p. B31.

Roane, K. (1999). "Spitzer threatens subpoena for police data on frisking." New York Times, May 16, p. B39.

Roberts, S. (1989). "Once again, racism proves to be fatal in New York City." New York Times, September 3, p. E6.

———. (1994). "In the strategy on policy, some promises remain unmet." New York Times, August 7, pp. B35, B36.

Robinson, D. (1970). "Leary to shift 200 to antinarcotics force." New York Times, February 27, p. 8.

Rohde, D. (1998). "Despite deal, family of man who died in arrest assails mayor." New York Times, October 3, pp. B1, B3.

———. (1999). "Crackdown on minor offenses swamps New York City courts." New York Times, February 2, pp. A1, B7.

———. (2000). "Drug arrests overloading court system." New York Times, February 17, pp. B1, B2.

Rohter, L. (1997). "In U.S. deportation policy, a pandora's box." New York Times, August 10, pp. A1, A6.

Rose, J. (1997). "The newest New Yorkers 1990–1994: An analysis of immigration to New York City in the early 1990s." New York: Department of City Planning.

Rosenblatt, R. (1981). "Why the justice system fails." Time, March 23, p. 28.

Rosenthal, A. (1993). "Problem-oriented policing: Now and then: Reprint of a 1977 article." Law Enforcement News, March 31, pp. 1, 10.

Rosenthal, E. (1997). "New York study finds uninsured are on the rise." New York Times, February 25, pp. A1, B5.

Sachs, S. (1999). "More immigrants are deported as officials' powers increase." New York Times, November 13, p. B3.

Safir, H. (1997). "Goal oriented community policing: The NYPD approach." The Police Chief, December, pp. 31–39, 56, 58.

———. (1999). Transcript of interview with reporter Lisa Evers. 1010 WINS radio, May 6.

Salins, P. (1990). "New York will rise again." New York Times, October 27, p. 23.

Saltonstall, D. (1996). "City coming back, New Yorkers roar." New York Daily News, September 29, p. 2.

Saltzman, J. (1997). "The streets are safer." Providence Journal Bulletin, September 11, pp. A1, A12.

Sanoff, A. (1996). "The hottest import: Crime." U.S. News and World Report, September 30, p. 49.

Saul, S. (1990). "Study: 1 in 100 use cocaine in U.S." New York Newsday, May 11, p. 15.

Schaffer, R. (1993). Socioeconomic profiles: A portrait of New York City's community districts from the 1980 and 1990 censuses of population and housing. New York: Department of City Planning.

Schill, M., Friedman, S., and Rosenbaum, E. (1998). Nativity differences in neighborhood quality. New York: NYU Law School, Center for Real Estate and Urban Policy.

Schmalz, J. (1986). "Cuomo plan fuels drug laws debate." New York Times, August 18, pp. A1, B5.

Schwartzman, P. (1998). "NYPD takes back streets." New York Daily News, May 10, pp. 20–21.

Sellin, T. (1938). Culture conflict and crime. New York: Social Science Research Council.

Serant, C., and Marzulli, J. (1996). "Cops hurry up and wait." New York Daily News, October 8, p. 2.

Shah, D. (1996). "Making the city safe: Good cop, bad cop." New York, April 1, pp. 26–27, 35.

Shannon, E. (1995). "State of the Union: Crime—safer streets, yet greater fear." Time, January 30, p. 30.

Shaw, C., and McKay, H. (1942). Juvenile delinquency and urban areas. Chicago: University of Chicago Press.

Shenon, P. (1990). "Cocaine epidemic may have peaked." New York Times, September 2, p. B32.

Sherman, L., Berk, R., and Smith, D. (1992). "Crime, punishment, and stake in conformity: Legal and informal control of domestic violence." American Sociological Review 57 (October), pp. 680–690.

Sherman, L., and Bridgeforth, C. (1994). Getting guns off the streets, 1993: A study of big-city police agencies. Report no. 8. Washington, D.C.: Crime Control Institute.

Sherman, L., Gartlin, P., and Buerger, M. (1989). "Hot spots and predatory crime: Routine activities and the criminology of place." Criminology 27, pp. 27–55.

Sherman, L., Shaw, J., and Rogan, D. (1994). The Kansas City gun experiment: NIJ Research in Brief (August). Washington, D.C.: U.S. Department of Justice.

Sherman, L., Steele, L., Laufersweiler, D., Hoffer, N., and Julian, S. (1989). "Stray bullets and 'mushrooms': Random shootings of bystanders in four cities, 1977–1988." Journal of Quantitative Criminology 5, pp. 297–316.

Sherman, W. (1998). "'Crackdown' on crime." New York Post, May 24, p. 8.

Shipp, E. (1981). "City makes a big issue of little crimes." New York Times, August 30, p. E4.

Short, J. (1997). Poverty, ethnicity, and violent crime. Boulder, Colo.: Westview.

Siegel, J. (1994). "Added cops don't patrol." New York Daily News, June 3, p. 4.

Siemaszko, C., and McCoy, K. (1998). "City's flooded melting pot." New York Daily News, April 10, p. 8.

Silberman, C. (1978). Criminal violence, criminal justice. New York: Random House.

Silverman, E. (1999). NYPD battles crime: Innovative strategies in policing. Boston: Northeastern University Press.

Smith, C. (1996). "The NYPD guru." New York Magazine, April 1, pp. 29–34.

Smith, S., Steadman, G., and Minton, T. (1999). Criminal victimization and perceptions of community safety in 12 cities, 1998. Bureau of Justice Statistics Report. Washington, D.C.: U.S. Department of Justice.

Smith, T. (1997). "New York: The ride." Fortune, November 10, pp. 191–201.

Sontag, D. (1994). "Porous deportation system gives criminals little to fear." New York Times, September 13, pp. A1, B9.

———. (1997). "U.S. deports felons but can't keep them out." New York Times, August 11, pp. A1, A8.

Sontag, D., and Dugger, C. (1998). "The new immigrant tide: A shuttle between worlds." New York Times, July 19, pp. A1, A28.

Spelman, W., and Brown, D. (1983). "Response time." Pp. 160–166 in C. Clockars (ed.), Thinking about police: Contemporary readings. New York: McGraw-Hill.

Spunt, B., Goldstein, P., Brownstein, H., Fendich, M., and Langley, S. (1994). "Alcohol and homicide: Interviews with prison inmates." Journal of Drug Issues 24, no. 1, pp. 143–163.

Spunt, B., Tarshish, C., Fendich, M., Goldstein, P., and Brownstein, H. (1993). "Research note: The utility of correctional data for understanding the drugs-homicide connection." Criminal Justice Review 18, no. 1 (Spring), pp. 46–60.

Stack, S. (1997). "Homicide followed by suicide: An analysis of Chicago data." Criminology 35, no. 3, pp. 435–449.

State Education Department of New York. (1978–1999). Distribution of high school graduates and college-going rate. Annual reports, 1977 to 1997. Albany: State University of New York.

Stein, A. (1988). "Drug shocker: The city itself is America's biggest crack-house landlord." New York Post, March 14, p. 21.

Stewart, B. (1997). "The Bronx: An all-American city, thonx." New York Times, November 19, p. B4.

Stone, M. (1990). "Hard times." New York Magazine, November 19, pp. 36–42.

"Strength in numbers." (1998). Law Enforcement News, July/August, p. 5.

"Study of gun seizures by police finds a 'shocking' absence of data." (1994). Law Enforcement News, September 30, pp. 1, 9.

Sullivan, J. (2000). "In New York and nation, chances for early parole shrink." New York Times, April 23, pp. B29, B34.

Swarns, R. (1997). "The issues: 320,000 have left welfare, but where do they go from here?" New York Times, October 29, p. B6.

———. (1999). "New York City admits turning away poor." New York Times, January 22, p. B3.

Talan, J. (1998). "The needle debate: Feds straddle issue of drug use, AIDS spread." Long Island Newsday, April 21, p. A5.

Tardiff, K., and Gross, E. (1986). "Homicide in New York City." Bulletin of the New York Academy of Medicine 62, pp. 413–426.

Tardiff, K., Marzuk, P., Leon, A., Hirsch, C., Stajic, M., Portera, L., and Hartwell, N. (1994). "Homicide in New York City: Cocaine use and firearms." Journal of the American Medical Association 272, no. 1 (July 6), pp. 43–46.

———. (1995a). "A profile of homicides on the streets and in the homes of New York City." Public Health Reports 110, no. 1 (January–February), pp. 13–17.

———. (1995b). "Cocaine, opiates and ethanol in homicides in New York City: 1990 and 1991." Journal of Forensic Sciences 40, no. 3 (May), pp. 387–390.

Thomas, P. (1997). Down these mean streets. New York: Vintage.

Thomas-Lester, A. (1998). "D.C. police ballistics backlog criticized; City, U.S. officers say ID system is underused." Washington Post, May 10, p. A1.

Tobier, E. (1984). The changing face of poverty: Trends in New York City's population in poverty, 1960–1980. New York: Community Service Society.

Topousis, T. (1997). "Cops take their time responding to fewer crimes." New York Post, August 15, p. 22.

Travis, N. (1998). "Gossip." New York Post, August 21, p. 6.

Treaster, J. (1990). "U.S. cocaine epidemic shows signs of waning." New York Times, July 1, p. A12.

———. (1994a). "Crime rate drops again in New York, hastening a trend." New York Times, June 2, pp. A1, B3.

———. (1994b). "Study says New York lags in seizing criminals' guns." New York Times, August 10, p. B2.

Tumposky, E. (1995). "Mayor denies move to oust poor." New York Daily News, April 29, p. 2.

Uchitelle, L. (1998). "The dark side of optimism." New York Times, March 8, p. E4.

United States Census Population Division. (1999). Current population survey, 1998, New York City. Washington, D.C.: U.S. Census.

Van Doorn, J., Ross, B., and Pelleck, C. (1980). "Crisis forum: City's growing peril." New York Post, March 20, p. 31.

Wakefield, D. (1992). New York in the fifties. New York: Houghton Mifflin.

Waldinger, R. (1996). Still the promised city? African-Americans and new immigrants in postindustrial New York. Cambridge: Harvard University Press.

Walker, S. (1998). Sense and nonsense about crime and drugs. 4th ed. Belmont, Calif.: Wadsworth.

Ward, J. (1997). "NYPD view: New procedures credited with crime drop." American City and County 112, no. 2 (February), pp. 28–31.

Wasserman, J., and Gonzalez, C. (1998). "Ed board posts progress, but HS is taking longer." New York Daily News, March 6, p. 7.

Weaver, W. (1952). "Dewey signs bills to curb narcotics." New York Times, February 20, p. 8.

Weinraub, B. (1967). "Crime reports up 72% here in 1966; actual rise is 6.5%." New York Times, February 21, pp. A1, A36.

Weiser, R. (1997a). "As Trade Center smoldered, suspect watched, jury hears." New York Times, October 23, pp. 1, B11.

———. (1997b). "Judge rejects Giuliani's attempt to kill bus ads using his name." New York Times, December 2, pp. A1, B4.

Weiss, M. (1996). "Report: Parole sets thugs free to strike again." New York Post, November 17, p. 3.

———. (1997a). "Recipe for a safe city: More officers and jails." New York Post, March 4, p. 18.

———. (1997b). "Crime stats show city hasn't been this safe in 30 years." New York Post, December 31, p. 8.

———. (1998). "Subway crime shocker." New York Post, January 19, p. 4.

Weiss, M., and Celona, L. (1997). "Cops told to flash cuffs and turn up their collars." New York Post, April 2, p. 8.

"Welcome to the new world of private security." (1997). The Economist, April 19, pp. 21–25.

Wendel, T., and Curtis, R. (2000). "The heraldry of heroin: 'Dope stamps' and the dynamics of drug markets in New York City." Journal of Drug Issues (forthcoming).

Widener, S. (1986). "State to take crack attack to school." New York Newsday, August 22, p. 17.

Wilgoren, J., and Cooper, M. (1999). "New York police lags in diversity." New York Times, March 8, pp. A1, B4.

Williams, D., Agrest, S., and Joshee, H. (1980). "Omega 7's killers strike in New York." Newsweek, September 22, p. 35.

Williams, T. (1989). The cocaine kids: The inside story of a teenage drug ring. Menlo Park, Calif.: Addison-Wesley.

Williams, T., and Kornblum, W. (1985). Growing up poor. Lexington, Mass.: Lexington Books.

Wilson, J. (1994). "Just take away their guns." New York Times, Sunday Magazine, March 20.

———. (1995). "What to do about crime: Blaming crime on root causes." Vital Speeches of the Day, April 1, pp. 373–376.

Wilson, J., and Kelling, G. (1982). Broken windows. Atlantic Monthly, March, pp. 29–38.

Wilson, W. (1987). The truly disadvantaged: The inner city, the underclass, and public policy. Chicago: University of Chicago Press.

———. (1996). When work disappears: The world of the new urban poor. New York: Knopf.

Wilt, S., Illman, S., and Brodyfield, M. (1997). Female homicide victims in New York City, 1990–1994. New York: New York City Department of Health Injury Prevention Program.

Winerip, M. (1993). "Kelly, a savvy insider, remakes police force." New York Times, May 22, pp. A1, B3.

Wish, E. (1987). Drug use forecasting: New York 1984 to 1986. NIJ Research in Action. Washington, D.C.: U.S. Department of Justice.

Witkin, G. (1998). "The crime bust." U.S. News and World Report, May 25, pp. 28–37.

Wright, L., and Smith, P. (1999). "Decrease in AIDS-related mortality in a state correctional system—New York, 1995–1998." U.S. Department of Health and Human Services, Morbidity and Mortality Weekly Report, January 8, p. 1115.

Wysocki, B., Jr. (1999). "The mixed blessings of low unemployment." Wall Street Journal, March 22, p. 1.

Young, R. (1978). "Dodge city: The deadliest precinct in town." New York Magazine, August 28, pp. 43–46.

Yurick, S. (1978). The warriors. New York: Holt, Rinehart, and Winston.

Zimmer, L. (1990). "Proactive policing against street-level drug trafficking." American Journal of Police 9, no. 1, pp. 43–74.

NAME INDEX

SUBJECT INDEX

ABOUT THE AUTHOR

Andrew Karmen received his Ph.D. in sociology from Columbia University in 1977. Since 1978, he has been a professor in the Sociology Department at John Jay College of Criminal Justice. He has taught courses on criminal justice, criminology, victimology, drug abuse, delinquency, social problems, race relations, research methods, statistics, and general sociology. He is a coordinator of the master's program in criminal justice and a member of the doctoral faculty.

Dr. Karmen has written a textbook, *Crime Victims: An Introduction to Victimology* (4th ed., Wadsworth, 2000), and has co-edited a reader, *Deviants: Victims or Victimizers?* (Sage, 1983). He has written chapters in books and journal articles on a number of subjects, including drug abuse, police use of deadly force, auto theft, provision of defense attorneys to indigents, victims' rights, the victimization of women, and predictions about the plight of crime victims in the future.